Learning Ransomware Response & Recovery

Stopping Ransomware One Restore at a Time

W. Curtis Preston and Michael Saylor

O'REILLY®

Learning Ransomware Response & Recovery
by W. Curtis Preston and Michael Saylor

Printed in the United States of America.

Published by O'Reilly Media, Inc., 141 Stony Circle, Suite 195, Santa Rosa, CA 95401.

O'Reilly books may be purchased for educational, business, or sales promotional use. Online editions are also available for most titles (*http://oreilly.com*). For more information, contact our corporate/institutional sales department: 800-998-9938 or *corporate@oreilly.com*.

Acquisitions Editor: Simina Calin	**Indexer:** Judith McConville
Development Editor: Sara Hunter	**Cover Designer:** Susan Brown
Production Editor: Jonathon Owen	**Cover Illustrator:** José Marzan Jr.
Copyeditor: Charles Roumeliotis	**Interior Designer:** David Futato
Proofreader: Laura K. Miller	**Interior Illustrator:** Kate Dullea

January 2026:   First Edition

Revision History for the First Edition
2026-01-21:   First Release

See *http://oreilly.com/catalog/errata.csp?isbn=9781098169589* for release details.

978-1-098-16958-9

[LSI]

Table of Contents

Part III.   Detect

Part IV.   Respond

Preface

On the very day I (Curtis) finished my final edit of this book to hand over to my amazing editor, Sara, the tech world fell apart, and I thought it would make a great story to open this book. While it doesn't appear to be ransomware related, it does show just how much we have all come to count on technology and how businesses don't know what to do when the tech they count on simply doesn't work.

The first thing my daughter, Marissa, noticed on October 20, 2025, was that Netflix wasn't working. Marissa, her husband Hunter, and my granddaughter Lily sat down to watch something together, and it just wouldn't play. "That's odd," they thought.

She went to work at a clinic, and some of her patients that she tells me are "tech people" told her there was a big outage. She thought, "Well, that has nothing to do with me." But later she noticed that she couldn't access some of her patient records. She had to resort to paper and pen for records. "That's super annoying," she thought.

Then she noticed that her patients couldn't use some of their streaming services. Weird. When she got home, she found out that Lily couldn't do her online classwork. *What is happening?*

The final straw, she told me, was when she couldn't turn on her bedroom lights. Apparently, she solved a problem by hooking them up to—you guessed it—Alexa. And Alexa was down.

On the same day, a friend of mine was in a hospital that was completely offline, and a restaurant that I'm a regular at (Hello, Beach Break Cafe in Oceanside!) had issues as well. Their POS system worked, but they couldn't enter tips.

All of this because DNS wasn't working on DynamoDB in the US-East-1 region of AWS. Imagine the pressure those folks were under that day and resolve to at least have a plan for when this happens to you because of ransomware.

Why This Book

I sent the initial idea for this book to O'Reilly almost three years ago, when I saw what was happening where I worked at the time. I was working for Druva, a SaaS-based backup and disaster recovery provider, and every Monday morning, we'd review the previous week's restore activity. It's the kind of meeting that should be routine and boring. Except it wasn't.

Week after week, I watched the ransomware restore numbers climb. Not the normal "Oops, I deleted a file" restores. These customers had been fully encrypted by ransomware and had to restore everything. Thankfully, they were always able to recover their data, but the numbers went from one or two a month to two or three ransomware restores a week!

These were our customers. They were the *lucky* ones because Druva by default secures your backups the way I recommend in Chapter 6 (e.g., separate credentials, air-gapped copy, immutable storage). But even then, we started seeing something that made my blood run cold: threat actors were getting smarter. They were clearly targeting the backup data. What used to be an afterthought for attackers had become target number one.

I'll never forget one customer whose attackers attempted to delete their backups. There was plenty of evidence of the attempts, and thankfully they had all been stopped. But I just couldn't help wondering, what if they had succeeded?

That's when I started making protecting our customers' backups against ransomware my number one priority. I didn't care about new platforms or additional features. I just wanted to make our customers' backups as secure as possible. (The good news is I wasn't alone; it's just that I had the luxury of being singularly focused on this.)

And the stories outside Druva kept coming as well. I'd read about attack after attack where the common thread was always the same: "Backups were encrypted or deleted prior to the attack." I can't tell you how much it hurts my heart to read that.

But here's what really got me: about 90% of these attacks could have been stopped at the very beginning. Not with some million-dollar security platform. Not with an army of SOC analysts. Just by following basic cyber hygiene practices that every IT person already knows they should be doing.

So I wanted to write a book that cut through all the noise and said this:

- Get decent unique passwords for everything
- Put multifactor authentication (MFA) on anything that matters
- Regularly patch your systems and monitor for critical patches
- Put one copy of your backups offsite (most likely in the cloud)

- Put one copy of your backups on truly immutable storage (so even you can't delete it)

That's it. If everyone just did these five things, we would see a drastic reduction in successful ransomware attacks. And for the attacks that still got through? You'd at least have a copy of your data that wasn't deleted or encrypted. Your restore process might take a while, but at least it would be *possible*.

As I'm now finishing this book, all of that is still true. And I believe it will always be true.

And seriously—if you're not doing anything on the preceding list, put this book down and go fix that *now*. There's not much point in everything else we discuss if you're not going to do the basics.

A Different Tack

Most ransomware books focus on prevention—trying to prevent you from getting it in the first place. A few also cover how to respond to an attack. But I didn't find any books that were dedicated to preparing you to be able to respond to *and recover from* an attack. So I set out to write one.

Odds are you're going to get ransomware. So let's acknowledge that fact and learn how to:

- Minimize the damage a single attack can cause
- Detect it sooner than later
- Fortify your backup system so it won't also get taken out
- Build an incident response plan (IRP) and an incident response team (IRT)
- Build up muscle memory on how to respond when the worst happens
- Know when to call in the pros

Bringing in the Cavalry

I initially thought I could write this one on my own, as I have for all my other books. But along the way, I realized that the readers would be much better served by someone with deep domain knowledge in the cybersecurity space. Which is why I decided to bring in a co-author for the first time—and I found the perfect co-author.

Besides being a great communicator and writer, Dr. Mike Saylor is a boots-on-the-ground warrior in this battle. He runs a managed security services provider (MSSP) called Blackswan Cybersecurity (*https://blackswan-cybersecurity.com*), and they are the folks you call on your worst day. They are the blue team—the guys you want in your corner before and during an attack.

We had him on *The Backup Wrap-Up* (*https://www.backupwrapup.com*) podcast, and he clearly knew what he was talking about. I asked him if he was interested, and he jumped at the chance. He is as dedicated to cyber as I am to backup and recovery.

He would write the cyber-heavy content, and I would write the backup-heavy content, and then we each reviewed the other person's work. The result is a very solid book that neither of us could have written by ourselves and that stands alone as the only book of its type. I'm going to write my acknowledgments now, so I'll stop talking about Mike.

Mike's Story

I have been in IT and cyber for about 30 years, in roles ranging from PC build technician and help desk to IT auditor, cybersecurity director, and CISO, while also teaching cybersecurity and computer science at colleges and universities since 1999. For the last 15 years, I've led IRTs and digital forensic investigations for clients on their worst day. I've worked with just about every law enforcement agency in the pursuit of cyber criminals and have contributed to three editions of a book on cybercrime and cyber terrorism with Bob Taylor.

The perspectives learned and experienced through these different roles and incidents have no doubt provided the content I share in this book. From the things that you must consider today in preparation for the inevitable, to descriptions and war stories of what to expect when it does happen—these are not theoretical/conceptual; they are facts that must be adapted for your organization ASAP.

How This Book Is Organized

This book follows the National Institute of Standards and Technology (NIST) Cybersecurity Framework 2.0, which organizes cybersecurity into five practical functions that form a complete defense lifecycle:

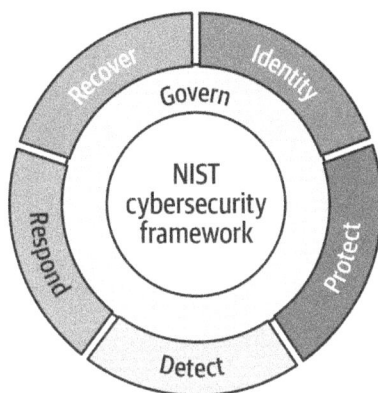

Identify (Chapters 1–2)

Understand what you're up against and which assets are most at risk. Spoiler: your backup system is now ransomware's primary target.

Protect (Chapters 3–7)

Build layered defenses before an attack happens. We'll cover backup fundamentals, basic cyber hygiene that stops 90% of attacks, blast radius containment, backup system hardening, and incident response planning.

Detect (Chapter 8)

Spot ransomware early with endpoint detection and response (EDR), security information and event management (SIEM), and backup monitoring so you find out in hours, not months.

Respond (Chapters 9–14)

Fight through the crisis when ransomware strikes. From the chaotic first 12 hours through containment, forensics, and permanent eradication.

Recover (Chapters 15–16)

Restore operations methodically without re-infection, then conduct post-mortem analysis to come back stronger than before.

Each section builds on the previous one, creating a complete playbook for ransomware defense and recovery.

Conventions Used in This Book

The following typographical conventions are used in this book:

Italic

Indicates new terms, URLs, email addresses, filenames, and file extensions.

Constant width

> Used for program listings, as well as within paragraphs to refer to program elements such as variable or function names, databases, data types, environment variables, statements, and keywords.

Constant width bold

> Shows commands or other text that should be typed literally by the user.

Constant width italic

> Shows text that should be replaced with user-supplied values or by values determined by context.

> This element signifies a tip or suggestion.

> This element signifies a general note.

> This element indicates a warning or caution.

O'Reilly Online Learning

O'REILLY® For more than 40 years, *O'Reilly Media* has provided technology and business training, knowledge, and insight to help companies succeed.

Our unique network of experts and innovators share their knowledge and expertise through books, articles, and our online learning platform. O'Reilly's online learning platform gives you on-demand access to live training courses, in-depth learning paths, interactive coding environments, and a vast collection of text and video from O'Reilly and 200+ other publishers. For more information, visit *https://oreilly.com*.

How to Contact Us

Please address comments and questions concerning this book to the publisher:

> O'Reilly Media, Inc.
> 141 Stony Circle, Suite 195
> Santa Rosa, CA 95401
> 800-889-8969 (in the United States or Canada)
> 707-827-7019 (international or local)
> 707-829-0104 (fax)
> *support@oreilly.com*
> *https://oreilly.com/about/contact.html*

We have a web page for this book, where we list errata and any additional information. You can access this page at *https://oreil.ly/learning-ransomware-response-recovery*.

For news and information about our books and courses, visit *https://oreilly.com*.

Find us on LinkedIn: *https://linkedin.com/company/oreilly-media*.

Watch us on YouTube: *https://youtube.com/oreillymedia*.

Acknowledgments (Curtis)

There is no "Mr. Backup" without all the people who supported me in my career, from the first person to give me a job in backup, to those who hired me along the way, acquired my companies, and let me stretch my wings.

I also have to thank those of you that have bought and read my books, listened to *The Backup Wrap-Up* (*https://www.backupwrapup.com*) podcast, read posts on Backup Central (*https://backupcentral.com*), attended my backup seminars, and responded to me on LinkedIn. You folks are why I do this. I hope I've helped.

Thank you to my family, starting with my wife and biggest fan, Celynn. It's not easy being married to an entrepreneur, but you always encourage me to follow my dreams. Thanks also to my daughters Nina and Marissa, and my granddaughter Lily. Killing zombie pirate skeletons with you in full-motion VR was the best way to celebrate finishing this thing. Thanks also to Hunter for taking care of Marissa and Lily. And finally, Brulee. Who's a good dog?

Thank you to my "everything advisor" and podcast co-host, Prasanna Malaiyandi. You are always a great sounding board and have the best advice and feedback. Don't ever change!

Thanks to Duane Laflotte for giving me that interview that made it into the book. Everyone has commented on how great it was. Keep up your great red-teaming!

Thank you to Dr. Mike Saylor, my coauthor. I'm so glad Legendary Podcasts booked you as a guest on *The Backup Wrap-Up*. Thanks for being the first to respond when I sent out a call for help. Thanks for your great content, and for jumping whenever Sara cracked the whip. I was terrified to bring in a co-author, but working with you was a breeze.

Thank you to Sara Hunter. You never gave up on me despite the many setbacks that were thrown my way during this project. How many times did I say "OK, *now* I have the time to work on this"? You were a constant positive influence, and I'm going to miss our Google Chats. Thank you so much.

Thank you to Simina Calin, who put up with me changing my mind on this book more than once. Thanks for sticking with me to the end, even when the page count ballooned on us. It's Mike's fault, I swear.

Thank you to our team of technical editors. You clearly believed in this book as much as we did, and it is so much better than it ever would have been without you. You gave me so much work to do! Thank you, thank you, thank you.

- Alex Hamerstone
- Gina Rosenthal
- Glenn Dekhauser
- Jack Poller
- Priyanka Neelakrishnan
- Stephen Manley
- Yaamini Mohan

Acknowledgments (Mike)

I'm incredibly grateful to have been part of this book, and I owe a huge thanks to Curtis for inviting me on this journey. Your vision and energy made this collaboration a joy, and I'm honored to contribute to your legacy in the backup world. Thank you, Sara Hunter, for keeping us on track with your relentless positivity and sharp oversight. To Simina Calin and the technical editors, your patience and keen insights elevated our work beyond what I thought possible. A special shoutout to Prasanna Malaiyandi for the wisdom shared on and off the podcast. To my wife Gina, kids Shelbe, Kyla, Ayden, and Knox, grandkids Bear and Laney—your support gave me the space to dive into this project. And to the readers, thank you for trusting us to guide you through how to respond and recover.

PART I

Identify

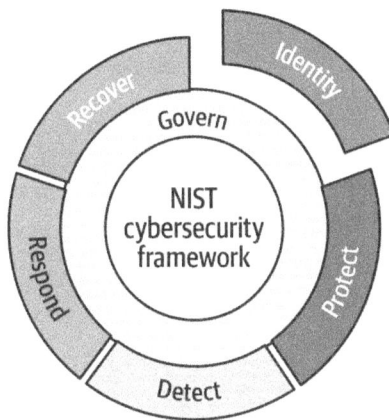

Understanding the Threat Landscape and Your Critical Assets

We wrote this book around the National Institute of Standards and Technology (NIST) Cybersecurity Framework 2.0 because it's one of the most practical, widely adopted approaches to cybersecurity that exists. The framework organizes cybersecurity activities into five functions: Identify, Protect, Detect, Respond, and Recover. Each function addresses a critical aspect of managing cybersecurity risk, and together they provide a complete lifecycle for defending against threats like ransomware.

This is the first section: *Identify*. You can't defend against threats you don't understand, and you can't protect assets whose vulnerabilities you haven't recognized. That's what Identify is all about—developing the organizational understanding you need to manage cybersecurity risk to your systems, people, assets, data, and capabilities.

For ransomware defense, identification starts with two critical questions: What exactly are we up against? And what are our most vulnerable assets?

Chapter 1, "What Is Ransomware?", answers the first question by breaking down the ransomware threat landscape. You'll understand what ransomware actually is, how it's evolved from simple encryption to sophisticated double-extortion campaigns, who the attackers are, and—most importantly—how attacks unfold from initial reconnaissance through final extortion. You can't build effective defenses if you don't know what you're defending against.

Chapter 2, "Your Backup System Is Under Attack", answers the second question, and it might surprise you. Your backup and disaster recovery system isn't just another IT asset—it's become the single most attractive target in your environment. Threat actors have figured out that a good backup system is the main reason organizations don't pay ransoms, so they've made disabling it their top priority. Worse, they've also discovered your backup system is the perfect tool for data exfiltration. Understanding this dual threat is essential for proper risk assessment.

Once you've completed this Identify section, you'll move into *Protect* (Chapters 3–7), where we'll show you how to harden your defenses based on what you've learned here.

CHAPTER 1

What Is Ransomware?

Imagine waking up to find all your files locked and a clock counting down until you pay up or lose everything. But that's just the beginning of your nightmare. While you're staring at that countdown timer, cybercriminals are already auctioning off your most sensitive data on the dark web, like your customer records, financial statements, employee information, or trade secrets, everything that could destroy your business and ruin lives. Your phones don't work, your email is down, your production line has stopped, and your employees are standing around helplessly while your company bleeds money by the minute. The attackers know exactly how much cyber insurance you have, when your backup administrator goes on vacation, and which systems will hurt you most when they're offline. They've been watching you for months, learning your weaknesses, and now they're squeezing you like a vice with a simple message: pay us millions in untraceable cryptocurrency or watch your company and reputation burn to the ground in front of your customers, competitors, and the evening news.

If your heart is racing right now, good. This first chapter might seem a little boring, so you need to know what's at stake. Let's take you on a journey through the fundamentals of ransomware, starting with a clear definition of what it is. We'll discuss how it has evolved to be more formidable by doing much more than just encrypting your data. We'll look into traditional encryption ransomware, the growing trend of data exfiltration, and the increasingly common tactic of double extortion. Understanding who the attackers are is just as important; we'll break down the roles of initial access brokers (IABs) and ransomware groups to shed light on the criminal ecosystem. Finally, we'll guide you through the typical sequence of a ransomware attack, arming you with the knowledge to better understand and combat this pervasive threat.

What Is Ransomware?

Ransomware is malicious software (*malware*) designed to block access to a computer system or encrypt its data until a ransom is paid. At its core, ransomware infiltrates a computer system (which may include servers, virtual machines [VMs], laptops, mobile devices, and more)—often through deceptive means like phishing emails or malicious downloads—and then encrypts the victim's files, making them inaccessible. Whatever that computer was supposed to be doing up to that point, it isn't doing it anymore. In more advanced attack scenarios, threat actors will use a type of ransomware capable of performing surveillance within victim systems and networks before strategically encrypting devices in a coordinated, larger scale attack that not only encrypts user data files but also impacts the organization's ability to conduct business by encrypting critical systems. This includes systems that support email, phones, internet, and business applications (e.g., invoicing, warehouse, payroll, etc.).

Ransomware has five fundamental objectives:

- Installing malware on victim computers without being detected
- Moving moving laterally across (i.e., traversing) the network to conduct reconnaissance and create an inventory
- Contacting the threat actor's command-and-control (C2) servers to negotiate the encryption keys
- Encrypting the target files
- Leaving a ransom note

The attackers, who are usually cybercriminals seeking financial gain, then demand a ransom payment, typically in the form of cryptocurrency like bitcoin, in exchange for a decryption key that can unlock the files. It's a bit like a digital kidnapping, where it's your files or systems that are held hostage. The appeal of ransomware to cybercriminals lies in its simplicity and effectiveness. With minimal effort and cost, they can disrupt entire organizations, from small businesses to large corporations, and even critical infrastructure like hospitals, water treatment plants, and government agencies. The disruption is not the goal, of course; it is a means to an end. It will give the attacker the leverage they need to extort the victim and get paid.

What makes ransomware particularly frightening is the pressure it exerts on victims, including the psychological and financial stresses for individuals, and the financial, operational, reputational, and regulatory pressure for organizations. The demand for ransom is often accompanied by a countdown clock, adding a sense of urgency and fear to the situation. Victims are told that if they do not pay within a specified time frame, the ransom could increase, their data will be permanently lost, or worse, it will be published online for all to see. This threat of data loss or exposure can lead to panic, pushing victims to pay the ransom even when there is no guarantee that the attackers will actually provide the decryption key, that the files will be recoverable, or that they'll honor their word in not publishing your data.

The evolution of ransomware over the years has also made it more dangerous. Early versions were relatively straightforward, simply locking users out of their systems until payment was made. However, modern ransomware has become more sophisticated, employing advanced encryption methods that are nearly impossible to break without the decryption key. Attackers have also developed new tactics, such as exfiltrating sensitive data before encrypting it and then threatening to release it publicly if the ransom is not paid—a tactic known as double extortion. This evolution has turned ransomware from a mere nuisance into a weapon of choice for cybercriminals worldwide, leading to billions of dollars in losses annually (Al-rimy et al., 2018 (*https://oreil.ly/Lec-Z*)). This evolution has made measuring the problem difficult.

True accounting for the impact and losses associated with ransomware has become more complicated over the years, primarily due to the evolution of the reconnaissance and extortion tactics we see today. For example, the Federal Bureau of Investigation's (FBI) annual Internet Crime Complaint Center (IC3) reported almost $60 million in losses in 2023. However, this data only captured *reported* incidents. The losses did not include lost business revenue or the wages, expense, and third-party remediation services related to recovering from the incident (Federal Bureau of Investigation Internet Crime Report, 2023 (*https://oreil.ly/rp_NP*)).

However, if you expand your research to include other perspectives on ransomware, like tracking crypto payments, you will begin to see the magnitude of the problem. The crypto-tracing firm Chainalysis published data that shows over $1.1 billion dollars in ransomware payments in 2023 (*https://oreil.ly/5vDSW*) (see Figure 1-1), a huge increase from the IC3 report and almost double the payments made in 2022.

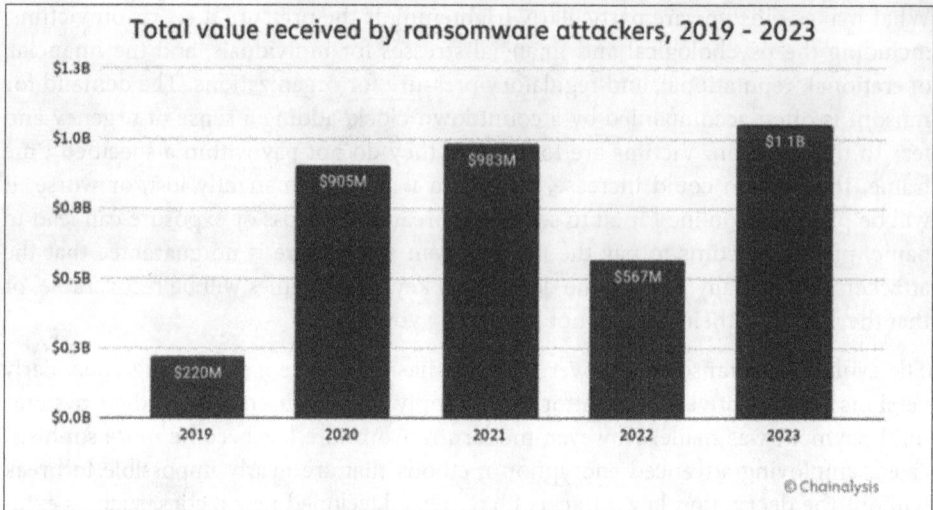

Figure 1-1. Ransomware crypto payments between 2019 and 2023, as reported by Chainalysis (source (https://oreil.ly/5vDSW))

In short, ransomware is a form of cyber extortion that preys on the fear of losing access to critical data, as well as having sensitive data leaked to the public and competitors. Its effectiveness and ever-evolving tactics make it one of the most challenging cyber threats to combat today. Understanding how ransomware works and the tactics used by cybercriminals is crucial for anyone looking to protect themselves or their organization from this growing threat.

> If you're new to either cybersecurity or backup and disaster recovery, this book is just for you. We also have a companion site, *StopRansomware.com*, that will have content just for you. We'll also be able to add updated content, since this world changes so quickly.

How Do You Get Ransomware?

Most ransomware infections start with social engineering, attempting to get the victim to download a file onto their computer or to interact with a malicious website. This is because, like most malware, ransomware typically requires interaction. (We say "typically" because some ransomware attacks are triggered by the threat actor, not the victim; we'll get to those later in Chapter 9.) This interaction is typically elicited via well-crafted phishing emails, containing malware or a link to a website with malware, that trick the victim into interacting. This opens the door for ransomware to download onto their device.

These phishing emails appear to be legitimate messages related to the victim's business, family, or topic of interest, or perhaps a free offer for something cool. Simply opening the email isn't enough to trigger the malware; it requires opening an attachment or clicking a link. If it's an attachment, then when the victim opens the file, the computer searches for the right application for viewing the attached file type (e.g., PDF, DOC, XLS, TXT, ZIP, RAR, etc.), and that operation often allows the ransomware to execute. If it's a website link, clicking it will take the victim to a malicious web address where malware could be automatically downloaded and installed in milliseconds.

Other common infection methods include Remote Desktop Protocol (RDP, which is used to remotely administer computers), software vulnerabilities, supply chain attacks, drive-by downloads, removable media attacks, network propagation, and stolen credentials.

Not securing RDP is like leaving your front door unlocked with a sign that says "Come on in." Attackers hammer away at poorly secured RDP connections with brute force attacks or use stolen credentials to waltz right into your systems. Once they're in through RDP, they can drop ransomware wherever they want or use that access as a launching pad to wreak havoc across your entire network.

Software vulnerabilities are the digital equivalent of broken windows that burglars love to exploit. Threat actors scan the internet looking for unpatched systems and applications, then use known exploits to break in without needing any help from users. This is why your IT team keeps nagging everyone about installing updates; those patches aren't suggestions, they're digital armor.

Supply chain attacks are particularly nasty because they turn your trust against you. Attackers compromise legitimate software updates or third-party tools, so when you install what looks like a routine update, you're actually rolling out the red carpet for ransomware. It's like getting poisoned by your own medicine cabinet.

Drive-by downloads happen when simply visiting the wrong website turns your browser into a delivery truck for malware. These compromised sites exploit vulnerabilities in browsers or plugins to automatically download and run ransomware without you clicking anything. It's digital food poisoning. You didn't mean to consume anything bad, but you got infected anyway.

Removable media attacks are the modern version of the old Trojan horse trick. Someone drops an infected USB drive in your parking lot, and curiosity kills the cat when an employee plugs it in to see what's on it. The malware springs to life and spreads through your network faster than office gossip.

Network propagation is how ransomware goes from "we have a problem" to "we're completely screwed." Once it gets a foothold on one machine, it spreads through your network like wildfire, using legitimate administrative tools and exploiting shared credentials. This is why network segmentation and proper access controls are so important; you want to contain the damage, not give it a highway system.

Stolen credentials let attackers walk through your front door wearing your own employee's badge. They use compromised usernames and passwords to deploy ransomware while looking like legitimate users to your security systems. It's the ultimate inside job, except the "insider" is actually a criminal wearing a disguise made of your own stolen data.

After the Initial Infection

Once inside your computer, the malware conducts reconnaissance, inventorying your entire network and any files you have access to and determining what privileges you have on your computer, the network, and possibly cloud environments like Microsoft or Google. These privileges will then be used to expand the scope of the attack. Once reconnaissance is done, and any exfiltration activities are conducted, the malware will begin encrypting files, making them inaccessible without a decryption key, which the attacker promises to provide in exchange for payment—often in hard-to-trace cryptocurrencies like Bitcoin (Bajpai, 2023 (*https://oreil.ly/CS6wX*)). The affected user is typically presented with a ransom note explaining the situation and providing instructions on making the payment.

One of the most notorious ransomware attacks in recent history was the WannaCry attack in 2017, which spread rapidly across the globe and infected more than 230,000 computers in over 150 countries (Mohurle and Patil, 2017 (*https://oreil.ly/UTHGQ*)). This attack exploited a vulnerability in Microsoft Windows, and the attackers demanded $300 in bitcoin for each infected machine. The impact was so severe that it caused disruptions in hospitals, businesses, and government agencies.

Then there was the Colonial Pipeline attack of 2021, when the DarkSide ransomware group pulled off one of the most devastating infrastructure attacks in US history. Colonial supplies about 45% of the East Coast's fuel. The attackers didn't need some sophisticated Hollywood hack; they got in through a compromised VPN password that probably should have been retired months earlier. Within hours, Colonial shut down their entire 5,500-mile pipeline system rather than risk the malware spreading to the operational technology systems that actually control fuel flow. Panic buying ensued, gas stations ran dry across the Southeast, and the US federal government declared a state of emergency. After six days of chaos and with their reputation bleeding out alongside their revenue, Colonial paid the $4.4 million bitcoin ransom. It was a masterclass in how ransomware doesn't just encrypt your files; it encrypts your ability to think clearly under pressure.

Case Study: Polymorphic Ransomware

To understand how polymorphic ransomware works in practice, let's examine Vir-Lock, the first self-reproducing polymorphic ransomware. This ransomware targets cloud or collaboration sites where its malware can spread through file sharing. The malware works by encrypting and repackaging victim files as an executable (e.g., your Word document *.doc* is now *.doc.exe*) but also infects each file with its ransomware. On the surface, each file looks normal and could be spread to coworkers or added to backups without anyone knowing they are infected.

When a file is infected with VirLock, it is repacked into a Win32 PE (Windows executable) file, and the *.exe* extension is added to its filename, unless it is already an executable file. When a victim opens an infected file, the ransomware decrypts the original file within its body, writes it to the current directory, and opens it. This behavior is one of the distinguishing characteristics of VirLock, as compared to typical file-encrypting malware.

VirLock then installs itself by dropping two non-identical polymorphic instances into the *%userprofile%* and *%allusersprofile%* directories. It also adds entries to the Windows Run registry keys to ensure these instances are executed with Windows startup. These instances contain only the virus code, with no host file to decrypt, and are launched immediately. Recent variants of VirLock also drop a third instance that is registered as a Windows system service. This mechanism provides self-preservation for the malware, automatically restoring terminated processes and deleted files.

The dropped instances are responsible for executing the malicious payloads. One thread focuses on file infection, with Win32/VirLock searching for host files across local and removable drives, network shares, and accessible cloud folders to enhance its ability to spread. The file extensions targeted for infection vary between VirLock versions, with recent samples focusing on *.exe*, *.doc*, *.xls*, *.zip*, *.pdf*, *.jpg*, and many others.

Specific to cloud-based collaboration targets, VirLock was especially successful at infecting and spreading across international boundaries. Let's look at an example of just two users (A and B) collaborating through a cloud platform with some form of file synchronization enabled. If user A gets infected with VirLock and all of their local files are infected, any file synced with the cloud folder then also becomes infected and subsequently syncs down to user B's computer. When user B opens any of the synced infected files, their local computer and all its files are then infected. Each infected file becomes an infector. Figure 1-2 depicts a typical corporate example where users (black dots) interact with shared files (grey dots)—all of the users within the grey boundary could become infected very quickly.

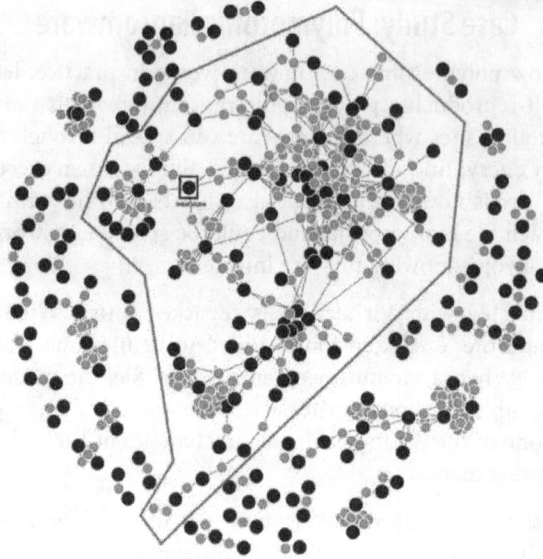

Figure 1-2. Example of VirLock spreading through typical corporate file sharing collaboration platforms (source (https://oreil.ly/iMjSK))

VirLock's ransom note varies by version and is either a straightforward threat actor demand for payment (Figure 1-3), or the alternative Operation Global III note that pretends to be an official notice from law enforcement related to pirated software detection and the requirement to pay a fine, in bitcoin (Figure 1-4).

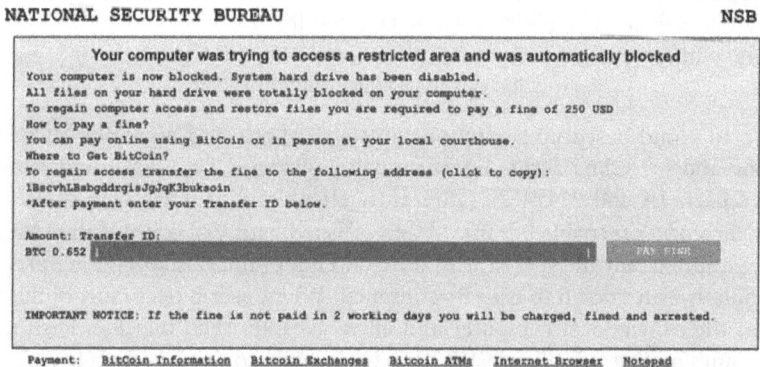

Figure 1-3. VirLock ransom note from ESET Security, December 22, 2014 (source (https://oreil.ly/ooaQ6))

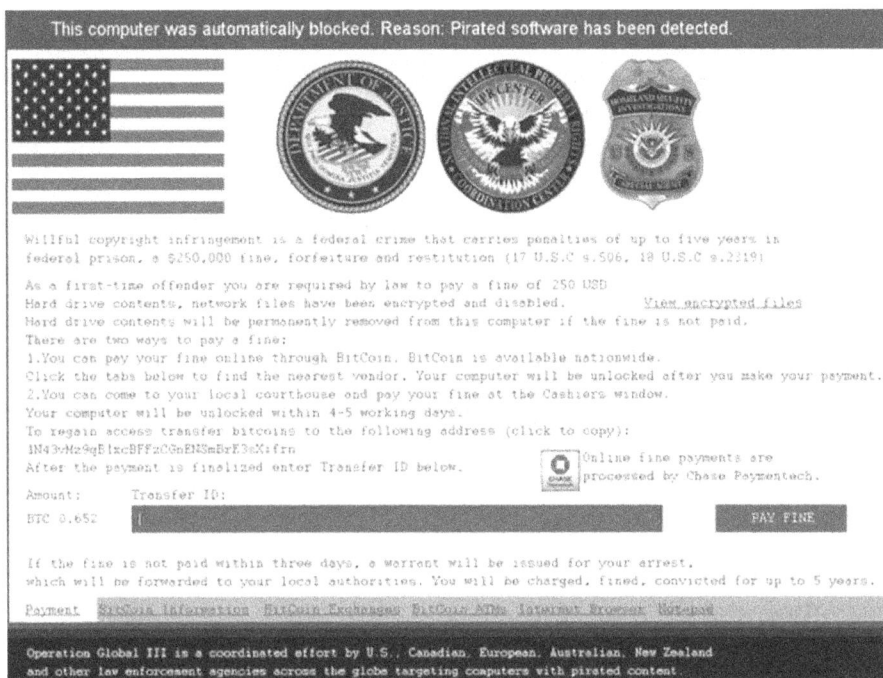

Figure 1-4. Operation Global III notice of software piracy fine from ESET Security (source (https://oreil.ly/ooaQ6))

For more information about this case study, see this article from Bleeping Computer (https://oreil.ly/tUC6M).

How Ransomware Avoids Detection

Ransomware is often detected through a combination of signature-based antivirus tools, behavioral analysis, and network monitoring systems that identify malicious patterns, such as unauthorized file encryption or suspicious network traffic. These detection mechanisms rely on recognizing known malware signatures, abnormal system activity, or communication with command-and-control servers. However, modern ransomware employs sophisticated techniques to evade these defenses, leveraging methods like polymorphism, obfuscation, and encryption to mask its presence. By constantly evolving its code, exploiting zero-day vulnerabilities (unknown, unpatched security flaws), or mimicking legitimate processes, ransomware can bypass traditional security measures, making it critical to understand how these evasion strategies work to effectively counter them.

Avoiding detection is an important skill for any malware developer. For ransomware, the malicious code is commonly hidden within a seemingly legitimate file or application, like a Microsoft Word file named *Invoice.doc* or *Resume.doc*. It can also leverage macros/basic code in Microsoft Office files (*.docx*, *.pptx*, *.xlsm*) as well as PDF files. It is also often disguised as system drivers or common executables living in the Windows system area.

This approach is described as a Trojan horse, similar to the ancient Greek history of Troy, where something appears to be one thing, tricking victims into accepting it, and resulting in something malicious. In addition to hiding the ransomware within another file, the malware is also encrypted to further disguise it from antivirus scanners.

Let's dive into the sophisticated techniques a ransomware developer uses to avoid detection. These techniques must evade security systems such as antivirus software, intrusion detection systems (IDS), and endpoint protection platforms. They have evolved significantly over time to maintain their infection success, making modern ransomware increasingly stealthy and difficult to detect.

Encryption and Obfuscation

There are two techniques that utilize encryption and obfuscation: code obfuscation and the packing or encryption of payloads. (In a ransomware context, the payload is the business end of the attack and is the actual malicious code that does the dirty work of encrypting your files once it's gotten into your systems. Think of it as the warhead on the missile.)

Code obfuscation
    Ransomware often obfuscates or disguises its code to make it difficult for static analysis tools to understand, utilizing techniques like encrypting strings, renaming functions to nondescriptive names, and using complex or redundant code structures to prevent easy identification of malicious code by antivirus programs.

Packing or encryption of payloads
    Attackers use packer and crypter programs to compress and encrypt the ransomware payload. The goal is to prevent antivirus solutions from analyzing the code until it is unpacked in memory on the target device, which can bypass signature-based detection systems. Traditional antivirus programs don't typically have AI or sandboxing capabilities (i.e., dynamic analysis) to identify the malware until its activities match an existing signature.

Polymorphism

There are two techniques that utilize polymorphism (like what happened in the case study mentioned earlier in this chapter): polymorphic code and metamorphic code:

Polymorphic code

This technique involves the ransomware slightly changing its code each time it infects a new system or replicates itself. These minor changes are often automated. The goal is to make it difficult for the signature-based detection methods of many antivirus programs to identify the malware, as each version of the ransomware looks different on the surface, even though it has the same core functionality.

Metamorphic code

A more advanced form of polymorphism where the entire code structure changes without altering the malware's functionality, further complicating detection by traditional security tools.

Fileless Malware Techniques

There are two fileless malware techniques: in-memory execution and script-based attacks:

In-memory execution

Ransomware increasingly operates filelessly, meaning it runs directly in the system's memory without writing files to disk. By avoiding the filesystem, the ransomware can bypass traditional file-based detection methods that scan for known malicious file signatures.

Script-based attacks

Ransomware may use PowerShell, Windows Management Instrumentation (WMI), or JavaScript to execute commands directly from memory, further reducing the likelihood of detection by antivirus systems focused on scanning files.

Exploiting Legitimate Tools

There are two techniques that exploit legitimate tools: living off the land and dual-use software:

Living off the land (LotL)

Ransomware often exploits legitimate system tools and administrative utilities like PowerShell, PsExec, or Windows Script Host (WSH) to perform malicious actions. Because these tools are commonly used in enterprise environments for legitimate purposes, it is difficult for security software to block or flag them without risking false positives.

Dual-use software

Attackers may also abuse widely used software (e.g., Microsoft Office macros) to deliver ransomware payloads. Since these are legitimate applications, security systems may not flag their usage unless specific anomalies are detected.

Stealthy Command-and-Control Channels

Command-and-control channels (also referred to as C2 channels) are the communication channels between the ransomware and the criminals running the show. Think of it as the bad guys' remote control system for managing their attack.

Once ransomware infects your systems, it doesn't just sit there quietly doing its thing: it needs to phone home. These C2 channels let the attackers communicate with their malware to do things like download additional payloads, get updated encryption keys, receive instructions on which files to target, or even get the "go" signal to start encrypting.

There are two techniques that utilize stealthy C2 channels: use of trusted platforms and use of the Tor network:

Use of trusted platforms

Ransomware can communicate with its command-and-control servers via trusted platforms such as Google Drive, Dropbox, Google Sheets, Slack, or even DNS. Since these platforms are widely used in enterprise environments, blocking them outright could disrupt business operations, making the ransomware's communications harder to detect. The DNS method is particularly stealthy, as it shows up as a normal DNS query. But it's for a very specific domain that would only be queried by ransomware looking for C2 instructions.

Use of the Tor network

Many ransomware variants use the Tor network for encrypted and anonymous communication with C2 servers. This prevents tracking and monitoring by network security tools since the traffic is encrypted and obfuscated.

Delaying Execution

There are two techniques that utilize delayed execution: delayed or timed execution and dormant phases:

Delayed or timed execution

Some ransomware delays its execution until after it has infiltrated the system to avoid immediate detection by behavioral analysis tools and to complete critical preparatory activities. This can involve waiting for a specific trigger (like a system reboot), implementing time delays before launching malicious actions, completing data exfiltration operations, or synchronizing encryption activities across multiple compromised systems to maximize the impact of the attack.

Dormant phases
Some ransomware lies dormant for a period after infection. It lies in wait so it can evade sandbox environments and analysis systems that monitor new software that is installed on a system. (*Sandbox environments* are isolated playgrounds where security folks can safely detonate suspicious files and malware to see what they actually do, without blowing up their real systems.) Once the ransomware detects it is no longer in a controlled environment, it can be remotely detonated by the attackers, request activation via C2 channels, or even self-activate its malicious functions, depending on the variant.

Behavioral Evasion

These techniques utilize behavioral evasion: environment detection and user-agent detection:

Environment detection
Ransomware often includes techniques to detect if it is running in a VM, sandbox, or other security research environment. If it detects such an environment, it may alter its behavior or terminate its execution to avoid detection. Common methods include checking for the presence of debugging tools, unusual memory configurations, or indicators of running in a VM.

User-agent detection
Some ransomware variants check for the type of system or user configuration before executing its payload. For example, it might verify whether the target machine is a specific operating system or belongs to a specific user profile, executing only when certain conditions are met.

Bypassing Endpoint Security

These techniques bypass endpoint security: privilege escalation and disabling security software:

Privilege escalation
Once ransomware gains access to a system, it may attempt to escalate its privileges to the level of a system administrator, allowing it to bypass user-level security measures and execute critical system commands without detection.

Disabling security software
Ransomware may attempt to disable security features such as antivirus, firewalls, and intrusion detection systems before launching its malicious payload. This can be achieved by modifying system settings or terminating security processes using

administrative privileges gained during the infection process, typically through privilege escalation exploits or by using stolen credentials obtained through phishing, credential dumping, or other compromise techniques.

Anti-Analysis Techniques

Some techniques that explicitly work against analysis include anti-debugging and control flow obfuscation:

Anti-debugging
Ransomware can employ anti-debugging techniques that prevent security researchers from using debugging tools (software that lets analysts step through code line-by-line) from examining the malware's behavior.

Control flow obfuscation
The malware's control flow can be intentionally altered to make it difficult for security analysts or automated tools to follow the logical sequence of the ransomware's actions. This includes adding meaningless loops, jumps, and conditional statements.

Self-Destruction and Anti-Forensic Techniques

Here are a couple of self-destruction techniques: log clearing and file deletion or encryption of logs:

Log clearing
Some ransomware variants delete logs, system event records, and other traces of their activities, making it difficult for forensic investigators to track how the infection occurred.

File deletion or encryption of logs
After completing its malicious actions, ransomware may delete itself or encrypt logs, making post-infection analysis difficult and reducing the ability of IRTs to identify the attack's origin or spread.

A Brief History of Ransomware

Ransomware started small but got scary fast. Most people consider the AIDS Trojan (see Figure 1-5) in 1989 to be the first ransomware attack; it was distributed on floppy disks at a health conference, demanding $189 sent to a PO Box in Panama. Quaint by today's standards, but it established the playbook: encrypt data, demand money.

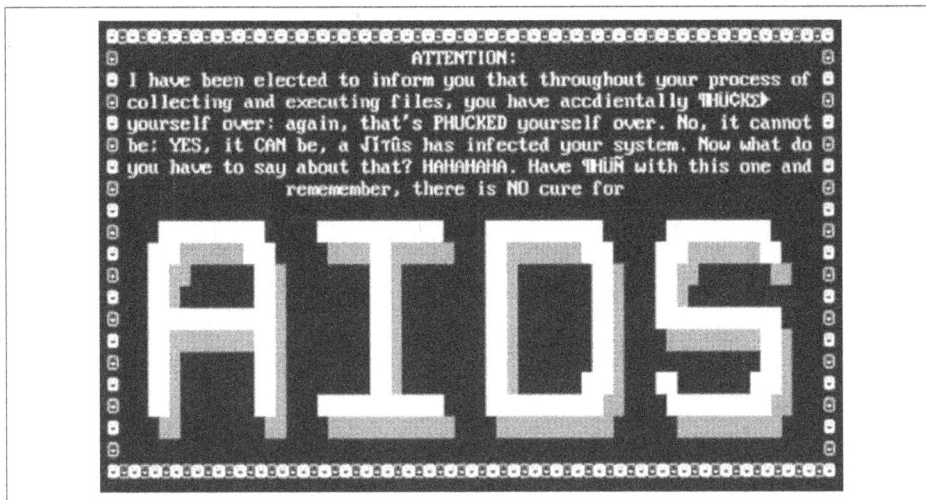

Figure 1-5. AIDS ransomware note

The real game-changer was CryptoLocker in 2013. It used military-grade encryption and demanded bitcoin payments, making it virtually impossible to recover data without paying (see Figure 1-6). Over 250,000 systems got hit, and attackers collected $3 million before law enforcement shut it down.

Figure 1-6. CryptoLocker ransom note

By the mid-2010s, ransomware-as-a-service (RaaS) democratized cybercrime and suddenly any script kiddie could rent professional ransomware kits and launch attacks. Then came the global nightmares: WannaCry hit 200,000 systems in 2017, crippling hospitals and businesses worldwide using leaked NSA tools.

In 2019, we started to see double extortion, where ransomware gangs started stealing data before encrypting it, threatening to leak your secrets if you didn't pay. Colonial Pipeline ($4.4 million ransom) and JBS ($11 million) showed how these attacks could disrupt entire industries.

Today's ransomware is a multibillion-dollar criminal enterprise (see Figure 1-7). Average ransom payments have skyrocketed from $170,000 in 2020 to over $1.7 million in 2023. Healthcare, critical infrastructure, and supply chains are prime targets because criminals know these victims "must pay" to keep operating.

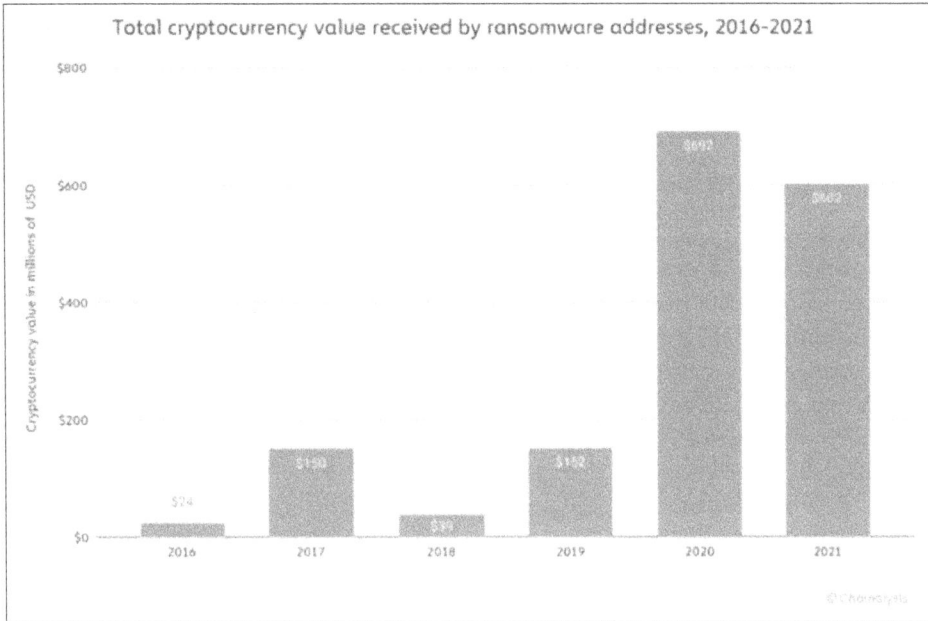

Figure 1-7. *Cryptocurrency value received by ransomware over time*

The bottom line: what started as a curiosity on floppy disks has become one of the biggest threats facing organizations today.

The Evolution of Ransomware

As you can see from the previous section, ransomware has evolved. What we would now call "traditional" ransomware locks up your most important files, like business documents, databases, family photos, tax records, using military-grade encryption like AES or RSA that's virtually unbreakable without the attacker's key.

Once your files are encrypted, you get a ransom note demanding cryptocurrency payment, often with a countdown timer cranking up the psychological pressure. Pay up or lose everything forever, they threaten.

But of course paying doesn't guarantee you'll get your data back. About 8% of victims who pay never receive working decryption keys, and even when they do, the recovery process often leaves some files corrupted. Worse yet, over 80% of victims who pay get hit again within six months.

The best defense against traditional ransomware is a solid backup and disaster recovery (DR) strategy, coupled with the ability to identify and respond to malware as quickly as possible 24 hours a day (this will be a recurring statement throughout the book). In recent years, many companies have implemented ransomware-specific recovery plans, for example, combining data restoration strategies with network segmentation and regular patch management to minimize the risk of infection. Additional methods and technologies will be discussed in more detail in subsequent chapters.

Double Extortion

Precisely because many organizations developed stronger backup and DR systems, ransomware attacks evolved, with one of the most significant trends being the incorporation of data exfiltration for use as leverage in extorting the victims to pay the ransom. In these modern attacks, cybercriminals encrypt the victim's files and steal sensitive information before demanding a ransom for both the decryption key and the promise not to leak the stolen data. *Double extortion*, which we've talked about already, heightens the stakes for victims, particularly organizations that manage confidential customer, client, or patient data. The threat of public exposure or sale of this data on the dark web adds additional pressure, often compelling victims to consider paying the ransom.

The financial, regulatory, or compliance implications of double extortion can be significant. While victims may believe they can recover their encrypted data from backups, the potential damage from a data leak can be far more damaging and longer lasting. Organizations are increasingly aware that the fallout from a data breach can lead to regulatory fines, loss of customer trust, and irreparable harm to their reputation. High-profile incidents involving healthcare providers and government agencies have underscored this risk, as leaked sensitive information can affect individuals' lives and jeopardize national security. As a result, many organizations feel they have no choice but to comply with attackers' demands.

Despite the push for improved security measures, ransomware payments' legal and ethical implications remain complicated. Some governments have proposed legislation discouraging or prohibiting ransom payments, arguing that compliance only fuels the ransomware economy. This has led to a contentious debate about the moral implications of paying ransoms. Organizations must weigh the immediate need for data recovery against potential legal repercussions and the ethical responsibility not to support criminal enterprises.

Collaboration among various stakeholders is essential to combat ransomware attacks that employ double extortion. Information-sharing initiatives between businesses, cybersecurity firms, and law enforcement agencies can enhance collective defenses against these threats. By sharing intelligence on emerging threats and known vulnerabilities, organizations can better prepare themselves to defend against potential attacks. Moreover, developing a coordinated response strategy can help minimize the impact of a successful ransomware incident, allowing affected entities to recover more quickly and effectively.

Case Study: Engineering Firm Compromised and Infected with Ransomware

It was a typical hot October Thursday morning in Texas, already 90 degrees by 10 a.m. My (Mike's) cell phone rings: it's the cybersecurity manager for one of the largest engineering firms in the US, to which we will give the fictional name Northforge. "Hey Mike, this is Bob from Northforge. We just got hit with ransomware, and we need help; about 80% of all our systems appear to be infected (approx. 2,300 computers and servers), and we aren't sure what to do about our engineering repository, but we think it's safe. Can you coordinate a call with our leadership team to help us respond to this?"

A few quick notes on this organization before we dig in. Northforge is a billion-dollar company with only two dedicated cybersecurity employees (a manager and an engineer) who report to the chief information officer (CIO). In late August of this same year, about five weeks prior to this incident, I moderated a ransomware tabletop exercise for this organization. The results from the tabletop identified several areas for improvement, including enhanced ability to detect and respond to malware, ensuring their critical systems are backed up offline, and testing their ability to recover from these backups, among other observations.

My firm coordinated Northforge's incident response (IR) call through our Microsoft Teams because the ransomware took down their network and phone system. Client executives and the IT team were all eagerly waiting to hear us explain to them what just happened, what to do next, how to respond, and lastly, that there was hope for getting through this. We could feel despair and anxiety coming through the phone, as they had no incident response plan (IRP) (except for "Call Mike"). They had not taken any action on the observations and recommendations from the recently completed ransomware tabletop exercise. In fact, it was later determined that the threat actors had compromised this organization's network several months prior to this incident and likely knew about the tabletop exercise and the recommendations for improving the environment.

On the call, we asked the typical briefing questions, like what happened, who has been involved, and what had been done so far. They educated us on all the business and operationally critical things. During this part of the conversation, it was determined through analyzing the ransom note and attributes of the encrypted files and the *.sz40* file extension that the threat actor was likely the Lorenz group. Figure 1-8 is the Lorenz ransom note that was placed on the computer's desktop and in every folder where files were encrypted. The Lorenz group is a sophisticated ransomware gang known for targeting large organizations with double-extortion attacks.

--=≡Lorenz. Welcome. Again. ≡=--

[+] Whats Happen? [+]

Your files are downloaded, encrypted, and currently unavailable. You can check it.
By the way, everything is possible to recover (restore), but you need to follow our instructions. Otherwise, you can't return your data (NEVER).

[+] What guarantees? [+]

It's just a business. We absolutely do not care about you and your deals, except getting benefits. If we do not do our work and liabilities - nobody will not cooperate with us. Its not in our interests.To check the ability of returning files, You should go to our website. There you can decrypt some file's for free. That is our guarantee. If you will not cooperate with our service - for us, it's does not matter. After deadline we'll publish all the contents of your company to site and we'll send all information to your client's and mass media. You will lose your time, data and reputation.Unfortunately many people if they see their personal info into web, will go to court. And for you it will be cost much expensive.

[+] How to get access on website? [+]

Using a TOR browser!

a) Download and install TOR browser from this site: https://torproject.org/
b) Open our website:
c) Check our website with leaks:

When you open our website, put the following data in the input form:
Company Key:

!!! DANGER !!!
DONT try to change files by yourself, DONT use any third party software for restoring your data or antivirus solutions - its may entail damage of the private key and, as result, The Loss all data.!!!
ONE MORE TIME: Its in your interests to get your files back. From our side, we (the best specialists) make everything for restoring, but please should not interfere.!!!

Figure 1-8. Lorenz ransom note

Also, during this initial call, we suggested involving federal law enforcement, like the FBI or Secret Service (collectively "the Feds"), due to their experience investigating related crimes, specifically the Lorenz gang. The thought was the Feds may already have a decryptor, which could provide intel for these threat actors and aid in forensic analysis. Additionally, involving them was a good demonstration of the company's due diligence in responding to the incident. We received approval to contact the FBI, and the incident was transferred to a field office specializing in the Lorenz gang.

The Lorenz group is a double extortion threat actor. In this case, Lorenz compromised the victim's network three months prior to the incident, conducted reconnaissance, compromised user accounts, and became knowledgeable about their business, revenues, insurance coverage, and vacation schedules. They strategically planned the infection for this particular Thursday because they knew the backup administrator was going on vacation the night before (Wednesday) and that Friday was a company holiday with limited coverage.

In addition, their persistent access up to this point also allowed them to use the victim's own network architecture to schedule the deployment and installation of the ransomware to every computer on the network at that time. At 8 a.m. Thursday morning, the automated delivery of the ransomware began, and within two hours, the damage had been done. Some computers were off at the time, some employees noticed something weird and turned their computer off, but the remaining online devices were completely infected.

Our team's next suggestion to Northforge was to contact their cyber insurance provider and brief them on the situation. The insurance company quickly connected us with their ransomware negotiator, who coincidentally works a lot with the Lorenz group. The negotiator informed us that this was already the fourth Lorenz call he'd had that day (it was 11 a.m.). The group's typical behavior is to compromise, learn and assess, exfiltrate your data, encrypt, and extort. He added that their extortion tactics involved a wall of shame website publishing their victims for the world to see, publishing victim data, selling victim data, and selling the access they gained in the initial compromise.

The negotiations began, and the initial volley was on Friday afternoon to ensure the victim's response was within two days of infection and prevent the initial posting on the wall of shame. The starting ransom demand was $8 million, and if they didn't receive a response by Monday, it would double to $16 million. Sunday afternoon we responded with an offer of $575,000.

I will note here that between Thursday morning and Sunday afternoon, the victim's critical engineering systems became infected. There were no backups for this data, which was one of the observations from the tabletop. The attackers likely knew the details of the victim's insurance coverage and countered with $4.5 million, which the company allegedly paid.

Northforge agreed to pay primarily because the Lorenz group offers not only the decryptor (unique to each infection), but also technical support to help you use it, tweak it, and test it. After the group received the money, most of the victim's data was recovered… except for the engineering data, because it was a proprietary system that the decryptor would not work on. ("Technical support" was no help.) It took the company approximately 7 weeks to finally recover from the ransomware attack at a total estimated cost of $7 million, including ransom payment, expenses, new systems, and lost revenue.

Understanding the Attackers: Initial Access Brokers

The ransomware ecosystem continues to evolve, with specialized roles emerging within cybercriminal organizations. One such role is that of an initial access broker (IAB). IABs play a crucial role in the ransomware ecosystem, serving as intermediaries between the attackers and the victims. These brokers specialize in gaining initial access to vulnerable systems and then selling that access to ransomware groups. IABs often exploit weaknesses in security protocols, using techniques such as phishing, social engineering, or exploiting unpatched software vulnerabilities to infiltrate organizations. (*Phishing* is a form of social engineering that includes phishing [email], smishing [SMS text], vishing [voicemail], pretexting, and now AI-driven deepfake phone and video calls.) By focusing on the entry point, IABs allow ransomware groups to bypass the often more challenging task of breaching well-defended organizations, thereby streamlining the attack process for cybercriminals.

IABs are a very organized and profitable part of the cybercrime landscape. They typically operate on a commission basis, earning a cut of the ransom collected from victims. This creates a symbiotic relationship where IABs provide the necessary access while ransomware groups can focus on what they do best: deploying the ransomware and negotiating the ransom. The profitability of this arrangement incentivizes IABs to continuously refine their techniques and tools, which can lead to more sophisticated and targeted attacks. However, some IABs may also directly affiliate with specific ransomware groups, leading to more collaborative attacks. This relationship can enhance the attack's efficiency, as IABs may have insider knowledge about the vulnerabilities that are most likely to lead to successful attacks.

IABs will also obtain access to victim systems, then post the access for sale. In 2024, large organizations with revenues over $1 billion were the most targeted, making up 27% of all initial access listings for sale. Most IABs charge between $500 and $2,000 for typical corporate access and upwards of $10,000 for high-value targets. The three primary types of access being sold by IABs are RDP at over 70%, VPN access credentials at 16%, and web shell access at 13%. The credentials for US organizations far outpace those of other countries as the most targeted, as shown in Figure 1-9 (for more information, see this article from Cyberint on IABs (*https://oreil.ly/wnVgE*)).

| USA 42% | France 19% | Brazil 9% | India 8.3% | Italy 4.1% |

Figure 1-9. IAB postings by country (source (https://oreil.ly/wnVgE))

As the landscape of cybercrime continues to evolve, the role of IABs will likely grow more significant. Their ability to quickly adapt and exploit new vulnerabilities makes them formidable adversaries. Organizations must remain vigilant and agile, continuously updating their security measures to counter the changing tactics of IABs and ransomware groups. By understanding the dynamics of this relationship and implementing robust defenses, organizations can reduce their risk of falling victim to ransomware attacks and protect their sensitive data from exploitation.

Understanding the Typical Attack Sequence

Ransomware attacks have become a persistent threat in today's digital landscape, targeting individuals and organizations alike with increasingly sophisticated methods. Understanding the typical attack sequence can provide valuable insights into how these attacks unfold and the steps that can be taken to mitigate their impact. From the initial reconnaissance phase, where attackers gather intelligence on their targets, to the final negotiation and recovery stages, each phase of a ransomware attack is carefully planned to maximize the threat actors' chances of success. By breaking down this sequence, organizations can better prepare themselves to defend against these potential threats and respond effectively in the event of an attack.

A typical ransomware attack follows a structured sequence of steps, each crucial for the attacker's success. Let's go through the common phases.

Reconnaissance

Attackers begin by gathering information about their target. This may involve blind internet queries, scanning the target's network, identifying vulnerabilities, and understanding the organizational structure. They might use tools to probe for open ports, outdated software, or weak security practices that could be exploited.

This phase can be broken down into several key activities:

Open source intelligence (OSINT) gathering
> Attackers often begin by collecting publicly available information from a variety of sources, such as social media profiles, company websites, and public databases. This information can reveal details about the organization's infrastructure, employees, and technologies, helping attackers to identify potential weak points. An example could be a LinkedIn search for employees at a target organization, their geographic locations, prior employment, recently posted accolades, vendor partners, and projects.

Network scanning
> Using tools like Nmap and Shodan, attackers target networks with live hosts (a device that responds to network requests), open ports, and the services running on those ports. This helps them understand the network's layout and pinpoint systems with unpatched vulnerabilities or misconfigurations. They will also scan your organization's use of the cloud and attempt to penetrate your cloud resources as well.

Identifying software vulnerabilities

Attackers search for known vulnerabilities in the software and hardware used by the target. They may refer to databases like the National Vulnerability Database (NVD) or exploit kits that catalog these weaknesses. Understanding which systems are outdated or poorly secured allows attackers to tailor their approach for maximum effectiveness.

Employee targeting

Social engineering plays a significant role in reconnaissance. Attackers may identify key employees, especially those in IT or executive positions, and gather information that could facilitate social engineering attacks. This includes analyzing email formats and internal communication styles or even using LinkedIn to identify roles and connections that may lead to more effective deception.

Third-party risks

Attackers may also assess third-party vendors or partners interacting with the target organization. Supply chain vulnerabilities can be a significant entry point, and attackers often look for ways to exploit less secure vendors to gain access to their primary target.

By conducting thorough reconnaissance, attackers can effectively customize their strategies, increasing their chances of success in the later stages of the attack. Organizations that understand this phase can take proactive measures, such as tightening access controls, enhancing employee training on social engineering, and regularly auditing their security posture to mitigate the risk of falling victim to ransomware.

Initial Access

Once reconnaissance is complete, attackers seek to gain entry into the target's systems. This can be achieved through various methods, such as phishing emails containing malicious attachments or links, exploiting unpatched software vulnerabilities, leveraging compromised credentials from previous data breaches, or even simply paying vulnerable employees to use their credentials. Initial access brokers may also facilitate this step by selling access to vulnerable networks. Here are some common methods used in this phase:

Phishing attacks

One of the most prevalent methods for gaining initial access is through phishing attacks that may include emails, SMS messages, and even voice and video messages created using AI. Attackers craft what appear to be legitimate messages that trick recipients into clicking on malicious links or downloading infected attachments. These emails may impersonate trusted entities, such as colleagues, service providers, or reputable companies, increasing the likelihood of a successful breach.

Malware delivery

In some cases, attackers may use malware delivery techniques such as drive-by downloads, where malicious code is executed on a user's system without their consent when they visit a compromised website. This method can infect systems quickly and stealthily, often without the target's knowledge.

Exploiting vulnerabilities

Attackers often exploit unpatched software vulnerabilities or misconfigurations in applications and operating systems. They may use exploit kits or custom scripts to target known vulnerabilities, gaining unauthorized access to systems. Common targets include outdated web servers, content management systems, and network devices.

Credential stuffing and brute force attacks

With access to stolen credentials from previous breaches or databases, attackers may employ credential stuffing techniques to log into accounts across various platforms. Alternatively, they might use brute force attacks to guess weak passwords and gain access to critical systems, particularly those with inadequate security measures.

RDP exploitation

Many organizations use RDP for remote access, but weak configurations and poor password practices can leave these systems vulnerable. Attackers may scan for exposed RDP ports and attempt to log in using compromised credentials or exploit vulnerabilities in the RDP protocol itself.

Employing these techniques can give attackers a foothold within the target's network, allowing them to execute the next stages of the ransomware attack.

Case Study: Compromised Employee Account Compromises Company

A client that we (Mike's company) provide 24/7 cybersecurity monitoring for called us in September 2024 about a data breach; their sensitive data was being posted for sale on a breach forum. We quickly determined that the source of the data was a system that our 24/7 monitoring team did not have visibility into. We also identified the user whose account was compromised. Speaking to the employee, they couldn't recall work-related incidents, like phishing emails or clicking anything out of the ordinary. Instead, they noted that their personal email was having a lot of issues.

We searched their personal email address in the recent data breach repositories and determined that their personal email was compromised in April 2024. Talking with the employee again, they indicated that their personal email issues began in July 2024, which correlated to the circumstances surrounding the company's data breach. We asked if they used the same password between home and work, to which they responded, "No, but I store many of my other passwords in my personal email account, including my work credentials."

Execution and Installation

Attackers deploy the ransomware payload after gaining initial access to the environment. This "access" can occur through attackers logging in with compromised credentials or an automated script triggered by the victim's interaction with an email attachment or a link they clicked. After breaching the system, the malware dropper file executes and starts its reconnaissance to determine its access, privileges, and the type of host it is installed on (e.g., workstation, point of sale, centrifuge) in preparation for encrypting files on the infected system. Attackers may also establish a foothold by installing additional malware, such as keyloggers or remote access tools, to maintain control over the system and facilitate further actions. Here's a detailed breakdown of the key steps in this stage:

Payload execution
  Attackers execute the ransomware payload on the compromised machine after obtaining access. This can occur in several ways depending on the method of entry. If access was gained through phishing, the payload might be disguised as a legitimate file (e.g., a document or a PDF) that triggers the ransomware upon opening. If the breach occurred through vulnerability exploitation or remote desktop access, attackers may manually run the payload once inside the system. Attackers often use scripting languages like PowerShell or command-line interfaces to automate this execution, bypassing traditional antivirus software.

Persistence mechanisms
  Once the ransomware is executed, attackers aim to establish persistence in the system, ensuring that they maintain control even if the system is rebooted or if the initial payload is detected. Common persistence techniques include creating scheduled tasks, modifying registry keys, or embedding the malware in system startup processes. This persistence ensures that even if part of the ransomware is removed, it can continue to spread or remain dormant until reactivated.

Privilege escalation
  After initial execution, attackers often attempt to escalate their privileges to gain deeper access to the organization's IT infrastructure. Privilege escalation allows attackers to gain the privileges of an administrative or system-level account, giving them full control over the infected machine or even the entire IT infrastructure. Attackers may exploit vulnerabilities in operating systems, use credential-stealing tools (like Mimikatz), or crack administrative passwords to gain higher privileges.

Installation of additional tools

Attackers often install other malicious tools alongside the ransomware to enhance their control over the network and facilitate further attacks. Commonly installed tools include:

- *Credential dumpers*: Tools like Mimikatz allow attackers to extract usernames and passwords from the system's memory or cached files. This is essential for lateral movement across the network and gaining access to high-value systems.

- *Remote access trojans (RATs)*: RATs provide attackers with ongoing remote access to infected systems, allowing them to execute commands, upload or download files, and monitor user activity in real time.

- *Cobalt Strike*: A legitimate penetration testing tool often repurposed by attackers, Cobalt Strike helps in lateral movement, reconnaissance, and payload delivery. It also supports beaconing, enabling attackers to maintain communication with infected systems. (*Beaconing* is when malware periodically "phones home" to its C2 servers, like a digital heartbeat that says "I'm still here and ready for orders.")

C2 communication

During this phase, the ransomware may communicate with a C2 server to receive instructions, download additional malicious files, or upload exfiltrated data. As previously mentioned, C2 traffic is often encrypted or obfuscated to avoid detection. Attackers often use encrypted communications (such as HTTPS or TOR) to prevent detection. These communications enable the attackers to adjust their tactics in real time based on the network environment or to receive confirmation that their ransomware is ready for deployment.

Obfuscation and evasion

Attackers often employ obfuscation techniques to avoid detection by antivirus software and other security measures during the execution phase. They may encrypt the ransomware payload or use polymorphic code, which changes its appearance with each infection. Other evasion methods include sandbox detection (where the ransomware can detect if it's running in a virtual environment and halt execution) and process hollowing, where the malware injects itself into legitimate processes to hide its activity.

Lateral movement

Once the ransomware is installed and attackers have administrative control, they begin moving laterally through the network to infect as many systems as possible. Let's take a look at this in more detail in the next section.

Expanding Scope and Data Gathering

Once the ransomware is in place, attackers often move laterally within the network to infect additional systems and servers. They may also exfiltrate sensitive data before encryption, increasing their leverage during ransom negotiations. This stage may involve gathering information on critical files, databases, and other valuable data that could be used to pressure the victim.

Lateral movement

Lateral movement involves attackers expanding their control beyond the initially compromised system by navigating through the network to access other critical systems and data. This allows them to infect more devices, escalate privileges, and locate high-value data that could be encrypted or stolen. Key techniques used in lateral movement include:

Mapping out network architecture
> If attackers can gain initial access to a lower-level system, they may use tools to further probe the network for additional information, such as Active Directory (AD) structures or domain trusts. This internal mapping helps them plan for lateral movement once they establish a foothold.

Credential dumping
> Attackers often use tools like Mimikatz or Local Security Authority Subsystem Service (LSASS) process injection to extract credentials from memory, allowing them to impersonate users or escalate their privileges. With administrative credentials in hand, they can access other machines, network resources, or even domain controllers.

Pass-the-hash and pass-the-ticket attacks
> Using stolen credentials, attackers may carry out pass-the-hash or pass-the-ticket attacks, which allow them to authenticate on other systems without needing to know the user's plaintext password. These attacks exploit weaknesses in authentication mechanisms within the network, making lateral movement swift and less detectable.

Remote execution
> Attackers often use legitimate tools and protocols, such as PowerShell, Windows Management Instrumentation (WMI), or PsExec, to move laterally. These tools allow them to run commands or scripts on remote machines, making it easier to distribute the ransomware across multiple systems. By using legitimate tools, attackers can evade detection, as their activities may appear normal to security teams and antivirus solutions.

Exploiting trust relationships

Attackers target systems with trust relationships, such as domain controllers, file servers, or AD. Compromising the domain controller gives attackers complete control over the network, allowing them to distribute ransomware more widely and target sensitive resources, such as backups, HR files, or finance systems.

Pivoting and network mapping

During lateral movement, attackers may perform internal reconnaissance to map the network and identify additional high-value systems, such as databases, file servers, or backup servers. They may also set up "pivot points" or use tunneling to route malicious traffic through compromised systems, which helps avoid detection by security teams monitoring network traffic.

Network propagation techniques

Attackers frequently use automated techniques, such as worms or self-spreading ransomware, to propagate across networks. These techniques exploit shared network drives, mapped drives, or known vulnerabilities to rapidly infect large portions of the network. Self-propagating ransomware like WannaCry and NotPetya used this method with devastating effects, spreading quickly within minutes.

Data exfiltration

By stealing sensitive data before encryption, attackers gain additional leverage over victims, threatening to release or sell the stolen information if the ransom is unpaid. This technique, typically called *double extortion*, has become the norm, and data exfiltration is essential to that strategy. Key techniques for data exfiltration include:

Identifying and targeting sensitive data

Before exfiltration, attackers typically search for and identify critical data. This may include financial records, intellectual property, personally identifiable information (PII), or health records, depending on the organization. Attackers may also steal email archives, internal communications, or legal documents, knowing these could damage the organization's reputation if leaked.

Encryption and compression

To avoid detection during the data exfiltration process, attackers often compress and encrypt the stolen data before sending it out of the network. Tools like 7-Zip or custom scripts are used to package large volumes of data into smaller, encrypted archives. This not only obscures the contents but also reduces the size of the data, making it easier to exfiltrate without triggering bandwidth-based alarms.

Stealthy exfiltration channels

Attackers use various methods to transfer data out of the network stealthily:

- *FTP or SFTP*: Standard file transfer protocols are often used to send stolen data to attacker-controlled servers.

- *Cloud storage abuse*: Attackers may use popular cloud storage services like Google Drive, Dropbox, or AWS S3 buckets to upload stolen data, knowing that these services are commonly allowed by organizations' firewall rules.

- *DNS tunneling*: By embedding stolen data within seemingly normal DNS queries, attackers can bypass detection by security systems. DNS tunneling allows data to be exfiltrated in small chunks over time without raising suspicion.

- *HTTP/HTTPS traffic*: Many attackers leverage HTTPS or custom C2 channels that use encryption to hide exfiltrated data within regular web traffic. This can make it difficult for security solutions to detect abnormal activity, especially when encrypted traffic is not inspected closely.

- *TOR and other VPN-like mechanisms*: Modern malware often routes this traffic through TOR, VPNs, or other anonymization services that not only hide the communication content but also mask the actual destination IP addresses and URLs. This makes it much harder for security teams to track down the real C2 infrastructure or block the communications.

Disabling security mechanisms

To further ensure successful data exfiltration, attackers may disable or evade security measures like data loss prevention (DLP) systems, IDS, or firewalls. This could involve using administrative privileges to alter logging configurations, silencing alerts, or exploiting blind spots in network monitoring tools. This means that the IDS or EDR solution is often only helpful in preventing or detecting the initial compromise.

Timing and throttling

Attackers often conduct exfiltration in small increments over an extended period, known as data throttling, to avoid raising suspicion. By sending data in smaller chunks, they evade network monitoring tools that may flag large or unusual data transfers. Attackers may also execute exfiltration during off-hours, such as late at night or during holidays, when security teams are less likely to notice the abnormal activity.

Once data exfiltration is complete, attackers will encrypt the victim's files. This combination of stolen data and encrypted systems gives the attackers immense leverage. They can demand two types of ransoms:

1. Payment for decryption to restore access to the victim's systems and files.

2. Payment to prevent data leaks, where they threaten to release or sell the stolen data if the victim refuses to pay.

This strategy forces organizations to face both operational disruption and reputational damage, as leaked data could lead to legal consequences, regulatory penalties, or loss of customer trust.

Ransom Demand

After the encryption process is complete and any sensitive data has been exfiltrated, attackers present their ransom demand. Victims receive a message detailing the ransom amount, typically in cryptocurrency, along with instructions on how to pay. The threat of data leaks or public exposure is often used to compel the victim to comply. If the ransom is not paid within a specified timeframe, attackers may threaten to release or sell the stolen data. Let's look at the components of this phase.

Ransom note delivery

Once the encryption process is complete, victims receive a ransom note or message that outlines the attackers' demands. This message is typically delivered in one of the following ways:

Pop-up messages
> The ransomware displays a prominent message on the victim's screen, blocking access to the system and making it clear that files have been encrypted.

Text files or HTML files
> The ransomware may leave ransom notes as text or HTML files scattered across affected folders. These files provide instructions on contacting the attackers and paying the ransom.

Desktop backgrounds
> Some ransomware variants go further by changing the victim's desktop background to the ransom message, ensuring visibility when the user attempts to log in.

Ransom note contents

A ransom note will likely contain the following components:

Description of the attack
> Attackers briefly explain what has happened, stating that the victim's files have been encrypted and/or sensitive data has been stolen.

Payment instructions
> Attackers provide specific instructions on making the payment, typically in cryptocurrency (e.g., Bitcoin or Monero), which offers anonymity for the attackers. They may also direct the victim to dark web portals where further communication can occur.

Deadline

To increase urgency, attackers often set a strict deadline for the ransom payment. The ransom note may include a countdown, and the consequences of failing to pay within the specified time:

- The ransom price doubles.

- The decryption key is destroyed, resulting in permanent data loss.

- The stolen data is publicly released or sold on the dark web.

Proof of decryption

Attackers sometimes offer to decrypt a few files for free as proof that they can restore the victim's data upon payment. This is intended to convince the victim that paying the ransom is a viable solution.

Ransom amounts

The ransom demand is often carefully calculated based on several factors:

Size of the organization

Larger organizations are typically targeted with higher ransom amounts, often in the millions of dollars, as attackers know that the financial loss from downtime and data breaches can far exceed the ransom cost. (This knowledge usually comes from financial reconnaissance, which is conducted at the same time or before cyber reconnaissance.)

Industry

Certain industries, such as healthcare, finance, and government, are more likely to be targeted with higher ransom demands due to the critical nature of their data and operations. For example, healthcare organizations are highly vulnerable because encrypted patient records can disrupt medical services, which increases the pressure to pay quickly.

Impact of data loss

In double extortion attacks, if attackers have exfiltrated sensitive data, they may adjust their demands based on the potential damage caused by a data leak. The more valuable or sensitive the stolen information (e.g., financial data, trade secrets, customer information), the higher the ransom amount.

Precedents

Attackers may base their demands on successful payments made by similar organizations in previous attacks, which are sometimes publicized in news reports or hacker forums.

Cryptocurrency payments

Ransom payments are almost always requested in cryptocurrency, as they offer attackers greater anonymity and are difficult for law enforcement to trace. The process of paying the ransom usually involves:

Setting up a cryptocurrency wallet
> Victims are instructed to create a cryptocurrency wallet and obtain the required amount of cryptocurrency, often Bitcoin or Monero. Attackers often provide detailed guides on how to do this, knowing that many victims may be unfamiliar with cryptocurrencies.

Payment through a dark web portal
> Attackers typically use a secure dark web portal to manage the transaction and further communication. These portals may be accessed via the Tor network, ensuring encryption and anonymity. The portal will provide a unique payment address and track the payment progress.

Escrow or payment verification
> Once the ransom is paid, attackers may either release the decryption key immediately or use an escrow-like system where the payment is verified before the key is delivered.

Why double extortion is so scary

Double extortion ups the ante and increases the pressure on victims to comply because the consequences extend beyond encrypted files:

Reputational damage
> A public data leak can severely harm an organization's reputation, especially concerning sensitive customer information or intellectual property. This can lead to long-term financial losses, regulatory penalties, and lawsuits.

Regulatory fines
> For organizations that handle regulated data (e.g., healthcare records or financial information), a data breach can result in substantial fines under laws such as GDPR or HIPAA. The threat of data exposure in ransomware attacks forces organizations to weigh the ransom cost against potential legal repercussions.

Customer trust
> Leaked customer data can damage trust in the organization, leading to loss of business and erosion of brand loyalty.

Ransom discounts
> In some cases, attackers may offer "discounts" if the victim pays within a certain timeframe, further increasing the urgency and pressuring the organization to make a quick decision.

Negotiation and Payment

After a ransom demand has been issued, victims of a ransomware attack must decide whether to negotiate, pay the ransom, or attempt recovery through other means. The negotiation and payment phase can be complex and risky, as it involves communication with cybercriminals who may not speak the same language as the victim, potential financial losses, legal concerns, and operational consequences. This phase often marks a turning point in the victim's response strategy, and the approach taken can have long-term effects on the organization's security posture and reputation. If the ransom is paid, the victim receives a decryption key, though there is no guarantee that it will work or that all data will be restored.

Decryption and Recovery

Organizations may also face the arduous process of restoring systems from backups, if available, and strengthening their security to prevent future attacks. Post-incident, organizations often conduct thorough investigations to understand the attack vector and improve their defenses.

If the ransom is not paid, the victim organization must rely on data restoring from backups in order to return systems to a fully operational state. In this scenario, every infected system must be rebuilt to ensure no traces of the ransomware remain. Key considerations during this step include:

Backup integrity
> Before restoring from backups, organizations must ensure that they have not been infected by ransomware. A significant portion of this book will be dedicated to this topic.

Digital forensics
> In some cases, digital forensics can be used to extract files from infected systems. If the infected system was powered off before the ransomware completed its infection, there may still be uninfected and unencrypted files that can be safely extracted. These files should still be scanned with anti-malware tools to ensure their integrity is intact. There are risks with this approach, though: keys may not work, or partial decryption may occur (especially with poor ransomware coding).

Summary

Ransomware has evolved from a curious floppy disk experiment in 1989 into a multibillion-dollar criminal enterprise that's holding the world hostage. What started as the AIDS Trojan demanding $189 sent to a PO Box has morphed into sophisticated operations where cybercriminals don't just encrypt your files—they steal your data first, then threaten to leak it if you don't pay up. These aren't lone wolves anymore; they're organized crime syndicates with specialized roles like IABs who sell network access to ransomware gangs for a cut of the profits. The attack playbook is disturbingly methodical: reconnaissance, initial access (usually through phishing), lateral movement, data exfiltration, encryption, and extortion—all designed to maximize pressure on victims who face operational shutdown, regulatory fines, and reputational damage. The kicker? Even if you pay the ransom (which averages over $1.7 million now), there's no guarantee you'll get your data back, and 80% of victims who pay get hit again within six months. The bottom line is that ransomware has become the weapon of choice for cybercriminals because it works, and understanding how these attacks unfold is the first step in defending against them.

CHAPTER 2

Your Backup System Is Under Attack

If you learn nothing else while reading this book, please learn this: your backup system is likely in grave danger. It is a prime target in an attack, and if they are successful at attacking it:

- It may be unable to perform its most vital function after an attack.
- It may be the reason that your organization ultimately ends up paying the ransom.
- The backup system may be the attack vector through which the ransomware attack happens in the first place.

Did we get your attention? We hope we did, because the only thing worse than knowing that you're not able to help during any events that would disable your organization is knowing that your backup system was the ultimate cause. You are patient zero. You are the one that let the bad guys in the backdoor.

> Some may think "backup system" refers to on-premises servers running backup software; however, in this context, it refers to any system (in the non-IT sense) that is designed to be able to restore your computers after an attack. This may be an on-premises system, a software as a service (SaaS)–based backup provider, or backup software running in cloud systems that you manage. No matter where it is, threat actors are coming for it.

Why Is the Backup System Under Attack?

If the situation is so dire, then why wasn't the backup system always the attack target? Backup systems have been a vulnerable part of the data center for a long time, so it's surprising that it took threat actors this long to finally pay some attention to them.

Once a threat actor understands just how vulnerable the typical backup system is, it may become the most interesting target in the environment! Yes, just like all security reporting, me acknowledging this in print will make it more true. Bad guys read O'Reilly books, too, right?

The initial reason that threat actors began targeting the backup system was that a good backup and DR system was the number one reason their victims did not pay a ransom. If you have a good backup and DR system and know that you can easily recover your entire environment within the time period your organization has agreed to, why would you even consider paying a ransom? But now they are also using it as a source of data exfiltration. But first, let's talk about the recovery part.

Quick Chat About RTO and RPO

When designing a backup or disaster recovery system, you must first decide what requirements it is going to meet, and the most critical requirements are going to be RTO and RPO. The *recovery time objective*, or RTO, is the amount of time that we all agree it should take to restore a system to working order. This isn't just restoring the data or even getting a database fully up and running. This is looking at an entire application and saying that the entire application should be able to accomplish its function again within a particular amount of time, such as 2 hours, 12 hours, or even 2 days. In the context of a ransomware attack, the recovery time will include the time it takes to clean your systems of malware before the restore begins. (This is why it is quite common to have a much longer RTO for ransomware attacks.) Determining that value in your environment is entirely up to your organization and how it will be negatively impacted by a particular application being down for a particular period of time.

> If you're new to the backup world, this book should explain much of what you need to know, especially the next chapter on basics. In addition, we have a companion site, *StopRansomware.com*, that will have additional content for the beginner.

Let's consider two ends of a spectrum to help illustrate this point. I, Curtis, once worked with a paper mill, and we were trying to determine their RTO. They said that their computer systems were not critical to the core function of the business, which was to produce paper. They felt that they could be down for weeks without any significant impact to the business, so their RTO was two weeks.

On the opposite end of the spectrum is a financial trading firm I worked with. They felt that they were losing millions of dollars every hour that they were down, so for them setting an RTO of one hour seemed totally reasonable. Obviously, since this place was essentially printing money, they had the money to pay for a system that could easily recover their environment within an hour. RTO can also differ based on time of year, such as a retail organization that may lose more money during the holiday shopping season.

Related closely to RTO is *recovery point objective*, or RPO. This is the amount of data everyone agrees is acceptable to lose in some sort of outage, as measured by time. In other words, we're agreeing that we can lose 24 hours' worth of data or one hour's worth of data. Again, thinking about the two businesses we discussed in the previous paragraphs, the paper mill had a much looser RPO than the financial trading firm. The financial firm actually wanted to set their RPO at zero, meaning that even in the worst of outages, they should not lose any data. This is possible with certain technologies like synchronous replication, but it is obviously expensive. They didn't seem to mind. And speaking of the different kinds of recoveries we covered in the preceding paragraph, there may also have to be a longer RPO during a ransomware attack due to the dwell time issue (meaning you may be able to recover to an older copy of data because the ransomware has been in your environment for a long time).

Closely related to RTO and RPO are RTA (recovery time actual) and RPA (recovery point actual). RTO and RPO are the *objectives*, or requirements that we are going to try to meet in an actual outage. RTA and RPA are what the system is currently actually *capable* of doing. This allows conversations that sound something like this: Our RTO is four hours, but we are nowhere near that. Our RTA is more like 24 hours. We will need to significantly rearchitect our system to have our RTA be anywhere near our RTO of four hours.

To return to the topic of ransomware, let's think about how a typical ransom demand is given. You are told to pay $10 million within 72 hours, and if you don't, the $10 million becomes $20 million. This is the threat actor wanting you to think that you really need to pay the ransom now, rather than attempting a recovery that would likely take longer than 72 hours.

But if your RTO and RTA are under 24 hours, why would you pay the ransom? This might even be true even if your RTA is nowhere near your RPO, if we're talking about a ransomware attack. For example, let's say you are able to easily restore your systems well within your RTO. Even if that's the case, it is unlikely that you will be able to successfully remove the ransomware from your environment *and* restore your systems within that amount of time. (We'll talk more about how difficult it is to remove ransomware in Chapters 14 and 15.)

Even if you're unable to meet your RTO (when you include the amount of time it takes to clean the environment of malware) you still might decide not to pay the ransom for many reasons, such as the ones given in the "The Ransom Dilemma: Legal Landmines and Empty Promises" on page 275 section of Chapter 9. Obviously, if you're going to do this, you must be absolutely sure that you can successfully restore your entire environment. Because if you tell the threat actors to go pound sand, it's going to be very difficult to go back to them two or three weeks later after you have cleaned the environment of malware and then realized that you're unable to recover.

Threat Actors Love/Hate Backups

Ransomware threat actors want to disable your backup and DR system so that it cannot be used against them in an attack. They really don't want a well-functioning backup and DR system.

However, they also *love* a good backup and DR system! They have discovered the backup system is a very valuable resource in conducting a *double extortion attack*. As discussed in Chapter 1, a double extortion attack is one where they have both encrypted and exfiltrated your data. You must pay the ransomware or you will never get your data back, and your sensitive data will be exposed to the world. Threat actors know your backup system contains the most sensitive data in your organization, and if compromised, it can be used to conduct exfiltration without any risk of being detected—for reasons we discuss in "Exfiltration" on page 44.

These two "features" of the backup system have moved from being just another computer system in your computing environment to the most popular person at the party. The 2024 Crowdstrike threat report mentioned that threat actors have adapted the methods that they use to gain initial access due to the existence of EDR sensors in many places. They are now beginning to target edge devices that they believe are either unmanaged or possibly unmonitored. Is it any surprise that backup storage is on the short list of types of devices that they're trying to attack? They believe, and justifiably so, that the likelihood of it being monitored is much lower than other systems.

Let me say it again: the backup system has become a prime target for threat actors because they see it as both public enemy number one and simultaneously their greatest ally trying to successfully extort money from you. Let this serve as a wake-up call to you and the cybersecurity team.

How Threat Actors Disable the Backup/DR System

As we previously mentioned, if you are able to successfully restore your environment from backup, you're much less likely to pay the ransom; therefore, the first goal of the threat actor is disabling your backup system. They want to injure your star quarterback so he cannot throw the winning touchdown. They want to "sweep the leg" so Daniel is unable to win the karate tournament. If they can disable your backup system, it will be useless in responding to their ransomware attack. However, before they disable it, they will definitely perform reconnaissance on your backup system to see if and how they will be able to disable it when the time comes.

Case Study: Travelex's Backups Were Deleted

Picture this: it's New Year's Eve 2019, and Travelex—those currency exchange kiosks you see in airports everywhere—gets absolutely hammered by the REvil ransomware gang. We're talking 1,500 stores worldwide, all locked up tight.

Now here's where it gets interesting. The attackers didn't just encrypt everything and call it a day. No, they went after the backups first. Deleted them. Gone. Which meant Travelex had exactly two options: pay up or lose everything. The gang initially wanted somewhere between $3 and $6 million, but after some negotiation, Travelex ended up paying $2.3 million in bitcoin.

But here's the kicker: even after paying, the company never really recovered. Between the ransomware hit and COVID-19 crushing the travel industry a few months later, Travelex went into administration. Over 1,000 people lost their jobs. And the really frustrating part? The whole thing was completely preventable. They hadn't patched their Pulse Secure VPN servers for over nine months. The patch had been available since April 2019, and they didn't get hit until December. That's just leaving the door open. Read more about this here (Abrams, 2020 (*https://oreil.ly/5bJPa*)).

They will determine the type of backup system you are using, enabling them to tailor their attack specifically for that system. They know the vulnerabilities and the strengths of different backup software products and SaaS offerings, including different versions. Once they determine you're using a particular backup system, they will try to find out which version it is and whether it has been configured securely or not. The more popular a backup system is, the more likely it is to be specifically targeted by threat actors.

Their attempts to disable your backup system take a variety of forms. The easiest way to take your backups out of the picture is simply delete them. If they can directly access and delete backup files, they are home free. These people are smart and will be able to figure out if you have multiple copies of your backups, and they will attempt to delete all copies.

However, since this is the ransomware world, what they're more likely to do is to encrypt your backups just like they do other servers. If they can gain sufficient privileges to do so, they will probably encrypt the backup files, or they might choose to encrypt critical files on the backup system, which would cause the backup system to become inoperable. This creates a catch-22 situation where you cannot restore your environment without your backup server, but you cannot restore your backup server without the ransomware decryption key. (Side note: make sure your encryption keys are stored somewhere secure, but not so secure that it becomes inaccessible in an attack.)

They might also attempt to gain administrative control of the backup software. (It's quite normal to have an authentication system for the backup system that is separate from the backup server.) If they can do that, their day just got better. If they have administrative control over the backup software, they can easily delete all your disk backups by simply setting the expiration date of the backups to today's date. Expiring backups deletes them out of the backup catalog, and if the backups happen to reside on disk, it will delete them from the disk. If they have time to do this, they might also simply delete resources from a particular backup job and allow those backups to simply age out. (This will take much longer but is harder to detect.)

If your backups are on tape, deleting them this way would not actually delete the backups, since they still reside on tape. However, if you have administrative control, you also have the ability to electronically relabel the tapes. This doesn't mean physically changing the paper label on the front of the tape; it means putting a new digital label on the front of the actual tape itself. Backups always write to tape in a sequential manner, and the last file on the tape always places an end-of-data marker at the end of the last file. By putting a new digital label on the front of the tape, you place an end-of-data marker after that label, which renders the rest of the data on the tape unreadable.

Although it is entirely possible to easily relabel all of the tapes in a tape library, you can take some solace in the thought that this is unlikely to happen for two reasons:

1. This is a ransomware attack. They want you to pay the ransom, and rendering all of your backup tapes completely useless isn't going to help their cause. (Unlike encryption, there is no turning back from relabeled tapes.)

2. This requires even more specialized knowledge that they probably do not have. But it is important to understand that this is a danger.

As we will discuss in Chapter 6 and others, this is why we are starting to talk more and more about immutable storage options for backups.

The Backup System as an Attack Surface

Besides being a target due to its data restoration capabilities, the backup system itself is an additional attack surface. This means that the backup system is another area of vulnerability itself, meaning that it can actually *assist the attackers* in furthering their goals.

Exfiltration

As we discussed in Chapter 1, double extortion attacks that include both encryption and exfiltration of your data are becoming the norm. Outside of the backup system, exfiltration should be monitored for and detected, but this is beyond the scope of this book. But if you have administrative control over the backup system—or at the very least can impersonate the owner of a particular data set—you can easily transfer any amount of data that you'd like to without setting off any alarm bells. Think about it; *the backup system's sole purpose is to transfer large amounts of data to other systems.*

If a threat actor would like to steal a customer database, they can simply tell the backup system to restore the database to a system that they control. This could be a VM of theirs in the cloud or simply a filesystem that they have access to anywhere outside the victim's environment. In many cases, organizations do not monitor the backup system for restores! An attacker that has the appropriate access to the backup system would be able to kick off a gigantic restore and no one would notice.

Think about this. Not only is the backup system this wonderful tool that you can use for exfiltration of data without anyone noticing, it is also the central repository for all valuable data. If you want to exfiltrate data, why hack dozens of systems when all you need to do is hack one and use that system to transfer any other system's data that you would like to wherever you want it to go?

Privilege escalation

If a threat actor has administrative access over the backup software, they can also use it to enable privilege escalation attacks. A privilege escalation attack is necessary when a threat actor has access to a system, typically via stolen credentials, but the account that they have access to does not have enough privileges to allow them to do what they want. The threat actor would want to *escalate* the privileges that they have, which would give them the power to do what they actually want to do. Let's say you have the ability to log into a basic, non-administrator account, and what you need is an administrator account. To get from one to the other you need a privilege escalation attack.

You might be wondering how a backup system could be used to do this. It's actually quite simple; remember that a backup system can read and write any file on any system in your environment that has been configured for backup. Perhaps you might want to back up the security account manager (SAM) file in Windows or the password file in Linux, edit it and change the password to NULL, back it up again, then restore it in place.

But with most backup systems, it's actually easier than that. Create a script that can be run on the command line that gives you the privileges you want, back that script up, restore it to the target system, and then tell the backup software product that it is a pre-backup script that must be run before each backup. When you run a backup, it will run that script as the backup service account, which has administrator access. The threat actor just gave themselves whatever access they wanted.

File access

Even if the threat actors don't have administrative access to the backup system, perhaps they might be able to exploit the backup service account to access data they're trying to steal. To understand what I'm talking about, let me first explain what a service account is and what's so special about the backup service account.

A service account is an account that allows another process to access either data or another process on the same computer. For example, backup software often communicates via the backup service account, meaning an account called *backup* that is used for this purpose. The backup service account is rather unique because it is specifically designed for a process that is going to access hundreds of thousands of files. Therefore, the backup service account allows you to access any file on the system without logging said access. If the service account that you use for backup is not configured in a secure manner, it might allow a threat actor to actually use that service account to access files as if they were the backup system—and no one would know.

Listen to the hacker

Duane Laflotte is an offensive cybersecurity expert, or what we used to call a white-hat hacker or an ethical hacker. He is hired by organizations to test their security. I, Curtis, recently had the opportunity to talk to him about backup systems as attack surfaces on my podcast, *The Backup Wrap-Up* (*https://www.backupwrapup.com*). This is a slightly edited transcript of that conversation:

> *W. Curtis Preston*: What do you know about backup systems as an attack surface?
>
> *Duane Laflotte*: We were doing a penetration test two weeks ago in an organization where we breached it over the backup system. So they were all virtualized, of course. They were backing up all of their VMs and we got access to the backup manager because the password for the backup manager was weak. It was actually a default password because people think to themselves, "It's a backup manager, what do I care? What are they gonna do, restore it?" And that's what we did. We actually took the backup of the domain controller and pulled it over the internet to us and restored it in my own lab. And then were able to tear it apart, pull every single username and password.
>
> So I would be careful. That repository is just as sensitive as your primary network. It's not only your path to recovering from disaster, but from an attacker. I'm always looking for backup systems, and what I can pull out of those systems, right?
>
> Backup accounts should have strong passwords and should be audited. Backup systems should be audited for who's trying to log in, etc.. Backup service accounts that are running on boxes, we've seen far too often, just have weak passwords. And it's super easy for us to then compromise.
>
> *[To a hacker]* Backup is awesome, actually. The backup service on Windows gives you the ability to read any file without being audited. So you have all these auditing tools looking for users like reading files and opening secure files. But if you can request the

service account *backup*? You can touch anything and nobody ever sees it. So from a surface of attack standpoint, backups are like a win button for us. We're always looking for, hey, do they have a backup system? Is there an account we can compromise that has backup rights? Because if so, you know—money—we can go open any file we want and nobody will know we were there. So yeah, I would absolutely say the surface of attack is large there.

So many cool things you could do. Privilege escalation from ransomware can be done through backups. I mean, there's so many cool things!

How Did We Get Here?

If you've been paying attention the last few paragraphs, you're probably a little freaked out right about now. You might be asking how is it possible that such a powerful system is not protected with an immense amount of security and monitored for the incredible vulnerability that it is? I feel your pain. In fact, I, Curtis, have felt your pain for the last 30 years. The answer to this question is a combination of human nature and people simply not thinking deviously enough.

Backup, recovery, and DR have always been extremely difficult, thankless jobs. No one remembers the millions of backups you got right—they only remember the one restore you got wrong. What this translates into is that nobody wants the job of being the backup admin.

This means that very few people are going to be thinking about backups when you are in important meetings. No one is going to raise their hand and ask important questions about whether or not a new system is being backed up, or whether or not the backup system is using modern cybersecurity methods.

We mean no one but you, of course. You care enough about your company's data to do just that—raise your hand. Be that champion that saves your company from a ransomware attack. But it is true that most people in the company aren't thinking about these things and don't want to.

This also means that the backup job is often given to the junior person. Just after the conversation recorded in the preceding transcript, Duane and I both said that backup was the first job that we got. Backup is often the first job that many people get in IT, because it's the hot potato that no one wants to hold, and the new person will take the job because they want a job. And then as soon as they get any type of seniority and you hire a new person, they will pass the job to them.

I got my first job in backup in 1993 because Ron Rodriguez wanted to become a regular system administrator, so that meant giving the job to me. I, of course, am incredibly thankful for that opportunity, especially since it launched a great career. But the reality remains—I was given an incredibly powerful position at a $35 billion bank with only a few months of UNIX experience.

It's also really important to understand that the junior person running the backup system is rarely well-versed in cybersecurity. They probably get the same cybersecurity training that all new employees get, but they do not get the specialized type of training that they should be getting as the administrator of one of the most powerful systems in your computing environment from a cybersecurity perspective.

Since no one wants to volunteer themselves to look into the backup system, and the person administering the backup system is usually a junior person, the result is a system that is often overlooked by the typical cybersecurity processes found in your organization. Hopefully this book will help to change that. Hopefully a cybersecurity professional is reading this and realizing that someone better take a look at the backup system and the person running it. Perhaps the backup administrator is reading it and realizing that they're in way over their head from a cybersecurity perspective and can gain a lot of organizational brownie points by bringing this to the attention of the cybersecurity team.

Disk Backups Made It Worse

Over the last 20 or so years, the entire computing industry has moved their backups from tape to disk. I, Curtis, was and am a huge proponent of this change; however, it's also important to acknowledge that moving from tape to disk for backups made the cybersecurity problem worse.

Backups stored on tape are simply harder to get to from a cybersecurity perspective. Manipulating a tape library, and reading and writing from a tape, is specialized knowledge that the typical system administrator or hacker might not have. As a sequential medium, it takes a long time to interact with thousands of backups on hundreds of tapes. Each tape is going to take a few minutes to load before you can do anything with it, such as erasing it by writing a new label. If anyone was near the tape library, they may hear all of the tape movement and begin to wonder what was going on. Perhaps this would allow them to stop a cyber attack that was going after the backup tapes.

Contrast this to backups stored on a filesystem. They are simply files just like any other files, and they can easily be accessed, deleted, or encrypted by anyone with the appropriate credentials. The threat actor could easily impact thousands of backups in a matter of seconds or minutes without anyone having any idea what they're up to—especially considering that no one is probably going to even see what they're doing. They can inflict a lot of damage in a very short period of time, and all they need is a privileged account on the backup server or the storage system being used as a backup target.

This is why we will be recommending the use of truly immutable backup storage. We want at least one copy of your backup to be stored on a device that even you cannot override—even if you are a superuser and have a really good reason. We will cover the topic of immutability in more detail in Chapter 6.

Sounds Pretty Bleak

Hopefully I've painted a very scary picture for you of just how poorly your backups are probably secured—or not. Hopefully you are now very scared about your backup system being used as an attack service, or you're worried that all of your backups are a few commands away from being deleted. If any of that is true, then I've accomplished my goal for this chapter.

The good news is that there are responses to each of these vulnerabilities, and all you have to do is follow my suggestions. We wish you the best of luck and we mean that with zero sarcasm.

Summary

Your backup system is in grave danger—it has become the favorite target of ransomware threat actors. This isn't hyperbole; attackers have realized that organizations with good backup and disaster recovery systems don't pay ransoms. If you can restore your environment within your RTO, why would you pay millions to criminals? The answer: you wouldn't, unless they take away that option—they've made it their mission to do just that.

But it gets worse. Threat actors have also discovered that your backup system is the perfect weapon for double extortion attacks like we discussed in Chapter 1. It contains all of your most sensitive data in one convenient location, and if they gain access to it, they can exfiltrate massive amounts of data without triggering a single alarm bell. After all, the backup system's entire purpose is to move large amounts of data around.

The attack methods are varied and effective. They might directly delete your backup files, encrypt them to create a catch-22 where you can't restore anything, gain administrative control to expire all your backups, or even digitally relabel your tapes to render them useless. Beyond simply disabling your backups, they can weaponize the system itself—using restore functions to steal data, exploiting backup service accounts that can access files without being audited, or leveraging the backup system's privileged access for privilege escalation attacks.

How did we get here? The backup administrator role has always been IT's unwanted job, typically given to the most junior person who rarely receives specialized cybersecurity training. The result is one of the most powerful systems in your environment being overlooked by typical security processes. Making matters worse, the industry's shift from tape to disk eliminated the natural air gap that made backups harder to compromise. Disk backups are just files that can be deleted or encrypted in seconds by anyone with the right credentials.

The situation is dire, but it's not hopeless. The vulnerabilities described in this chapter all have responses, and we'll cover them throughout this book, particularly the critical topic of truly immutable backup storage we discuss in Chapter 6. The question isn't whether your backup system is under attack—it's whether you'll be ready when it happens.

PART II

Protect

Govern

NIST
cybersecurity
framework

Recover

Identify

Respond

Protect

Detect

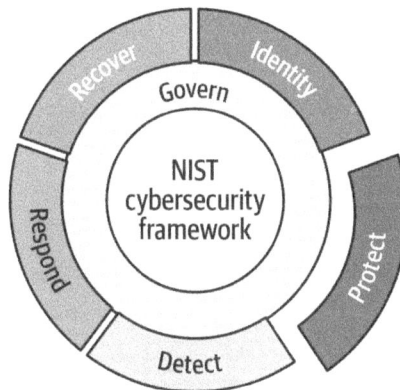

Building Your Defenses Before the Attack

The NIST Cybersecurity Framework's *Protect* function is about implementing appropriate safeguards to ensure delivery of critical services and to limit or contain the impact of potential cybersecurity events. Now that you've identified the ransomware threat and your critical vulnerabilities, it's time to build the defenses that will reduce your risk and minimize damage when attacks occur. We're not trying to prevent every attack, but we are going to make attacks harder and easier to recover from.

Chapter 3, "Backup and Recovery Basics", establishes the fundamental concepts you need to understand before securing your backup system.

Chapter 4, "Stop Most Ransomware", covers the prevention basics that will stop most attacks before they start. We'll tackle the table stakes (patching, multifactor authentication [MFA], password management) and comprehensive cyber hygiene.

Chapter 5, "Minimize the Blast Radius", focuses on limiting how much damage ransomware can do if it gets in. We'll harden endpoints, segment networks, lock down access controls, and protect data so that a ransomware attack doesn't become a disaster.

Chapter 6, "Get Ready for Battle", is where we secure your last line of defense: the backup system itself. We'll talk about cyber professionals, forensic tools, and immutable storage. This chapter transforms your backup system from a vulnerable target into a fortified stronghold.

Chapter 7, "Make Your Incident Response Plan", establishes decision frameworks, roles, and procedures before crisis strikes. You'll build out your IRP and IRT with RACI accountability and test everything through tabletop exercises and war games.

By the end of this Protect section, you'll have layered defenses in place that dramatically reduce your attack surface and ensure you can recover even from sophisticated ransomware campaigns.

CHAPTER 3

Backup and Recovery Basics

Many readers (especially those predominantly specializing in cyber) may not be familiar with many basic backup and DR concepts. If that describes you, then this chapter is for you! But even if you think you have the basics down, you may want to read on. You'd be surprised at some of the basics that many people misunderstand.

This chapter covers only the basics of backup and recovery and doesn't really delve too much into the ideas of ransomware. Chapter 6 will go into more detail on how to prepare your backup system for a ransomware attack. This chapter is just making sure you understand the vocabulary we'll use later in the book.

> If you'd like to learn more about modern backup and recovery methods, I recommend the book *Modern Data Protection* (O'Reilly). It was written by yours truly, W. Curtis Preston. We also have a companion site for this book, *StopRansomware.com*.

Backup or Disaster Recovery?

Many people often view backup and DR systems as completely separate concepts and completely separate systems. I, Curtis, do not see it that way.

The Same System

Historically people viewed backup as what you used for operational recovery. Someone deleted a file, or a DBA accidentally dropped a table in a database. Maybe it might be used to recover an entire server if a RAID array blew up.

But for really big problems—like a ransomware attack—people think of a completely separate disaster recovery system. This is because historically most backup systems were incapable of providing the kinds of recovery speed that organizations were looking for. So for mission-critical data, they used a completely different system that was typically based on replication. However, modern backup and recovery systems that use disk and cloud storage can provide automated, very quick recovery speed— even instantaneous.

A Different Process

Backup and recovery is a relatively simple concept to understand. A file was deleted, so we went to the backup system and restored it. Not a lot of process. DR, on the other hand, is all about process.

DR is so much more than the system you use to actually recover the data. When we talk about DR, we're also talking about all of the processes that you have to wrap around the backup system to make sure that you have something clean to restore to. It might include ordering new systems; heck, it might even mean getting new buildings (after a natural disaster, for example). In the case of a ransomware attack, it includes the process of identifying what needs to be restored, and either cleaning or replacing many systems before you actually perform a restore. So while backup and DR may be performed by the same computer system, they will be a different system of processes.

But since the backup and recovery system will be part of the DR system, it also means you need a good grasp of basic backup and recovery concepts to have a good DR system. So let's take a look at those.

Case Study: Atlanta Had No Backups

Atlanta's story is just maddening. Picture this: it's March 2018, and the new mayor, Keisha Bottoms, has been on the job for five weeks. She gets hit with SamSam ransomware that tears through the city's systems like a freight train.

Now here's where it gets really frustrating. Two outdated Windows Server machines were hosting 104 city applications. And get this: they *apparently had no active backup systems*. None. Zero. Zilch. Real estate transactions? Frozen. Email? Gone. City payments? Offline. The encryption was so strong that even the NSA couldn't crack it.

The attackers wanted $51,000 in bitcoin. That's honestly pocket change for a major city. But Baltimore refused to pay, which was actually the right call. The problem was, without backups, recovery became an absolute nightmare.

Here's the part that should make every IT person's blood boil: two months before the attack, an audit found between 1,500 and 2,000 vulnerabilities in the city's systems. Fifteen hundred to two thousand! And they just... ignored them. The attackers didn't even need to be sophisticated: they just used brute-force attacks to guess weak passwords.

Recovery took several months. The final cost? Nearly $18 million. All because they had weak passwords and ignored a mountain of warnings.

The real kicker? The same two Iranian hackers who did this had already hit Hollywood Presbyterian back in 2016. They were eventually indicted in November 2018, but the damage to Atlanta was done.

Defining Backup System Requirements

First let's focus on the business and political aspects of building or enhancing your data protection system. While technical requirements are important, getting buy-in from stakeholders who'll benefit from (or fund) the system is equally crucial.

Data protection isn't the exciting part of IT. It reminds organizations of their vulnerabilities and requires resources that don't directly contribute to the product you're selling. You're essentially trying to sell an insurance policy that no one wants to buy. Despite this challenge, your data protection plan will be one of your organization's most critical investments.

Before allocating a significant amount of money to data protection, ensure your plan properly addresses organizational needs. An insurance policy is worthless if it won't cover your losses when disaster strikes. Let's create a structured process and develop tools for building an effective plan.

What Does Your Organization Do?

As we do everywhere in this book, we use the word *organization* to be inclusive of all entities that might need backups. This could be a single person looking to protect their own personal data, a for-profit company looking to preserve shareholder value, a nonprofit looking to protect their interests, or a government entity trying to protect itself.

A successful backup system requires more than just technical expertise in data protection systems. You need to understand your organization's purpose and any external requirements from laws and regulations. Even if you are only tasked with a single business unit or department, you should always start with the purpose of the entire organization.

For example, here are just a few considerations:

- Are you a government organization? What IT-dependent services do you provide?
- Do you operate through an ecommerce model?
- Are you a commercial business with R&D and manufacturing cycles?

- Are there external requirements governing how you store certain data types?

Each aspect has different requirements, and as the data protection person, you'll need to architect a solution that protects everything for everyone.

Start by understanding your organization and its services or products to grasp your data's importance. You should also think about regulations and standards for your type of organization. Find someone (or multiple people) willing to explain what your organization does, its product portfolio, and how it serves its customers. This complete picture will guide your journey.

IT Does Not Determine Requirements

While the following sections are primarily written with large organizations in mind, small organizations should not overlook the need for this kind of process. It just needs to be scaled down to fit your organization.

Make sure that those who are driving the business are the ones that are making these kinds of decisions. Even in a two-person company, where one is the businessperson and the other is the IT person, the IT person should be consulting the businessperson on IT requirements.

For example, many of the roles discussed in the requirements gathering section will likely exist even in a small organization. It's just that they are often found in one person. For example, in a small organization, the upper management, compliance, and governance "people" might be one person. Also, the institutional and technical knowledge might be found in one person. Try and identify those who play these roles in your organization and get them involved in the process.

This includes reviewing requirements with stakeholders and determining service level agreements (SLAs). In a small organization, this may be a simple meeting between two people where you discuss what you believe the requirements are and how you're going to meet them. A bigger organization is going to hold much bigger meetings.

The point of these sections is that you really do need to design your backup and recovery system to fit the needs of the organization. Remember that IT should not be determining requirements. Requirements should come from the business or data owner. IT will then design a system to meet those requirements.

Requirements and Service Levels

Identifying key stakeholders and understanding their needs is crucial. These requirements will drive your RPO and RTO. We'll define these in more detail later in this chapter, but for now just understand it's about how fast you can recover (RTO) and how much data you can lose (RPO).

Gather requirements

Gathering requirements starts with identifying those who might care what those requirements are. The usual term for such a person is *stakeholder*. Here are some examples of who might be on your key stakeholders list and what types of requirements they would request:

Upper management

Upper management provides valuable insight into organizational operating speed and timeline expectations. While they typically want everything protected constantly, they're best at helping understand organizational flow and priorities. Be prepared for discussions about acceptable downtime and cost constraints to determine RTO.

Department heads

These are the people that really understand the different parts of your organization. Create a list of internal customers by department. Find those with institutional knowledge of your organization, who can describe each group's activities, protection needs, and criticality.

Data owners

You need to know where data originates. This helps determine data recreation complexity and appropriate RPO levels. Work with those who actually understand how and where data is created to understand RPO implications and get insights into transaction volumes and storage requirements.

Compliance and governance

Ensure compliance with relevant laws and regulations, particularly regarding privacy (like GDPR and CCPA). Consult legal or governance teams to confirm your design meets the requirements for backup and archive access.

Review requirements

After collecting requirements, get everyone aligned by reviewing the requirements you believe you have gathered from them. Make sure you understand and can present your understanding of all of the following:

- Data location and volume
- Data generation and change rates
- Service/product creation timelines
- Organizational outage tolerance

Present these findings to key stakeholders, including management representatives and technology team members. Define the problem clearly and present each department's requirements.

Determine service level agreements

After the requirements are clear, establish service level agreements (SLAs) based on agreed-upon RPOs and RTOs. Consider the physical constraints of network resources, storage devices, and potential tape usage. Remember data protection typically uses more network bandwidth than other services.

Design, Implement, and Document Your System

Once your requirements and SLAs are clear, you can design your backup system to meet those requirements. This may be servers or VMs running backup software, or it may be a SaaS product that can meet them for you. Here are some other things to consider during this process.

Depending on the size of your organization, you may need to submit your design for review. Once the design has been accepted, you can move forward with implementation.

It should go without saying that any new backup design should undergo rigorous recovery testing, and the results of those tests should be compared to the requirements and SLAs you already agreed to.

As you're implementing it, make sure to document the new system, why and how it was designed, as well as how it will be used:

- Requirements and design documents
- Operational procedures and runbooks
- Contact information for vendors and key personnel
- Incident tracking and resolution procedures

Consider maintaining printed copies for emergencies when electronic documentation might be inaccessible. But make sure to store them in a binder to allow you to update them by adding or removing pages.

Backup and Recovery Basics

Now that we've covered how to gather requirements to design and implement a backup and DR system, we need to explain some basic backup and recovery concepts. We'll start with discussing the all-important concept of recovery testing, followed by backup levels. We then look at many backup system metrics, especially RTO and RPO and how they (more than anything else) determine backup design. We'll then address image-level versus file-level backups, and how the contents of backups are selected. The first, and possibly most important basic backup concept, however, is that all backups must be tested.

Is it *restore* or *recover*? There is no hard-and-fast rule here, and that's saying a lot, since I (Curtis) can be very pedantic about such things. You'll usually see *recover* when we're talking about the overall process (e.g., we'll eventually recover from this) and *restore* when we're talking about physically copying from the backup system (e.g., restore the server to just before the attack). But honestly, many people in the business use the terms interchangeably. It's not something I worry about. If it does bother you, don't worry; I'm sure you'll recover.

Recovery Testing

The only reason you back up things is to be able to restore them. And the only way you're going to know if you can restore the things you're protecting is to test your ability to do so. Regular recovery testing should be a fundamental part of your backup system.

Testing serves two crucial purposes: (1) validating the backup system and its documentation and (2) training your personnel. If the first time they're executing a big restore is during a production crisis, such a restore will be much more stressful and error prone. If they've performed such restores many times during testing, they should be able to follow their usual procedure confidently.

You should regularly test the recovery of anything and everything you're responsible for, from small items to very large systems. The frequency of testing each item should relate to (1) how often a restore of such a thing happens in production and (2) how difficult a restore test will be. You tend to do small file and VM restores quite often, and testing such restores is quite easy. So you should therefore test those recoveries quite often. On the other hand, doing a full DR test is quite the operation and will cost a lot of time and money. And it's also something you're not likely to do very often—at least we hope not.

It's important for the reader to understand that when we say "full recovery," we are essentially starting from bare metal. We start with a blank computer, or virtual machine (typically running in the cloud), then install or restore the operating system (e.g., Windows or Linux), then install or restore the application (e.g., Oracle, Apache web server, SAP, etc.), and then restore the data. It is a complicated, multistage process that can be quite difficult. This is why you must frequently test the process to develop muscle memory of how to do it when the feces hits the rotary oscillator.

One real challenge with testing, though, is that you need hardware to test the recovery on. You can't just restore your production servers while they're doing their job! What if it doesn't work? What about the downtime associated with a restore? This is why you need alternate hardware (or virtual hardware in the cloud) to do restores to.

This is why the cloud has made testing much easier by eliminating resource con-straints. You don't have to fight for resources to use for recovery; you just configure the appropriate resources in the cloud and then restore to those resources. This is especially true of large DR resources; someone who is familiar with the process should be able to configure everything you need to do a full DR test in the cloud. Regular testing in this environment will make production recoveries much smoother. Tests should also include restoring common items in SaaS services, including users, folders, and individual files or emails.

> *A backup isn't a backup until it's been tested!*
> —Ben Patridge

Deduplication

Because it's going to come up in the following pages, let's also talk about deduplica-tion—possibly the biggest advancement in backups in the last 25 years. Deduplication is one of those technologies that sounds complicated but is actually pretty straightfor-ward when you get down to it. Think of it this way: your users are creating the same PowerPoint templates, the same Word documents, the same everything over and over again. Why the heck would you want to back up 17 copies of the company logo? Deduplication looks at all that data, figures out what's identical at the block level, and says "Hey, I only need to store this once." The result? A 90+% reduction in the amount of disk needed to store your backups.

There are two main flavors of deduplication, and like most things in backup, each has its place, depending on what you're trying to accomplish:

Source-side deduplication
    Source-side dedupe happens on the client before anything hits the wire. The beauty of this approach is that you're not shoving duplicate data across your network—and if you've ever tried to push terabytes of backup data across a WAN link, you know why that matters. Your backup software does all the heavy lifting locally, figures out what's unique, and only sends the good stuff.

Target-side deduplication
    This is where the magic really happens. All your backup data lands on your storage appliance first, then the system looks across everything—and I mean everything—from all your clients to find duplicates. Since you're analyzing data from your entire environment, you get much better deduplication ratios. Sure, you're still pushing all that data across the network, but you're getting the benefit of global deduplication. It's like having a really smart librarian who can spot that the same book exists in 17 different departments.

Backup Levels

There are essentially two very broad categories of what the backup industry calls backup levels: backing up everything (traditionally called *full backup*) or backing up only what has changed (traditionally called *incremental backup*). Each of these broad types has variations that behave slightly differently. Most backup levels are throwbacks to the tape era, but understanding their definitions remains valuable:

Traditional full backup
> A traditional full backup copies everything from the system being backed up (except anything specifically excluded) to the backup server. This includes all files in a filesystem (unstructured data) or all records in a database (structured data). It requires significant I/O, which can create a substantial performance impact on your application.

Traditional incremental backup
> A traditional incremental backup captures all files or database records that have changed since a previous backup. Unless otherwise specified, incremental backups are full-file incremental backups, meaning they will back up an entire file or record if it has changed at all. Even if only one byte changed, the complete file gets backed up.

However, several other types of incremental backups exist:

Cumulative incremental backup
> Backs up all data changed since the last full backup. While requiring more I/O and bandwidth than typical incrementals, it simplifies restores by needing only the full backup and latest cumulative incremental. This saves time compared to typical incrementals, which require restoring the full backup and each subsequent incremental.

Incremental backup with levels
> Uses numbered levels (0–9) where 0 represents a full backup, and 1–9 represent other incremental levels. An incremental backup of a certain number will back up everything changed since a previous backup one level down. This allows various combinations for different results, such as monthly level 0, weekly level 1, and daily increasing levels. These are now very uncommon and are only here for completeness.

Block-level incremental backup
> Up to this point in the discussion, all incremental backups did things only on a file level; if anything in a file changed, the whole file got backed up. But a block-level incremental backup only backs up bytes or blocks that have changed since the last backup. Something must track which bytes or blocks have changed, typically through changed block tracking (CBT). This requires significantly less

I/O and bandwidth than full-file approaches. It's especially popular in hypervisor backups, where the hypervisor maintains a bitmap of changed blocks.

Source-side deduplication
An extension of block-level incremental backup that applies additional processing to new or changed blocks before sending them to the backup server. It identifies if "new" blocks have been seen before anywhere in the backup system, saving even more time and bandwidth than standard block-level incremental backups.

Synthetic full backups
Created to solve the restore inefficiency of traditional incremental approaches while avoiding the load of regular full backups. Synthetic backups leverage data that already exists in the backup system to avoid re-copying that data from the source system to the backup system.

Three main methods exist:

Synthetic full via copying
Creates a full backup by copying data from available backups based on the backup system's catalog of current versions. Can be run anytime without impacting backup clients but may create I/O load on backup storage.

Virtual synthetic full
Possible only with target deduplication systems, creating a full backup by pointing to existing blocks without data movement. Requires backup product integration but is very efficient.

Forever incremental
Modern approach that never requires another full backup, synthetic or otherwise. Requires disk as the primary target and stores each changed item as a separate object. Every backup behaves as a full backup for restores without creating one. This is now the most common type of incremental backup in modern systems.

Metrics

Several crucial metrics determine backup system design and maintenance. They include recovery metrics, capacity metrics, and operational metrics, and they govern everything from system design to performance monitoring and capacity planning.

Recovery metrics

No metrics are more important than those involving recovery. One of the things I, Curtis, say a lot is that nobody cares how long backups take; they only care about restore speed. I say this somewhat facetiously, since many people are worried about backup time, and bad things can happen if your backups take too long. But I still say that people care much more about how long your recovery takes than how long your backups take. Two metrics determine if your backup system works: restore speed and data loss during recovery.

Recovery time objective.   It's important to understand that when measuring your adherence to an RTO, the clock starts when the incident occurs and ends when business returns to normal—not just when data restoration completes. This includes hardware ordering, logistics, and post-restore activities.

Recovery point objective.   It's also important to measure adherence to any agreed-upon RPOs. Like RTO, multiple RPOs throughout an organization are common, depending on data criticality. And you must determine whether or not you are adhering to those metrics.

Negotiating RTO and RPO.   Most organizations initially want zero RTO and RPO: no downtime or data loss. This isn't technically possible, even with the best systems, and would be prohibitively expensive to approach. You must negotiate what is both possible and financially reasonable for your organization.

For example, financial trading firms might seek near-zero RTO, while other organizations might accept weeks of downtime. For government or nonprofit organizations, RTO calculations might focus on overtime costs for catching up after outages rather than lost revenue. Multiple RTOs across an organization are normal, with tighter RTOs for critical applications.

For RPOs, most organizations settle on values higher than one hour, typically 24 hours or more, because tighter RPOs require more frequent backups. There's little point in agreeing to a one-hour RPO while running daily backups; you'll achieve 24-hour RPO at best.

Present cost estimates for requested RTOs and RPOs. Organizations justifying tight recovery objectives should provide potential outage cost analysis. Negotiate between technical feasibility, affordability, and current capabilities.

Recovery time actual (RTA) and recovery point actual (RPA).   These metrics measure how well you meet RTO and RPO during actual recoveries or tests. If your RTA or RPA fails to meet your RTO, as is the case for most organizations, either adjust objectives or redesign the backup system—there's no point in having objectives if you can't get close to meeting them.

Testing is essential because most organizations rarely perform production recoveries. Regular testing reveals:

- Backup system reliability

- Resource requirements for large recoveries
- Actual RTA and RPA values
- Recovery process familiarity

Having participated in large-scale recoveries without knowing system capabilities, I can confirm the first question is always "How long will this take?" Without regular testing, you can't answer confidently.

Capacity metrics

Capacity metrics track the capacity of your system to back up and restore data, like how much it can store, how fast it can back it up, how fast it can restore it, how long data is being kept, and others. Let's look at some examples of capacity metrics you may want to use in the following.

License/workload usage. Most backup systems are licensed or charged based on the number of systems that are backed up, but the devil is in the details of how vendors count what you're backing up. Some count physical servers, others count virtual machines, and still others count by the amount of data you're protecting. Some vendors charge by "sockets" (CPU sockets in servers), while others use more granular metrics like "cores" or even "protected capacity." Cloud-based solutions often charge by consumption—either data stored or data transferred—which can create billing surprises if you're not paying attention.

The key is understanding exactly what your vendor counts and how they count it. I've seen organizations get blindsided by license compliance issues because they assumed their VM-based licensing covered containers, or they thought their "unlimited" backup plan actually meant unlimited.

Track license utilization religiously to anticipate needs before you hit limits. Nothing ruins your day quite like discovering you can't back up that critical new server because you're at your license cap. Monitor workload numbers even without immediate license implications to understand backup system growth patterns. This historical data becomes invaluable when negotiating renewals or planning migrations.

Backup storage capacity and usage. Backup storage capacity is the amount of capacity you have to store your backups. You need to monitor available capacity and usage trends. Failing to do so can force emergency decisions violating organizational policies, like deleting older backups prematurely.

There are two types of storage typically used for modern backups: block storage and object storage. Block storage is found on regular disk and tape, and object storage is typically found in the cloud. Block storage must be provisioned up front and will eventually fill to its provisioned capacity, where object storage automatically provisions additional capacity as needed. This is why cloud object storage simplifies capacity management.

Throughput capacity and usage. Backup systems have finite daily backup volume capabilities, usually measured in MB/s or TB/hour. Monitor this to prevent backups extending into workday hours. If you're using tape, tape throughput monitoring is particularly crucial; backup speed must match tape drive minimums to prevent device failure. Consult the manufacturer for details.

The cloud offers both advantages and challenges here. While cloud throughput is virtually unlimited with properly designed systems, many cloud-based products using traditional backup software in VMs face bandwidth limitations. You'll need to upgrade VM types or add instances to increase throughput. Some systems can automatically scale bandwidth with needs.

The cloud's main throughput limitation is your site's upload bandwidth. The more bandwidth you have, the more data you can back up to the cloud. But even the best bandwidth has limitations. Even if you are using byte-level replication or source deduplication, you may exceed site capacity, requiring bandwidth upgrades or vendor changes.

Compute capacity and usage. Backup system capability depends on underlying compute power. Insufficient processing capability in backup servers can slow backups into workday hours. Monitor system performance to prevent this.

Cloud-native backup systems can automatically scale compute resources. Some even scale up and down throughout the day, reducing costs. However, traditional backup software running in cloud VMs lacks this capability, requiring manual compute additions and associated licensing.

Backup window

The backup window is defined as the window of time during which a backup can or does run. Backup systems can significantly impact the performance of the backed-up system during backup. Full backups are resource-intensive, and even incremental backups can be challenging if they're full-file incrementals. You should agree in advance on allowable backup times.

Traditionally, a typical window might be 6 p.m. to 6 a.m. Monday to Thursday, and 6 p.m. Friday to 6 a.m. Monday for environments with minimal weekend activity. However, this is highly environmentally dependent. Monitor window utilization to see if you're approaching window limits, then either reevaluate the window or redesign the system. This is because running backups outside the acceptable backup window can cause performance issues for the systems you are backing up, which violates one of the rules I, Curtis, have for backups. It's kind of like the Hippocratic Oath—first do no harm. Backups should be done but not seen, or something like that. If you're running backups during production hours, you may be doing more harm than good. And in an extreme case, you can get a race condition where the next backup can't start because the last backup hasn't finished. This is why you need to track whether or not you are adhering to your backup window.

Let backup products handle scheduling within their window rather than overengineering with external schedulers. The built-in scheduler typically manages resources more efficiently.

Organizations using block-level incremental-forever techniques often don't need strict windows. These methods run briefly (minutes) and transfer small amounts (megabytes), with minimal performance impact. Such systems typically run throughout the day, as frequently as every five minutes, making the backup window point moot.

Backup and recovery success and failure

Track backup and recovery quantities and success rates. A backup is successful when it completes within the acceptable window and backs up everything it is supposed to back up. A restore is successful if it restores everything it is supposed to bring back/restore, while also meeting your RTO and RPO. While 100% success is ideal, it's unlikely, especially for backups. Too many things conspire against a 100% success rate, like network blips, system performance issues, etc. The important thing is to monitor what happens and respond appropriately. Address all failures. Successfully rerunning failed backups or restores resolves immediate concerns, but track failures for trend analysis. Also be sure to monitor trends over time to identify improvements or degradation in your success rate.

Retention

While not technically a metric, monitor retention policy adherence. If your organization has agreed to retain all HR data for seven years, then make sure you are doing that. But make sure that IT doesn't determine retention periods; these should come from legal, organizational, and regulatory requirements.

Modern systems use multiple storage tiers. Retention should specify duration for each tier, not just overall retention. Review system settings against organizational policies periodically and adjust as needed.

Using metrics

It's not good to just have metrics; you need to use them to show your system is (or is not) meeting them. If you are not meeting your metrics, the numbers can be helpful in diagnosing the problem. The other purpose of metrics is to build confidence in the backup system by publishing them. Be sure to share:

- Performance against design goals
- Backup and recovery success rates
- Capacity forecasts
- RTO/RPO achievement capability (i.e., RTA/RPA)

Being transparent about RTA and RPA limitations serves everyone better than hiding shortcomings.

Item Versus Image-Level Backups

There are two very different ways to back up data. You can either back up items or images. An item-level backup backs up discrete items like files or objects, typically using in-system agents. Advantages include:

- Easy to understand
- Straightforward implementation
- Direct file (item) selection
- Simple restore process

An image-level backup backs up entire physical or virtual volumes at the block level. It's very popular in virtualization environments. Benefits include:

- Faster backups and restores
- More efficient incremental backups
- Better DR capabilities
- Simplified recovery of an entire server from scratch (i.e., bare metal recovery)

Modern systems often combine both approaches, performing image-level backups while maintaining file-level restore capabilities through mounting or indexing.

Backup Selection Methods

Understanding how systems are included in backups is crucial for ensuring complete protection. First, ensure servers and services are registered with your backup system. Although most modern backup systems can detect new VMs in monitored environments, no backup system automatically detects new SaaS applications, and very few can detect new physical servers. This is why the backup system must be aware of new servers and new SaaS applications in the environment so they can be added as necessary.

Two broad categories exist for backup inclusion:

Selective inclusion
> Administrators specify which filesystems, databases, or objects to back up. Example: backing up only the D:\ drive or specific databases.

Selective exclusion (automatic inclusion)
> Backs up everything except specifically excluded items. Example: backing up all filesystems except */tmp* or user media directories.

While selective inclusion might save storage, it's riskier than selective exclusion. Configuration changes require backup reconfiguration, or new resources never get backed up.

Some people may feel they are saving space using selective inclusion and not including things like the OS drive. However, with deduplication, excluding operating systems saves less space than you might think. The OS is typically stored only once across all backups. Consider leaving default configurations and letting deduplication handle efficiency.

One of the best methods for automatic inclusion today is tag- and folder-based inclusion. It is popular in virtualization and cloud environments, where new VMs or databases can receive tags or folder placements indicating their type. This can automatically apply appropriate backup policies.

> If you're using tag-based inclusion, be sure to create a default backup policy for untagged resources. Monitor this policy for new systems that might need different backup approaches. Without a default policy, this functionality risks leaving systems unprotected.

Backup Methods

There are myriad ways you can meet the backup requirements you agreed to in your environment. This is our attempt to summarize the pros and cons of the various methods.

Is Everything Backup?

Many people have a narrow view of backup. They immediately think of tape drives and batch processes encapsulating files into formats like tar, dump, or commercial backup formats. While they might expand this to include disk targets, they often don't consider replication, snapshots, or continuous data protection as backup methods. We respectfully disagree.

We define backup broadly as any copy of data stored separately from the original that can restore the original system if damaged. Not everything mentioned here qualifies as backup when used alone. Replication and snapshots, for instance, aren't valid backup methods individually. However, combined, they create near-continuous data protection (near-CDP), a robust solution.

First, anything called backup in this chapter must conform to the 3-2-1 rule. What is that, you ask? The 3-2-1 rule is as fundamental to backup design as $E = mc^2$ is to physics. Use it as one of the ways to verify if your backup design is proper.

The rule states: have at least three versions of your data on two different media, one of which should be somewhere else. (This has typically been written as "one copy offsite." In the cloud world I, Curtis, prefer to say "somewhere else," which may be another region, another cloud vendor, etc.) Let's break this down in the following.

Three versions of your data

Some backup specialists include the original when totaling up their number of versions; others do not. Multiple versions protect against corrupted backups or unnoticed mistakes. Three is the minimum, not maximum. Modern systems often create many more versions—office apps create multiple daily versions, database logs create thousands of versions, and laptop backups might run every minute.

On two different media

The original idea here is to store the backup on something with a different risk profile than the original. For example, the best thing to do is to have at least two different types of media, like disk and cloud, tape and disk, etc. This is becoming harder in a cloud world. But one idea would be to store your primary data on block storage and the backup copy on object storage. That would follow the original idea of spreading out risk.

Somewhere else

Never store all backups on the same media as the original. For example, many people like to refer to Microsoft's delayed, replicated copies of Exchange. But those are all stored in the same place as the original! At least one copy must also be in a different location—preferably very physically distant from the original system. The way to do this in a cloud world is to use a different region, or even a different vendor. This way a single disaster won't take out both copies.

The 3-2-1-1-0 rule

As ransomware attacks have evolved, so has the 3-2-1 rule. Many experts now advocate for the 3-2-1-1-0 rule, which adds two critical protections against modern threats. The additional "1" means at least one copy should be immutable or air-gapped, meaning it can't be altered or deleted, even by administrators with full access. This protects against ransomware that specifically targets backups for encryption or deletion. The "0" stands for zero errors, meaning you need to regularly verify your backups actually work and can be restored successfully. If you follow the suggestions in this book, you will conform to the 3-2-1-1-0 rule.

Two Ways to Restore

Let's categorize backup solutions based on one of two ways in which they restore data:

Traditional restore
    Copies data from backup to the system after initiating restore

Instant recovery
    Makes backup usable as primary without performing traditional restore

Backup methods supporting a traditional restore

These backups require you to restore the data from the backup for it to be useful. Until that time, the backups are stored in some kind of container that makes it impossible to use them directly.

Traditional full and incremental backups.   Let's start with the granddaddy of them all. You do a full backup, then you do incrementals until you're ready for another full. Back in the day, this meant weekly fulls with daily incrementals. Now most organizations have moved to monthly fulls, weekly cumulative incrementals, followed by daily incrementals.

Advantages
    It's dead simple. Your grandmother could understand this backup strategy, and that's not nothing. It's been around forever, every traditional backup product supports it, and it just works.

Disadvantages
    You're doing the same work over and over again. Every month, you are backing up data you already have. Every full backup is basically saying "I'm going to pretend I've never backed up this data before." It's wasteful, and when disaster strikes, you're stuck restoring that full backup plus every single incremental in sequence. Fun times.

File-level incremental forever.   Here's where things get interesting. You do one full backup—ever—then it's incrementals from here to eternity. The system is smart enough to never duplicate work, which means you're not backing up the same files repeatedly like some kind of digital *Groundhog Day*.

Advantages
    You eliminate the waste of traditional fulls, and restores are faster because you're not shuffling around redundant data. But here's the kicker—these systems had to

be built from scratch with this approach in mind. You can't just bolt this onto your existing traditional backup system.

Disadvantages

If you're still married to tape, forget it. This approach laughs at tape. And not every vendor actually delivers true incremental forever—some sneak in synthetic fulls when you're not looking. Read the fine print.

Multiplexing. Multiplexing interleaves multiple slower backup streams into one faster backup stream in order to keep those expensive (and finicky) tape drives fed. This is one of those "seemed like a good idea at the time" solutions.

Advantages

It will indeed make your tape drives happy, but it comes at a cost. It's frankly the only way to do so. If you want to back up to tape, multiplexing is your friend.

Disadvantages

The real problem is that when you need to restore just one stream—a very normal situation—then you have to read all the streams and throw away all but one. It's very inefficient. Today's implementations use bigger chunks and better memory management, which helps with the traditional multiplexing nightmare of trying to restore data that's been scrambled across the tape like a jigsaw puzzle.

Block-level incremental forever. Now we're cooking with gas. Instead of looking at files, we're looking at the actual bits and bytes on the disk. CBT tells you exactly which blocks changed, and you only back up those blocks.

Advantages

Your VM moved a 10 GB file? File-level backup sees a 10 GB change. Block-level sees maybe a few KB of metadata changes. This is why block-level incremental forever is the darling of VM backups—it just makes sense.

Disadvantages

You need CBT, you need disk-based storage, and you need systems that actually support this properly. Not every backup product does this well, despite what the marketing brochures claim.

Source deduplication. This is incremental forever on steroids. The deduplication engine at the source looks at every chunk of data and says, "Have I seen this before?" If yes, it doesn't back it up again. Ever.

Advantages

This is as efficient as it gets for network utilization. If you're backing up to the cloud or across slow WAN links, this is your friend. The catch? You might need to change backup software, and change is hard.

Disadvantages

Besides the fact that it usually requires a complete replacement of your backup system to use this technology, there are no inherent downsides to source dedupe. However, there are often downsides to the way some source dedupe vendors store backups, which can lead to slow restores.

> Picture this: It's Patch Tuesday, and you've got 100 Windows VMs that just got the same updates. File-level backup backs up all those new files 100 times. Block-level backs up all those changed blocks 100 times. Source dedup? It backs up the new stuff once and says, "The other 99 VMs have the same stuff." Boom.

Methods supporting instant recovery

Everything we've talked about so far still requires you to restore data when disaster strikes. These next methods flip the script—your systems come back instantly because the "restore" is really just pointing to a different copy of the data.

Replication.   Replication is the process of continuously copying and maintaining data across multiple servers or storage systems to ensure availability, fault tolerance, and sometimes improved performance. (We will use the term *primary* to refer to the main, production server, and *replica* to refer to the copy/backup server.) There are two very broad types: block-based and database-based replication. Block-based replication replicates blocks as they change in the storage, where database replication replicates records as they change in the database.

With synchronous replication, changed blocks (in the case of block-based replication) or records (in the case of database replication) are copied to the replica servers as they are written to the primary server—before the write is considered complete. This ensures strong consistency but introduces latency since the primary must wait for confirmation from any replica.

With asynchronous replication, changed blocks or records are copied to the replica at some point after the initial write to the primary (source) server. This provides better performance and lower latency but creates a window where replicas might be slightly behind the primary, risking some data loss if the primary fails before replication completes.

Advantages

Replication is very efficient. It is quite possibly the most efficient way of creating a continuous backup of your data that is ready to go at any time.

Disadvantage

Replication *by itself* is not backup. It has no "oops" button. If someone drops a table or ransomware encrypts your data, guess what? It replicates that too. You still need something that behaves like backup.

Continuous data protection (CDP).   CDP is like "replication with an undo button." It combines replication with a journal of every change, so a full CDP system can instantly present a fully functioning copy of your data at any point in time.

Advantages

A continuously updated copy of your data that can recover instantly, plus point-in-time recovery. It's like having your cake and eating it too. You get operational recovery (oops, I deleted that file) and disaster recovery (the building burned down) in one solution.

Disadvantages

CDP is resource-heavy and expensive. Plus, try explaining to a panicked executive exactly which of the 50,000 possible recovery points they want. It's not as simple as it sounds.

Snapshots.   Snapshots are virtual copies of your data at various points in time. They are virtual copies because they rely on the original to function. This gives you multiple versions of your data while using minimal additional space by referencing the original data for anything that hasn't changed.

Advantages

Snapshots are perfect for "I'm about to do something stupid" protection. Upgrading software? Take a snapshot first. They're also great as a backup source because they give you a consistent point-in-time view.

Disadvantages

Like replication, snapshots by themselves are not backup. They live on the same storage as your primary data. If that storage dies, your snapshots die with it. Don't let anyone tell you otherwise.

Near-continuous data protection (Near-CDP).   This is where vendors try to have it all— snapshots plus replication equals a complete solution. You can snapshot the primary and replicate the snapshots or replicate first and then snapshot at the target.

Advantages

You get instant recovery, multiple versions, offsite copies, and integration with your hypervisor. It's not as resource-heavy or expensive as CDP, and you have a much more manageable number of points in time from which to recover.

Disadvantages

You're typically locked into one vendor's ecosystem, and if that vendor has a bad day, you have a bad day. Plus, getting applications to play nicely often requires custom scripting that nobody wants to maintain.

The Bottom Line

There's no perfect backup method. Each approach makes trade-offs between simplicity, efficiency, recovery time, and cost. The trick is picking the one that matches your actual requirements, not the requirements you think you should have. And remember—any backup strategy that you can't successfully restore from is just an expensive way to feel good about yourself.

Deciding on a Backup Method

No perfect backup and recovery method exists. Each approach has pros and cons. To narrow your choices, determine which advantages you can't live without and which disadvantages you won't accept.

Do You Need to Change?

The grass often looks greener with other backup solutions. Before switching, ask yourself some key questions:

- Does our current system meet RTOs and RPOs?
- Are costs within budget?
- How are operational costs?
- How much troubleshooting time is required?
- What's the cost of switching, including training?

Consider consulting product experts before replacement. Most backup system problems stem from configuration (wetware) rather than software or hardware issues. The cost of expert consultation is usually less than system replacement.

Tips for Considering a New Backup System

The following list includes some considerations to keep in mind when deciding on a backup system. It's also important to understand that—like the rest of this chapter—this is a very high-level overview of these considerations. You can consult *Modern Data Protection* (O'Reilly) for more details.

Recovery time considerations:

- Traditional restore methods can't match instant RTOs.
- An RTO of zero is often requested but rarely justified
- An 8-hour RTA is acceptable if you have a 24-hour RTO.
- Don't pay for speed you don't need.

Recovery point considerations:

- Traditional approaches that back up only once a day can only support a 24-hour RPO.
- Many methods achieve one-hour RPO.
- An RPA of zero is possible, but extremely expensive.
- Match method to actual requirements.
- Consider cost versus benefit.

Virtualization and Kubernetes support:

- Most methods handle VMware and Hyper-V well.
- Most vendors are also finally supporting Kubernetes, although not equally well.
- Since Nutanix AHV and KVM hypervisors are not typically supported, they may require additional support.
- Consider the backup roadmap for virtualization and Kubernetes.
- Verify specific platform support. Do not take a vendor's word for it.

Cloud Considerations

When thinking about the cloud, you need to consider both how you are going to back up data that is resident in the cloud and how (if at all) you are going to leverage the cloud as a place to back up data to. When thinking about protecting cloud resident data, make sure to consider the 3-2-1 rule and ensure that at least one copy of your data is as far from your primary copy as possible. In the cloud world, that means copying it to a different region using a different account and possibly even copying it to a different company (e.g., from AWS to Azure).

When thinking about using the cloud as a place to send your backups, here are some things to think about:

Primary backup storage type (object versus block)
    Object storage (e.g., Amazon S3) is much cheaper (10× less or more) than block (e.g., Amazon EBS), but you need to make sure your backup system can properly handle object storage. It's a myth that it's slower.

Cloud-native versus traditional design
> A backup design that fully leverages how the cloud works will save you money in the long run. Simply lifting and shifting backup servers into the cloud costs much more.

Resource scaling capabilities
> Find out whether or not the system you are considering has the ability to automatically scale up *and down* without you having to manually do it. This gives you performance when you need it and saves you money when you don't.

Bandwidth requirements
> If you're going to back up to the cloud, make sure you know how much bandwidth you need and how much you have.

Backup and Archive Myths

Before we leave this backup and recovery basics chapter, let's look at some common backup and archiving myths and respond to each one:

Myth: "You don't need to back up RAID"
> False. RAID, or a redundant array of independent drives that helps protect you from losing data if one drive fails, only protects against physical device failure. It can't help with file deletion, ransomware encryption, or database corruption. RAID protects the volume, not the filesystem above it.

Myth: "You don't need to back up replicated data"
> False. Replication copies everything, including mistakes and corruption. If someone drops a database table accidentally, replication ensures that mistake reaches all copies.

Myth: "You don't need to back up infrastructure as a service (IaaS)/platform as a service (PaaS)"
> False. Cloud vendors typically provide backup capabilities but don't automatically back up your resources. While cloud resources offer high availability, this doesn't protect against user mistakes or attacks. Make sure to review your SLAs and contracts.

Myth: "You don't need to back up SaaS"
> False. Major SaaS vendors rarely include comprehensive backup. Check your service contract: backup, recovery, and restore terms typically aren't included. Built-in features like versioning and recycle bins don't replace proper backups.

Myth: "Backups should be stored for many years"
> False. Traditional backup products aren't designed for long-term retention. Without proper archive functionality, using backups for long-term storage cre-

ates expensive e-discovery challenges. Most restores come from recent backups; consider 18-month retention for regular backups and proper archive systems for longer retention.

Myth: "Tape is dead"
False. While we haven't used tape for primary backups in years, tape sales continue growing. Tape excels at long-term archives, offering reliable, cost-effective storage with minimal power requirements. Cloud providers often use tape behind the scenes for cold storage.

Regarding myths, claims that you don't need to back up certain technologies are almost never true. Get backup coverage in writing from any vendor claiming it's included.

Summary

This chapter provided a foundational understanding of backup and DR concepts, starting with the critical business aspects of building stakeholder buy-in and gathering requirements. We covered the framework needed to design and implement a backup system, including documentation templates, review boards, and the importance of finding subject matter experts.

We then explored core backup concepts, from basic backup levels to essential metrics like RTO and RPO. The chapter emphasized that recovery testing is fundamental—a backup isn't truly a backup until it's been tested. We examined different backup methods, from traditional full/incremental approaches to modern techniques like source deduplication and near-CDP.

The 3-2-1 rule emerged as a foundational principle: maintain at least three versions of your data on two different media types, with one copy kept offsite. This rule serves as a fundamental benchmark for evaluating any backup design.

Whether choosing traditional restore methods or instant recovery solutions, the key is matching your approach to organizational requirements while considering factors like virtualization support and cloud integration. Remember: there's no perfect backup solution—focus on finding the best match for your specific needs while ensuring compliance with fundamental principles like the 3-2-1 rule.

CHAPTER 4

Stop Most Ransomware

This book takes an "assume breach" stance because we're realists: some ransomware attacks will get through. But here's the thing—"some" is a lot better than "all." Let's talk about doing what we can to stop ransomware in the first place.

Most ransomware attacks succeed because organizations fail at basic cyber hygiene: they don't patch systems, they don't enable multifactor authentication, and they ignore password management. If you implement the measures in this chapter, you should stop almost all ransomware. Most attacks would never become the crisis scenarios we'll prepare for in other chapters.

So yes, this chapter is a departure from our assume-breach philosophy—but it's a necessary one. Prevention doesn't contradict preparation; it complements it. Every attack you stop is one less incident your team has to respond to, one less backup you have to restore, one less ransom demand you have to consider. Prevention reduces the frequency and severity of the breaches we're assuming will happen.

Think of it this way: Your car has brakes AND airbags. You assume you might get in an accident (that's the airbag), but you also have brakes to prevent running into other cars. This chapter gives you some brakes. The rest of the book is your airbag, crumple zones, and emergency glass breaker.

We'll cover proactive cybersecurity measures like vulnerability management and system hardening, and employee training that turns your people into a defensive asset rather than a liability.

If you're new to cybersecurity, don't worry. We've tried very hard to explain everything you need to know, as well as show when it's best to call in a pro. We also have a companion site, *StopRansomware.com*, that will have more (and updated) resources.

No, prevention isn't foolproof. Attackers constantly evolve their tactics. But the organizations that survive ransomware aren't just the ones that recover well—they're the ones that stop most attacks before they start, so they only have to recover from the sophisticated ones that slip through.

Table Stakes

You really should follow all of the recommendations in this chapter; however, if you're not doing the three things in this section, you simply aren't doing your job at this point. These aren't aspirational goals or advanced techniques; they're fundamental requirements that every organization must implement. If you did nothing other than these three things, you'd stop approximately 90% of ransomware attacks. Let that sink in: nine out of ten attacks fail when you get these basics right.

Continuously Update Your Patches

Keep your systems patched. Period. Ransomware groups predominantly exploit known vulnerabilities—weaknesses that vendors have already identified and released fixes for—sometimes months or even years before the attack. When Colonial Pipeline, one of the largest pipeline operators in the United States, suffered a ransomware attack in 2021 that disrupted fuel supplies across the East Coast, the attackers exploited a VPN account that lacked MFA—a completely preventable entry point. Similarly, the WannaCry ransomware that infected hundreds of thousands of computers worldwide in 2017 exploited an SMBv1 vulnerability that Microsoft had patched two months before the attack began. Organizations that had applied available patches were immune; those that hadn't became victims.

Establish automated patching for workstations and develop a systematic process for testing and deploying patches to servers within 7–14 days of release for critical vulnerabilities. Don't let perfect be the enemy of good. Even if you can't patch everything immediately, prioritize internet-facing systems, critical infrastructure, and systems handling sensitive data. Every day a critical vulnerability remains unpatched is a day attackers can exploit it.

Enforce MFA or Passkeys

Require MFA for every account that uses a password and has administrative privileges, provides remote access to your network, or accesses business-critical systems and data. No exceptions. Stolen credentials are the most common initial access vector for ransomware attacks because attackers know that many organizations still rely solely on passwords for authentication. With credential-stuffing attacks, phishing, and password-spraying techniques readily available, passwords alone provide virtually no protection against determined attackers.

MFA adds a critical second verification layer that dramatically reduces the effectiveness of stolen credentials. Even if attackers obtain a user's password through phishing or a data breach, they cannot access the account without also compromising the second factor, typically a time-based code from an authenticator app, a hardware token, or biometric verification.

Start with your highest-risk accounts: domain administrators, email administrators, cloud console access, VPN connections, and email accounts (which attackers use for password resets to other services). Then expand MFA requirements to all users accessing company resources remotely and finally to everyone accessing any business-critical application. Ensure MFA is properly configured by disabling "trust this device" options that allow users to bypass MFA for extended periods, and require re-authentication at reasonable intervals. If you're not enforcing MFA on administrative and remote access accounts, you're essentially leaving your front door unlocked with a welcome mat for attackers.

Passkeys: The future of authentication

If you really want to level up your authentication security, implement passkeys wherever possible. *Passkeys* are a passwordless authentication method that uses cryptographic key pairs—one public key stored on the server and one private key that never leaves your device. When you authenticate, your device proves it has the private key without ever transmitting it, making passkeys fundamentally immune to phishing, credential stuffing, and data breaches that expose passwords.

Passkeys are built on FIDO (Fast Identity Online) standards, an open authentication framework developed by the FIDO Alliance, which is a consortium that includes Apple, Google, Microsoft, and other major technology companies. FIDO standards ensure that passkey implementations work consistently across different platforms and devices, so a passkey you create on your iPhone can authenticate you on your Windows laptop. The FIDO Alliance developed these standards specifically to eliminate the security vulnerabilities inherent in password-based authentication.

Passkeys are superior to strong passwords with MFA for several reasons:

- They can't be phished because there's nothing for users to enter on fake websites.
- They can't be stolen in database breaches because the private key never leaves your device.
- They can't be guessed or brute-forced because they're not based on memorable information.
- They eliminate password reuse entirely because each passkey is unique to a specific service.

Users typically authenticate with biometrics (fingerprint or face recognition) or a device PIN, making the experience both more secure and more convenient than typing passwords.

The challenge? Passkey adoption is still emerging. Not every application or service supports them yet, and some organizations face technical hurdles implementing them across legacy systems. That's why passwords and MFA remain the practical baseline requirement for now. But as passkey support expands, transition your authentication strategy toward them. Start with services that already support passkeys. Many major platforms like Apple, Google, Microsoft, and password managers now offer passkey functionality. Every account you convert from password and MFA to passkeys is one less credential that can be compromised.

Case Study: Year-Long Hack That MFA Would Have Stopped

In fall 2025, an unnamed company discovered that Chinese state–backed hackers from Flax Typhoon spent over a year inside their ArcGIS server, turning trusted mapping software into a covert backdoor. They modified legitimate server extensions into a web shell, established a VPN bridge to appear as part of the internal network, targeted IT personnel workstations, and harvested credentials across multiple systems. When defenders tried to recover from backups, they just reinstalled the malware.

The technique was so sophisticated that ArcGIS had to rewrite their security documentation. This was the first documented case of a malicious server object extension being weaponized this way.

But here's the thing: MFA would have stopped this cold.

One compromised credential gave them the keys to the kingdom. Everything that followed—the year of undetected access, the network reconnaissance, the credential dumping, the backup persistence, the complete server rebuild—all of it traces back to that single administrative login. Since the customer didn't have MFA turned on, the hackers were able to waltz right in undetected.

Sometimes the most sophisticated attacks have the simplest prevention: just turn on MFA. You can read the full story at Feminella and Ziang, 2025 (*https://oreil.ly/ws-YR*).

Enforce Solid Password Management

Want to get scared? Take a look at Figure 4-1, which shows the amount of time it would take to crack passwords of various lengths and complexity in 2025. (Reprinted with permission from Hive Systems.)

Number of characters	Numbers only	Lowercase letters	Upper and lowercase letters	Numbers, upper- and lowercase letters	Numbers, upper- and lowercase letters, symbols
4	Instantly	Instantly	Instantly	Instantly	Instantly
5	Instantly	Instantly	57 minutes	2 hours	4 hours
6	Instantly	46 minutes	2 days	6 days	2 weeks
7	Instantly	20 hours	4 months	1 year	2 years
8	Instantly	3 weeks	15 years	62 years	164 years
9	2 hours	2 years	791 years	3k years	11k years
10	1 day	40 years	41k years	238k years	803k years
11	1 week	1k years	2m years	14m years	56m years
12	3 months	27k years	111m yeats	917m years	3bn years
13	3 years	705k years	5bn years	56bn years	275bn years
14	28 years	18m years	300bn years	3tn years	19tn years
15	284 years	477m years	15tn years	218tn years	1qd years
16	2k years	12bn years	812tn years	13qd years	94qd years
17	28k years	322bn years	42qd years	840qd years	6qn years
18	284k years	8tn yers	2qn years	52qn years	463qn years

Figure 4-1. Time it takes to crack a password

What should you learn from this table? First, numbers-only passwords are easy to guess, unless they're really long. But the real lesson you should get from this table is that length is what matters. A 6-character password with numbers, uppercase and lowercase letters, and symbols can be guessed in only two weeks! Compare this with a 15-character password of only lowercase letters, which would take *477 million years*. Even if you use all numbers, a 15-character password will still take 284 years to crack.

Based on that information, here are our recommendations regarding password length and complexity: choose length over complexity every time. But if you can only have 8 characters, it does need to be complex:

- This will get guessed immediately: fewer than 8 characters
- Bare minimum: at least 8 characters, with a combination of uppercase, lowercase, and numbers.
- Better: at least 15 characters (requiring some letters)
- Best: at least 18 characters, and they could be anything

A 15-character passphrase like "coffee-purple-laptop-mountain" is dramatically stronger than an 8-character password with mixed cases, numbers, and symbols like "P@ssw0rd!" Yet the passphrase is also easier to remember and type, reducing user frustration and the likelihood they'll write passwords down or reuse them across systems.

Eliminate mandatory periodic password changes, which research consistently shows leads to weaker passwords as users make predictable modifications (Password1, Password2, Password3) or forget new passwords and require frequent resets. Passwords should only change when there's evidence of compromise.

Implement blocklists that prevent users from selecting commonly used passwords (Password123, Welcome2024) or previously compromised passwords found in breach databases. Services like Have I Been Pwned provide APIs that organizations can integrate into their authentication systems to check passwords against billions of known compromised credentials. This single control prevents users from unknowingly selecting passwords that attackers already possess and actively use in credential-stuffing attacks.

Use a password manager

The single most effective tool for implementing strong password policies is deploying password managers throughout your organization. Password managers solve the fundamental conflict between security and usability: they enable users to maintain genuinely unique, randomly generated 20+ character passwords for every service without any memorization burden. Users need to remember only one strong master password (or use biometric authentication) to unlock their password vault, and the password manager handles everything else, like generating complex passwords, storing them securely with encryption, and automatically filling credentials when needed.

This transforms password security from a user burden into an automated capability. Without password managers, asking users to create and remember unique 15+ character passwords for dozens of services is unrealistic and leads to predictable workarounds: password reuse across services, writing passwords on sticky notes, or using simple patterns with minor variations. With password managers, users can maintain a 32-character random password like "7$mK9#pL2@vN8qR3&xW5*hT6^jF4!dS1" for every single account without ever seeing or typing it. They simply unlock their password manager once per session, and it handles authentication automatically.

Enterprise password managers like 1Password, Bitwarden, or Keeper provide centralized management capabilities that let IT administrators enforce password policies, require minimum password lengths and complexity for generated passwords, monitor for weak or reused passwords across the organization, and maintain access to company credentials even when employees leave. Many integrate with single sign-on (SSO) solutions to provide seamless access to cloud applications while maintaining strong unique passwords behind the scenes. Password managers also reduce help desk burden by dramatically decreasing password reset requests; users no longer forget passwords because they're not trying to remember dozens of them.

From a ransomware defense perspective, password managers provide critical protection against credential-based attacks. When every account has a unique password, credential stuffing attacks fail. Even if attackers obtain a user's password from a breach at an unrelated service, they can't use that password to access your systems. Password managers also protect against keyloggers and clipboard-monitoring malware by directly injecting credentials into applications without ever exposing them to system memory where malware could intercept them. Many password managers include breach monitoring that alerts users when their credentials appear in data breaches, enabling immediate password changes before attackers can exploit the compromised credentials.

Implement password managers organization-wide and make their use mandatory for all business accounts. Provide training on how to use them effectively: generating strong passwords for new accounts, storing existing credentials securely, using secure password sharing features for team accounts rather than emailing passwords, and enabling two-factor authentication on the password manager itself to protect the master vault. Some organizations subsidize or provide password managers for personal use as an employee benefit, recognizing that improving employees' personal security posture indirectly protects the organization by reducing the risk that personal account compromises lead to business impacts. The relatively modest cost of enterprise password manager licenses—typically a few dollars per user per month—delivers outsized security value by solving one of the most persistent challenges in cybersecurity: making strong, unique passwords practical for everyday use.

> ## Case Study: The LastPass Breach (Why Password Length Matters)
>
> Anytime I, Curtis, recommend password managers, someone ultimately brings up the LastPass hack. I used to be able to say that I knew of people that got hacked because they didn't use a password manager, but I never knew anyone that got hacked because they used one. And then the LastPass hack happened.
>
> In August 2022, attackers breached LastPass's development environment and eventually gained access to backup data containing encrypted customer password vaults. This represented a worst-case scenario for password manager users: attackers possessed the encrypted vaults and could attempt offline brute-force attacks without rate limiting or detection, essentially having unlimited attempts to guess master passwords and decrypt the stored credentials.
>
> Here's what happened next: attackers successfully decrypted some vaults and were able to compromise some crypto wallets, but only those protected by shorter master passwords were vulnerable. Security researchers and breach analysis revealed that users with master passwords of 12 characters or fewer were at significant risk of hav-

ing their vaults cracked. Those with 8–10-character passwords, even with complexity (uppercase, lowercase, numbers, symbols), were compromised relatively quickly using modern GPUs and password-cracking techniques. However, users with master passwords of 15+ characters remained secure. Even with unlimited offline cracking attempts, the computational resources required to brute-force longer passwords made them effectively unbreakable with current technology.

This real-world breach validated everything we've discussed about password length. Complexity didn't save the shorter passwords, but length created an insurmountable barrier. A 15-character password has exponentially more possible combinations than a 10-character password, turning a cracking attempt that might take days or weeks into one that would take decades or centuries.

The LastPass breach taught the security community several critical lessons. First, even encrypted passwords need protection through length. Encryption buys you time, but only if the underlying password is long enough that cracking it isn't feasible. Second, password managers remain valuable security tools despite this breach. The users who were compromised had failed to follow the fundamental rule: use a long master password. Those who followed best practices—15+-character master passwords—kept their data secure even after the breach. Third, this incident reinforced that password length is the most important factor in password security, more important than complexity, more important than periodic changes, more important than any other single factor.

The breach also highlighted the importance of the other security layers we've discussed. Users who had multifactor authentication enabled on their critical accounts remained protected even if their password vault was compromised. Attackers with passwords still couldn't access accounts requiring a second factor. This demonstrates why defense in depth matters: the password manager failure didn't result in complete compromise for users who had implemented multiple security layers. For more information on this hack, see this article (Krebs, 2023 (*https://oreil.ly/Qdvz8*)).

These three controls—patching, MFA, and strong passwords—are table stakes because they address the most common attack vectors with proven, readily available solutions. They don't require expensive tools or extensive expertise to implement. They don't depend on cutting-edge technology or sophisticated security teams. They're basic cyber hygiene that every organization, regardless of size or industry, can and must implement. If you take only one thing from this chapter, make it this: get these three fundamentals right, and you'll prevent the vast majority of ransomware attacks before they begin.

People, Process, and Technology

Effective ransomware defense requires balancing three essential pillars: people, process, and technology. This framework isn't new to cybersecurity, but it's particularly critical when defending against ransomware because attacks exploit weaknesses across all three dimensions. The most sophisticated technical controls fail when employees click malicious links. The best-trained workforce struggles without clear processes for identifying and reporting threats. And even perfect processes become ineffective without the technology to implement and enforce them.

While "people, process, technology" is the traditional ordering, we'll address them in implementation order: process first to define your security standards and policies, technology second to deploy the controls that enforce those standards, and people last. Not because they're least important, but because effective training requires showing employees the concrete processes they should follow and the specific tools they'll use. Training people before you've defined your policies or deployed your controls leaves them with abstract concepts rather than actionable guidance.

This chapter walks through each pillar systematically, starting with understanding your environment—the foundation upon which everything else builds—then establishing your processes, implementing your technical controls, and finally equipping your people to work effectively within this security framework. These elements collectively form what's often called *cyber hygiene*: the basic, routine practices that keep digital systems secure and healthy. Good cyber hygiene includes asset inventory, system hardening, patch and vulnerability management, email filtering, authentication and encryption standards, employee training, advanced endpoint protection, and continuous monitoring. All of these require an organization to understand its purpose, the technologies it relies on, the location and value of its data, and its users. Organizations that excel at ransomware defense don't just invest in one area; they build strength across all three pillars—people, process, and technology—creating layered protection where each element reinforces the others. If implemented strategically, this comprehensive approach provides effective defense against ransomware that's greater than the sum of its parts.

Know Your Environment

Before implementing any cybersecurity measures, organizations must first understand what they're protecting. A comprehensive inventory of your entire IT environment is the foundation of effective cyber hygiene. This includes cataloging all physical and virtual servers, workstations, mobile devices, network equipment, software applications, cloud services, third-party vendors, and any other technology assets within your organization. Without this complete picture, you cannot effectively secure, patch, monitor, or backup systems you don't know exist.

Think of your environment inventory as a detailed blueprint of your entire digital infrastructure. Just as a building's blueprints show not only what rooms exist but also how they connect, what they contain, and their importance to the structure, your IT inventory must go beyond a simple list of assets. This living document becomes the roadmap for all subsequent security efforts—from vulnerability management and patch deployment to incident response and recovery planning.

What to Document

Your inventory should capture multiple dimensions of information about each asset

Basic asset information

Document the fundamentals: hostname, IP address, physical or virtual location, operating system, hardware specifications, and installation date. Include serial numbers, asset tags, and purchase information that helps track warranties and support contracts. For cloud resources, document the service provider, region, account details, and configuration specifics.

Business context and criticality

This is where many organizations fall short. Understanding the business impact of each system is essential for prioritization during both prevention and recovery efforts. Classify each asset by its criticality to business operations:

Mission-critical
> Systems whose failure stops core business operations (e.g., production databases, payment processing, manufacturing control systems)

Business-critical
> Systems that severely impact operations but have short-term workarounds (e.g., CRM systems, internal communications platforms)

Important
> Systems that reduce efficiency when unavailable but don't stop business operations (e.g., reporting systems, analytics platforms)

Low impact
> Systems that are convenient but not essential for business continuity (e.g., test environments, archived systems)

This criticality assessment directly informs your response priorities when ransomware strikes. If you can only restore 10 systems immediately, which 10 would keep your business running? The answer should be clear from your inventory.

System dependencies and relationships

Modern IT environments are interconnected webs where systems rely on one another. Document these dependencies explicitly. For example, your customer-facing web application might depend on an application server, which depends on a database server, which depends on a storage array and backup system. All of these might depend on Active Directory for authentication and DNS for name resolution.

Understanding these dependency chains is critical during both attack and recovery scenarios. If ransomware compromises your DNS server, what else stops working? If you're restoring systems after an attack, what must come back online first to enable other systems to function? These dependency maps prevent you from wasting valuable recovery time trying to restore systems that can't operate because their dependencies are still offline.

Identify single points of failure in your environment—those systems whose compromise or failure would cascade throughout your infrastructure. These assets deserve extra security attention and redundancy planning.

Data mapping and classification

Document what types of data each system processes, stores, or transmits. Identify systems that handle regulated data (personally identifiable information [PII], personal health information [PHI], payment card industry [PCI], financial records) or intellectual property. Understanding your data landscape helps you recognize what attackers might target for double-extortion scenarios where they exfiltrate data before encrypting it.

Map how data flows through your environment. Which systems regularly exchange information? What external parties connect to your systems? Where do backups get stored? This data flow documentation reveals potential attack paths and helps you implement appropriate security controls at critical junctures.

Recovery requirements

Make sure to document the RTO and RPO of each system. We discussed these important concepts in Chapter 3.

These metrics aren't arbitrary IT decisions—they require business stakeholder input. The finance team must tell you how much data loss they can accept in the accounts payable system. Operations must specify how quickly the manufacturing control system must be restored. Document these requirements now, during calm times, so you don't have to determine priorities during a crisis.

Ownership and contacts

Every system should have clear ownership. Document the technical owner responsible for maintaining the system, the business owner who depends on it, and any vendors or third parties involved in its support. Include contact information, escalation procedures, and after-hours contacts.

During a ransomware incident, you need to quickly reach the people who understand each system's nuances, can authorize recovery decisions, and can validate that restored systems are functioning correctly. An inventory without ownership information leaves your IRT guessing who to call at 3 a.m. when critical systems are down.

Security context

Document security-relevant details: patch levels, antivirus/EDR status, backup schedules, monitoring coverage, firewall rules, and authentication methods. Note systems that are exceptions to standard policies—perhaps legacy systems that can't be patched or isolated systems with relaxed security controls. These exceptions often become attack vectors and deserve special attention in your monitoring and IR planning.

Third-party connections

Identify all systems that connect to external parties: vendors with remote access, cloud service integrations, electronic data interchange (EDI) connections, API endpoints, or B2B partnerships. Ransomware groups increasingly exploit trusted third-party connections to move laterally between organizations. Understanding these external connections helps you implement appropriate boundary controls and informs your incident response when determining whether an attack might have spread beyond your organization.

Making Your Inventory Actionable

A comprehensive inventory is only valuable if it remains current and can be easily referenced. Store your inventory in a format that supports quick searching and filtering. During an incident, you need to instantly answer questions like "Which systems are running this vulnerable software version?" or "What's the RTO for our customer database?"

Consider maintaining your inventory in a configuration management database (CMDB) or dedicated asset management platform that can automatically discover assets, track changes, and integrate with your other security tools. At minimum, use a structured format (database or detailed spreadsheet) rather than narrative documents.

Update your inventory whenever systems are added, retired, or significantly modified. Make inventory reviews part of your change management process. Assign someone specific responsibility for inventory accuracy—orphaned inventories quickly become useless as environments evolve.

This inventory directly enables the security measures discussed throughout this chapter. Your patch management program needs the inventory to know what systems require updates. Your vulnerability scanning prioritizes based on system criticality documented in the inventory. Your monitoring tools use the inventory to understand what normal looks like for each system. Your backup strategy uses RTO and RPO requirements to determine backup frequencies and restoration priorities.

Most importantly, when ransomware strikes, this inventory becomes your recovery roadmap. You'll know exactly what you're dealing with, what must be restored first, how the restoration sequence should flow, and who needs to be involved. Organizations that struggle through ransomware recovery often discover they're essentially reverse-engineering their own environment under pressure. Build the map now, while you have time to be thorough.

Process: Policies and Procedures

Security technology is only as effective as the policies and processes that govern its use. This section establishes the systematic approaches and standards that define how security works across your organization. We're talking about the documented frameworks that specify how systems should be configured, how authentication should work, what encryption standards apply, and how vulnerabilities get identified and remediated. These aren't abstract governance documents gathering dust in a Share-Point folder; these are actionable standards that directly reduce your attack surface and guide daily security operations. Strong processes ensure consistency across your environment, prevent configuration drift that creates vulnerabilities, and provide clear procedures for maintaining security over time. We'll cover everything from baseline configuration policies and authentication standards to the ongoing processes of patch management and vulnerability assessment. Think of these processes as the playbook that coordinates your people and technology into a unified defensive strategy, ensuring that security isn't dependent on individual heroics but instead becomes a repeatable, scalable capability embedded throughout your organization.

Configuration Policies and Implementation

You need to develop comprehensive configuration policies that define the acceptable security settings for each type of system in your environment. Create separate policy frameworks for different system categories, such as Windows servers, Linux servers, Windows and Apple workstations, network devices, and peripheral equipment like USB drives and Bluetooth devices. These policies should specify which services are permitted to run on each system type, with particular attention to internet-facing systems where administrative services like the Remote Desktop Protocol (RDP) must be prohibited and only essential, hardened services should be exposed externally.

Many people, including me, Curtis, say RDP stands for Ransomware Deployment Protocol. Many, many ransomware deployments have been made possible by exploiting vulnerabilities in RDP. Please consider disabling it everywhere. There are also tools to re-enable it when you need it.

Many vendors, including Microsoft, provide baseline security configuration templates that serve as excellent starting points for developing your organization-specific policies. These industry-standard baselines can be customized to meet your operational requirements while maintaining strong security postures. Your configuration policies should also establish role-based access controls built on least-privilege principles, ensuring users and service accounts have only the minimum permissions necessary to perform their functions. The concept of least privilege is covered in more detail in Chapter 5.

Once policies are defined, implement them systematically across every system in your environment using tools like Group Policy Objects (GPOs) for Windows environments or configuration management platforms for mixed environments. Establish regular configuration review schedules to verify policy compliance and identify any configuration drift that may have occurred over time. These systematic reviews help ensure that security configurations remain consistent and that no systems have reverted to insecure default settings or developed new vulnerabilities through unauthorized changes.

Common configuration policies that significantly strengthen ransomware defenses include:

Account and access controls
- Disable or rename default administrative accounts that attackers commonly target
- Implement least-privilege access where users receive only the permissions needed for their roles
- Disable dormant accounts that haven't been used in 90+ days

Network and remote access
- Restrict RDP to authorized users only and require VPN access for remote connections
- Never expose RDP or other administrative interfaces directly to the internet
- Disable legacy protocols like Server Message Block version 1 (SMBv1) that ransomware frequently exploits

Script and application controls
- Disable PowerShell on systems where it's not required for business operations
- Configure Microsoft Office to block macros by default, as malicious Office documents remain a primary ransomware delivery method
- Implement application allowlisting or blocklisting to control what can execute

Removable media and data protection
- Disable USB storage devices or require encryption for all portable drives

- Disable autorun features that automatically execute programs from USB drives or network shares

Firewall and segmentation
- Configure host-based firewalls to deny all traffic by default and permit only necessary connections
- Implement network segmentation to prevent lateral movement if systems become compromised

Logging and updates
- Enable comprehensive logging of authentication events, privilege escalations, and file access
- Establish automatic update policies that install critical security patches within defined timeframes (typically 7–14 days of release)

These practical policies directly address tactics that ransomware groups actively exploit and can be implemented using built-in operating system capabilities and standard enterprise management tools.

Authentication and Encryption Policies

Authentication and encryption policies form the second critical layer of your security framework, governing how users prove their identity and how data is protected throughout its lifecycle. Authentication policies define who can access which systems and resources, what methods they must use to verify their identity (passwords, MFA, biometrics), and under what conditions access should be granted or denied. Encryption policies specify when and where data must be protected through cryptographic methods, both when stored on disk (encryption at rest) and when transmitted across networks (encryption in transit). These policies are particularly crucial for ransomware defense: strong authentication prevents attackers from using stolen or weak credentials to gain initial access, while encryption protects your data if attackers do breach your perimeter. Without clear authentication standards, organizations end up with inconsistent password requirements, optional MFA, and weak access controls that ransomware groups routinely exploit. Without encryption policies, sensitive data sits unprotected on disk and travels across networks in plaintext, making exfiltration trivial for attackers conducting double-extortion attacks. This section establishes the authentication and encryption standards your organization should implement across all systems and data.

As we've already mentioned earlier in the chapter, you need to define multifactor authentication (MFA) requirements for all administrative accounts, remote access, and access to business-critical applications. Specify appropriate authentication methods for different user categories and system access levels, ensuring MFA is properly configured to prevent token saving or "trust this device" options that can bypass the additional security layer.

Create detailed encryption policies that specify when and where encryption must be implemented throughout your environment. Define requirements for encryption at rest using tools like BitLocker for Windows endpoints and equivalent solutions for other platforms. Establish policies for encryption in transit, covering network communications, email, file transfers, and API connections. Include storage-level encryption requirements for databases, file servers, and backup systems, ensuring that sensitive data remains protected whether stored locally, in the cloud, or during transmission.

We covered this already in "Enforce Solid Password Management" on page 82, but we'll say it again because it's so important. Develop comprehensive authentication policies based on current NIST guidelines that prioritize password length over complexity. Require a *bare minimum* password length of 8 characters with a strong preference for 15 characters or longer, allowing passwords up to at least 64 characters to accommodate passphrases. Avoid enforcing arbitrary complexity requirements such as mixing character types, as research shows these rules often lead to predictable patterns. Instead, encourage unique, lengthy passphrases that are both more secure and easier for users to remember.

Eliminate mandatory periodic password changes, as frequent resets often lead to weaker passwords and predictable modifications. Passwords should only be changed when there's evidence of compromise. Implement blocklists that prevent users from selecting commonly used or previously compromised passwords, and prohibit password hints or knowledge-based authentication questions that can be easily guessed through social engineering.

Implement these policies systematically across all systems using automated deployment tools and centralized management platforms. Ensure password storage uses salted hashing with computationally expensive algorithms to protect against offline attacks. Once your hardening policies are finalized and tested, create standardized golden images for each system type (e.g., Windows servers, Linux servers, workstations, and specialized devices). Store these golden images securely offline, as they serve as clean, hardened baseline configurations for new deployments and provide critical restore points during ransomware recovery operations. (We will discuss these golden images again in Chapter 15, when we talk about how best to recover systems.)

Regular policy compliance audits should verify that authentication and encryption standards are being maintained consistently across your environment. System hardening isn't about making systems impossible to use, it's about finding the balance between security and functionality. Removing unnecessary components, enforcing secure configurations, and strengthening user authentication make it harder for malicious actors to attack your systems and infect them with ransomware or other types of malware, or to exfiltrate your data.

The NIST has a National Checklist Program (NCP) for just about any technology. The NCP was established by the NIST Special Publication 800-70 and is the United States government repository of publicly available security checklists. Each checklist or benchmark provides detailed low-level guidance for setting security configurations of operating systems and applications. The NCP is free to use and can be found at *https://ncp.nist.gov/repository*, and it would be a very good resource to use when developing your cyber hygiene program. Figure 4-2 is their checklist for installing Ansible.

UNCLASSIFIED

Canonical Ubuntu 18.04 STIG Ansible Documentation, V2R15   DISA
24 January 2024   Developed by DISA for the DOD

2. INSTALLATION

The following instructions are for standalone installation using ansible-playbook[1] for testing purposes. A production environment may additionally use Ansible Tower. See here[2] for details.

2.1 Installing Ansible

On Ubuntu, Ansible is available on their official PPA. To install it, run the following:

```
$ sudo apt update
$ sudo apt install software-properties-common
$ sudo apt-add-repository --yes --update ppa:ansible/ansible
$ sudo apt install ansible
```

Figure 4-2. Installing Ansible checklist from the NIST Checklist Program

Patch and Vulnerability Management

Patch management controls, like enforcing automatic Windows updates and keeping track of all the third-party application updates (e.g., Java, Adobe, Microsoft Office), are key to mitigating a network intrusion-based ransomware attack. Attackers often exploit known network and application layer vulnerabilities in sophisticated ransomware attacks, so ensuring all software is patched and up to date can reduce the chances of these vulnerabilities being exploited. As noted in Chapter 1, vulnerabilities in outdated systems have been a consistent entry point for ransomware. They may provide an internal foothold from which attackers can coordinate a much larger-scope infection.

Patches and vulnerability management are tightly intertwined but serve different purposes. A cybersecurity vulnerability is a weakness in a system that can be exploited to compromise security. A software patch is an update to a system designed to fix or improve it. Patches can address security vulnerabilities and other bugs, improve usability or performance, or add functionality.

Patch management ensures your systems have the latest version of every software component to mitigate all known vulnerabilities that have available fixes. It focuses on software versions, systematically tracking and deploying updates across your environment. However, patch management alone is insufficient because vulnerabilities can exist that are not addressed by any patches. These include unknown bugs (zero-days), known bugs without fixes yet, bugs that vendors have decided never to fix, misconfigurations, and unnecessary services running on your systems. Vulnerability management helps you identify and manage the vulnerabilities that exist in your environment, even when your systems are fully patched and up to date.

To move into the technology pillar for a moment, vulnerability scanners examine your systems for known vulnerabilities, providing you the opportunity to remediate or mitigate risks even without patches. You may disable unnecessary services, restrict access to vulnerable components, apply compensating controls, or in some cases, accept the risk after proper evaluation. The process part would be to make sure that regular vulnerability scans are part of your process.

Regular vulnerability assessments help you identify missed patches and any new potential risks across your network, applications, and devices. This dual approach —maintaining current patches while actively scanning for vulnerabilities—ensures comprehensive coverage against both known threats with available fixes and those requiring alternative mitigation strategies.

For example, a vulnerability scanner can find outdated software, weak encryption protocols, unnecessary services running, or open ports that could provide attackers with a foothold. While the volume of potential vulnerabilities may seem overwhelming, prioritization is key. Not all risks are created equal. You must focus on the vulnerabilities that pose the greatest threat to critical systems or those actively exploited in the wild.

Most vulnerability scanners, including the free Nessus scanner, provide internet reference links for additional vulnerability details and the Common Vulnerability Scoring System (CVSS) score for each. The CVSS score is a good initial indicator to help you prioritize your remediation efforts. This doesn't mean lower-scoring vulnerabilities shouldn't be reviewed or considered for remediation. It depends on your unique environment. You may have to invest more time up front on the initial scan results to truly understand the findings as you become more familiar with your environment. Eventually, this will lead to less effort and better prioritization in subsequent scan results.

The first Nessus scan I, Mike, ran on a production network resulted in over 15,000 pages of findings, which took our team of four about a month to review, validate, and prioritize. In such a situation, make sure to prioritize critical systems and vulnerabilities with a higher criticality.

Vulnerability scans can also identify system misconfigurations. Even the most secure systems can be exposed if they're not set up correctly. Default passwords, user accounts with excessive permissions, or improperly configured firewalls can all serve as entry points for ransomware. Regular configuration reviews and adherence to best practices, like least-privilege access, can significantly reduce your attack surface.

Vulnerability management isn't a one-time effort; it's an ongoing, continuous process. Cyber threats are constantly evolving, and new vulnerabilities emerge almost daily. That's why many organizations integrate vulnerability management into their broader cyber hygiene practices. You can stay one step ahead of attackers by combining automated tools, like vulnerability scanners, with human oversight and consistent updates. In the fight against ransomware, vulnerability management keeps us from becoming complacent while helping identify new and evolving vulnerabilities.

Case Study: The Decryption Key Doesn't Work

A Fortune 500 organization suffered a ransomware attack that infected its core production systems. Management decided to pay the ransom primarily because the IT team indicated that the core system backups were corrupt and unusable for recovering the environment. Management coordinated with the company's insurance provider to negotiate the ransom payment, and the threat actors provided the decryptor tool and basic technical support.

As the IT team and the threat actors worked to use the decryptor on the core production systems, they soon determined that the tool was not working, and the files remained unusable. This continued for two days until the threat actors suggested the company pay them an additional $100,000 for continued support, or they would disengage. The company decided not to pay the additional sum and continued to be offline for the next three weeks while the systems and data were rebuilt.

The after action found that the organization could have avoided paying the initial ransom if they had simply tested the decryptor on one of their files immediately. They would have seen the poor results and rejected the threat actors' offer.

Technology: Technical Controls and Monitoring

With your security processes and policies defined, it's time to implement the technical controls that enforce those standards and provide visibility into threats. This section covers the tools and systems that form your technical defense layers, from hardening individual endpoints and filtering malicious emails to deploying advanced detection capabilities and maintaining continuous monitoring across your environment. These aren't standalone solutions; they're integrated controls that work together to create defense in depth. System hardening reduces your attack surface by eliminating unnecessary services and enforcing the secure configurations you defined in your policies. Email filtering blocks threats before they reach users. Endpoint protection tools identify and stop malicious behavior in real time. And continuous monitoring provides the 24/7 visibility you need to detect threats that slip through other defenses, giving your team the early warning required to respond before ransomware can spread. We'll explore each technology layer and explain how they complement each other, creating multiple opportunities to detect and stop attacks. Remember: attackers only need to succeed once, but defenders get multiple chances to stop them—if the right technical controls are in place and properly monitored.

System Hardening

Ransomware attackers are like burglars, always looking for an easy way in. System hardening (which includes both physical data centers and cloud resources) is the process of locking every door, securing every window, and putting alarms in place to make sure they can't get in. It's about reducing the attack surface, which simply means eliminating vulnerabilities or opportunities in your systems, applications, and devices. The smaller your footprint and the more secure your environment, the harder it is for threat actors to find a crack in the perimeter.

The first step in system hardening is removing what you don't need. Every application, service, or account running in your environment is a potential entry point for attackers. Start by understanding the systems in your environment, the types of users, and the applications they (systems and users) need to do their job. Be sure to document this information and use it to disable unnecessary services, uninstall unneeded software, and remove inactive user accounts, templates, demo files, etc. For instance, old software versions often contain unpatched vulnerabilities, new servers and workstations come with unnecessary software, and many devices have services running that don't support the system's purpose or role. Removing unused services eliminates potential attack paths and opportunities for attackers to exploit unknown bugs and reduces the burden on administrators by removing the need to patch/keep the service up to date in the future.

Disable common services

Common services that should be disabled when not required include:

Windows systems
- RDP on systems that don't need remote access

- SMBv1, which has known vulnerabilities exploited by ransomware like WannaCry
- Print Spooler on servers that don't handle printing
- Windows Remote Management (WinRM) on endpoints where remote administration isn't needed
- Remote Registry service
- Telnet client
- Simple Network Management Protocol (SNMP) unless actively used for monitoring
- Bluetooth support on desktop systems and servers
- Xbox-related services that serve no business purpose
- Web server components like IIS on workstations and non-web servers

Linux systems
- Telnet and FTP services (use ssh and sftp instead)
- R-commands (rsh, rlogin, rexec)
- Trivial File Transfer Protocol (TFTP)
- Network File System (NFS) and Samba/SMB file sharing when not required
- Avahi daemon for zero-configuration networking
- Common UNIX Printing System (CUPS) printing services on servers without printers
- X11 forwarding on headless servers

Both platforms
- Bluetooth (often enabled by default but rarely needed on servers)
- Database services on non-database servers
- Web services on non-web servers
- Server-class services on workstations

Review services specific to your environment and apply role-based principles: database services shouldn't run on web servers, web services shouldn't run on database servers, and workstations rarely need server-class services running at all.

Advanced endpoint protection

Consider deploying advanced endpoint protection tools to combat modern ransomware threats. Traditional antivirus software, reliant on signature-based detection, is increasingly ineffective against modern polymorphic or zero-day malware strains that can rapidly evolve to evade pattern detection. Next-generation anti-malware solutions, such as the tools discussed in Chapter 8, which leverage AI, are more capable of proactively identifying and blocking ransomware before it can cause harm.

A critical component of these solutions is EDR, which provides comprehensive protection through multiple layers of security. EDR systems excel at identifying and stopping ransomware by detecting suspicious activities, such as mass file encryption attempts (e.g., the rapid encryption of hundreds of files across a system) or unauthorized data exfiltration efforts, where attackers attempt to steal sensitive data before deploying ransomware in a double-extortion scheme. By analyzing behavioral patterns, such as unusual file access rates, modifications to critical system files, or outbound network traffic to unknown servers, EDR can isolate affected endpoints, terminate malicious processes, and roll back unauthorized changes in real time. EDR platforms also enforce robust data security policies, such as restricting the use of portable storage devices (e.g., USB drives) to prevent data leaks or malware introduction via removable media. These policies can include blocking unapproved devices, encrypting data transfers, or logging all external device activity for forensic analysis. By integrating AI-driven anomaly detection, real-time response, and strict policy enforcement, EDR solutions provide a dynamic, multifaceted defense that significantly reduces the risk of ransomware disrupting operations or compromising sensitive data.

Firewalls and IDS also play a critical role in protecting endpoints. An endpoint firewall can block malicious activity that is not caught by the corporate network firewall because that activity originates inside the protected domain. Similarly, an endpoint firewall can prevent malware on a system from connecting to other systems in the network, while an IDS protects the endpoint from seemingly benign traffic that either bypasses the network firewall or originates from inside the protected network domain. By monitoring for signs of exploitation or suspicious behavior, these tools enable organizations to detect ransomware early in the attack lifecycle, allowing for a rapid quarantining process before the attack spreads. In addition, strict firewall and IDS configurations such as geo-IP blocking, blocking known bad IP addresses, and DNS lookups of strange or known bad domains can possibly prevent a device infected with ransomware from being able to contact its master (a.k.a. the command-and-control systems) to negotiate the encryption keys.

Email Filtering

Email systems have evolved over the years from on-premises systems that had to be purchased, maintained and patched, backed up, licensed, and managed. Today, most email systems are hosted by a third party, like Microsoft 365 or Google Workspace. The good news is that modern cloud email services like these can significantly reduce exposure to phishing if properly configured.

Email filtering serves multiple critical security functions by automatically blocking or quarantining dangerous content before it reaches users. Effective email filtering should target spam messages that waste time and resources, suspicious attachments that may contain malware or ransomware, phishing emails designed to steal credentials or trick users into malicious actions, and prohibited content such as inappropriate material, data exfiltration attempts, or communications that violate organizational policies.

Phishing emails represent one of the most significant threats, as they're specifically crafted to appear legitimate while attempting to harvest login credentials, install malware, or manipulate users into transferring funds or sensitive information. Advanced email filters analyze message content, sender reputation, link destinations, and attachment characteristics to identify these sophisticated attacks.

The placement of filtered messages significantly impacts security effectiveness. Quarantine systems provide the strongest protection by keeping suspicious messages completely out-of-sight and out-of-mind, preventing curious users from accessing them entirely. This approach recognizes that even security-aware users often succumb to curiosity and click on suspicious content when it's easily accessible in their inbox or junk folder. While users are improving at identifying suspicious emails, human nature and curiosity still lead many to interact with questionable messages when they remain visible and accessible.

In contrast, sending filtered messages to junk folders still presents them to users, creating opportunities for accidental clicks or deliberate investigation of "interesting" subject lines. Quarantine systems remove this temptation entirely while still allowing administrators to review and release legitimate messages that were incorrectly filtered, providing both security and operational flexibility. An example of email filtering can be seen in Figure 4-3, showing where to enable strict protection in Microsoft 365.

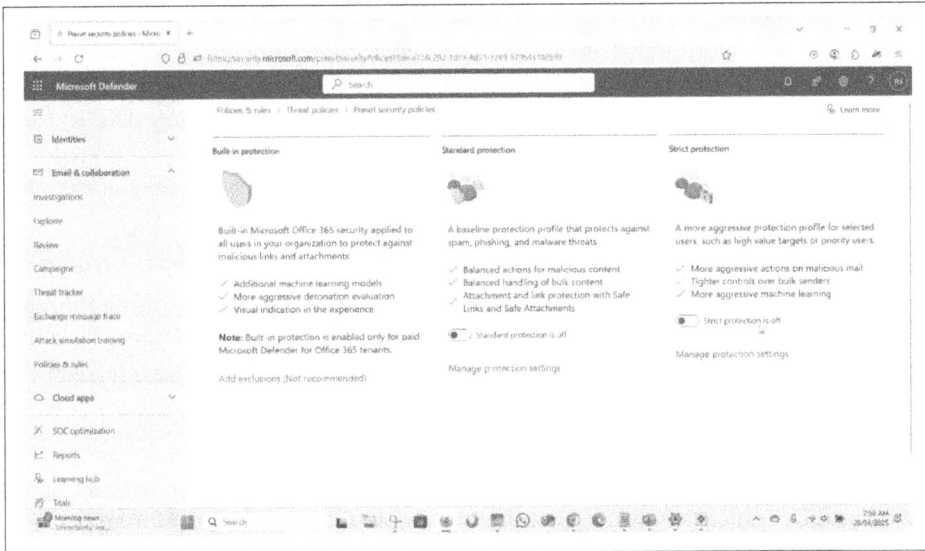

Figure 4-3. Strict protection on Microsoft 365

Detect and Monitor

Even with hardened systems and well-trained employees, sophisticated ransomware attacks can still find ways through your defenses. This is where continuous monitoring becomes critical, giving you the visibility and early warning you need to detect threats before they cause catastrophic damage. Modern ransomware attacks rarely succeed instantly; attackers typically spend days or weeks probing your environment, testing credentials, and positioning themselves before striking. Effective monitoring catches these warning signs early, transforming what would be a devastating surprise attack into a detected threat that your team can respond to and contain. This section covers the tools and strategies that provide 24/7 visibility into your environment, enabling you to spot anomalies, investigate suspicious behavior, and respond rapidly when threats emerge. Combined with a defense-in-depth approach that layers multiple security controls, continuous monitoring ensures that even if attackers bypass one defense, others remain in place to detect and stop them.

Continuous monitoring

Ransomware doesn't just appear out of nowhere, and it usually leaves clues. Attackers often move silently through networks, probing for weak spots, testing credentials, or exfiltrating data before launching their final strike. This is where continuous monitoring comes in. Think of it as having a security guard who never sleeps, constantly watching for suspicious activity and sounding the alarm before things spiral out of control. By proactively monitoring your systems, networks, and endpoints, you can catch the warning signs of ransomware early and stop it in its tracks.

At its core, continuous monitoring involves using tools to collect and consolidate data from sources on the network. This data helps observe network activity, system performance, and user behavior 24/7. Solutions like security information and event management (SIEM) systems, EDR, extended detection and response (XDR), and security orchestration, automation, and response (SOAR) platforms play a vital role here. We discuss these tools in more detail in Chapter 8, so please consider this section a primer.

SIEM systems collect and correlate log data from across your entire IT infrastructure to identify potential threats. Think of SIEM as a security guard monitoring multiple surveillance cameras simultaneously. While providing broad organizational visibility, SIEM requires significant expertise and can generate overwhelming false positives.

EDR tools play a vital role in monitoring, in addition to the prevention role we previously mentioned. They focus on device-level activity, continuously monitoring laptops, servers, and workstations for suspicious behavior patterns. Unlike traditional antivirus, EDR watches how processes behave rather than just looking for known bad signatures. EDR excels at forensic analysis but is limited to endpoint visibility.

XDR evolves beyond SIEM and EDR limitations by creating unified platforms spanning endpoints, networks, and cloud services. XDR follows threats as they move across different infrastructure components and coordinates responses across multiple domains, though integration with existing security investments remains challenging.

SOAR platforms automate security responses based on predefined playbooks. When threats are detected, SOAR can automatically isolate endpoints, disable accounts, and collect evidence within seconds. While powerful for routine tasks, SOAR requires careful balance between automation and human oversight for complex incidents.

When integrated with SIEM or XDR platforms, EDR telemetry provides the device-level visibility needed to correlate suspicious endpoint behavior with network-level indicators, creating a complete picture of how ransomware moves through your environment. The forensic logs captured by EDR—detailing exactly what processes ran, what files were accessed, and what network connections were established—become critical evidence during incident investigation and recovery planning.

These tools collect and analyze massive amounts of data in real time, flagging unusual behavior such as unexpected file encryption, unauthorized access attempts, or large amounts of data being transferred outside your network. For example, if an employee's account suddenly starts accessing critical systems it shouldn't, continuous monitoring tools will alert your security team before it becomes a full-scale attack.

Another key benefit of continuous monitoring is its ability to identify zero-day threats—previously unknown vulnerabilities that haven't been publicly disclosed or patched yet—by detecting abnormal behavior rather than relying on known signatures. This capability directly addresses the gap in vulnerability management where traditional patch management and vulnerability scanners cannot protect against threats that are completely unknown to the security community.

As discussed in "Patch and Vulnerability Management" on page 96, even fully patched systems remain vulnerable to zero-day exploits because no patches exist for unknown vulnerabilities. Continuous monitoring fills this critical security gap by establishing baselines of normal system and network behavior, then alerting when activities deviate from these patterns. Ransomware groups frequently exploit zero-days to bypass traditional signature-based defenses, making behavioral monitoring a crucial line of defense against these advanced threats.

The ability to detect abnormal behavior in real time can mean the difference between catching ransomware early and watching it wreak havoc across your systems. Monitoring tools can recognize suspicious activity—such as unusual file encryption patterns, abnormal network traffic, or unexpected system processes—by correlating data patterns and spotting anomalies even when a ransomware variant is brand new and has never been seen before. This behavioral approach complements traditional vulnerability management by providing protection against the unknown threats that patches and vulnerability scanners cannot address.

Continuous monitoring, however, still requires skilled people to configure the platforms, review the alerts, and escalate issues to be addressed. Automated systems are powerful, but they're most effective when paired with trained security teams who can investigate alerts and act quickly. A well-monitored system combines real-time detection with rapid incident response. For example, if ransomware has been detected encrypting files, the response team can isolate the affected device, shut down network access, and prevent the infection from spreading. Though this chain of events could be automated through a SOAR tool, the impact and scope of the response is typically more accurate and limited when done by skilled people.

Continuous monitoring allows you to see threats as they emerge and respond before they escalate. It's not just about catching the attack but about building confidence that your systems are being watched and protected at all times. This is especially true when, in the absence of continuous monitoring, most company employees are sleeping, and threat actors are just clocking in.

Comprehensive protection with defense in depth

In today's threat landscape, where ransomware is becoming increasingly sophisticated, relying on a single security measure is no longer effective, and it really hasn't been for some time. A layered security approach, combining proactive measures such as employee training, advanced endpoint protection, and secure data backups, offers a more robust defense against ransomware attacks. This multifaceted strategy ensures that even if one defense layer is bypassed, others will still provide protection.

By integrating these tools and practices, organizations can create a security infrastructure that minimizes vulnerabilities and maximizes their ability to prevent or quickly contain a ransomware attack. These layers aren't just for prevention; they are also designed to give us (network defenders) the opportunity and time to identify the attack and slow down the attackers so that we can begin responding before they reach their target.

An analogy we often use is the visualization of a suburban house. There is usually a street, a curb, a sidewalk, a yard, maybe a fence, motion lights, the walls and doors of the house, locks on the windows and doors, maybe an alarm system or dog, and the people inside. These are all layers between a potential threat actor and the valuables inside the house. None of these layers can truly deter or stop a determined criminal from getting what they want. But they can help identify the attack, slow them down, and give the occupants time to respond.

People: Building Your Human Defense

With your processes documented and technology deployed, there's one critical element remaining: your people. All the policies and technical controls in the world won't stop ransomware if employees don't understand their role in the defense. Attackers know this, which is why phishing emails and social engineering remain the most common initial attack vectors for ransomware campaigns. An employee who clicks a malicious link can bypass millions of dollars in security investments in seconds. Conversely, a well-trained employee who recognizes and reports that same phishing attempt becomes an early warning system that prevents an attack entirely. This section focuses on transforming your workforce from a potential liability into an active defensive asset through comprehensive security awareness training. Now that your security framework is in place—with well-defined policies and properly deployed technology—your training can be concrete and actionable rather than abstract. We'll cover the essential topics every employee should understand, from recognizing phishing attempts and using the multifactor authentication you've deployed to properly handling sensitive data according to your policies. The goal isn't to turn employees into security experts; it's to give them the knowledge and confidence to work securely within the framework you've built, recognize threats, follow security protocols, and report suspicious activity before it escalates into a full-scale ransomware incident.

Employee Training

While technology plays a significant role in defending against ransomware, human error remains one of the most common causes of successful attacks. Phishing emails, which trick users into clicking malicious links or downloading infected attachments, remain a primary method of delivering ransomware. Employee training is essential to help individuals recognize suspicious emails, links, or attachments. By creating a cybersecurity awareness culture, employees become the first line of defense against these threats. Examples of concepts all employees should be familiar with are listed here:

Phishing recognition
> Identifying suspicious emails, links, and attachments

Login/password security
> Creating passwordless login systems, or using strong, unique passwords and password managers

MFA
> Understanding and properly using additional verification steps

Social engineering tactics
> Recognizing manipulation attempts via phone, email, or in-person

Safe web browsing
> Avoiding malicious websites and suspicious downloads

Physical security
> Securing devices, clean desk policies, and visitor protocols

Wi-Fi and network safety
> Using secure networks and avoiding public Wi-Fi for business

Incident reporting
> How and when to report suspected security issues

Data handling and classification
> Proper storage, sharing, and disposal of sensitive information

Mobile device security
> Securing smartphones, tablets, and remote work devices

Software updates
> Importance of keeping systems and applications current

Removable media risks
> USB drives, external storage, and unknown devices

Remote work security
> Securing home offices and video conferencing

Ransomware awareness
> Recognizing signs and proper response procedures

Compliance requirements
    Industry-specific regulations affecting data protection

The importance of continuous employee education cannot be overstated. Training should not be a one-time annual event but an ongoing process that reflects the evolving nature of ransomware attacks. As ransomware evolves, so must the training programs, ensuring that employees know the latest tactics and threats. This proactive approach can significantly reduce the likelihood of an attack being successful, as informed employees are less likely to fall victim to phishing scams and other social engineering techniques and are less likely to circumvent the cybersecurity controls put in place to protect them. To help incentivize them, explain how these same concepts can be used to keep their own data safe.

Testing and Reinforcement

Training becomes truly effective when combined with regular, realistic testing that measures comprehension and identifies areas needing reinforcement. Simulated phishing campaigns, where employees receive fake phishing emails designed to mimic real attacks, provide invaluable insights into how well your training translates to real-world behavior. Services like KnowBe4, Cofense, and similar security awareness platforms automate these testing programs, sending periodic simulated attacks and tracking employee responses. However, the philosophy behind testing matters as much as the testing itself.

Focus on positive reinforcement rather than punishment. When employees report suspicious emails to your security team—even if those emails turn out to be legitimate—celebrate that behavior. Consider implementing recognition programs that acknowledge employees who consistently demonstrate security awareness by reporting potential threats. Some organizations publicly recognize top reporters (with employee consent), offer small rewards, or incorporate security awareness into performance reviews as a positive factor. This approach encourages a "see something, say something" culture where employees feel comfortable reporting suspicious activity without fear of looking foolish if it turns out to be benign.

Conversely, when employees click on simulated phishing links or provide credentials, treat it as a learning opportunity rather than a punishable offense. Automatically redirect clickers to brief, targeted training that explains what indicators they missed and how to recognize similar attacks in the future. This just-in-time education is often more effective than generic annual training because it occurs at the exact moment when the employee is most receptive to learning—immediately after making a mistake.

Track repeat offenders not for disciplinary purposes, but to identify individuals who may need additional one-on-one coaching or more frequent training interventions.

At some point, however, you may need to consider terminating those who seem unwilling or unable to follow basic cyber hygiene.

Make testing frequent and varied. Monthly, or even weekly, simulated phishing attempts keep security awareness top-of-mind far better than quarterly campaigns. Vary the sophistication level, starting with obvious phishing attempts and gradually introducing more sophisticated social engineering tactics as your organization's detection rates improve. Rotate through different attack vectors: credential harvesting, malicious attachments, invoice fraud, CEO impersonation, and urgent requests that pressure users into hasty decisions. This variety ensures employees develop broad threat recognition skills rather than learning to identify only one type of attack. Most importantly, share aggregate results with the organization (never publicly singling out individuals for poor performance) to demonstrate progress, highlight common attack patterns, and maintain organizational focus on security awareness as an ongoing priority rather than a checkbox compliance exercise.

If you'd like to explore some of these concepts further, please check out *The GC+CISO Connection*, written by Shawn E. Tuma.

Summary

This chapter broke from our "assume breach" philosophy, but for good reason. Yes, we believe you're going to get attacked eventually. But here's the thing: if you implement the basics in this chapter, you'll stop about 90% of ransomware attacks before they start. That's not hyperbole; it's reality.

We started with the three table stakes that every organization must do, no exceptions: keep your systems patched, enforce MFA everywhere (not just on "important" accounts), and implement solid password management. Length beats complexity every time, and password managers make strong unique passwords actually practical. If you're not doing these three things right now, stop reading and fix that first.

We organized everything else around people, process, and technology, but we tackled them in implementation order, not the traditional order. We started with process because you need to define your security standards before you can deploy technology or effectively train people.

Process means establishing the policies that define how security works in your organization. Configuration policies that specify which services can run on which systems. Authentication standards that require MFA and prioritize 15+ character passwords over arbitrary complexity rules. Encryption policies that protect data both at rest and in transit. And patch and vulnerability management processes that create a continuous cycle of finding and fixing weaknesses, including zero-days that don't have patches yet.

Technology implements the controls that enforce those policies. System hardening removes what you don't need and locks down what remains. Email filtering blocks threats before users ever see them. Advanced endpoint protection with EDR catches malicious behavior in real time. And continuous monitoring through SIEM, XDR, and SOAR platforms provides 24/7 visibility into what's happening across your environment. Defense in depth means attackers have to bypass multiple layers, and each layer gives you another chance to detect and stop them.

People are last in implementation order but absolutely critical. Your employees need to understand the processes you've defined and the tools you've deployed. Training covers everything from recognizing phishing attempts to properly using the MFA you've implemented to handling data according to your policies. Regular testing with simulated phishing campaigns—focused on positive reinforcement, not punishment—validates that training is working and builds security awareness into your culture.

Prevention and preparation aren't opposites; they work together. Every attack you stop with good cyber hygiene is one less incident you have to respond to, one less backup you have to restore, one less ransom demand you have to consider. Get these fundamentals right, and you'll dramatically reduce how often you need those disaster recovery procedures we're building throughout the rest of this book.

CHAPTER 5

Minimize the Blast Radius

Imagine you're sitting at your desk, going about your day, when you begin to notice your desktop files change before your eyes. Then when you try to open them, it appears you don't have access! Then a ransom note fills your screen and demands payment in exchange for your data. It's a nightmare scenario and one that's becoming all too common. It finds its way into environments where users don't have proper awareness training, technical defenses are weak or outdated, security gaps have been overlooked, and attackers can exploit vulnerabilities without being detected. It also finds its way into environments that do all the right things.

The difference between a bad day and a bad month is preparation. This chapter is about doing what you can in your environment to minimize how much damage the ransomware attack can do. Another way to say that is to minimize the *blast radius*.

This chapter assumes compromise (i.e., the user clicked something they shouldn't have, the vulnerable system was compromised, etc.) and focuses on implementing the controls that will diminish the impact of the attack while also slowing the attack down so you can react. Those include technical strategies, such as access controls, endpoint hardening, network segmentation, real-time monitoring, and threat detection. We'll also discuss practical tips for isolating infections, mitigating lateral movement (i.e., attackers moving around inside your network), and building long-term resilience against ransomware threats.

This chapter isn't about implementing flashy, overcomplicated solutions or spending endless amounts of money on the latest cybersecurity solutions. Instead, it's about understanding your technology environment, layering proven defenses, understanding the risks, and making smart, strategic investments in your security posture. By the end of this chapter, you'll have a clear roadmap for reducing the technical vulnerabilities ransomware attackers love to exploit and the confidence to defend your systems when it matters most.

Lastly, this chapter recommends some fairly technical solutions at a high level and is not intended to be a lengthy technical manual. Please use this information to search for and obtain the technical information, best practices, and procedures needed to implement the pieces that are applicable to your environment.

Know Thyself

The first thing to do to reduce the blast radius is to know what you have. Revisit and enhance the environment inventory you did in Chapter 4. It is imperative that you know what you are protecting, the ingress and egress points, the priority and dependencies of different assets, and the capabilities of your team and support partners.

> *If you know the enemy and know yourself, you need not fear the result of a hundred battles.*
> *If you know yourself but not the enemy, for every victory gained you will also suffer a defeat.*
> *If you know neither the enemy nor yourself, you will succumb in every battle.*
> —Sun Tzu, *The Art of War* (*https://oreil.ly/Wsb0J*)

Developing and maintaining detailed asset inventories forms the foundation of effective cybersecurity. These inventories should encompass servers, workstations, network architecture, applications, and cloud assets, along with their respective stakeholders and criticality levels. Rather than existing in isolation, these inventories should be integrated into other security activities such as EDR deployment, vulnerability assessments, and network monitoring. The output from these ongoing activities will help maintain the accuracy and relevance of your asset documentation.

Understanding your environment extends beyond mere cataloging. You must comprehend your business operations, the data that drives them, and the systems and applications required to support company functions. This comprehensive knowledge, combined with an honest assessment of your available resources, enables you to develop a realistic and effective IRP.

The process of developing this IRP will inevitably reveal gaps in your current resources and capabilities that demand immediate attention. These gaps commonly involve skills and technologies, but may also include critical elements like cyber insurance coverage, established law enforcement contacts, and relationships with outside legal counsel.

Preparing for a Ransomware Incident

An effective response starts long before an attack happens. Organizations need a clear, well-documented incident response plan (IRP) that outlines roles, responsibilities, and response procedures.

We'll talk about the IRP in depth in Chapter 7, so the following is just a basic primer.

Develop a ransomware playbook:

- Define specific actions for IT, security, legal, and executive teams.
- Include decision trees for scenarios such as partial versus full network compromise. You can see an example decision tree in Figure 5-1.

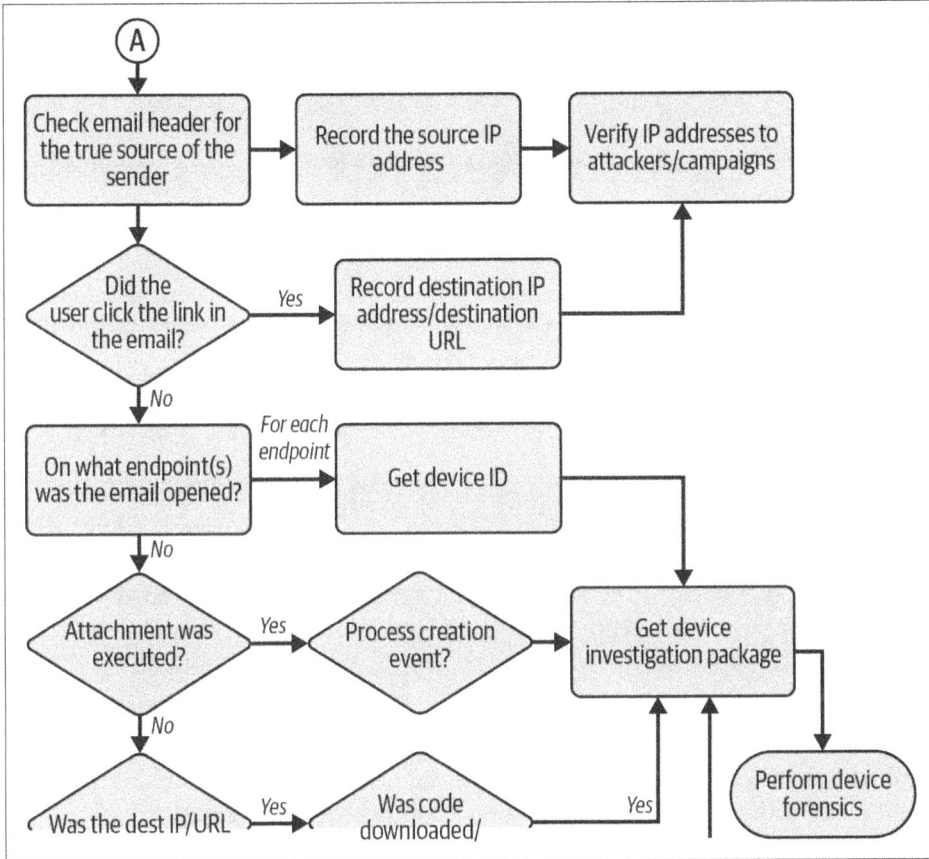

Figure 5-1. An example decision tree

1. Assemble an incident response team (IRT):

   - Use the Responsible, Accountable, Consulted, and Informed (RACI) matrix discussed in Chapter 7 to assign roles to security analysts, system administrators, legal counsel, public relations, and senior management, and make sure they understand these roles
   - Conduct periodic training exercises and tabletop simulations.

2. Establish communication protocols:

- Consider using out-of-band communication channels like encrypted messaging apps (e.g., Signal) or external email services.

- Make sure these communication channels are compliant with applicable regulations.

3. Engage external support:

- Establish relationships with cybersecurity firms, ransomware negotiators, crisis response communication experts, legal advisors, and law enforcement before an attack occurs. Many of the professional services firms that support IR will do a $0 retainer in order to get all the paperwork out of the way ahead of an incident. Note: doing the paperwork while the house is on fire typically incurs a 2- to 6-hour delay.

Incident response will only be as effective as the resources and knowledge you bring to bear. Even a rudimentary outline in a notebook with phone numbers, IP addresses, and important steps is better than trying to objectively and calmly think through those things during the stress and potential chaos of a ransomware event. Create or update your IRP today, including all of the applicable resources, contacts, and procedures.

Endpoint Security: The First Line of Defense

When it comes to ransomware attacks, endpoints are often the most vulnerable and likely entry points. Whether it's a workstation, a smartphone, or an Internet of Things (IoT) device, attackers frequently target these systems because they're the weakest link in most organizations' defenses. The good news is that a well-configured endpoint security strategy can significantly reduce the risk of an infection and contain its spread if ransomware does find a way in.

In this section, we'll explore practical, technical recommendations for securing endpoints and turning them from liabilities into fortified checkpoints.

Deploying Endpoint Detection and Response Tools

Modern ransomware strains are designed to evade traditional antivirus solutions. That's where EDR comes into play, which we covered briefly in Chapter 4. Now let's look at the topic in a little more detail and how it can help minimize the blast radius of an attack.

Unlike basic antivirus software, EDR tools monitor endpoint activity in real time, looking for suspicious behavior such as unusual file encryption, changes to registry keys, or attempts to disable security tools. Newer EDR solutions also incorporate AI and sandboxing in their analysis capabilities, letting the files execute in a safe environment to determine how they behave.

The EDR solution will help you stay abreast of the current and evolving threats to endpoints. You can also use the EDR's threat intelligence capabilities to keep up with the latest ransomware tactics. Well-established EDR solutions, those big names with millions of deployments around the world, collect tons of data and perform extensive analysis that helps make the EDR solution better and contributes to threat intelligence reports and updates.

Here are the key steps for implementing EDR:

1. Before deploying an EDR solution, the organization must define policy, objectives, and how EDR will be utilized and enforced. An analogy for this would be ensuring that once you buy the car, you are familiar with the motor vehicle laws that govern its use. Applicable policies include acceptable use, information security, IT asset policy, and incident response:

   Acceptable use policy
   Effective policy must include acceptable use to define how the organization's devices can and cannot be used, and how to communicate issues, incidents, and observations to the appropriate personnel. The appropriate personnel to report incidents to are often the organization's Information Security Team, which is governed by the information security policy and incident response plan.

   Information security policy
   This policy is typically comprehensive of all information security objectives and controls across the company, such as anti-malware, vulnerability management, and system hardening. These policy components must be defined and adhered to in order to ensure that an EDR solution is proactively effective and reactively timely. EDR-specific provisions typically define the solution's configuration, technical policy for endpoint restrictions (e.g., USB device connections, file downloads, and installations), management, monitoring, and response (e.g., quarantine, auto-deletion).

   IT asset policy
   Defines how an organization manages its technology resources throughout their lifecycle—from procurement and deployment to maintenance and disposal. It covers standards for hardware and software acquisition, inventory management, configuration requirements, access controls, and proper decommissioning procedures to ensure assets are tracked, secured, and utilized effectively.

   Incident response plan
   An effective incident response plan (IRP) defines the procedures, roles, and workflows for detecting, responding to, and recovering from security incidents identified by the EDR solution. The IRP must establish clear escalation

paths, notification procedures, and decision-making authority for security events that the EDR flags as high-priority threats. EDR-specific provisions should define alert thresholds that trigger formal incident response procedures, specify who receives automated alerts and under what circumstances, and outline the containment actions (such as device isolation or network disconnection) that can be initiated through the EDR console. The plan should also address evidence preservation requirements for EDR logs and forensic data to support post-incident analysis and potential legal proceedings. (Chapter 7 provides comprehensive guidance on developing an incident response plan.)

2. Choose a solution that integrates with your organization's broader security stack. As with any new technology, it must play well with your existing environment and users and be manageable. Considerations for choosing the EDR should include an analysis of its capabilities (centralized management console, policies, AI, sandboxing, offline mode), the overhead it creates for the host, and integration with a SIEM tool. (We'll cover SIEM and other tools in Chapter 8.)

3. Configure the EDR to automatically isolate suspicious files, applications, and devices to prevent lateral movement. The effectiveness of an EDR solution is its ability to timely identify and quarantine or prevent malicious activities. The EDR solution must be configured to be as aggressive as possible in quarantining files and devices. Implementing this approach will require coordination and patience with users, ensuring that all trusted files and applications are whitelisted during the initial implementation and follow a formal process for reviewing future changes.

4. Manage the EDR. Implementing the EDR is not a point-in-time activity and must be managed on a daily basis. Once the baseline policies are implemented, the EDR must be reviewed daily to ensure policies are current, endpoints are updated and checking in, and alerts are reviewed and responded to in a timely manner.

Using Next-Gen Anti-Malware Solutions

Now let's talk about antivirus and anti-malware solutions. Antivirus software traditionally focuses on detecting and removing known viruses, worms, and trojans using signature-based detection methods that identify specific malware fingerprints. Anti-malware software is broader in scope, designed to combat all types of malicious software including viruses, spyware, adware, ransomware, and zero-day threats, often using behavioral analysis and heuristic detection alongside signatures.

In practice, the distinction has blurred significantly as most modern "antivirus" products now incorporate comprehensive anti-malware capabilities, making the terms largely interchangeable in today's security landscape. The key difference is that anti-malware represents a more holistic approach to threat detection, while traditional antivirus was more narrowly focused on specific types of file-based malware.

Antivirus and anti-malware software are an important layer in a ransomware defense strategy. While these tools alone may not be sufficient to stop sophisticated ransomware campaigns, they are critical for detecting and blocking known threats, particularly in the early stages of an attack. When properly configured and maintained, they act as a strong safety net, reducing the risk of infection and giving your organization valuable time to respond.

Role of real-time scanning

Real-time scanning is one of the most effective features of antivirus and anti-malware tools. It works by continuously monitoring your systems and files for any suspicious or malicious activity. Real-time scanning can detect and block the malware before bad things happen.

Real-time scanning differs significantly from the traditional approach of scanning the entire device every time. Instead, the EDR does a full system scan on day one to establish a baseline and then only scans what changes or is interacted with. This approach makes better use of device resources and limits the impact on the user.

Advanced features

Many anti-malware tools now include advanced capabilities specifically designed to combat ransomware. When selecting or upgrading your solutions, look for the following features:

Heuristic analysis
> This feature detects threats based on their behavior rather than relying solely on known signatures. This is critical for identifying new or unknown ransomware strains.

Ransomware rollback
> Some modern solutions provide a rollback feature that allows systems to revert to a pre-infection state. This is particularly useful for minimizing downtime and recovering encrypted files.

Machine learning integration
> AI-powered threat detection analyzes patterns in malware behavior to detect and block zero-day ransomware attacks.

File integrity monitoring (FIM)
> This feature monitors critical files and systems for unauthorized changes, such as encryption attempts or sudden file renaming.

Cloud-based threat intelligence
> Leverage real-time updates from global threat intelligence networks to identify and block the latest ransomware variants.

Configuration best practices

Even the best anti-malware solution can fail if not configured correctly. To maximize the effectiveness of an EDR, consider the following best practices:

Enable full coverage
> Ensure real-time scanning is enabled on all endpoints, including desktops, laptops, mobile devices, and servers. Extend coverage to cloud-based storage solutions where ransomware can reside.

> A specific note here to address the gap in coverage at most organizations with mobile devices. Businesses allow users to receive company email and files on their mobile devices, but they often fail to require equal anti-malware protection on these devices. Even if the devices are not owned by the company, anti-malware protection must be required by policy before the user can access company data from these devices.

Scan network shares
> Ransomware often targets shared drives. Enable scanning of network shares to identify and block threats attempting to propagate through shared folders.

Quarantine suspicious files
> Configure the software to immediately isolate and quarantine suspicious files rather than attempting to delete them. Preserving files helps during forensic analysis. Quarantine allows security teams to analyze the file before deciding on the next steps.

Schedule regular full-system scans
> Set up regular full-system scans during off-peak hours to catch dormant malware or threats that may have evaded real-time detection.

Whitelist/allowlist known safe applications
> Reduce false positives by creating a list of trusted applications (known as a *whitelist or allowlist*), while maintaining strong monitoring for unknown or unauthorized software.

Ensuring anti-malware tools are up-to-date

Ransomware evolves rapidly, and attackers are constantly finding new ways to bypass outdated software. Keeping your anti-malware tools updated is critical to ensuring they can recognize and respond to the latest threats:

Automatic updates
> Enable automatic updates for both the EDR software and its threat signature database across all endpoints.

Vendor communication
> Stay in contact with your software vendor to receive notifications about major updates or newly discovered vulnerabilities.

End-of-life management
> Whenever possible and practical, replace outdated software no longer supported by the vendor, as it will lack updates and pose a security risk.

Integrating anti-malware with a broader security ecosystem

While antivirus and anti-malware solutions are essential, they work best when integrated with other security measures. For example:

- Feed the EDR threat data into a SIEM system (covered in detail in Chapter 8) to analyze patterns and uncover broader attack campaigns.
- Use them alongside firewall and network monitoring tools to block malicious payloads before they reach endpoints.

Common mistakes to avoid

The following common security mistakes can really increase the blast radius of an attack, making it much more dangerous:

Relying solely on default settings
> Default configurations may not align with your specific environment or needs. Customize settings for your unique use cases and company workforce environment.

Delaying license and maintenance renewals
> Expired EDR software is effectively useless. Ensure timely renewals to maintain uninterrupted protection.

Ignoring alerts
> Don't treat EDR alerts as noise. Each alert deserves investigation to ensure threats aren't missed, and any accepted anomaly is documented.

Running multiple antivirus programs
> Installing multiple antivirus solutions on the same device can cause conflicts and reduce the overall effectiveness of both.

By effectively utilizing antivirus and anti-malware solutions with real-time scanning and the advanced features available today, organizations can significantly reduce their risk of ransomware infections. While these tools are not a standalone solution, they are a foundational part of a comprehensive ransomware defense strategy. Combined with other endpoint and network security measures, they can provide critical protection against even the most determined attackers.

Importance of Endpoint Hardening

Endpoints are only as strong as their configuration. These configurations must be intentional, documented, and periodically reviewed to ensure they remain relevant and maintained. By hardening endpoint devices, you can reduce the likelihood of exploitation and increase the ability to identify deviations from the build standards.

Here are some key hardening techniques, which we'll discuss in more detail in the following:

Role-based configurations
  Each endpoint should be built and configured for its purpose, and these build standards should be documented, approved, and used for all new device builds.

Disable unused ports and services
  Minimize the attack surface by disabling unnecessary features like RDP and file sharing.

Enforce application whitelisting
  Allow only preapproved applications to run, blocking unauthorized or malicious software.

Control USB device access
  Use tools to restrict unauthorized USB storage devices, which are common vectors for ransomware delivery.

Harden operating system and software configurations
  Apply security baselines and remove unnecessary features, accounts, and permissions to reduce potential attack vectors.

Enforce strong user permissions
  Implement least-privilege access principles, ensuring users only have the minimum permissions required for their job functions.

Perform regular security patching
> Maintain current patch levels for operating systems and applications to close known security vulnerabilities.

Monitor endpoint activity
> Deploy logging and monitoring solutions to detect suspicious behavior and potential security incidents in real time.

Role-based configurations

Endpoints, such as servers, workstations, laptops, smartphones, and IoT devices, are common entry points for ransomware attacks. By hardening endpoints, you can eliminate weaknesses that attackers exploit to deliver ransomware, execute malicious code, or propagate an infection across a network. Endpoint hardening involves reducing the attack surface, securing configurations, and limiting opportunities for attackers to exploit vulnerabilities.

For each endpoint or endpoint type (e.g., accounting PC or web server), the organization should define the appropriate hardware configuration, BIOS settings, OS, OS configuration, authorizations, third-party applications, backup and recovery strategy, and network connectivity and placement. These requirements should then be formalized into the Secure Build Guideline for your organization and relied upon for the deployment of all new assets. Ideally, the Secure Build Guideline would also require a build checklist to be completed and archived for each device.

Disabling unused ports and services

Many endpoints come with unnecessary ports, services, software, and features enabled by default, creating potential entry points for attackers. Removing or disabling these reduces the number of pathways ransomware can use to infiltrate a device.

Using your newly documented Secure Build Guideline, begin disabling or removing everything that is unnecessary or doesn't support the device's purpose. Be sure to monitor for compliance or drift of the system from its preconfigured setup—significant deviations should be captured in a ticket or other form of documentation.

In the US, the NIST offers best practice guides for various devices, and the US Cybersecurity and Infrastructure Security Agency (CISA) published guidance specifically for IoT devices in January 2025. If you live in the United Kingdom, the National Cyber Security Centre (NCSC) developed a Code of Practice for Consumer IoT Security that became the basis for UK legislation requiring manufacturers to meet baseline security requirements, which took effect in April 2024. If you live in Australia, the Australian Cyber Security Centre (ACSC) has published IoT Secure-by-Design Guidance and a voluntary Code of Practice for manufacturers, with new mandatory security standards for IoT devices taking effect in March 2026 under the Cyber Security Act 2024. If you live in the European Union, the European Union Agency for Cybersecurity (ENISA) has published comprehensive guidelines covering the entire IoT supply chain and lifecycle, including an interactive online tool to help organizations identify threats and implement security measures. For more information on similar resources throughout the world, see "Cybersecurity Resources Around the World" on page 190.

Here are some general key steps:

Turn off unneeded services

Services like remote desktop, file sharing, and print sharing are often not required by all endpoints. Services running on a device consume resources like memory and processing but are also potential targets for system exploitation. FTP and Telnet services, for example, are configured by default to always listen for an incoming connection. If an authentication configuration file wasn't created, null access may be allowed. Disabling unnecessary services, like FTP and Telnet, will often disable unnecessary communication ports, like ports 21 and 23.

Disable unnecessary ports

Communication ports are used by specific services and applications to establish a connection between devices on a network. These ports can also be used by malware to send and receive data during an attack. Use a network scanner, like Wireshark, to identify open ports and either disable the associated service or close the ports that aren't in use, such as FTP (port 21), Telnet (port 23), or unused RDP (port 3389).

Host firewall configuration

Configure endpoint firewalls, such as the Windows firewall, to block inbound and outbound traffic on unused ports and restrict traffic to trusted IPs. This can be managed as part of the Secure Build Guideline and the deployment of Active Directory Group Policy.

Enforcing application whitelisting

Ransomware often relies on executing unauthorized or malicious programs on endpoints. Application whitelisting is one of the most effective ways to prevent this, as it only allows preapproved programs to run on a device—as you no doubt defined in your role-based Secure Build Guideline.

Here are some tips for implementing application whitelisting:

- Only allow software to be obtained from legitimate sources, ideally centralized with the IT or technical department for approval, procurement, and deployment. This workflow will also ensure an accurate inventory of software, licensing, uses, and stakeholders.

- Use tools like Microsoft AppLocker or third-party solutions to create and manage whitelists. An EDR solution can also support whitelisting applications through policy.

- Block executable files from running in directories commonly used by ransomware, such as temporary folders (*%AppData%*, *%Temp%*).

Controlling USB device access

USB devices are a common vector for ransomware delivery. Attackers can use USB drives loaded with malicious payloads to infect endpoints. Infected mobile devices that connect to PCs through a USB port may cause an infection. Limiting USB device access minimizes the risk of malware infection and spread. Here are some best practices for USB device access:

Restrict USB access

Use endpoint management tools, like Microsoft Intune, or operating system policy to disable USB ports unless explicitly required. Alternatively, the PCs could be configured to allow USB power charging but not to allow for transferring data. Some EDR solutions can also enforce policy that restricts the use of USB devices.

Enable read-only mode

Configure USB ports to allow only read access where necessary, preventing malicious files from being written to the endpoint. There aren't very many use cases for a read-only USB port, and this approach really only prevents the spread of malware from the PC to the USB, not necessarily the other way around.

Monitor USB usage

Use DLP solutions to track and control USB device activity. Some EDR and SIEM solutions can alert on USB usage if the event log data is available.

Harden operating system and software configurations

Default settings in operating systems and applications often prioritize usability over security. Hardening these configurations ensures your endpoints are less vulnerable to ransomware attacks. Here are some key steps in this process:

Secure operating systems
- Disable unnecessary features like Windows PowerShell, which is often exploited by ransomware.
- Enable security features such as BitLocker encryption (for Windows) or FileVault (for MacOS).
- Turn on secure boot to ensure only trusted software loads during startup.

Limit macro execution
- Ransomware is commonly delivered through malicious macros in Office files. Disable macros unless required and enforce policies to only allow macros signed by trusted developers.

Remove bloatware
- Pre-installed applications that aren't needed increase the attack surface. Uninstall or disable unnecessary software.

Enforce strong user permissions

Improperly configured user, system, and service accounts often provide attackers with an easy way to escalate privileges or access sensitive data. Here are some steps to enforce strong permissions:

Implement principle of least privilege
- Ensure that accounts only have the access and permissions they need for their roles. Don't let a vendor persuade you to provide an account, like a service account, with administrative privileges during deployment or troubleshooting— these are often targets of threat actors and malware.
- Regularly audit and revoke unused permissions.

Limit administrative access
- Reduce the number of users with administrator privileges to an absolute minimum.
- These administrator accounts must also be named, like MikeAdm or SuperMike, instead of using the built-in admin accounts. This creates accountability and traceability for admin activities, also known as *nonrepudiation*.
- Use separate accounts for administrative tasks and everyday use.

- Use separate credentials between the production environment and any test or development environments. Also, Test/Dev credentials should not have access to any production environments.

Implement role-based access control (RBAC)
- Define access levels based on job roles, ensuring that employees have access only to what's necessary for their responsibilities. This can be done on a case-by-case basis in smaller organizations. In larger organizations, these roles should be built into templates with input from stakeholders and approved by management. In either scenario, be consistent with your approach to limiting access, and you will then only need to manage the approved exceptions.

Perform regular security patching

Outdated software is one of the most significant risk factors for ransomware infections. Unpatched endpoints leave vulnerabilities open for exploitation. Here are some tips for effective patch management:

- Define a formal patch management policy and procedure, and review it regularly. This establishes approval from stakeholders for how and when patches are applied, and accountability for getting it done. (There also needs to be a process for mitigating the risk from systems that cannot be patched, such as an isolated network segment.)

- Create and maintain an inventory of all the software in the organization, including firmware, operating systems, databases, and apps.

- Ideally, you want to automate patch deployment across all endpoints using endpoint management tools. These can be expensive, so alternatives are to upgrade your remote management tools like Kaseya or Manage Engine to add the patch management module.

- Another good practice is to incorporate patch management into your vulnerability management process. After every vulnerability scan (OpenVAS or Nessus are free scanners), use the results related to missing patches to help prioritize your efforts.

- Prioritize patches for critical vulnerabilities, especially those with active exploits in the wild. However, don't discount non-critical findings because even the mediums and lows can add up to potential entry points.

Endpoint isolation

If an endpoint is compromised, quick isolation can prevent ransomware from spreading to other systems. Here are some strategies you can use to be able to more quickly isolate an infected endpoint:

- Use EDR tools (explained in Chapter 4) to automatically isolate infected devices.

- Configure VLANs or network segmentation to limit communication between endpoints.

- Develop incident response playbooks with clear procedures for isolating infected devices.

- Implement a SIEM or XDR solution, like Stellar Cyber, with SOAR capabilities. (SIEM, XDR, and SOAR are all explained in Chapter 4.) Then configure the SOAR playbook to automatically address compromised user accounts and endpoints. SOAR playbooks could also modify firewall rules and cloud infrastructure configurations where applicable.

Monitor endpoint activity

Continuous monitoring helps identify suspicious activity early, reducing the chance of a full-scale ransomware attack. Here are some monitoring best practices:

- Deploy endpoint monitoring tools to log file changes, application behavior, and network activity. Ideally, these endpoint tools, like an EDR, would send their logs to a SIEM to be correlated along with events and logs from other data sources.

- Enable alerts for common ransomware behaviors, such as mass file encryption, registry modifications, or attempts to disable security tools.

- Regularly review logs and reports for indicators of compromise (IOCs).

- 24/7 monitoring is often a missing component in most organizations, especially small- to medium-sized businesses. Threat actors know this and will wait until after hours or weekends to make their move. One of the important keys to surviving an incident is timely identification that leads to timely and appropriate response.

Implementing these endpoint-hardening techniques, organizations can significantly reduce the attack surface available to ransomware. Hardened endpoints make it more difficult for attackers to compromise systems and limit the potential damage if an attack does occur. In the next sections, we'll explore how network security and other technical measures can further improve your ransomware defense strategy.

Network Security: Limiting Lateral Movement

While endpoints are often the initial targets of ransomware attacks, a compromised network can amplify the impact, enabling ransomware to spread laterally and disrupt operations on a much larger scale. Strengthening network security is a critical part of reducing the impact of ransomware, as it provides the digital equivalent of locks, like MFA, speed bumps, like network segmentation, and the obvious alarms to keep attackers out, slow them down and contain them if they get in, or lock them out by blocking their internet traffic.

These network defenses work in layers: firewalls act as the main gate, controlling what traffic can enter or leave your network; VLANs and network segmentation serve as speed bumps that force attackers to navigate through multiple checkpoints as they try to move between systems; MFA functions as additional locks that require more than just stolen passwords to open doors; and IDSs work like security alarms, alerting your team when someone is trying to break in or move around where they shouldn't be. Just as a burglar might give up when faced with multiple physical barriers, ransomware attackers often look for easier targets when confronted with well-implemented network security layers that slow their progress and increase their chances of detection.

In this section, we'll cover essential network security measures to reduce the risk and impact of ransomware, prevent lateral movement, and maintain control over your IT environment.

Network Segmentation: Containing the Blast Radius

One of the most effective ways to limit the spread of ransomware is through network segmentation. By dividing your network into smaller, restricted segments, you can reduce the ability of ransomware to move laterally and infect other systems. It's like segmenting a warehouse into multiple rooms. In an open warehouse, the bad actor can steal anything in the entire warehouse. In a segmented warehouse, the bad actor can't move room to room, so they can only steal stuff from the room they originally accessed.

Case Study: UCSF's $1.14 Million Lesson in Segmentation

In June 2020, the University of California, San Francisco was hit by Netwalker ransomware that encrypted servers in the School of Medicine. The attackers demanded $3 million. After negotiation, UCSF paid $1.14 million to decrypt critical COVID-19 research data.

But here's what didn't make all the headlines: the attack was contained to the School of Medicine's IT environment. The broader UCSF campus, including other schools, the hospital system, and administrative functions, continued operating normally. Students kept learning, patients kept receiving care, and researchers in other departments kept working.

Why? Network segmentation.

UCSF had implemented network segmentation between different schools and departments. When ransomware infected the School of Medicine network, it couldn't jump to the School of Engineering. It couldn't reach the hospital's patient care systems. It

---

couldn't spread to the main campus infrastructure. The segmentation created boundaries that ransomware couldn't cross.

Without segmentation, this attack could have crippled the entire UC San Francisco system—hospitals, all schools, research labs, administrative systems. Recovery costs would have been exponentially higher, and the impact on patient care and research could have been catastrophic. Instead, the blast radius was limited to one segment, allowing most of the university to continue functioning while the School of Medicine recovered.

Yes, they still paid a ransom. Yes, it was still expensive and disruptive. But network segmentation turned what could have been a complete organizational shutdown into a contained incident affecting one department. That's the difference between a bad week and a bad year.

Implement network segmentation before you need it. Separate critical systems from general-purpose networks. Isolate departments from each other. Create boundaries that force attackers to overcome multiple barriers rather than having free run of your entire infrastructure. For more information on this story, see here (UCSF Campus News, 2020 (*https://oreil.ly/YM3sT*)).

Here are the key steps to implementing segmentation:

1. Create zones based on sensitivity

   Separate critical systems (e.g., financial databases, production servers) from general-purpose systems like user workstations or guest Wi-Fi.

2. Use virtual local area networks (VLANs)

   Implement VLANs to logically separate traffic within your network. Common examples include putting the VoIP phone traffic on its own network, creating separate segments for different floors of an office building, and isolating the data backup network.

3. Restrict communication

   Limit communication between segments to only what is absolutely necessary. For example, end-user devices should not directly communicate with servers unless explicitly required, and the production network should not directly communicate with the test or development environments.

4. Micro-segmentation

   For high-security environments, use micro-segmentation to enforce communication policies at the application level.

Most of these are easier to implement in virtual or cloud environments that were built with segmentation in mind. However, most network devices are capable of creating VLANs, and their interfaces are fairly intuitive.

Firewalls and Traffic Control

Firewalls are the first line of defense in monitoring and filtering network traffic to prevent unauthorized access. A properly configured firewall can block ransomware-related activity, such as downloading payloads or communicating with command-and-control (C2) servers. Here are some best practices for firewalls:

Deploy next-generation firewalls (NGFWs)
NGFWs provide advanced features like deep packet inspection, intrusion prevention, and application awareness to identify and block malicious activity. The effectiveness of these capabilities requires good maintenance and management to ensure bad-IP lists are current, rules are updated and appropriate, and any changes follow a formal review and approval process.

Restrict outbound traffic
Block outbound connections to unapproved or suspicious IP addresses and domains to prevent ransomware from communicating with C2 servers. Some firewall vendors provide updates to known bad-IP and C2 server IPs, which can change several times a day. There are also subscription services that ensure you have the most accurate list of IPs to block.

Use geo-blocking
If your organization doesn't interact with certain regions, block traffic to and from those areas to reduce exposure to international ransomware threats. Though this is highly effective at stopping the automated attacks, if bad guys really wanted to attack you, then they will find a compromised host within your geolocation and use that as an attack point.

Log and monitor activity
Regularly review firewall logs for unusual traffic patterns or blocked attempts that may indicate reconnaissance or attempted ransomware delivery. Most firewalls have a good dashboard, but the view is focused on network traffic without context like user behavior, EDR alerts, etc. Ingesting your firewall logs into a SIEM or OpenXDR platform is the most effective way to monitor your firewall while also correlating those events with the cybersecurity events from other data sources (yes, I will continue to harp on getting a SIEM-type solution throughout the book).

Network Monitoring and Behavioral Analytics

Continuous monitoring of your network is essential for detecting ransomware-related activity early. Threat hunting adds a proactive layer by identifying potential threats before they escalate.

Case Study: CNA Financial's $40 Million Wake-Up Call

In March 2021, CNA Financial—one of the largest insurance companies in the United States—was hit by Phoenix Locker ransomware. The attack ultimately cost them approximately $40 million in ransom payment, making it one of the largest known ransomware payments at the time.

But here's what's often overlooked: CNA's security team detected unusual activity and began shutting down systems proactively to limit the spread. Their monitoring tools caught suspicious behavior, and they made the difficult decision to take systems offline before encryption was complete. According to reports, this early detection and rapid response prevented the ransomware from encrypting significantly more systems than it otherwise would have.

The lesson: detection buys you time, and time limits damage.

Imagine if CNA hadn't detected the attack until Monday morning when employees couldn't log in. The ransomware would have had the entire weekend to spread unchecked, encrypt more systems, and potentially exfiltrate more data. Instead, their continuous monitoring detected anomalies quickly, giving them the opportunity to act while the attack was still in progress.

Yes, CNA still paid a massive ransom. Yes, recovery was expensive and time-consuming. But their monitoring and detection capabilities—likely including SIEM, EDR, and behavioral analytics—identified the threat early enough to take defensive action. They could isolate infected systems, shut down network connections, and prevent the worst-case scenario.

This is why continuous monitoring isn't optional. Deploy SIEM tools that aggregate logs from across your infrastructure. Implement EDR on every endpoint. Enable alerts for suspicious behavior like mass file access, privilege escalation, or unusual network traffic. Monitor 24/7, because ransomware groups specifically attack after hours and on weekends when they think nobody's watching.

Early detection won't prevent every ransom payment, but it can be the difference between recovering in days versus weeks, between losing some data versus losing everything, between a contained incident and a company-ending catastrophe. For more information, see Gatlan, 2021 (*https://oreil.ly/WnXYd*).

Behavioral analytics capability is a newer and evolving approach to detecting the pre-cursors to a ransomware infection before it happens. Here are the steps for effective monitoring and threat hunting:

1. *Deploy SIEM tools*

   Use security information and event management (SIEM) solutions to aggregate and analyze logs from across your network. The more data sources the better, and they should include at a minimum, the firewall, Active Directory or other authentication source, EDR, and server logs.

2. *User and entity behavior analytics (UEBA).*

   Some SIEM or OpenXDR platforms are UEBA capable and establish baselines for each user, device, and network segment. Even if a behavior isn't yet a security concern, if it deviates from the baseline, it will alert you. Examples include robotic beaconing, which may hit an IP address 500 times a second, which is not humanly possible and likely abnormal for Bob's laptop. Another example might be Sally downloading large files or files with extensions that she has not done before.

3. *Monitor for common IOCs.*

   Examples include large numbers of encrypted files, unusual lateral movement, or unauthorized privilege escalation.

4. *Monitor common attack vectors.*

   Monitor things like remote access (RDP, VPN, remote monitoring and manage-ment [RMM]), email, all internet-facing systems, and user downloads. RDP allows users to remotely control Windows computers over a network connection. A VPN creates an encrypted tunnel for secure access to corporate networks from external locations. RMM tools enable IT administrators to remotely monitor, maintain, and troubleshoot multiple systems from a centralized console.

5. *Automate alerts and response.*

   Set up automated alerts for activities associated with ransomware, such as mass file renaming or spikes in outbound traffic. Ideally, someone would be available 24/7 to receive these alerts and respond accordingly. Alternatively, the SIEM could be configured with a SOAR playbook to automatically respond.

DNS Filtering

Ransomware is often delivered through malicious websites or phishing emails with links to compromised domains. DNS filtering and web security tools can block these threats before they reach users. For example, when the Emotet banking trojan attempts to communicate with its C2 servers, DNS filtering can block those known malicious domains, preventing the malware from downloading additional payloads like ransomware. Similarly, web security gateways can identify and block access to freshly compromised websites that host exploit kits designed to deliver ransomware through drive-by downloads, stopping the infection chain before it begins. Here are some best practices for DNS filtering:

Block known malicious domains
Use threat intelligence feeds, like DarkTrace or OpenDNS, to block access to domains associated with ransomware campaigns.

Enforce safe browsing policies
Implement an acceptable use policy to define what is acceptable internet use and what is expressly prohibited. Restrict access to prohibited, high-risk categories, such as file-sharing, adult content, or newly registered domains.

Monitor DNS queries
Look for suspicious DNS queries, such as frequent lookups for random domain names, which may indicate ransomware beaconing to C2 servers.

Network Vulnerability Assessments

Routine assessments help identify weaknesses that ransomware attackers could exploit. This is important because ransomware is not only delivered by email, and the most significant ransomware attacks typically start with a network intrusion that allows attackers time to perform reconnaissance and staging for their coordinated ransomware deployment. Here are some best practices for vulnerability assessments:

Network vulnerability assessment

All internal network assets and all internet-facing network assets must be scanned in order to fully assess the network. You wouldn't hire a home inspector and ask that they only review the front of the house; you want to know where all the potential issues are before you decide to live there.

Do these assessments as often as possible because technology changes every day. Attackers find new ways to exploit systems every minute, and users present a constant risk to the network. The appropriate assessment frequency should be unique to your environment and the availability of resources (time, skill, budget, etc.). However, I would recommend at least quarterly, plus anytime the environment changes (e.g., new switch, firewall, internet-facing application, etc.).

Effective vulnerability assessments will find open ports, running services, software versions and missing patches, and configuration issues, among other things. Of course, conducting the assessment is only part of the process… now verify, prioritize, and fix these issues.

Network penetration testing

At least annually, simulate an attack on your network. An effective penetration test will be conducted by a third party familiar with threat actor tactics, techniques, and protocols (TTPs). The approach will include conducting reconnaissance to find data from the internet about your company, the networks, DNS leaks, registrations, social media, etc. and use this information to design the simulated attack. During the attack, vulnerabilities are exploited to gain access and demonstrate the extent and impact of unauthorized access. The exercise also assesses your ability to detect the attack and the effectiveness of your response to stopping it.

By implementing these network security measures, you can significantly reduce the risk and impact of a ransomware attack. A well-segmented, monitored, and actively defended network is a substantial part of an effective ransomware defense strategy. Next, we'll explore how access control and identity management play an important role in ransomware prevention and containment.

Access Control and Privilege Management

Ransomware attacks often exploit weak or misconfigured access controls to gain entry and escalate privileges within an organization. Attackers frequently use stolen credentials, brute-force techniques, or privilege escalation to move laterally and maximize damage. Implementing strong access control and identity management practices is critical to minimizing ransomware risks and limiting its spread. These controls and practices should align with established frameworks like NIST's Cybersecurity Framework or the CIS Critical Security Controls, which provide proven methodologies for implementing least-privilege access, regular access reviews, and identity verification processes. For example, following NIST guidelines for identity and access management helps ensure that user accounts have only the minimum permissions necessary to perform their job functions, while CIS Control 6 (Access Control Management) provides specific implementation guidance for managing user access rights and preventing lateral movement during ransomware attacks.

In this section, we'll cover some of the essential strategies to secure user accounts, enforce strict authentication, and prevent ransomware operators from exploiting identity-based weaknesses. (We covered some of these concepts in "Endpoint Security: The First Line of Defense" on page 114. This section will focus more on access to the core of the organization's computing infrastructure.)

Implementing the Principle of Least Privilege

One of the most effective ways to limit ransomware impact is by restricting user permissions to the minimum level required for their job functions. This is referred to as the principle of *least privilege*. The more privileges an account has, the more damage an attacker can do if they compromise it. Here are some best practices for enforcing least privilege:

Restrict administrative privileges
- Minimize the number of users with administrative rights.
- Use separate admin accounts instead of giving standard user accounts admin privileges.
- Don't allow users to be local administrators.

Role-based access control
- Assign permissions based on job roles rather than individuals.
- Regularly review and update role assignments to ensure users only have the necessary access.
- Implement automatic access expiration for critical systems, requiring users to recertify their need for access on a quarterly or semi-annual basis.
- When employees change roles, establish overlapping access periods with defined end dates to ensure business continuity while preventing indefinite accumulation of privileges from previous positions.

Monitor and audit privileged accounts
- Use privilege management tools to track administrative access and detect anomalies. SIEM platforms can alert on privileged access policies, especially ones with UEBA capabilities.
- Implement just-in-time (JIT) access, granting admin privileges only when needed and revoking them automatically after use.

Enforcing Multifactor Authentication

We touched on this in Chapter 4, but MFA is one of the better defenses against credential-based attacks. Even if an attacker steals a password, they cannot access the account without an additional authentication factor, such as a one-time password from an MFA app on a smartphone or MFA dongle (e.g., YubiKey or SecurID). Of course, the implementation of MFA and related policies must also be effective. Here are some key MFA recommendations:

Build your MFA policies
- MFA must be accompanied by well-designed technical and administrative policies to be effective. The administrative policy must define how MFA will be used, like all logins will require MFA every time. This will drive the technical policy that prohibits a device or user from being "trusted" or "remembered" on subsequent logins that wouldn't then require MFA.

Require MFA for all access points

- Enforce MFA on everything possible, including domain authentication, remote access (VPN, remote desktop, etc.), cloud services (O365, social media, backups, etc.), and applications.

Use phishing-resistant MFA methods

- Hardware security keys (e.g., YubiKey), MFA or authenticator applications, or biometrics are more secure than SMS-based authentication, which can be intercepted. Hardware security keys that support FIDO2/WebAuthn standards provide the strongest protection against phishing attacks, as these protocols verify the authenticity of the website before allowing authentication to proceed.

Monitor failed MFA attempts and credential theft

- Unusual patterns of failed MFA logins may indicate an attacker attempting to bypass security. SIEM platforms can alert on MFA failures and abnormalities (UEBA) as part of their authentication policies.

- Subscribe to dark web monitoring services or solutions (e.g., Recorded Future, Searchlight) for alerts related to possible credential theft of employees, administrators, and executives. Something to consider and incorporate in company password policy is to require that company passwords be especially unique and not coincidental with any other account. The policy could also extend to vendors, especially managed service providers, who may use the same credentials across multiple clients.

Educate users on the importance of MFA

- Users will likely develop MFA fatigue from being required to provide MFA for each login. Periodically educating users on the importance of MFA, including the risks of circumventing policy by clicking "trust this device" or "remember me" and the consequence and impact of a resulting compromise can help keep them compliant with policy and the company safe.

By enforcing strict access control policies and strengthening identity management, organizations can significantly reduce the risk of ransomware infiltrating their network through compromised credentials. In the next section, we'll explore incident response strategies to contain ransomware and mitigate its damage when an attack occurs.

Data Protection Strategies

Ransomware primarily focuses on two tactics: encrypting your data so that it can't be used and stealing your data to use for leverage in double-extortion schemes. In both scenarios, the focus is your data. Protecting your data and ensuring its rapid recovery are critical components of minimizing ransomware's blast radius. This section explores strategies that reduce the impact of data encryption, prevent data exfiltration, and enable quick restoration of operations.

Data Classification and Segmentation

Not all data is equally valuable or sensitive, and ransomware attackers know this. By classifying and segmenting your data, you can focus protection efforts on the most critical assets and limit the blast radius when an attack occurs.

Implement data classification policies

Categorize data based on sensitivity and business impact:

Critical
Data essential to business operations (financial records, customer databases, intellectual property)

Sensitive
Regulated data requiring compliance protection (PII, PHI, payment card data)

Internal
Business data not for public consumption but not highly sensitive

Public
Information that can be freely shared

Document which systems and storage locations contain each classification level. This inventory becomes crucial during incident response when you need to prioritize recovery efforts and assess breach notification requirements.

Separate critical data

Store your most valuable data in isolated environments with enhanced security controls:

- Use separate file servers or storage arrays for critical business data
- Implement network segmentation (covered earlier) to isolate critical data stores
- Require additional authentication factors for accessing high-value data repositories
- Limit the number of systems and users with access to critical data stores

When ransomware hits a general file server, isolated critical data remains protected. Attackers who compromise a workstation or standard server won't have immediate access to your most valuable assets, significantly limiting the blast radius.

Control data proliferation

Prevent critical data from spreading uncontrolled throughout your environment:

- Prohibit copying sensitive data to local drives or unauthorized locations
- Implement policies preventing email attachments of classified data without encryption
- Use DLP tools to automatically enforce data handling policies
- Regularly scan for and remediate "shadow IT" data stores where employees save copies outside approved systems

Every additional copy of critical data represents another potential ransomware target. Centralizing and controlling where sensitive data resides reduces the attack surface and simplifies protection efforts.

Data Encryption

Encrypting your data is a common recommendation for protecting it, but it's important to understand how and when encryption actually protects against ransomware attacks.

Understanding encryption's role in ransomware defense

Data encryption on endpoints, like Microsoft BitLocker for workstations and servers, is only effective when the storage drive is not mounted and the user is not logged in. When a user logs into a workstation that is infected with ransomware, that same malware can also access and encrypt or exfiltrate the data from the device. Even if BitLocker encrypts the workstation storage drive, the data for that logged-in user exists in an unencrypted state and would be available to the ransomware.

If users are logged in as local administrators, ransomware would have access to all data on the device. Therefore, storage-level encryption like BitLocker primarily defends against physical theft of devices, not ransomware attacks where the threat actor impersonates or compromises an authenticated user.

Encryption that actually helps against ransomware

While endpoint encryption doesn't prevent ransomware encryption, other forms of encryption can limit the blast radius:

Encrypt data in transit
    Use TLS/SSL for all network communications, especially:

- Backup traffic between systems and backup repositories
- Replication traffic between data centers

- Cloud synchronization traffic

Encrypted network traffic prevents attackers from intercepting backup credentials or identifying backup locations through network sniffing, limiting their ability to compromise your recovery capabilities.

Encrypt backup repositories

Apply encryption at the backup system level, not just the source data level. This prevents attackers who gain access to backup storage infrastructure from simply reading or destroying your backups. Ensure encryption keys for backups are stored separately from production systems, ideally in a password manager or hardware security module (HSM), so compromising production doesn't automatically compromise backups.

Backup and Recovery Strategies

We cover backup and disaster recovery extensively in Chapters 2, 3, and 6. However, since backups are critical to limiting ransomware's blast radius, here are the essential strategies you should implement:

- Implement immutable backups that cannot be modified or deleted for a specified retention period
- Create air-gapped backup copies on media completely disconnected from the network
- Use separate credentials for backup systems that aren't used anywhere else
- Store backup credentials in password managers separate from production systems
- Restrict network access to backup infrastructure through firewall rules and segmentation
- Maintain multiple backup versions (daily for 30+ days, weekly for 90+ days, monthly for 1+ years)
- Test restores from multiple time points to ensure you have clean data predating any infection
- Verify backup integrity using checksums before full restoration during recovery
- Document RTOs and RPOs for each critical system
- Pre-stage recovery resources (spare hardware, cloud instances, clean installation media)
- Practice recovery procedures quarterly to validate your team can execute quickly
- Maintain detailed recovery documentation and dependencies

- Use database-native backup tools (SQL Server backup, Oracle RMAN) that create consistent point-in-time copies
- Enable transaction log backups for point-in-time recovery capability (recover to moments before ransomware struck)
- Test database restores regularly, as database recovery is often more complex than file restoration

---

Case Study: The One Server That Saved Maersk

In June 2017, the NotPetya ransomware devastated Maersk, one of the world's largest shipping companies. Within minutes, the malware spread from a Ukrainian accounting software update to 4,000 servers and 45,000 PCs across 130 countries. It encrypted everything—email servers, domain controllers, file servers, even the systems that track where ships are in the ocean. The company estimated losses at $300 million, and recovery took weeks.

But here's the remarkable part: Maersk survived because of one domain controller in Ghana.

That single domain controller happened to be offline during the attack due to a power outage. When IT teams scrambled to rebuild Active Directory from scratch—a process that would have taken weeks—they discovered this one Ghana-based server still had a clean, functioning copy of their domain. They flew someone to Ghana, retrieved the server, and used it as the seed to rebuild their entire global infrastructure.

The lesson: air-gapped and offline systems save companies.

If that power outage hadn't occurred, Maersk would have had no clean domain controller to rebuild from. The attack spread so fast because everything was connected and accessible. While Maersk didn't have proper network segmentation to prevent the initial spread, the accidental "air gap" created by that power outage became their lifeline.

This is why we emphasize creating intentional offline backups—not relying on accidents. Rotate backup drives offsite. Create immutable backups that can't be deleted even by administrators. Maintain air-gapped copies completely disconnected from your network. When ransomware compromises everything online, these offline copies become your recovery foundation. Maersk got lucky. You shouldn't rely on luck. For more information, see Control Engineering Staff, 2021 (*https://oreil.ly/ YRhf5*).

For comprehensive guidance on backup strategies, testing procedures, and recovery planning, see Chapters 2, 3, and 6.

Data Loss Prevention

While encryption is the primary ransomware threat, data exfiltration for double-extortion attacks is increasingly common. DLP technologies help detect and prevent unauthorized data transfers, limiting the extortion leverage attackers can gain.

Implement network-based DLP

Monitor and control data leaving your network:

- Configure DLP to block uploads of sensitive file types to unauthorized cloud services.
- Alert on large file transfers or bulk downloads that deviate from normal patterns.
- Monitor and restrict data transfers to external drives, cloud storage, and email attachments.
- Use DLP to enforce data classification policies automatically.

When ransomware groups like Maze began threatening to release stolen data, DLP became critical. Organizations with DLP are better positioned to detect exfiltration attempts early, enabling them to contain the threat before significant data left the network, dramatically reducing potential extortion leverage.

Deploy endpoint DLP

Protect data at the device level:

- Prevent copying sensitive files to USB drives or unauthorized cloud sync folders.
- Monitor clipboard operations that might extract sensitive data.
- Control screen capture and print-to-file operations for classified documents.
- Alert when applications attempt to access large numbers of files rapidly (potential ransomware behavior).

Monitor for data staging

Ransomware groups typically stage data for exfiltration before encryption. Watch for:

- Large archives (*.zip*, *.7z*, *.rar* files) created in unusual locations
- Multiple large files moved to common directories
- Compressed files named with dates or "backup" that aren't part of normal operations
- Network traffic to cloud storage services from unexpected hosts

Detecting staging activity gives you a window to respond before both encryption and exfiltration occur, potentially preventing double extortion entirely.

Database-Level Protections

Databases often contain an organization's most valuable data and deserve specific protection strategies beyond general file protection.

Enable database auditing

Configure database auditing to detect suspicious activity:

- Log all administrative actions, especially bulk operations
- Alert on mass UPDATE or DELETE operations outside normal business processes
- Monitor for suspicious queries that access entire tables (potential data exfiltration)
- Track unsuccessful authentication attempts that might indicate credential stuffing

When ransomware targets databases directly (encrypting database files or using SQL commands to scramble data), audit logs often provide the earliest warning signs, enabling faster response and reducing blast radius.

Restrict database access

Limit who and what can access your databases:

- Use service accounts with minimum necessary permissions, not administrative accounts
- Implement network-level restrictions so only application servers can reach databases
- Disable direct SQL access from workstations unless specifically required
- Use database firewalls or query filtering to block suspicious SQL patterns

Shadow Copies and Volume Snapshots

Operating system-level snapshot technologies provide rapid recovery options that significantly reduce blast radius by enabling near-instant restoration.

Enable Windows Volume Shadow Copy Service (VSS)

Configure shadow copies on Windows file servers:

- Enable VSS on all data volumes with appropriate scheduling (multiple times per day).

- Allocate sufficient shadow copy storage (minimum 10% of volume size, preferably 20%).

- Set retention policies to keep multiple restore points over several days.

- Educate users on self-service recovery through "Previous Versions."

When ransomware encrypts files on a Windows server, shadow copies often provide the fastest path to recovery—sometimes within minutes—dramatically limiting downtime. However, ransomware increasingly targets VSS, so this cannot be your only protection.

Protect shadow copies from deletion

Ransomware specifically targets shadow copies for deletion. Protect them:

- Configure EDR to alert on *vssadmin.exe* and *wmic.exe* shadow copy commands.
- Restrict permissions on VSS to prevent unauthorized management.
- Monitor for and block PowerShell commands that manipulate shadow copies.
- Consider third-party VSS protection tools that lock shadow copies from deletion.

Implement SAN/storage array snapshots

Enterprise storage arrays provide snapshot capabilities superior to VSS:

- Configure automated snapshots at the storage array level (hourly or more frequently).
- Ensure snapshots are read-only and cannot be deleted by compromised servers.
- Keep snapshots on separate storage pools from production data.
- Test rapid recovery from storage-level snapshots regularly.

Storage array snapshots sit below the server operating system, making them much harder for ransomware to compromise. Organizations with NetApp, Dell EMC, or similar enterprise storage can often recover entire servers in minutes using storage-level snapshots, minimizing blast radius through rapid restoration.

File Access Controls and Monitoring

Controlling and monitoring who accesses what data helps detect ransomware early and limits the scope of damage.

Implement granular file permissions

Configure filesystem permissions restrictively:

- Use the principle of least privilege for shared folders.
- Implement separate read and write permissions (many users only need read access).
- Restrict "modify" and "full control" permissions to small groups.
- Regularly audit and remove unused permissions.

Ransomware operating under a compromised user account can only encrypt files that user can modify. Restrictive permissions limit blast radius by preventing ransomware from accessing files beyond the compromised account's authority.

Enable file access auditing

Configure comprehensive file access logging:

- Enable success and failure auditing on sensitive file shares.
- Log all file modification, deletion, and encryption events.
- Alert on rapid access to large numbers of files (strong ransomware indicator).
- Monitor for access patterns inconsistent with a user's normal behavior.

File access auditing provides early warning of ransomware activity. When an account suddenly accesses and modifies thousands of files in minutes—behavior virtually impossible for human users—you can detect and respond before encryption completes, potentially saving substantial data.

Deploy file integrity monitoring (FIM)

FIM solutions detect unauthorized changes to files in real time:

- Configure FIM on critical data directories and shares.
- Alert immediately on bulk file modifications or extensions changing (*.docx* → *.encrypted*).
- Monitor for suspicious file operations like or file header modifications or rapid renaming.
- Integrate FIM alerts with SIEM for correlation with other security events.

FIM often provides the earliest possible detection of ransomware encryption in progress, giving security teams precious minutes to isolate infected systems before the entire dataset is encrypted.

Virtualization

Virtualization can be a powerful tool for protecting your data through frequent snapshot backups, as well as using the virtual host environment to isolate infected systems.

Isolation and containment

VMs can be isolated from one another and the host system. If a VM becomes infected with ransomware, it can be quickly isolated by disconnecting its virtual network adapter, preventing spread to other VMs or other parts of the network. Modern hypervisors allow instant network isolation through management consoles, often faster than physically disconnecting servers.

It is also possible to pause an infected VM, which immediately stops it from spreading its infection to other systems, and it preserves a complete forensic image of whatever was in memory. This can be very helpful during the analysis phase.

Snapshots and rollbacks

Virtualization platforms support snapshots—point-in-time copies of a VM's complete state including memory, disk, and configuration. A VM infected with ransomware can be rolled back to a previous snapshot very quickly, often within minutes. This minimizes downtime and data loss and provides a very effective rapid response if you are confident in the integrity of the snapshot being used (i.e., it's not also infected).

Configure automated VM snapshots:

- Take snapshots before major changes or updates.
- Schedule regular snapshots (every 4 to 12 hours for critical systems).
- Retain multiple snapshot generations to ensure clean restore points.
- Store snapshots on separate storage to prevent ransomware from destroying them.

Segmentation and micro-isolation

By segmenting critical applications and data into separate VMs, you limit the impact of a ransomware attack. Modern virtualization platforms support micro-segmentation policies that control traffic between VMs, even on the same host, creating additional barriers that ransomware must overcome to spread.

Consider implementing:

- Separate VMs for different business functions (finance, HR, operations)
- Network isolation between development/test and production VMs

- Security zones for VMs handling sensitive data requiring additional controls
- Virtual firewalls between VM groups to restrict lateral movement

Rapid cloning for recovery

Virtualization enables rapid deployment of clean systems during recovery:

- Maintain golden images of configured, hardened VMs.
- Clone clean VMs in minutes rather than hours of bare-metal installation.
- Deploy multiple recovery instances simultaneously across hosts.
- Scale recovery resources dynamically based on need.

When ransomware encrypts virtual infrastructure, the ability to rapidly clone and deploy clean VMs from templates dramatically reduces recovery time compared to traditional physical server restoration, directly minimizing business disruption.

By implementing these data protection strategies, you create multiple layers of defense that limit ransomware's ability to destroy or steal your data. No single control is sufficient—DLP without good backups leaves you vulnerable to encryption, file permissions without monitoring won't detect attacks in progress—but together these strategies dramatically reduce the blast radius of ransomware attacks. The key is implementing them before an attack occurs, when you have time to do them properly.

Summary

When ransomware breaches your defenses—and this book assumes it will—the difference between a manageable incident and a catastrophic disaster comes down to how well you've prepared to minimize the damage. Reducing the blast radius isn't about preventing every attack; it's about containing the spread, slowing attackers down, and limiting how much they can encrypt or steal.

Start by knowing your environment inside and out. You can't effectively defend systems you don't understand. Maintain detailed asset inventories that document not just what you have, but system dependencies, data criticality, and recovery priorities. This knowledge forms the foundation for every defensive control and becomes your recovery roadmap when attacks occur.

Endpoint security transforms vulnerable devices into fortified checkpoints. Deploy EDR tools that detect behavioral patterns rather than relying solely on signature-based detection. Harden endpoints systematically through role-based configurations, disabled unnecessary services, application whitelisting, and least-privilege permissions. When endpoints are properly secured and monitored, ransomware struggles to establish footholds and spread laterally.

Network security creates barriers that slow attackers and limit their movement. Segment your network to contain breaches within isolated zones. Deploy firewalls with geo-blocking and C2 server blacklists. Implement continuous monitoring through SIEM platforms that correlate events across your entire infrastructure. Use DNS filtering to block access to malicious domains before threats reach users. These layered defenses force attackers through multiple checkpoints, increasing detection chances and response time.

Access control and privilege management address ransomware's favorite attack vector: compromised credentials. Implement least-privilege principles rigorously, enforce MFA everywhere, and regularly audit who has access to what. Even when attackers steal passwords, proper access controls limit how much damage those credentials can cause.

Data protection strategies acknowledge that some data will be at risk despite all other controls. Classify and segment data so critical assets receive enhanced protection. Implement DLP to detect exfiltration attempts. Use granular file permissions so compromised accounts can't encrypt files beyond their authority. Deploy file integrity monitoring to catch encryption in progress. Leverage virtualization's snapshot and isolation capabilities for rapid recovery. While backups (covered extensively in Chapters 2, 3, and 6) provide ultimate recovery capability, these data protection layers minimize how much you'll need to recover.

The chapter's core message: effective blast radius minimization isn't about expensive, complicated solutions. It's about understanding your environment, layering proven defenses strategically, and preparing thoroughly before attacks occur. No single control suffices—EDR without network segmentation allows lateral movement, network segmentation without access controls lets compromised credentials bypass barriers, strong access controls without data protection leave too many vulnerabilities. The power comes from how these controls reinforce each other, creating multiple opportunities to detect, slow, and contain ransomware before it causes catastrophic damage.

Organizations that survive ransomware with minimal impact aren't those with the most advanced technology; they're those that have prepared thoughtfully and implemented fundamental controls properly and thus can respond decisively. The investment you make now in these defensive layers will determine whether ransomware becomes a bad day or a bad month.

CHAPTER 6

Get Ready for Battle

This book starts from an "assume breach" position, which means that we assume that you are going to get attacked. We do that for several reasons. First, there are many books that will attempt to explain how to *prevent* ransomware. So we didn't feel another book on that topic would be helpful. In contrast, there didn't appear to be another book like this one—a book specifically designed to help you *respond* to a ransomware attack.

Finally, and perhaps most importantly, we believe the chances of successfully defending yourself against every ransomware attack are virtually nil. To do that, you would have to be successful at defense 100% of the time; the threat actors only have to be successful once. Their chances of success are much greater than your chances of success. It reminds me of the hilarious posters from despair.com (*https://oreil.ly/p2Qgp*), one of which is called DEFEAT. It says "For every winner, there are dozens of losers. Odds are you are one of them."

Therefore, since your odds of needing to respond to a ransomware attack are very high, you should simply assume that you're going to be attacked and prepare accordingly. In other words, like this book, you should begin from an *assume breach* position. It's simply the most logical starting point when beginning a ransomware defense strategy. Before your organization is infected with ransomware, take the time to follow the suggestions of this chapter.

We have created a companion site, *StopRansomware.com*, that can help you learn and implement the things you see in this and other chapters.

Table Stakes: Do These Five Things First

Before we dive into the technical details, let's be clear about the absolute minimum requirements for backup security. These aren't optional. These aren't "nice to have." These are table stakes—the bare minimum you need just to sit down at the poker table. If you're not doing all five of these right now, stop reading and fix that first.

1. Contract with a blue team NOW.

Not next month. Not after you get budget approval. Now. When ransomware hits, you need professionals on speed dial, not a list of companies to research. The contracts take time to negotiate—time you won't have during an attack.

2. Enable MFA on every backup system component.

Backup servers, storage systems, cloud accounts, tape libraries—everything. If it touches your backups and it doesn't require MFA, you're one stolen password away from losing everything.

3. Implement truly immutable storage for at least one backup copy.

Not "hard to delete." Not "protected by the immutable flag in Linux." I mean nobody-can-touch-it-even-with-root-access immutable. If you can manually expire those backups, so can an attacker.

4. Segregate your backup infrastructure completely from production.

Separate servers, separate networks, separate authentication systems. Your backup system cannot share Active Directory, Okta, or any other identity and access management (IAM) system with production. When production gets compromised, your backups must remain untouchable.

5. Schedule a disaster recovery test as soon as possible

Not "someday." Not "when we have time." This quarter. Actually restore something from your backups and verify it works. If you haven't tested recovery in the last 90 days, you don't have backups—you have wishes.

Everything else in this chapter builds on these five fundamentals. Get these right first, then we'll talk about the advanced stuff.

Engage with Cyber Professionals

One of the best things that you can do to prepare for a cyber attack is to engage with cyber professionals in advance of the attack. Cyber professionals are often categorized as *blue teams* and *red teams*. Blue teams are responsible for the defensive side of security, meaning they help you build and strengthen your defenses and are the first responders during an attack. Red teams, on the other hand, are offensive. They simulate attacks on your infrastructure and systems to test the effectiveness of your existing defenses.

Find a Blue Team Now

In the midst of a cyber attack, every moment is critical. This is not the time to be searching online for "cyber defense professionals" or "ransomware blue team." You should have a pre-existing relationship with experts and a clear line of communication, such as a dedicated hotline or even direct mobile numbers for your response team, depending on your company's size.

Please understand that ransomware recovery is a complex and high-stakes process. One wrong move can have irreversible consequences. A technique that might seem logical to a novice could be instantly detected by a threat actor. For example, unplugging a compromised server to contain the threat might seem like a good idea (one that we actually suggest in previous chapters), but doing so could erase critical evidence from its memory needed for a forensic investigation. Similarly, actions like kicking an attacker out of an account or running full antivirus scans must be done at the right moment. An experienced professional knows the precise timing for these actions to avoid escalating the situation and giving the attacker an advantage.

It's also natural to feel anger during an attack and to want to retaliate with emotional messages to the threat actor. However, such responses are unprofessional and could provoke the attackers to change their behavior for the worse.

A seasoned cyber professional, who is not personally under attack, can respond to the situation with dispassion and objectivity. This detachment gives them the insight to understand how a threat actor might react to a given response. Additionally, most ransomware attacks are not carried out by individuals but by large, organized groups. An experienced blue team professional has likely dealt with many of these groups before and understands their typical tactics. This knowledge can be crucial for predicting how a particular group might respond to ransom negotiations or whether they're likely to detect your forensic investigation.

They will know what you can say and what you cannot say, as well as what tools you can and cannot use to attempt to respond to the attack. Using cyber professionals gives you a much greater chance of successfully defending against the attack without having to pay the ransom.

Get a Red Team Too

Once you have negotiated a relationship with a professional blue team that can help you defend against an actual cyber attack, it's time to hire a red team to assess your current defenses, potential vulnerabilities, and reduce the chances of threat actor success. While it is our position that you cannot stop all attackers and attacks, hiring a red team is a great way to at least make it harder for the threat actors.

Red teams can conduct everything from basic automated port scans to physical penetration tests. They can start by making sure you're not doing anything obvious to make yourself a target and help you slowly harden your infrastructure. Make sure to have them specifically target the backup and disaster recovery infrastructure because (as this chapter is going to repeatedly say) it is your last line of defense and the first point of attack by a threat actor who has infiltrated your environment. It needs to be as solid as it can be.

It is important to say that an inexperienced red team can be worse than no red team at all. They might give you a false sense of security. Make sure to check references and hire a team that knows what they're doing. Also, don't take their findings personally; you want them to find vulnerabilities. That's literally why you hired them.

Find a Cyber Insurance Carrier

One of the other teams you're going to want on your side is a cyber insurance provider. Perhaps it goes without saying, but insurance only works if you get it before an attack, so sooner is better than later.

Backup Tape to the Rescue

Consider the company Spectra (*https://oreil.ly/f0I-4*), which (interestingly enough) is actually a robotic tape library provider in Colorado. A few years ago they suffered a ransomware attack and were quite pleased to realize that they had contracted a cyber insurance company only one month prior to the attack. The cyber insurance company honored the contract and was instrumental in their successful defense against the attack. Spectra's backups were on tape. (Many companies today use disk or cloud storage as their primary storage for backup. Spectra still uses backup tapes, such as LTO, for their backup infrastructure.) They successfully defended themselves against a ransomware attack without paying the ransom—and they did it with tape.

Like everything else in this chapter, you need to select the insurance provider before you need one. The first thing you need to take the time to do properly is search for and vet potential companies. Cyber insurance providers and cybersecurity professionals are not all created equal, and you need time to properly examine the differences between these different providers and select which one is most appropriate for your business.

> Make sure your cyber insurance policy is not easily accessible by a threat actor. If they can find out you have cyber insurance, and see what your coverage limits are, that will most likely turn into your ransomware demand number.

You have time for a full request for proposal (RFP) process. Reach out to different vendors with your requirements and let them propose to you how they would help you. When developing your RFP, make sure to include stakeholders in your organization, such as the legal department and whatever resources you have in the cyber defense category.

If you are a reasonably sized organization with a chief information security officer (CISO), they will help you create the questions for your RFP. If you are a small organization without a CISO, you will need to be a little bit more creative. You might even have to hire a consultant to help you craft it. But again, doing this in advance gives you so much more time to do things properly. Waiting until the moment of disaster to start contacting cyber defense professionals just means you're likely to get whoever has the best SEO—which may have little to do with whether or not they're any good at cyber defense. And, of course, insurance companies will just laugh at you if you call them in the midst of an attack.

Once you have finished your RFP process and successfully vetted and selected both a cyber defense team (a.k.a. your blue team) and a cyber insurance provider, you will need to create contracts with them on what they will charge you for the different services that they will provide. This is another process that can take time. At a minimum it is probably going to take several days to review contracts and agree on pricing. That's not a problem if you're doing things in advance; it's a disaster if you're doing it in the middle of a cyber attack.

So if you do not already have a cyber insurance carrier and a blue team, it's time to find them and hire them immediately.

Consider choosing a cyber insurance carrier in two rounds. Assuming it doesn't include a large up-front investment or a severely long-term contract, I'd do a very quick RFP for both types of companies and quickly hire the ones that feel right in the beginning. Then once you have them under contract, start a second RFP round to ensure you made the right decision. But at least you'll have someone on your side if the worst happens while you're trying to find the perfect team.

Identify Forensic Tools

Just like the cyber defense professionals we discussed in the previous section, you will want to find time to select these tools and become familiar with their operation. Again, don't take too long to pick your first tool. Pick one and make sure someone knows how it works before you spend weeks or months finding just the right tool.

There are two primary categories of forensic tools. First are forensic imaging tools, which create exact bit-for-bit copies of systems and memory to preserve evidence while allowing safe offline analysis. Second are log analysis platforms, which aggregate, normalize, and analyze the massive volumes of log data generated across your environment to reconstruct the attack timeline and identify the scope of compromise. Imaging tools preserve the evidence, while log analysis tools help you understand what that evidence reveals about the attack.

We will again state that this is a job best left to the professionals. Your blue team needs to help you select these tools and will most likely be the ones using them (or directing you how to use them) in an attack.

Forensic Imaging Tools

Here's a list of things you should consider when picking a forensic imaging tool for battling a ransomware attack:

Accuracy is number one
> If your imaging tool isn't giving you a perfect bit-for-bit copy, you might as well not bother. Make sure it captures everything, including deleted files, hidden data, all of it. When you're defending against an attack (or presenting evidence of one), you need to be 100% certain your copy is identical to the original. No exceptions.

Live capture
> It's essential that your forensic imaging tool is capable of capturing an image (i.e., full byte-by-byte copy) of a live system. This allows you to capture an image of what's in memory before you shut down an infected system. You can then examine what's in that image passively without it being active on your network.

Speed
> Your imaging tool needs to handle large drives and servers without breaking a sweat. I've seen cases crater because someone picked a tool that couldn't handle the volume. Losing the fight with a threat actor because your tool is crawling is not a place you want to be.

Rock-solid reliability
> Your imaging tool needs to work every single time, no matter what you throw at it. I don't care if it's an ancient Windows machine or the latest SSD. When you're in the field, you can't afford tools that throw tantrums over different operating systems or file formats. Reliability isn't a feature; it's a requirement.

Legal defensibility
> If you want to be able to assist law enforcement in prosecuting your threat actors, your imaging process needs to be bulletproof. That means proper audit trails, documented chain of custody, and adherence to standards like the Scientific Working Group on Digital Evidence (SWGDE). If you're not worried about assisting law enforcement, this may be a lower priority for you.

Here are some widely used forensic imaging tools for capturing full system images during cyber attacks.

Commercial tools

When you're dealing with a real attack and need tools that work every time, commercial forensic imaging tools are your best bet. They've been battle-tested in courtrooms and come with full support for when things go sideways:

EnCase Imager
The gold standard that attorneys can't argue with and judges trust

FTK Imager (AccessData/Exterro)
Reliable workhorse that handles whatever you throw at it, with a free version to get you started

X-Ways Forensics
Fast and efficient when you're racing against time with massive drives

Cellebrite UFED
Your go-to for mobile devices, but don't overlook its computer imaging capabilities

Magnet AXIOM
Modern platform that actually understands live systems matter

Open source/free tools

Don't have the budget for commercial tools? These open source options can get the job done, but you better know what you're doing because there's no support desk to call at 2 a.m.:

dd (Linux/Unix)
The old reliable that's been creating perfect copies since before ransomware was a thing

Guymager
For those who want dd's reliability with a GUI that won't scare the management

DEFT Linux
Complete forensic toolkit on a bootable drive—just don't expect handholding

Autopsy
Solid open source platform that handles imaging without the commercial price tag

PALADIN
Purpose-built Linux distribution that gets straight to the point

Specialized tools

Sometimes you need more than just imaging software—you need hardware and environments that won't contaminate your evidence or let you shoot yourself in the foot:

Tableau hardware write blockers
Because accidentally writing to evidence drives is a career-ending mistake

WinFE (Windows Forensic Environment)
Bootable Windows that won't touch your evidence but still lets you work

CAINE
Everything you need in one package, assuming you know how to use it

Log Analysis Platforms

When investigating a ransomware attack, the quality and capability of your log analysis platform can make the difference between understanding what happened or being left in the dark. The following is a set of criteria for evaluating these platforms:

Data ingestion and normalization
The foundation of any effective log analysis platform is its ability to ingest and normalize data from diverse sources. Your environment likely generates logs from numerous systems, everything from network devices and firewalls to server logs, security tools, authentication systems, and cloud services. The platform must be able to ingest these varying formats and normalize them into a consistent, searchable format. It also needs to maintain the original log data while creating these normalized versions because sometimes normalized data obscures crucial details present in the original logs, leading investigators down incorrect paths. Your platform should give you the best of both worlds: normalized data for efficient searching and the original logs for verification.

Search capabilities and performance
When investigating an incident, time is critical. Your analysis platform must provide robust search capabilities that operate at scale. Beyond basic full-text search, you need support for regular expressions, field-based filtering, and complex Boolean logic. The platform should allow you to save searches and create templates for common investigation patterns. Also be sure to test search performance at scale. You don't want a large investigation to cripple your search.

Timeline analysis and correlation
Understanding an attack's sequence of events is perhaps the most crucial aspect of incident investigation. Your platform should provide clear visual timeline representations while correlating events across multiple sources. Don't forget time zone normalization, which becomes critical when dealing with geographically

distributed systems or cloud services. The system should also help identify gaps in logging data, as these could indicate either system issues or deliberate log deletion by attackers.

Event classification and automated analysis
While human analysis remains crucial, modern platforms should provide both manual and automated analysis capabilities. The ability to classify and tag events during analysis helps track investigation progress and facilitates collaboration among team members. But remember that automated analysis features like anomaly detection and pattern recognition should augment human analysis, not replace it. Relying entirely on automated analysis can cause you to miss crucial evidence.

Integration and scalability
Your log analysis platform shouldn't exist in isolation. It should integrate seamlessly with your other security tools, including threat intelligence platforms, SIEM systems, and case management systems. These integrations should be bidirectional, allowing both import and export of relevant data. Scalability becomes increasingly important as log volumes grow. The platform must handle increasing data volumes while maintaining performance under load. Support for multiple concurrent analysts is essential during large-scale investigations.

Cost considerations and evaluation
Remember to consider both initial and ongoing costs. This includes licensing, storage requirements, training needs, and support costs. But also understand that cost may sometimes take a backseat to functionality and performance. Don't attempt to save money by using inadequate tools. Also be sure to test everything thoroughly with your actual log volumes and verify performance with historical data—before signing that purchase order. Perhaps most importantly, verify support responsiveness, remembering that they will be at their best during testing. It only goes downhill from there.

Here are some key log analysis tools commonly used during cyber attack investigations.

Enterprise SIEM/log analysis platforms

These are the heavy hitters designed to handle the log tsunami that modern networks generate. They cost real money, but when you're drowning in logs during an active attack, you'll understand why:

Splunk
The 800-pound gorilla that everyone knows how to use, with more apps than you'll ever need

Stellar Cyber
> OpenXDR platform that can be deployed in hours and is capable of ingesting practically any data source and providing fast actionable analysis with the help of AI

IBM QRadar
> Correlation engine that actually works when you need to connect the dots fast

ArcSight (now part of Micro Focus)
> Enterprise-grade tool that compliance auditors love to see

LogRhythm
> Timeline analysis that doesn't make you want to pull your hair out

Elastic Stack (ELK)
> Scalable search that won't choke when you feed it terabytes of logs

Sumo Logic
> Cloud platform that actually understands modern infrastructure

Open source/free tools

Budget-friendly options that pack serious punch, but remember—free tools still cost time and expertise to set up and maintain properly:

Graylog
> Centralized logging that doesn't require a PhD to configure

OSSIM/AlienVault OSSEC
> Open source SIEM that correlates events without breaking the bank

Fluentd
> Data collector that unifies your logging mess into something manageable

Apache Kafka
> High-speed log streaming for when you need to handle serious volume

Grafana + Prometheus
> Visualization stack that turns data into insights you can actually use

Specialized analysis tools

Purpose-built tools that do one thing really well—perfect for when your big SIEM platform isn't cutting it for specific analysis tasks:

Chainsaw
> Windows event log analysis that's actually fast enough to be useful

Hayabusa
Timeline generation that doesn't take forever to process

Sigma
Universal signatures that work across different log platforms

YARA
Pattern matching that finds the needles in your log haystacks

Timeline Explorer
Excel-based analysis for when you need to show results to people who speak spreadsheet

Cloud-native solutions

Platform-specific tools that understand cloud infrastructure because generic solutions often miss the nuances of cloud logging:

AWS CloudTrail + CloudWatch
Native AWS tools that actually understand how AWS works

Microsoft Sentinel
Cloud SIEM with AI that might actually help instead of generating false positives

Google Chronicle
Massive-scale analytics for when your log volume makes other tools cry

Azure Monitor
Comprehensive monitoring that integrates with everything Microsoft

Learn Your Tools

Once you select your forensic tools, it's time to try them out. You want to be very familiar with how a tool behaves well before you need it. Start with some non-production systems. See how long it takes to image them and how easily you can analyze those images. Try to analyze a large set of logs to see what you can find out.

This is another area where a red team can be useful. They can conduct a planned attack against your environment, which you should be able to detect using your forensic tools. The more you use these tools in simulated attacks, the better you will be at using them during an actual attack.

Just like everything else in this chapter, waiting until you need a tool to figure out how to use the tool is definitely not the way to go. I still maintain that the best strategy is to develop a relationship with the blue team and bring them in when an actual attack occurs. However, there's nothing wrong with learning how to use the tools as well.

Secure the Backup System

Just as this book assumes that your environment will eventually be compromised by ransomware, you also have to assume that your backup system will be compromised as well. Assume a threat actor will gain the username and password for the most powerful accounts in your backup system. Therefore, it is vital that you are able to stop them from using that login information or at least minimize the damage that they can do with that account. As you will read in the coming pages, you must be able to prevent the deletion of the backups that you will need to respond to the attack. The good news is that stopping this particular attack is actually relatively easy.

> This section covers a few topics that were already covered in the previous chapter, such as password security, MFA, and passkeys. We are covering these topics again with a focus on securing your backup system. Because, as we've already said: it's where you make your last stand.

When it comes to cybersecurity and ransomware attacks, you should consider your backup system Helm's Deep. For those unfamiliar with the amazing trilogy *The Lord of the Rings* by J. R. R. Tolkien, Helm's Deep is a fortress valley, with a huge wall blocking its entrance and a castle at one end. When the kingdom of Rohan comes under attack by the evil wizard Saruman's massive army, King Théoden leads his people there for a desperate last stand.

The defenders, outnumbered five to one, hold off the enemy until Saruman's forces breach the wall using explosives. Just when defeat seems certain at dawn, the wizard Gandalf arrives with reinforcements, and a mysterious forest of walking trees appears to trap and destroy the enemy army.

Every element of the backup system should be designed with security in mind. The following is a list of non-negotiable security design elements for your backup system. You may notice that some of the advice given here is very similar to the previous chapter, but the purpose is different, and the urgency is higher. Things that may be optional in other areas of your environment (e.g., MFA) are table stakes (i.e., you cannot begin without them) here in Helm's Deep. Take a look at Figure 6-1, which shows you all the different parts you may have within your backup infrastructure.

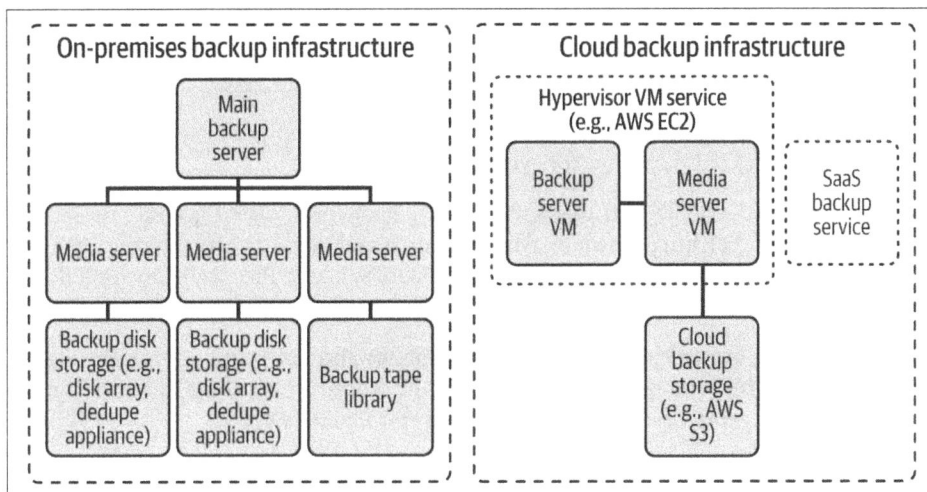

Figure 6-1. Backup infrastructure

Remember that when we are talking about the backup system and its security, we are talking about the main backup server, any media servers, any disk arrays or purpose-built backup appliances (e.g., dedupe arrays), any cloud accounts where backups may be running (e.g., AWS EC2), any cloud storage systems where backups are stored (e.g., AWS S3), and any tape libraries. We're also talking about the physical security where any hardware or media is found. If we're talking about a SaaS application, the good news is that most of this is taken care of for you, and all you have to worry about is the security of the app itself; however, some apps allow you to use other cloud providers' storage. If so, you must include that.

Case Study: They Didn't Know Their Backups Were Broken

So here's a story that should make every IT person check their backup logs right now. We're talking about a farm supplies retailer with 150 computers across seven locations that got absolutely hammered by ransomware in 2024.

The attackers wanted $500,000. That's a pretty hefty ransom, but here's where it gets really ugly. The company's most recent backup disk had been malfunctioning for months—and nobody knew. When they went to restore, they discovered their recovery point was 30 days old. Thirty days! Their backup policy said it should never be more than five days old, but clearly nobody was monitoring those backups.

But wait; it gets worse. You know what the attackers did? They timed the attack to hit just before the scheduled backup was supposed to run. These guys weren't just smart; they were patient. They'd obviously been inside the network long enough to know exactly when the backup window was, and they struck right before it.

The company refused to pay the ransom, which was the right call. But without good backups, they were in a world of hurt. They had to try to rebuild everything they could from that 30-day-old backup and manually re-create the rest.

And here's the kicker: 18 months later, their data showed up online anyway. All that data they lost? It's out there now for everyone to see.

The root causes? Classic stuff that should never happen: outdated firewall, no password policy, no patching schedule. And of course, nobody was actually checking to make sure the backups were working. Everyone just assumed they were fine until they needed them; by then it was way too late.

This is a perfect example of why you need to monitor and test your backups. Having a backup system isn't enough. You need to know it's working before the bad guys come knocking. Read more here (Kinsinger, 2024 (*https://oreil.ly/bHtgQ*)).

Taking Backups Out of the Equation

The first thing a threat actor is going to want to do is delete or encrypt your backups, in order to remove them as an option for you. That forces you to rely on them as your only way of recovering your data, which means you'll be paying the ransom. Since encrypting your backups can take some time and deletion can be done near instantaneously, what they are most likely to do is attempt to delete your backups.

There are two ways a threat actor can delete your backups. The first method would be to target the backup data itself by directly accessing and deleting files on disk, in the cloud, or on backup tapes. This means that you need to be sure to properly secure all of the ways that you can access backup data outside of the actual backup software so that they are as secure as the backup system.

The second method a threat actor might use to delete your backups is to get your backup system to do it for them. If they can become a privileged user in the backup system, they can mark all of the backups "expired." Most backup systems will then immediately delete any disk-based copies of expired backups.

If you have backups on tape, it will be a bit harder for them to delete them, as backup data on tape must be manually erased before it will disappear. Even if they delete the tape out of the backup software database, the data on the tape remains and can be re-ingested in a crisis. Depending on how proficient they are with your particular backup application, they may try to actually delete the data on the tapes as well.

Depending on the backup software in question, deleting backups on tape can be a one- or two-step process. Some backup software packages will allow them to simply tell the tape library to relabel the tapes. The software assumes that if you ask it to relabel tapes that you want the backups on them deleted. That would be the one-step process. Other packages will not allow you to relabel the tape if it has backup data on it. In that case, the first step would be the same as with disk—tell it the backups on a given tape are expired.

Once the software allows you, you simply tell it to put a new electronic label on the front of the tape. If the tapes are in a tape library and accessible to the backup system, that will happen almost as quickly as deleting backups on disk. Once a tape has a new electronic label at the beginning of the tape, it places an end of data (EOD) mark directly after the label, and all of the data on the rest of the tape is completely inaccessible—effectively deleting all the data on that tape in a few seconds. You can see this in Figure 6-2, which shows a typical backup tape with some backups on it. Notice that at the end of the tape on the top, you have the EOD mark, which is always written after writing data to the tape. If you wanted to append additional backups to this tape, the drive would fast forward to the beginning of the EOD mark and then start writing. It cannot go past the EOD mark.

The second image shows what the tape would look like after being relabeled. When the new label is written to the tape, it will then write an EOD mark after it, because it always does that when writing data to tape. Any read or write operations will start and stop at the EOD mark; they will not be able to go past it. That means that the backups to the right of it in the image—which are technically still on the tape—are inaccessible to the drive. This effectively erases them, without actually having to overwrite them.

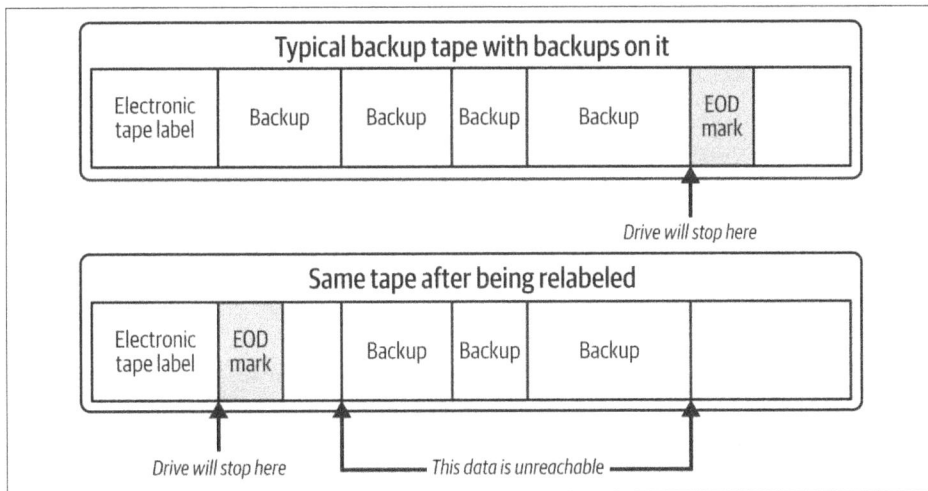

Figure 6-2. Making backups on tape inaccessible

This means that one rather effective way of preventing this is to simply not keep all of your tapes online and accessible via the tape library. A threat actor will not be able to write a new label to a tape if it is sitting on a shelf somewhere outside of the robotic tape library.

Friendly Fire

I (Curtis) saw firsthand how quickly all of the tapes in a tape library can be rendered useless on site with a Legato NetWorker client many years ago. I was one of two specialists on site, and the other one was a Legato employee—and we were using a new version of NetWorker. Prior to this new version, relabeling a large number of tapes took a long time, since it only used one drive at a time. A large relabeling operation also had to be babysat, because you had to say yes to the "Are you sure?" message for each tape.

But this new version of NetWorker had a new feature called "fast and silent" that allowed you to use all of the tape drives in the tape library to do a relabeling operation, without being bugged by the "Are you sure?" notifications. It was indeed a very nice feature if you had to relabel a large number of tapes.

Unfortunately, however, this feature came out at a time where there also was a bug where if you double-clicked on one tape in the library, it would actually select all of the tapes in the library.

This consultant needed to relabel one tape—so he double-clicked it. Because of this bug, he actually selected all tapes in the tape library. For whatever reason, he also clicked the fast and silent option. Clearly, he was distracted, and he did not realize what he was doing at the moment he did it. But what he did was—in just a few clicks—relabel (i.e., erase) every tape in the tape library of a production customer. A few minutes later, he realized what he had done, but the damage had already been done.

The point of this story is to show just how easy it is to delete all backups in a tape library. It's even easier if the backups are on disk.

All of these attempts to delete your backup data require privileged access. You need root or administrator access in order to delete backup files on disk—or at least one would hope so. You also need root or administrator access to do the kinds of commands that would relabel tapes outside of the backup system. And of course you're going to need privileged access to the backup system in order to convince it that the backups should be expired early and deleted, or that backup tapes should be relabeled.

This risk is why we must do our best to prevent unauthorized privileged access to the backup system and its software, and to limit the damage that a particular user can do if their account is breached.

Role-Based Administration

Before we start talking about locking down various privileged accounts, it's important to discuss the concept of role-based access control (RBAC). It is a natural outcome of implementing the concept of least privilege discussed in Chapter 5. The idea is to create roles that have various levels of power within the backup system and to assign those roles to different people that perform various functions.

While RBAC has been commonplace in other parts of the computing world for many years, it is sometimes seen as nascent in the backup world. So let us explain why not using RBAC is a particularly bad idea in the world of backups. Here's a quick list of some of the operations a typical backup person might perform, and how they could be used by a threat actor for nefarious purposes:

Create backup configurations
> A threat actor could create a custom backup configuration that backs up all of the sensitive data they are looking for, such as password files and important spreadsheets with configuration information. No one would look twice at new backup configurations. Also, if they have the ability to create backup configurations, that also means that they can change existing backup configurations, such as reducing the retention period of certain backups, which could have the effect of deleting existing backups made with that policy.

Setting retention policies
> It's not quite backup, but it is related. Think about the data protection capabilities in SaaS products like Microsoft 365. I (Curtis) personally assert that you need to back up such things, but many people rely on the retention capabilities of these products as a method of backup. It's not a backup as far as I'm concerned, but stick with me. One of the things a threat actor might do is reduce your number of versions down to one, which again has the net effect of deleting all previous versions of files. Once again, this is probably not something that anyone is watching for either.

Manually expiring backups
> This is easily the most dangerous operation. If a threat actor can perform this function, they can use it to expire all backups in your environment in a matter of seconds. And if those backups are on disk, they will be deleted as well.

Perform restores
> This task could be used to exfiltrate data. Even if they were unable to create custom backup configurations, they can easily restore data to a location that they could control—even a location outside of your firewall. This is because most modern backup software has the ability to restore any file to anywhere. Since most environments don't monitor restores, a threat actor could probably do this without anyone noticing.

Expire backups and relabel tapes

This was already mentioned in the previous section. This could be used to delete every backup you have in a matter of minutes. Even if you replicated those backups to another location, the backup software will delete those backups as well.

Scheduling backups that have already been configured and monitoring those backups are relatively harmless functions. Even manually rerunning already-configured backups is relatively harmless. This means that a backup operator could be allowed to do their job without needing access to the more dangerous functions of creating new backups, performing restores, and expiring backups prematurely.

This means you could create a backup operator role that only has access to the safer operations, and a backup administrator role with access to the riskier operations. The backup administrator role could be locked up behind tighter security and receive much tighter scrutiny when it is being used.

Secure Your Logins

The first and foremost method of stopping a threat actor from taking control of your backup system is login security. (Remember when we say "system" here, we are referring to the entire system—in the generic sense of that word—not an individual server.) If they cannot log in to the backup system or any part of it, they will be unable to take it out of the ransomware equation. So if any part of your backup infrastructure allows you to log in to a privileged account simply by entering a username and password—that needs to be addressed immediately. That would mean that all a threat actor needs to compromise your backup environment is to steal one set of credentials. And sadly, there are innumerable ways that can be done. So if you only need a password to login to your backup system, fix that now.

We've already covered the fundamentals of password managers, MFA, and passkeys in earlier chapters. But here's the thing: backup systems present unique authentication challenges that deserve special attention. Your backup infrastructure is both your last line of defense and attackers' favorite target, so the authentication protecting it needs to be bulletproof. Let me explain why the general security advice we've already discussed becomes absolutely critical—and more complicated—when applied to backup environments.

Passwords and password managers for backup systems

I (Curtis) have walked into more data centers than I care to count and found backup servers with passwords like "backup123" or "Password1." The excuse is always the same: "It's just the backup server." Just the backup server? It's the system that has read access to literally everything in your environment!

The password manager discussion from Chapter 4 becomes even more critical when we're talking about backup infrastructure, but with some backup-specific twists. First, you're not just dealing with user accounts—you're managing service account passwords that need to run automated processes 24/7. These service accounts often get overlooked in password policies because they're "just for backups."

Here's where it gets interesting: backup environments typically have multiple types of accounts that all need strong, unique passwords managed by password managers:

- Backup service accounts are the backbone of your backup infrastructure, but they're often configured once and forgotten. I've seen organizations where the backup service account password hasn't been changed in five years because "we don't want to break anything." Your password manager needs to track these accounts, and you need a process for rotating these passwords without bringing down your backup operations.

- Administrative accounts for backup software often get shared among multiple administrators. This is where password managers become essential—each admin should have their own account with unique passwords generated and stored in the organization's password manager. No more "admin/password" shared among the backup team.

- Storage system credentials for your backup targets (whether disk arrays, cloud storage, or tape libraries) need the same treatment. These systems often have default passwords that never get changed, or simple passwords because "they're on the internal network."

The challenge with backup systems is that password rotation can be tricky. Unlike a user account where you can change the password and update it in your browser, backup service accounts often have passwords embedded in configuration files, scheduled tasks, and service configurations across multiple servers. This is why password managers with API integration become valuable—they can help automate the rotation process.

One backup-specific consideration: make sure your password manager itself isn't dependent on the systems you're trying to protect. If your password manager runs on infrastructure that could be compromised in the same attack, you might find yourself locked out of the very systems you need to recover. Strongly consider keeping critical backup system passwords in a separate, offline password manager or secure physical location.

Multifactor authentication for backup infrastructure

We covered MFA extensively in Chapter 5, but backup systems often become the exception to every security rule. I can't tell you how many times I've heard "We can't put MFA on the backup system because we need emergency access" or "What if the backup fails at 3 a.m. and we can't get the MFA code?" These concerns aren't entirely wrong, but they're not a reason to skip MFA—they're a reason to implement it more thoughtfully.

The emergency access problem is real. When your primary domain controller is down and your backup system requires MFA through that same domain, you've created a chicken-and-egg problem. This is why backup systems should have completely separate authentication systems, and why emergency access procedures become critical. You might need offline MFA methods or emergency break-glass procedures that don't depend on your primary infrastructure.

Service account MFA presents unique challenges. Your backup software runs automated jobs that can't respond to MFA prompts. This is where certificate-based authentication or service account–specific MFA solutions become necessary. Some organizations solve this by using dedicated service accounts that authenticate via certificates or API keys rather than traditional MFA.

MFA fatigue in backup environments has its own flavor. Picture this: it's 2 a.m., backups are failing, and the on-call administrator is getting bombarded with MFA requests from an attacker who compromised their credentials. The tired admin, just wanting the noise to stop so they can fix the backup issue, approves the request. This is why backup environments need particularly robust MFA policies.

The solution isn't to skip MFA—it's to implement it correctly:

- Use backup-specific MFA that doesn't depend on your primary infrastructure.
- Implement proper break-glass procedures for emergency access.
- Consider hardware security keys for backup administrators.
- Use certificate-based authentication for service accounts where possible.
- Monitor MFA requests from backup systems more closely than other systems.

Case Study: Colonial Pipeline Paid $4.4M, Then Used Their Backups Anyway

In May 2021, DarkSide ransomware hit Colonial Pipeline, responsible for 45% of fuel consumed on the US East Coast. The company shut down 5,500 miles of pipeline, causing gas shortages, panic buying, and prices spiking to six-year highs. CEO Joseph Blount decided to pay 75 bitcoin—$4.4 million—within hours, calling it "the right thing to do for the country."

The attackers provided the decryption key as promised. But here's what the headlines missed: the decryption tool was so slow that Colonial Pipeline abandoned it and restored from their own backups instead. The ransom bought them nothing—their

---

own business continuity measures proved faster and more reliable than the attackers' buggy decryption tool.

The attack exploited a VPN account without MFA. Once inside, attackers spent two weeks mapping the network before striking. Better access controls and backup segregation—exactly what this chapter recommends—would have made this attack far more difficult.

The lesson: even when criminals keep their word, their tools are often useless. Backups beat ransom payments every time. The FBI eventually recovered $2.3 million of the ransom, but that doesn't change the fundamental truth: invest in backup security before an attack, not in bitcoin payments after one. For more information, check out Kerner, 2022 (*https://oreil.ly/rj7Zf*).

Passkeys and FIDO for backup systems

FIDO and passkeys represent the future of authentication, and we covered their general benefits in Chapters 4 and 5. But implementing them in backup environments requires some special consideration.

The biggest challenge is that many backup software packages are, frankly, behind the times when it comes to authentication. Many backup systems still don't support modern FIDO authentication. If your backup software doesn't support FIDO, that's not a reason to avoid it—that's a reason to seriously consider replacing your backup software.

The lockout concern is more serious with backup systems than with other applications. If you lose access to your FIDO device and get locked out of your email, that's annoying. If you lose access to your FIDO device and get locked out of your backup system during a ransomware attack, that's catastrophic. This is why backup environments need robust backup plans for authentication—multiple FIDO devices, secure recovery codes, and documented emergency procedures.

Legacy system integration is another backup-specific challenge. Your shiny new backup software might support FIDO, but what about the tape library interface that's older than anyone currently working there? Or the cloud storage gateway that hasn't been updated in three years? You'll need to plan for mixed authentication environments and secure the weakest links.

Our recommendation is to implement FIDO where you can, but don't let perfect be the enemy of good. If your backup software supports FIDO, use it. If it only supports traditional MFA, use that. If it only supports username and password, then seriously consider replacing it ASAP. In the meantime, see what you can do to firewall off that system to shore up the vulnerability.

The key point is this: if any component of your backup system—whether application, server, or storage—doesn't support MFA and/or passkeys, seriously consider replacing it. The integrity of your backup system is your last line of defense. When everything else fails, these security measures could be all that stands between you and complete data loss.

Remember, we're not just talking about convenience here. We're talking about the difference between paying a ransom or restoring from backups. The difference between weeks of downtime and hours of downtime. The difference between losing customer trust and maintaining business continuity. Your backup system's authentication deserves the same level of attention—if not more—than any other critical system in your environment.

Update Your Backup Software

Like many other topics covered in this chapter, we have already covered keeping your software up to date in earlier chapters. However, the importance of the security of your backup system is important enough that we must reiterate it now: make sure your backup software is up to date.

The main concern here is if you are running your own backup system. (If you are using a SaaS backup vendor, they will handle server upgrades.) I can't tell you how many times I (Curtis) have walked into a data center and found backup servers running operating systems and application versions that went end-of-life years ago. Or they're running current versions, but their patches are not up to date. The excuse is always the same: "We don't want to break anything that's working."

Your backup server is one of the most privileged systems in your environment. It needs access to pretty much everything to do its job. Running it on an out-of-date system is like giving the keys to your house to someone you know is a burglar.

What you need to do:

- Keep your backup server's operating system patched and current.
- Update your backup software regularly (even if the current version "works fine").
- Update any agents or components running on protected systems (this applies even if you're using a SaaS-based product).
- Keep your backup target systems (like deduplication appliances) current as well.
- Monitor security advisories (e.g., *https://cve.mitre.org*) for your backup infrastructure.

You may ask: what if an update breaks something? That's why you test updates in a lab environment first. Yes, it's more work. Yes, it takes more time. But it's a lot less work than trying to explain to your CEO why all the backups are gone because you got hit with a vulnerability that was patched six months ago.

Segregate All Backup Infrastructure

Your backup system should share nothing in common with your production system, except the network. Your backup system should share no security infrastructure in common with your production systems. It should be on separate servers, inside a separate virtual data center (if using virtualization), on separate storage, etc.

Most importantly, it must not share your corporate network's IAM system. It doesn't matter if it's Okta, Entra ID, Active Directory, or LDAP. If that system is compromised, it might also compromise your backup system. Use a completely separate IAM system. If possible, use a different technology altogether, such as using Okta when the rest of your company uses Entra ID, or vice versa. If you're using the same system, just make sure it is a completely separate administrative account with no crossover to the production side. There should be no "super user" account that controls both environments.

Shut Off Remote Desktop Protocol

As we've already mentioned in Chapter 4, RDP is one of the most common attack vectors used by ransomware groups. Ransomware attacks via RDP are so common that some of us say RDP stands for Ransomware Distribution Protocol. If you absolutely must have RDP enabled on your backup servers (and you probably don't), consider securing it using these methods:

Restrict it to specific IP ranges
> First, restrict access to specific IP ranges inside your LAN. (Obviously, RDP must never be allowed externally.) I mean completely locked down—no connections allowed unless they're coming from known, trusted addresses.

Require VPN access first
> Even inside your LAN, consider a separate firewall that requires VPN access before allowing any RDP connection. This means potential attackers can't even see your RDP port unless they've already compromised that VPN.

Enable Network Level Authentication (NLA)
> NLA forces users to authenticate before establishing an RDP session, not after. This might sound like a small distinction, but it prevents attackers from exploiting vulnerabilities in the RDP protocol itself.

Use nonstandard ports
> You should also consider moving RDP to a nonstandard port. Yes, this is security through obscurity, and no, it won't stop a determined attacker. But it will keep

your servers from showing up in automated port scans, which is how many attacks begin. Think of it as locking your backdoor, even though someone could still break a window—it's not perfect, but it's better than leaving the door wide open.

Disable RDP entirely
> The best solution is to simply disable RDP entirely and use your backup software's built-in console access. Modern backup solutions have spent considerable time and effort building secure remote access capabilities. Use them. They're almost always more secure than RDP, and they're certainly more appropriate for backup system management.

Lock Down SMB

The Server Message Block (SMB) protocol (sometimes incorrectly referred to as Common Internet File System [CIFS]) is how Windows servers share files with one another. Its security is another critical area we need to discuss, particularly when it comes to backup servers. Too many organizations treat their backup servers like any other file server, and that's a recipe for disaster. Just like RDP, SMB is also used to deploy ransomware and to interrogate your network for vulnerable information. Lock down SMB access to only what's absolutely necessary:

Shut down SMBv1
> First and foremost, if you're still running SMBv1, stop reading right now and go disable it. I mean it. A Rapid7 report from March 2020 found that between 500,000 and 1.3 million devices worldwide were still running SMB services, with around 343,000 using SMBv1 and lacking authentication. Most were Unix-based, but many were Windows. This version of the protocol has been obsolete for years and was the primary attack vector for WannaCry and several other devastating ransomware variants. There is absolutely no excuse for running SMBv1 in a modern environment. If you have legacy applications that require it, those applications need to be upgraded or replaced—immediately.

Restrict SMB to certain IPs
> Just like with RDP, you need to restrict SMB access to specific IP ranges. Your backup server has no business accepting SMB connections from arbitrary network segments. Lock it down to only the specific systems and networks that absolutely require this access. There are many documented incidents where unrestricted SMB access gave attackers free rein to explore—and eventually encrypt— entire backup repositories.

Use modern authentication methods
> Modern authentication methods are crucial here. This means using at least SMBv3 with encryption enabled, and implementing strong authentication

protocols. The days of NT LAN Manager (NTLM) and basic password authentication should be long behind us. If your backup software supports it, consider using its native protocols instead of SMB.

Implement monitoring

Finally, you must implement robust monitoring for unusual SMB access patterns. This means watching for things like excessive file access, unusual access times, or connections from unexpected sources. Modern ransomware often behaves differently than legitimate backup processes—it tends to access files much faster and in different patterns than normal backup operations. Having proper monitoring in place can alert you to an attack in progress before it's too late.

Secure Backup Storage

This recommendation will come as a complete shock to many: keep your disk-based backups inaccessible from users—including admins—as much as possible. Threat actors should not be able to log in to your backup server and see your backups, especially not in *D:\backups*! Keeping them where you can see them (i.e., in user space) is a bad idea for multiple reasons.

First, it makes your backups vulnerable to the same attacks that might hit your user systems. Second, it often means your backups are accessible to regular users, which violates the principle of least privilege. And third, it makes it really easy for ransomware to find and encrypt your backups.

If no one has ever told you this before, you might find yourself wondering how you're supposed to do that. Let's discuss your options.

Use Direct Storage Connections (Like Veeam's Direct SAN Access)

One of the most secure ways to store your backups is to bypass the filesystem entirely. Modern backup solutions like Veeam offer direct storage access capabilities that connect straight to your storage infrastructure. This isn't just about performance—it's about security. When your backups never touch the filesystem, they're essentially invisible to filesystem-based attacks. I've seen organizations survive ransomware attacks specifically because their backups were stored this way, completely out of reach of the malware that encrypted their production systems.

Store Backups in Dedicated Backup Appliances

Purpose-built backup appliances (e.g., Data Domain, Exagrid, Quantum) exist for a reason. These systems are designed from the ground up to securely store and manage backup data. They typically include their own storage, their own operating system, and their own security controls. These appliances often include features like built-in encryption, deduplication, and immutability—all crucial for secure backup storage.

I've worked with organizations that tried to save money by using general-purpose storage for their backups, only to spend far more recovering from a security incident that a dedicated appliance would have prevented.

Use Object Storage Instead of File Shares

Object storage represents a fundamental shift in how we store backup data. Unlike traditional filesystems, object storage systems provide inherent security features that make them ideal for backup storage. They're not mountable as drives, they're not browsable like file shares, and many offer built-in immutability features (more on immutability in the next section). I've seen organizations completely transform their backup security postures simply by moving from traditional file shares to object storage. Finally, object storage systems are typically a lot easier to scale up.

Here's what proper backup storage looks like in practice: separate networks, separate authentication, separate storage systems, and separate access controls. Yes, this makes things slightly more complicated to manage. Yes, it might cost a bit more. But I can tell you from experience that the cost of properly segregating your backups is nothing compared to the cost of losing them in an attack.

Remember, your backup storage isn't just another place to put data—it's Helm's Deep. It's your last line of defense against data loss. Every decision about where and how to store your backups should start with security considerations. If you're still storing backups in filesystem locations or on general network shares, you need to rethink your approach. The threat landscape is too sophisticated, and the stakes are too high, to continue with these outdated practices.

Use Immutable Storage

At least one copy of your backups should be stored on truly immutable storage. True immutability is the best way to ensure that your backups cannot get encrypted or deleted in a ransomware attack. Immutable simply means cannot be changed. In backup parlance, it means that once written, backups cannot be changed, encrypted or deleted by anyone—including the administrator. It can, of course, expire based on its retention period, after which it will automatically get deleted. But it will not and cannot be expired or deleted before that time.

Different meanings of immutability

Having your backups on truly immutable storage ensures that you will have at least one copy available to you even after the worst cyber attack. This is why many people are starting to ask their backup vendors whether or not they have immutable backups. Virtually all of them are now saying yes, but what they are calling immutable is often a variety of things. All of the following types of backup storage are being called immutable. Remember that outside of computing circles, the word *immutable* simply means "cannot be changed":

The restored/retrieved file is the same as the original file
This is what we would call "old school immutability." Someone familiar with a particular backup system could testify in court that the backup system is immutable, and that you can prove with a chain of custody and various logs that the file that was restored is exactly the same as the file that was backed up. It is not possible to change it without it being noticed. However, that doesn't mean that someone can't modify the backed up item: it just means that if they modify a backup, you will know.

Backups cannot be directly modified (unless you have root access)
There are products that support the use of the immutable flag in the Linux filesystem. This means that when they write backups, the software tells Linux that the file is immutable and that it cannot be deleted until the assigned expiration date (system specified at time of creation). Again, this sounds great. And again, it is great, but it has limitations.

The immutable flag in Linux is changeable if you have root access. If the threat actor wants to delete backups on this system and they have root access, they can simply unset the immutable flag and then delete or encrypt all the files they want.

Backups cannot be directly modified/encrypted/deleted at the storage layer
Some backup software products make the claim that once they have written backups to storage, those backups cannot be directly modified or encrypted via that storage. This means that even if you log in with a privileged account on the backup server, you would not be able to directly access the files and encrypt or delete them.

This sounds great, right? It is good, but it's also important to understand whether or not the backup system itself can modify those files. If you can log in to the backup administrator account and expire those backups (as mentioned in "Taking Backups Out of the Equation" on page 160), then so could a threat actor if they gain control of the backup system.

Backups cannot be modified even by privileged account at any layer
The only functionality that we would consider truly immutable is one where backups cannot be deleted by anyone at any time until they have expired. That includes privileged accounts like root or administrator. That includes people with administrator accounts within the backup software itself. This includes the customer calling in to the backup software company and saying that they really need those backups deleted. If no one can delete or prematurely expire any backups for any reason, no matter how privileged this person might be, then we

would say that such a system is truly immutable. We discuss in the next section the different ways this can be accomplished.

Unfortunately, all of the above are referred to as immutable. Here's the standard: If even you, the backup administrator, cannot manually expire and delete the backups, then neither can a threat actor.

Good: Filesystems that support immutability

One way to implement immutable storage is to use an on-premises file system that has built-in immutability features at the filesystem level, such as Linux. This means the immutability is enforced by the filesystem itself, not just the application or storage layer. While this approach can be effective, remember that anyone with root access to the filesystem can typically disable these controls. That's why you need additional security measures around these systems.

Better: Purpose-built appliances with immutability features

These systems, such as those provided by Oootbi, are designed specifically for backup storage and include built-in immutability capabilities. When you write data to these appliances, you can specify a retention period during which the data cannot be modified or deleted—by anyone. And I mean anyone—not even a system administrator with root access can alter this data until the retention period expires.

Best: Immutable storage in the cloud

On-premises immutable storage is a solid start—but you can do more. There's still that risk of physical access, although it's a very remote possibility in a typical ransomware attack. Cloud immutable storage adds another crucial layer of protection, and it does so in a way that's both elegant and cost-effective. Think of it as your insurance policy's insurance policy.

Let's talk about the major players. AWS led the charge with S3 Object Lock, and it's still one of the most robust implementations available. Once you enable Object Lock on a bucket and set a retention period, that data is untouchable—even if someone compromises your AWS root credentials. Azure followed suit with their Blob Immutable Storage, offering similar capabilities but with their own twist on the implementation. Google Cloud's Object Lock rounds out the big three, providing comparable features for those invested in the Google ecosystem.

What makes cloud immutable storage particularly compelling is its inherent separation from your primary site. I've investigated incidents where organizations lost both their primary and local backup storage because both were affected by the same disaster—whether that was a flood, fire, or particularly aggressive ransomware attack. Cloud immutable storage would have saved them.

Here's another reality check: these cloud providers have security teams that are larger than most IT departments. They have physical security that would make Fort Knox envious. When you store your immutable backups in their facilities, you're essentially hiring their security team to protect your data.

The scalability aspect is crucial too. I've watched organizations struggle to predict and provision enough local immutable storage, often either overprovisioning (and wasting money) or underprovisioning (and compromising their backup strategy). With cloud storage, you pay for what you use and can scale instantly when needed.

And let's talk about costs. Yes, cloud storage has ongoing operational costs that can add up. But when you factor in the total cost of ownership for local immutable storage—hardware, maintenance, power, cooling, floor space, and the expertise to manage it all—cloud storage can come out ahead. I've helped organizations run these numbers, and they're frequently surprised by how cost-effective immutable storage in the cloud can be.

Just remember: while immutable storage in the cloud is powerful, it's not magic. You still need to properly configure it, monitor it, and most importantly, test your ability to recover from it regularly. I've seen too many organizations assume their cloud backups were working correctly, only to discover problems during a crisis.

Case Study: Yuba County's Immutable Backups Made Ransom Negotiations Irrelevant

In 2021, Yuba County, California suffered a sophisticated multistage attack involving Dridex, Cobalt Strike, IcedID, PowerShell scripts, and a Kerberos Golden Ticket attack giving attackers domain admin access. By the time IT discovered DoppelPaymer ransomware, 50 PCs and 100 servers were encrypted.

Paul LaValley, the county's CTO, described discovering the attack's scope through forensic analysis. But he had an unusual reaction: "Even with essential data encrypted by the attackers, I knew we wouldn't have to pay the criminals to have the files restored—and that it wouldn't take long to get the county back up and running."

Why such confidence? Yuba County had implemented truly immutable backups using Rubrik. The attackers could see the backups on the network but couldn't delete, encrypt, or modify them. The county simply restored from clean backups and brought systems back online. No ransom payment. No negotiations. No wondering if decryption keys would work.

The lesson: This is what this chapter is about—fortifying Helm's Deep before the attack. Yuba County spent money on backup security beforehand, saving hundreds of thousands (possibly millions) they didn't have to spend on ransom, emergency recovery, or extended downtime. Even sophisticated attackers with domain admin

---

access couldn't compromise the one system that mattered most: the backups. For more information, see Barrett, 2025 (*https://oreil.ly/RXjO6*).

Encrypt All Backups

Let's talk about encryption. If you're not encrypting your backups, stop reading right now and go fix that. We'll wait. Are you back? Good.

Backup encryption isn't just a nice-to-have security feature; it's your insurance policy against both regulatory nightmares and ransomware catastrophes. When attackers steal your backup data (and they will try), encryption ensures they get useless gibberish instead of your customer records, financial data, and trade secrets. From a compliance perspective, encrypted backups can be the difference between a minor incident report and massive GDPR fines, HIPAA violations, or PCI Data Security Standard (DSS) penalties. Many regulations actually require (or strongly encourage) encryption of backup data. Even when they don't explicitly mandate it, encryption demonstrates due diligence that can significantly reduce legal liability after a breach.

Two things to talk about here are the difference between at-rest and in-flight encryption, and the importance of good key management.

At-Rest Encryption

Your backup data needs to be encrypted anywhere it sits—whether that's on disk, tape, or in the cloud. This is your first and most critical line of defense against unauthorized access. Start with AES-256 encryption at a minimum; anything less is simply inadequate for modern security requirements. Skimping on encryption strength to save processing overhead is a false economy if I've ever seen one.

Every single copy of your backups must be encrypted—no exceptions. This includes primary copies, replicas, and especially anything stored offsite. And here's the crucial part: you need to regularly test recovery operations with your encrypted backups. I've seen too many organizations discover during a crisis that their encryption strategy had holes in it.

In-Flight Encryption

Data in motion is just as vulnerable as data at rest—maybe more so. Every piece of backup traffic moving across your network needs encryption. Implement TLS 1.2 or higher for all network communications—version 1.1 and below have known vulnerabilities that make them unsuitable for backup traffic. This applies to everything: backup agent communications, replication traffic, and especially any data moving between sites.

Ensure your backup server-to-agent communications are encrypted with modern protocols. I've investigated incidents where organizations encrypted their backup data but left the control channel vulnerable—that's like putting a steel door on a cardboard frame.

Key Management

This is where I see organizations stumble most often. You can have the strongest encryption in the world, but it's worthless if you manage your keys poorly. First rule: never, ever store encryption keys alongside the data they protect. I once worked with a company that stored their encryption keys in a text file on their backup server—don't be that company.

Implement a secure process for key rotation. This means having clear procedures for generating new keys, securely distributing them, and maintaining access to older backups encrypted with previous keys. Keep secure backups of your encryption keys, stored separately from your backup environment. Document every aspect of your key management procedures thoroughly, and store that documentation securely—but not with either the keys or the backups.

Remember: encryption isn't just about making your data unreadable to unauthorized users. It's about ensuring your entire backup and recovery process remains secure and reliable. Test everything regularly, document meticulously, and never assume your encryption is working without verifying it.

Watch Everything: Monitoring Your Backup Environment

You know what's worse than getting hit with ransomware? Finding out you got hit three months ago and nobody noticed. This is why monitoring your backup environment is crucial. Watch for unusual data transfer patterns (especially outbound), excessive restore operations, mass deletion attempts, failed login attempts, configuration changes, and access from unusual locations or times.

Let's look at each of these in detail:

Unusual patterns in data transfer (especially outbound)
Your backup system should have a fairly predictable pattern of data movement. You know roughly how much data you back up each day and where it's supposed to go. When you see unexpected outbound data transfers, especially large ones, alarm bells should start ringing. Attackers can use backup systems as exfiltration points precisely because organizations often don't monitor these patterns carefully enough.

Excessive restore operations

Sudden spikes in restore operations are a red flag. Your restore patterns should be predictable—either scheduled tests or legitimate restores that follow your documented processes. If you're seeing numerous concurrent restores or restores of unusual scope, that could indicate someone trying to extract data through your backup system.

Mass deletion attempts

Any attempt to delete multiple backups simultaneously should trigger immediate alerts. Normal backup deletion follows retention policies and happens in a predictable pattern, and it's usually not done manually. There are many documented incidents where attackers tried to delete entire backup sets before launching their main attack. Your monitoring system needs to catch these attempts before they succeed.

Failed login attempts

Failed authentication attempts often precede successful breaches. Pay special attention to failed logins happening outside normal maintenance windows or from unusual source addresses. Attackers can probe backup systems for weeks looking for vulnerabilities in authentication. Every failed login attempt tells a story—make sure you're reading those stories.

Configuration changes

Your backup system's configuration should be relatively stable. Any changes to backup policies, retention settings, or security configurations should be documented and approved. Unexpected configuration changes, especially those reducing retention periods or disabling security features, often precede attacks. Monitor these changes religiously and verify every single one.

Access from unusual locations or times

Backup systems typically operate on well-defined schedules. When you see access attempts outside normal maintenance windows or from unexpected locations, you should get concerned. This is especially true for administrative access—your backup administrators should have predictable work patterns. Any deviation from these patterns deserves investigation. Access during odd hours is often the first sign of compromise.

Set up alerts for anything that looks suspicious. Yes, you'll probably get some false positives. But it's better to investigate ten false alarms than miss one real attack.

Create a Disaster Recovery Plan

Our next chapter explains creating your IRP. One key component of that is your DRP. Once the blue team has finished ridding your environment of ransomware, it'll be the backup person's job to activate their DRP and restore everything. So let's talk about the different ways you might actually accomplish restoring your entire environment.

Full Hot Site

Let's talk about the Cadillac of disaster recovery solutions—a *hot site*. This is exactly what it sounds like—a complete duplicate of your production environment, sitting there ready to take over at a moment's notice. This isn't just backup hardware gathering dust; it's a fully operational duplicate of your environment that's kept in sync with production continuously. Yes, it's expensive. Yes, it's complex to maintain. But for organizations that simply cannot tolerate downtime—think financial trading systems or critical healthcare applications—it's the only real option. When you need to be back online in minutes instead of hours or days, this is how you do it:

Duplicate hardware/infrastructure
> A hot site requires a complete mirror of your production environment. Every server, every switch, every storage array needs to be replicated. I've seen organizations try to cut corners here, only to discover during a disaster that some crucial piece of infrastructure wasn't duplicated. You're either fully redundant or you're not—there's no middle ground with a hot site.

Regular replication
> Your hot site needs to stay synchronized with production, usually through continuous replication. This means substantial bandwidth requirements and sophisticated replication technologies. You're typically looking at synchronous or near-synchronous replication with recovery point objectives measured in seconds or minutes.

Automated failover capabilities
> Manual failover procedures are too slow and error-prone for a proper hot site. You need automated systems that can detect failures and initiate failover without human intervention. If you're investing in a hot site, you'd better be testing it regularly. We recommend quarterly full failover tests at minimum. Yes, it's disruptive. Yes, it's expensive. But it's nowhere near as expensive as discovering your hot site doesn't work during an actual disaster.

Clear activation criteria
> You need crystal clear, documented criteria for when to activate your hot site. I've investigated incidents where organizations delayed failing over to their hot site because no one was sure who could make the call. Every minute of indecision costs you money and potentially data.

Cold Site Recovery

A cold site is fundamentally different from a hot site, and it's the more common approach. Instead of maintaining a duplicate environment, you're essentially starting with an empty room and a set of backup copies. When disaster strikes, you'll be building your environment from scratch using these backups. It's much slower than a hot site, but it's also *far* less expensive to maintain. This approach makes sense for organizations that can tolerate hours or days of downtime in exchange for lower ongoing costs. Here are some key considerations:

Hardware acquisition
> This is the first question you need to answer with a cold site strategy. You need guaranteed access to hardware that matches your specifications, usually through vendor agreements. I've seen organizations assume they could just order hardware when needed—then discover during a disaster that their required equipment had a 12-week lead time.

Networking concerns
> Your network infrastructure needs to be just as recoverable as your servers and data. This means documented IP schemes, routing configurations, and firewall rules.

Process for declaring a disaster
> You need clear procedures for who can declare a disaster and under what circumstances. This needs to be documented and practiced.

DNS and other external services
> External services like DNS need to be part of your recovery plan. I've seen perfectly executed server recoveries fail because no one remembered to update DNS records. Document every external dependency and how to handle it during recovery.

Cloud Recovery

Cloud recovery has revolutionized disaster recovery over the past decade, offering a middle ground between hot and cold sites. Instead of maintaining your own recovery facility, you can leverage the virtually unlimited resources of a cloud provider. Using the concept of infrastructure as code, you can even script your way into a full-functioning virtual data center. This allows you to automatically provision your recovery data center exactly as you want it to be during the time of recovery—while only paying for it when you use it. The cloud offers the same level of hot and cold recovery as a traditional recovery, but without the cost.

Figure 6-3 depicts the three different cloud recovery options: the solid lines indicate which parts of the recovery infrastructure you will pay for every month, and the dotted lines show what parts you will pay for when you test or declare a disaster. The cheapest option would be a cold recovery, where you only provision any resources when testing or declaring a disaster recovery, and then restore your data from backups once the environment is provisioned. Next would be a warm recovery, where you can keep an up-to-date copy of your data by regularly restoring it from your cloud backups. In this instance, you're paying for the primary storage needed for your recovery environment, but only paying for compute resources when you test or declare a disaster recovery. Finally, the cloud does offer full hot-site capability as well, which would mean you're using replication to keep the recovery copy in sync with your primary copy, and you've created your VMs in advance of a recovery. In this case, you're continually paying for the storage taken up by those images, then during a disaster, you pay to actually turn on those VMs. Each of these levels of recovery offer a faster actual recovery time (RTA), but at an additional cost.

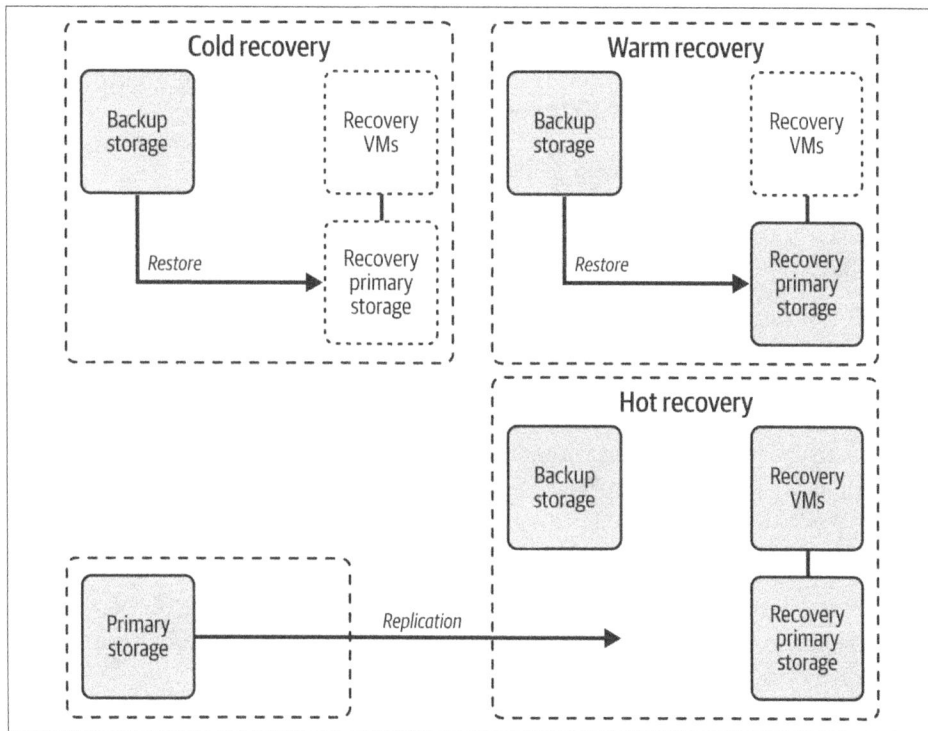

Figure 6-3. Cold, warm, and hot recovery in the cloud

The beauty here is flexibility—you can choose exactly how "hot" or "cold" you want your recovery to be, and you can adjust it on the fly based on your needs and budget. You're essentially trading capital expenses for operational expenses, and gaining a level of scalability that's simply impossible with traditional DR approaches. Some key considerations with cloud recovery include:

Understand cloud costs

Cloud recovery can be cost-effective, but only if you understand the pricing model. Egress charges can be especially shocking if you're not prepared. I've seen organizations get hit with massive bills during recovery testing because they didn't understand the cost implications of moving large amounts of data out of the cloud.

Test your recovery procedures regularly

Cloud recovery procedures need regular testing, just like any other DR strategy. The cloud adds its own complexity—API changes, service updates, security requirements. I recommend monthly testing of critical system recovery procedures at minimum.

Document network requirements

Cloud networking is different from on-premises networking. You need to document exactly how your recovered environment will connect to users and other systems. I've seen organizations successfully recover their servers to the cloud, only to realize they had no plan for how users would access them.

Have clear procedures for accessing cloud resources

Cloud access during a disaster needs to be carefully controlled. This means having documented procedures for accessing cloud consoles, APIs, and recovered systems. I've investigated incidents where organizations compromised security during recovery because they hadn't planned their access procedures properly.

Maintain security during recovery

Security often takes a backseat during recovery operations—and that's a massive mistake. Your recovered environment needs to be just as secure as your production environment. I've seen organizations recover from one disaster only to create another by standing up insecure systems in their rush to restore operations.

Failback

After a disaster is over—during which you *failed over* to some type of recovery environment—you need to go back to normal. The processing of undoing the failover process is called *failback*.

In DR planning, everyone focuses on failing over, but failing back is just as critical. You need a clear plan for how to return to normal operations once the disaster is over. I've worked with organizations that executed their failover perfectly but had no plan for getting back to normal operations. They ended up running their production systems in their DR environment for months, paying premium costs and operating in a configuration they never intended for long-term use.

The dirty secret about failback

Here's what nobody tells you about failback: it's often harder than the original fail-over. During a disaster, adrenaline is pumping, everyone's focused, and there's clear urgency. Failback happens weeks or months later when the crisis has passed, budgets are tight, and management attention has moved elsewhere. I've seen more problems during failback operations than during the original disaster recovery.

Data synchronization challenges

The biggest technical challenge in failback is data synchronization. While your systems were running in the DR environment, data changed. Users created files, databases were updated, configurations were modified. Now you need to get all of that back to your primary site without losing anything. This isn't just about copying files—you need to understand what changed, in what order, and how to merge those changes back without creating conflicts.

For database systems, this often means taking your DR environment offline during the synchronization process. I've seen organizations try to keep systems running during failback sync, only to end up with corrupted data when transactions occurred during the copy process. Plan for downtime during failback—it's unavoidable if you want to do it safely.

Network reconfiguration

Your network configuration during DR was probably a temporary compromise. DNS entries were changed, firewall rules were modified, VPN endpoints were reconfig-ured. All of this needs to be changed back, and it needs to happen in the right order. I've investigated outages where organizations successfully moved their data back but forgot to update their load balancer configurations, sending traffic to systems that were no longer running.

Document every network change made during the disaster response. I know it seems obvious, but during a crisis, documentation is often the first casualty. If you don't know exactly what was changed to make DR work, you can't reliably reverse those changes.

Testing your failback procedures

Failback testing is just as important as failover testing, but it's often ignored. You need to practice the entire cycle—failover, run in DR mode for a realistic period, then failback. This means your DR tests need to be longer and more complex than most organizations are comfortable with.

I recommend annual full-cycle tests that include at least 48 hours of operation in DR mode before attempting failback. This gives you time to discover all the little issues that only show up after systems have been running in the DR environment for a while. It also forces you to practice failback under more realistic conditions.

The politics of failback

There's a political dimension to failback that's rarely discussed. During the disaster, IT is the hero for keeping systems running. During failback, IT is the department asking for another outage to fix something that's already working. I've seen management push back on failback operations because "everything's working fine where it is."

You need executive sponsorship for failback operations, documented in advance. The decision criteria for when to failback should be as clear as your criteria for when to failover. Is it when the primary site is repaired? When costs reach a certain threshold? When performance degrades below acceptable levels? Document this before the disaster, when everyone's thinking clearly.

When NOT to failback

Sometimes the right answer is not to failback at all. If your primary site suffered significant damage, this might be an opportunity to relocate permanently to your DR site or to the cloud. I've worked with organizations that used a disaster as a catalyst for infrastructure modernization, ultimately ending up with a better environment than they started with.

The decision not to failback needs to be made consciously, with full understanding of the long-term implications. Your DR site probably wasn't designed for permanent operations—network capacity, cooling, power, and physical security might all be compromised compared to your primary site.

Summary

Look, I've walked into enough data centers to know what's going to happen when you finish reading this chapter. You're going to think, "This all sounds great, I'll get to it next quarter." Don't do that.

Your backup system is Helm's Deep—your last stand when everything else falls. But here's the thing: Helm's Deep worked (for a while, anyway) because the defenders prepared it in advance. You can't fortify a castle while the army is already at the gates.

So here's what needs to happen immediately:

Get help lined up now
> Find your blue team, contract with a red team, and get cyber insurance before you need any of them. These relationships take weeks to build and contracts take days to negotiate. During an attack, you'll get whoever has the best SEO—and that's not the same as whoever's best at cyber defense.

Lock down your backup infrastructure like it's Fort Knox

MFA everywhere, even when it's inconvenient. Segregate it completely from production. Disable RDP or lock it down so tight nobody can find it. Update everything—I don't care if "it's working fine." And implement RBAC so your backup operators can do their jobs without having the keys to delete everything.

Make your backups truly immutable

Not "hard to delete" immutable. Not "Linux immutable flag" immutable. I mean nobody-can-touch-them-even-with-root-access immutable. At least one copy needs to be stored this way, preferably in the cloud where it's physically separated from your primary site.

Monitor everything obsessively

Unusual data transfers, excessive restores, mass deletion attempts, failed logins, configuration changes, odd-hour access—all of it needs alerts. Yes, you'll get false positives. That's infinitely better than missing the real attack.

Plan the complete DR cycle—including failback

Everyone focuses on failing over. Nobody thinks about getting back to normal. I've seen organizations execute perfect disaster recovery only to run in their DR environment for months because they had no plan for failback. Test the entire cycle, not just the exciting disaster part.

Here's the bottom line: everything in this chapter assumes you're doing the work before you need it. Waiting until you're under attack to figure out your backup security is like waiting until the orcs are scaling the walls to ask, "So, uh, how does this fortress work anyway?"

The threat actors only have to be successful once. Your backup system needs to be secure every single time. Time to get to work.

CHAPTER 7

Make Your Incident Response Plan

Ransomware has developed into a formidable weapon that you must prepare your response to. What started as an annoyance targeting individual users has become a full-blown criminal operation that often involves nation states, and is aimed at businesses, governments, and even critical infrastructure. In recent years, we've seen major ransomware attacks bring down supply chains, cripple healthcare systems, and cost organizations billions in ransom payments, recovery costs, and lost productivity. The growing sophistication and frequency of these attacks make one thing clear: you need a solid incident response plan (IRP) in place before your number comes up in the ransomware game.

A good ransomware response plan is like a playbook for disaster. It lays out exactly how your team will detect, contain, remove, and recover from an attack. Without one, you're looking at longer downtime, bigger financial losses, and a greater chance of losing sensitive data, or having it leaked to the public. A well-executed plan can mean the difference between getting back on track quickly or being stuck in damage-control mode for weeks (or longer).

But a written plan is only the first step. The real test is whether your team can execute it under pressure. That's where tabletop exercises (TTXs) and cyber war games come in. Running a simulated ransomware attack in a controlled environment helps you see how prepared your team really is. It's the best way to spot gaps in your plan, sharpen decision-making, and make sure everyone knows their role when things get messy. Start with high-level tests, and be sure to include executives in the planning and evaluation process. Perform additional tests that are more technically detailed.

In this chapter, we'll break down the components of an incident response plan for ransomware that works, from setting clear goals and defining roles to developing containment and recovery strategies. We'll also talk about how to design and run effective TTXs and war games so you can test and improve your plan before a real attack happens. By the end, you'll have a clear roadmap for handling ransomware with confidence.

> This chapter provides the blueprint for building your incident response plan, which is the strategic framework and decision points you need to document before an attack occurs. You'll see procedural details throughout, but these are here to help you understand what belongs in your plan, not to serve as step-by-step execution instructions during a live incident. Think of this chapter as the architect's drawing, not the construction manual. The detailed, hands-on technical procedures for actually executing your response come in Chapters 9–16. Build your IRP now using this chapter as your guide, so when ransomware hits, your team already knows the playbook.

Table Stakes: Before Writing Your IRP

Before you fire up Word and start cranking out incident response procedures, we need to talk about what you actually need to have in place first. I'm talking about the foundations—the stuff your IRP sits on top of. Think of it like building a house: you wouldn't start framing walls before you pour the foundation, right? Same deal here.

These five things aren't part of your IRP. They're the prerequisites. If you're missing even one of them, your IRP won't be very valuable. Not because the plan itself is bad, but because you're not set up to execute it properly. So here's what you need locked down before you write anything.

1. Get Executive Sponsorship

You need a real, live executive who gets it. Not someone who nods along in meetings and then ghosts you when budget season rolls around. I'm talking about a C-level champion who understands that incident response isn't just "nice to have" and has the juice to make things happen when you need them.

This person needs to be able to approve emergency spending at 2 a.m., break through corporate red tape, and make the hard calls when things go awry. Without this person in your corner, your IRP is nowhere near as valuable as it could be. They're how you get a budget and make changes if necessary.

2. Name Names, Not Job Titles

Here's where things get real. You need a roster with actual human names on it. Who specifically is leading the incident response? What's their cell number? Who's the backup if they're on a beach in Cancun when ransomware hits? Who from legal? Who from comms?

Build your IRT list right now with real people who've actually agreed to be on it. Each role needs a primary and an alternate, with current phone numbers, emails, and backup contact methods like Signal or Teams. Be sure to get consent before you put their names down.

Please don't think, "Well, whoever's on duty in IT will handle it," or "We'll figure that out later."

3. Write the Templates Now—Not During the Crisis

Picture this: It's 3 a.m., your systems are encrypted, your CEO is freaking out, and legal is demanding to review every word before you send anything. This is not the time to be crafting the perfect email to customers or trying to wordsmith a press release.

Get with your legal team and your communications people right now and hammer out pre-approved templates: internal notifications, customer emails, regulatory reports, media statements, all of it. These should have the legal language baked in, the right tone already set, and blanks where you'll drop in incident-specific details when the time comes.

Having these ready means you can communicate in minutes instead of wasting time while your customers are panicking on social media.

4. Contract the Help Before You Need It

When ransomware hits at 2 a.m. on Saturday, you can't start shopping for vendors. You can't negotiate contracts. You definitely can't sit through three rounds of vendor presentations and an RFP process. But that's exactly what'll happen if you don't sort this out now.

Identify your incident response firms, forensic specialists, legal counsel who actually know cybersecurity, and PR pros who've handled crisis communications before. Then get the contracts signed. Establish response time commitments. Get their emergency contact procedures. Figure out the money stuff now so you're not arguing about retainer fees in the middle of a crisis.

These relationships take weeks to build properly. Don't wait until you need them to start looking.

5. Know What Tools You've Got (and Where to Find Them)

Your IRT needs actual tools to do their jobs. At minimum, you need forensic imaging tools for preserving evidence, log analysis platforms for investigating what happened, secure communication channels that don't go through your (potentially compromised) corporate email, and isolated environments where you can safely analyze malware.

You don't need to be a forensics expert yet, that's what training is for. But you do need to have this stuff available, and your team needs to know it exists. We've seen too many organizations waste the critical first hours of an incident trying to find, purchase, and deploy forensic tools while ransomware is actively spreading.

Get the tools identified. Get them purchased, or at least get approvals in place to purchase them immediately if needed. Know where they are and how to access them.

So before you keep reading, take a hard look at this list. The things on it are what you need to get started.

Cybersecurity Resources Around the World

Before beginning the discussion about how to build your IRP, we thought it would be helpful to know what resources your government might provide in this area. We both live in the US, so we're most familiar with CISA and what they offer. The nice thing is that pretty much every developed country has its own version of CISA, and they're all sitting there with free resources, guidance, and incident response assistance specifically designed to help organizations like yours deal with ransomware. And most people have no idea these exist.

So before you go it alone or start Googling "ransomware help" during an attack, let's talk about what's actually available to you, wherever you're located.

Who's Got Your Back?

Here's a quick rundown of the major national cybersecurity agencies. These aren't just websites with PDFs; they're actual organizations with real people who will help you when things go sideways:

Australia
Australian Cyber Security Centre (ACSC): These folks have a 24/7 hotline (1300 CYBER1) and will actually talk you through an incident.

Canada
Canadian Centre for Cyber Security (CCCS)

European Union
European Union Agency for Cybersecurity (ENISA): covers all EU member states

France
Agence nationale de la sécurité des systèmes d'information (ANSSI)

Germany
Bundesamt für Sicherheit in der Informationstechnik (BSI)

Israel
Israel National Cyber Directorate (INCD)

Japan
National Center of Incident Readiness and Strategy for Cybersecurity (NISC) and JPCERT/CC

Netherlands
National Cyber Security Centre (NCSC-NL)

New Zealand
Computer Emergency Response Team New Zealand (CERT-NZ)

Singapore
Cyber Security Agency of Singapore (CSA)

South Korea
Korea Internet & Security Agency (KISA)

United Kingdom
National Cyber Security Centre (NCSC)

If your country isn't on this list, don't panic. Search for "[your country] national cybersecurity centre" or "[your country] CERT" (Computer Emergency Response Team). Nearly every country has one these days.

These agencies aren't just sitting around waiting for disasters. They've got practical stuff you can use right now to get better prepared.

Free Frameworks and Tools

Australia's ACSC has something called the "Essential Eight," and it's basically eight things that, if you do them right, will stop most ransomware dead in its tracks. They also run free training through their Cyber Wardens program. The UK's NCSC provides an "Exercise in a Box" toolkit that lets you run your own TTX without hiring consultants. Germany's BSI, France's ANSSI, and Canada's CCCS all publish ransomware-specific playbooks that actually make sense, even if you're not a security expert.

If you've got a small team and a tiny budget, Singapore's CSA and New Zealand's CERT-NZ have toolkits specifically designed for organizations like yours. They know you don't have a security team of 50 people, and their guidance reflects that reality.

Early Warning Systems

Here's something most people don't know: many of these agencies will actually monitor for signs that *you specifically* are being targeted and give you a heads up before the attack happens. The UK's NCSC runs an Early Warning service that does exactly this. Australia's ACSC has a similar alert service. They're watching for the bad guys doing reconnaissance on your systems and will tell you about it.

Think about that for a second. Free early warning that ransomware actors are poking around your network. That's a pretty good deal for "free."

What They Do When You're Actually Under Attack

This is where these agencies really prove their worth. When ransomware hits and you're scrambling, most of them offer immediate, expert help:

24/7 incident hotlines
Australia's ACSC hotline (1300 CYBER1), the UK's NCSC incident reporting service, and Canada's CCCS all have people standing by who can walk you through what to do right now. Not next business day—right now. And it's free.

Hands-on support
Australia goes even further with their Small Business Cyber Resilience Service. If you've got fewer than 20 employees, they'll provide tailored, hands-on support to help you both respond to the incident and recover afterward. The UK's Funded Cyber Essentials Programme helps eligible small businesses and charities implement baseline security with expert support.

These services can guide you through critical decisions: Should you pay the ransom? How do you contain the infection? What steps do you take to recover? And most importantly, they can help you figure out if your backups are actually going to work.

How to Actually Use This Stuff

Here's what you should do right now, before you need any of this:

Step 1: Find your agency
Go to your country's cybersecurity agency website. Bookmark it. Save their emergency contact number in your phone. Seriously, do this now. You don't want to be hunting for this information at 2 a.m. when you're under attack.

Step 2: Sign up for alerts
Most of these agencies have free alert services that'll send you notifications about emerging ransomware campaigns, new vulnerabilities being exploited, and specific threats targeting your region or industry. Sign up. The intel is usually solid and you'll get it before it shows up on the news.

Step 3: Grab their toolkits

Download their ransomware response guides, checklists, and assessment tools. These are usually PDFs or online tools you can access anytime. Have them ready. The EU's ENISA has an "Awareness Raising in a Box" toolkit that's particularly good for building your organization's cybersecurity program.

Step 4: Make contact before you need them

If your country's agency offers consultations or has regional representatives, reach out now. Introduce yourself. Ask questions. Build that relationship when things are calm. When you call them during an actual incident, it's a lot better if they already know who you are.

The Bottom Line

Dealing with ransomware is hard enough without trying to figure it all out on your own. Your government has already invested millions in building these cybersecurity agencies and filling them with experts who've seen it all before. Use them. They exist specifically to help organizations like yours.

And before you think "this is probably just for big enterprises," think again. Most of these agencies specifically prioritize helping small and medium businesses because they know you don't have the resources that big companies do. They want to help you. Let them.

The difference between a manageable disruption and a business-ending catastrophe often comes down to getting expert help quickly. Know who to call before you need to make that call. Now let's start developing our plan, shall we?

Setting Objectives and Scope

Before you start building your IRP, you need to nail down two things: what you're actually trying to accomplish, and what you're covering. Skip this step and your plan becomes a useless document that nobody understands or follows. Let's walk through how to set clear goals and boundaries so your team can handle an attack smoothly and successfully.

Defining the Goals of the Incident Response Plan

So, what's the point of this plan? It's all about giving your team a clear target to aim for when ransomware strikes. Without that focus, everyone's just guessing, and that's a recipe for trouble. Here are a few targets you might want to focus on:

Minimize downtime

Get your business back online quickly. No one wants operations grinding to a halt for longer than necessary.

Protect key data

Keep sensitive information (e.g., personal data and intellectual property) safe from compromise or theft. That's a top priority.

Limit the damage

Reduce the financial and reputational fallout, including ransoms, legal headaches, or bad media coverage.

Stay compliant

Make sure you are meeting any applicable regulatory requirements, like SOX, PCI, GDPR, HIPAA, or CCPA, to name a few. If you have compliance requirements, then having an IRP isn't optional.

Preserve evidence

Hold onto logs or files that could help with investigations later, whether it's for insurance, legal, law enforcement or internal reviews.

Get stronger

Learn from the experience to improve your processes, skills, and defenses for next time.

Protect reputation

Being able to respond effectively and communicate to customers/vendors will do just that.

Something to keep in mind while you build out your IRP goals is to use SMART. SMART stands for Specific, Measurable, Achievable, Relevant, and Time-bound. It's a straightforward way to keep things practical. Here are some sample goals that pass the SMART test:

- Restore critical systems within four hours of detecting the ransomware.
- Contain the spread within 30 minutes of the first alert.
- Notify affected stakeholders, like customers or regulators, within an hour of confirming the incident.

These activities set expectations and can be measured. Did you hit that four-hour mark? Were we able to stop it in 30 minutes? It keeps your team on track and gives you a way to gauge how you're doing. Clear goals, expectations, and metrics will help everyone keep a pulse on the progress of the response.

What Does the Incident Response Plan Cover?

This is where you draw the lines—what's in, what's out, and what you're actually going to defend when ransomware hits. Get this wrong and your team will be arguing about whether they should respond to issues they never knew they owned.

What types of ransomware are you dealing with?

Ransomware is not just one thing; it has different flavors and attack types, and your plan needs to be ready for all of them. There is the old-school encryption kind that locks up your files and demands a payout in order to unlock them. Then there is locker ransomware that just kicks you out, no fancy encryption required. Double extortion ransomware is yet another, and it encrypts your stuff while the attackers siphon your data out to the dark net *and* threaten to post it publicly if you don't pay.

Ransomware-as-a-service (RaaS) is a franchise anyone can buy into, where bad guys rent out their tricks to other bad guys or wannabe cybercriminals. Lastly, we have wiper ransomware that will "burn it all down" if you don't pay, forensically wiping everything with no way back. Knowing this helps you spot it, stop it, and clean up the mess.

Which systems are you covering?

Start with what actually matters. Your critical data—customer info, financial records, intellectual property, anything regulators care about. Then map the stuff that touches that data: the servers that store it, the systems that process it, the networks that move it around.

Your scope should include the endpoints that access critical systems, such as laptops and mobile devices used by key personnel, as well as any workstations that handle sensitive data. Include the servers essential for critical business processes or that house important data, whether on-premises or in the cloud. Network infrastructure like firewalls, VPN devices, and core routers that protect or enable access to critical systems should also be in scope. For organizations with operational technology, include any OT systems or IoT devices that could impact safety, production, or business operations if compromised.

Don't forget to inventory both your primary data and backup systems—including cloud backups, offline storage, and any managed backup services—since attackers increasingly target backup systems to prevent recovery.

Establish clear boundaries by defining what's out of scope. Not every device or system needs the same level of incident response attention. That dusty desktop in the break room might not warrant inclusion unless it actually processes sensitive data. Prioritize your assets into tiers (critical, high, medium, low) so your response team knows where to focus their efforts during an actual incident.

How's this going to affect the business?

Now you need to consider the impact. What are the critical things you need to keep critical processes running, like orders or payroll? What data is required to support these processes, such as customer details, financial records, and HR data? Is there any legal stuff to worry about, like GDPR or HIPAA rules? What's the financial impact, including ransom costs, downtime, lost deals, third-party labor, and overtime? Determine where the biggest impacts are, and you'll have a head start on prioritizing your IRP focus.

Who's in and who's out?

Draw your boundaries now, or you'll be drawing them at 3 a.m. when nobody agrees on anything. Does your IRP cover the whole company or just headquarters? What about that subsidiary in Europe? The contractors who have VPN access? Figure this out now.

Clarify vendor and supply chain responsibilities up front. If a vendor's system is compromised and affects your operations, who leads the response? What information will they share with you? What support can you expect during business hours versus after hours? Document these boundaries clearly in your IRP and create a visual diagram showing:

- Which entities are covered by your response procedures
- Which have separate but coordinated response plans
- Communication and escalation paths between organizations
- Who has authority to make decisions affecting different parts of the business

This prevents confusion during an actual incident, where team members otherwise might waste valuable time wondering whether they should respond to an issue affecting a subsidiary, partner system, or vendor service.

Communications

We covered this in "Table Stakes: Before Writing Your IRP" on page 188, but it bears repeating: have your communication templates ready. Emails, press releases, internal updates—all prewritten and preapproved by legal. An incident is not the time to start working on things like this.

Metrics of Effectiveness

So how do you know if your plan actually works or if it's just expensive paperwork? You need numbers. Real metrics that tell you whether you're getting better or just spinning your wheels. Here's what actually matters:

Mean time to detect (MTTD)
> How fast can you catch the problem? Industry research shows the average is around 200+ days for many attack types, but high-performing organizations aim for hours or days, not months.

Mean time to respond (MTTR)
> How quickly can you respond and begin dealing with the situation? This measures from detection to initial response actions. Leading organizations target response times in minutes to hours for critical incidents.

Mean time to restore (MTTR)
> How long until things are back to normal? This tracks full recovery time and is often the most business-critical metric, as downtime directly impacts revenue and operations.

Containment rate
> How many of these attacks did you stop before they achieved their objectives? This measures your success at preventing attackers from reaching their goals (data theft, system encryption, etc.).

Data recovery rate
> How much of your encrypted or compromised data did you successfully recover? This is particularly important for ransomware incidents.

MTTD and the response/recovery MTTR metrics are the most widely adopted, as they're part of standard incident management frameworks like NIST and ISO 27035. Many organizations start with these three since they're easier to measure and directly correlate to business impact.

Track these metrics over time, and you'll spot if you're getting better or if you need to tweak something, like more practice or better gear.

Matching the Plan to Business Priorities?

This incident response plan (IRP) can't be all about what IT thinks should be in scope; it has to reflect the whole company's priorities and strategic objectives. When you tie the IRP into your enterprise strategy and risk management approach, you get more than just buy-in; you get a unified framework that prevents chaos during a crisis.

Industry frameworks like NIST's Cybersecurity Framework and ISO 27035 specifically emphasize that incident response must align with business context and organizational risk tolerance. This isn't just best practice—it's essential for effective response.

Here's how to make it work:

Get the bosses involved
> Bring in the C-suite so they understand their role, approve resource allocation, and can make executive decisions during incidents. When leadership is engaged from the planning stage, they won't second-guess response decisions during a crisis.

Align with disaster recovery plans

Integrate your IRP with your broader DRP or business continuity plan (BCP). This ensures consistent priorities: if manufacturing is deemed more critical than corporate systems in your BCP, your IRP should reflect that same priority during cyber incidents.

Pull in other teams

Legal, compliance, HR, and communications teams must provide input during planning, not just during incidents. They understand regulatory requirements, notification timelines, employee communication needs, and external stakeholder management that IT might miss.

Establish clear priorities up front

When your IRP reflects enterprise-wide priorities, business units won't fight over whose systems get restored first during an incident. Everyone already agreed on the priorities during planning, eliminating costly delays and infighting when every minute counts.

Find the balance

Keep critical business processes running while implementing security controls. Your IRP should define acceptable risk levels that let the business operate even under incident conditions.

This alignment pays dividends beyond incident response. You'll get business support for regular TTXs, adequate funding for security tools, and cross-functional teams that actually know their roles before a crisis hits.

Assembling Your Incident Response Team

Your ransomware IRP is only as good as the people on your IRT. You need a tight and cohesive IRT that can hit the ground running and deal with a ransomware mess using the muscle memory they developed from all their preparation. And it's not just the IT crew; you must include others from across the business to manage everything from stopping the attack to preventing legal and PR disasters. So, how do you set up the roles, keep everyone ready around the clock, and make sure nobody's stepping on toes when it all goes down? The following sections will help you figure it out.

Sorting Out Who Does What

First things first, everyone needs to know their job. You can't afford to be scrambling to figure out who's responsible for what when ransomware is encrypting your data and locking you out of critical systems. Define these roles now, so when it's game time, your team's not just standing there like, "Wait, is that on me?" Let's look at the roles you need to assign and remember that every role should have a primary and backup person, in case the primary is unavailable.

Three external resources that we covered in Chapter 6 are critical to modern ransomware response: cyber insurance to cover costs and potentially handle ransom negotiations, law enforcement agencies like the FBI for recovery assistance and intel, and professional incident response firms for specialized expertise. Understanding your insurance coverage and establishing these relationships before an attack occurs can make the difference between swift recovery and prolonged disruption.

Now let's look at the roles that need to be filled in an IRT:

Incident response leader
> This is your quarterback, the one calling the plays, steering the ship, etc. They are the go-to person, keeping tabs on everything from spotting the attack to getting things back on track. They communicate with the response team, management, maybe even law enforcement or outside experts. Pick someone who doesn't crack under pressure, communicates well, and can be effective in both technical and business conversations.

Technical response team
> These are your technical subject matter experts. (While many of these roles are unlikely to exist in separate people in smaller organizations, you will still have someone filling this role—perhaps one person filling all of them.) You need:

Cybersecurity analysts
> The ones playing detective, figuring out where it started and how bad the situation is.

Network engineers
> The lockdown crew, shutting off systems, collecting data from the firewall, and stopping it from spreading.

System admins
> The repair crew, killing processes, pulling backups, and getting stuff running again.

Malware analysts
> The people familiar with ransomware, determining what variant you're working with, and possible decryption options (these are usually part of the law enforcement, insurance, or expert IRTs).

Threat intel analysts
> The ones doing internet and dark net searches to see who's behind it and what they might do next, understanding their tactics, techniques, and procedures (TTPs).

Legal and compliance team

You need the legal team in on this because ransomware can be a messy tangle of laws. They're sorting out if paying's even an option, handling those "we got hacked" notices (like SOX, GDPR, or HIPAA stuff), and talking with law enforcement if it escalates. They're your shield from bigger trouble, so don't hesitate to involve them as soon as you know there's trouble.

Communications and public relations

When everyone's eyes are on you, these are the ones that are going to make sure you effectively communicate what is happening to the world. These people should be tasked with providing clear updates, prepping what to say to the press, and reassuring customers it's under control. They'll even tackle the social media chaos.

Consider an external team specializing in such public relations disasters. Your PR team is likely quite skilled at day-to-day communications, but this is a horse of a different color. A specialist isn't likely to make rookie mistakes, like overpromising when it will all be over. Like everything else in this book, the key is to vet them and get them under contract long before you actually need them.

Executive leadership

Big decisions need big players, like whether to pay the ransom or shut everything down. Their perspective can weigh security against keeping the business alive, brief the board, approve requests for additional help, and involve insurance.

Identify the primary contact from the leadership team, with at least one backup contact.

Human resources (HR)

HR is your people department. They're helping to address staff questions and payroll snags, communicating new updates, and setting up training later so this doesn't happen again. They've got the human side covered.

Make sure you get to know your primary HR contact and at least one alternative contact.

Third-party vendors and partners

Sometimes you need extra resources, specific skills, or just the A-Team. These may include managed security service providers (MSSPs), professional incident response firms, or insurance, and ransom negotiators. They bring experience and perspectives gained from other incidents, extra know-how, and extra hands.

Identify these resources today, and get the paperwork out of the way so they're ready when you need them.

Who's Calling the Shots?

You need to be clear about who's in charge. There is no time for arguing when the clock's ticking. A great tool for determining who does what is called a RACI matrix.

Create a RACI matrix

Ever been in a crisis where everyone's standing around going, "Wait, who's doing this?" while the clock's ticking? That's what a RACI matrix prevents. It's dead simple:

- Responsible = You do the actual work
- Accountable = The buck stops with you, you own the outcome
- Consulted = We need your input before we decide
- Informed = We'll tell you what happened

Here's how it plays out: Your security analyst is responsible for isolating infected endpoints, so they're doing the work. Your CISO is accountable for the overall incident response, because they own it. Legal counsel gets consulted before you make public statements, because you need their input first. And your board of directors is informed of major developments because they need to know, but they're not in the war room making technical calls.

The beauty of this thing? It stops the paralysis. Without a RACI matrix, you get two disasters: everyone assumes someone else is handling the critical stuff, or three people jump on the same problem while something important gets ignored. During a ransomware attack, that kind of confusion doesn't just slow you down, it can shut you down.

Make this matrix *now*, during peacetime, when people can think straight and ask questions. Not at 2 a.m. when systems are burning and everyone's running on adrenaline.

How a RACI works

Table 7-1 shows you how RACI works. Here are a few things to note about this matrix:

One "A" per row
> See that? Every single task has exactly one person who's Accountable. No "well, we're both kind of responsible for this" nonsense. One person owns each decision. This prevents the "too many cooks" problem where critical calls get delayed because everyone's waiting for someone else to decide.

The CEO isn't doing technical work
> The CEO stays Accountable for the big business calls, like paying the ransom or public communications, that level. But they're not Responsible for isolating infected systems. Can you imagine the bottleneck if technical recovery stopped every time you needed executive sign-off? Keep executives where they belong: making executive decisions.

Legal is Consulted, not running the show
> Notice legal counsel appears as Consulted for most decisions? That's their role—advisory. They're not Accountable for technical response. They tell you what's legally risky, you make the call.

It scales up or down
> Small company? Same person might appear in multiple columns wearing different hats. Big enterprise? You might need separate matrices for different business units. The principle stays the same.

Build this during calm times and get everyone to agree on it. Because when ransomware's encrypting your files and everyone's freaking out, you want to be fighting the attack—not arguing about whose job it is to make the call.

Table 7-1. Example RACI matrix

Task	Sec. analyst	IT mgr.	CISO	CEO	Legal	HR dir.	Comms
Initial threat detection	R	I	A	I			
Isolate infected	R	A	C	I			
Access scope	R	C	A	I			
Involve law enforcement	C	C	R/A	C	C		
Activate IRT		R	A	I			
Talk to insurance		C	R	A	C		
Pay ransom?	C	C	C	A	C		C
Employee comms			C	A		R	C
Media/PR			C	A	C		R
System recovery ops	R	A	C	I			
Evidence preservation	R	C	A	I	C		
Vendor coordination	C	R	A	I			
Business continuity		C	C	A		R	
Post-incident review	C	C	R	A	C	C	C

Here is a list of the roles you're going to want to make sure you have covered:

Primary incident lead
> The main shot-caller, making moves and signing off on the big stuff.

Backup incident lead
> Jumps in if the lead is MIA, even if they're on a beach somewhere.

Departmental leads and stakeholders
> Each group (IT, legal, comms) has a go-to person keeping their team looped in and on-task.

Executive sponsor
> The primary executive contact that monitors the response activities, updates the leadership team and board, and provides approvals as needed.

Making Sure You're Covered 24/7

Ransomware doesn't care about your sleep schedule. Though most coordinated attacks happen on Thursday or Friday morning, the response efforts will no doubt carry into the early morning hours. Your team has to be ready anytime. Here's how:

Shift rotation
> Set up a schedule so a contact from each of the IT, legal, and comms teams is always capable of responding. Rotate them so nobody is "always on."

Contact list
> Keep a list of everyone's primary and backup phone numbers, and alternate contact methods like Signal or the Microsoft Teams app on their smartphone.

Alert system
> Get a loud "RANSOMWARE!" alarm that goes off when it hits. This could be the subject line of the email, an SMS text message, phone call, etc. Train everyone to jump when they hear it. No holes, no slack—24/7 is the deal for the IRT members.

Cross-Training and Alternate Plans

These attacks can drag on for days and sometimes weeks. Your response can't be hindered because someone is on vacation, sick, or unresponsive. Cross-training among IRT members can be critical for an effective response where one or more members aren't in the game:

Cross-train
> Share basic skills and responsibilities across teams to establish familiarity with activities that may need to be reassigned if the primary resource isn't available.

Write it down
> Keep playbooks and quick reference guides handy so that any IRT member can access them and follow basic procedures.

Practice swaps

Run drills where alternate resources from other teams take over. Can they handle it? This exercise can build your IRT's confidence.

Teaming Up with Outside Help

You don't have to fight this alone; build your ecosystem of support to call upon when things get bad. Many of the groups on this list bring expertise to the table that is not typically found in an average IT team.

Law enforcement

Get friendly with the law enforcement organizations of your country. In the US, that would the FBI, US Secret Service, CISA, or your local police department. In the United Kingdom, contact the National Cyber Security Centre or your local police force's cybercrime unit. In Australia, reach out to the Australian Cyber Security Centre via their 24/7 hotline (1300 CYBER1) or the Australian Federal Police. In Canada, contact the Canadian Centre for Cyber Security or the Royal Canadian Mounted Police's cybercrime units. In the European Union, you can report to your national cybersecurity agency or Europol's European Cybercrime Centre (EC3). These organizations have skills, resources, and experience.

Insurance company

Know your policy and understand what it covers. Have a claims plan and a contact ready. Insurance typically wants to be notified as soon as you've determined there is a problem, even if it turns out to be a false positive.

Response firms

Connect with a professional incident response firm to back you up. Your insurance company may already have pre-approved firms to use, so reach out and get connected. Even if you don't need their whole IRT, it is often very helpful to have an extra set of eyes and ears from someone that's been in the trenches and can be your IR coach or advisor.

Recovery pros

These data experts may be necessary to help your IRT with decryption, data restoration, or rebuilding. The key here is to be certain that they understand your environment, any data dependencies, and especially your recovery priorities.

Build these connections now, reach out, meet for coffee, get direct phone numbers, and get the paperwork out of the way as soon as possible. Support vendors do not typically do work without a signed agreement, and getting those reviewed and approved can take hours if not days.

You've got your team assembled and your vendors on speed dial. Now let's talk about what everyone actually *does* when ransomware hits.

Now that we have assembled our IRT, including outside and government resources, and we've defined our objectives and scope, it's time to document the response procedures that will guide your team during an attack.

The following sections outline the procedures that need to be included in your written IRP. They will contain the strategic decisions, policies, and procedural frameworks that should be established now, during planning. These aren't the detailed technical steps for executing during a crisis (those come in Chapters 9–16). Instead, you're documenting the decision frameworks and protocols your team will follow: detection criteria, containment strategies, communication channels, and recovery priorities. Make these decisions now, when you can think clearly, so your team isn't improvising under pressure when ransomware strikes.

Detection and Initial Response Procedures

Your IRP should document how ransomware will be identified and what immediate actions your team will take upon detection. This includes defining detection indicators your team should watch for, establishing assessment criteria to determine attack type and scope, and documenting the decision framework for those critical first moves—whether to power off systems immediately, pause VMs, or isolate while preserving evidence. These decisions need to be made during planning, not during the panic of an active attack. Here's an overview of what your detection and initial response procedures should address:

Initial Detection and Assessment

Detecting ransomware quickly is critical. The earlier you identify it, the more likely you are to contain it and keep things from really getting messy. Review the list of monitoring and response tools discussed in Chapter 8 and develop a plan on how they will be used during an attack.

What does ransomware look like? CISA has a stop ransomware website (*https://www.cisa.gov/stopransomware*) with tons of information and indicators for various ransomware.

A few common symptoms to look out for include:

- The obvious file extension changes to *.locked*, *.crypt*, etc.
- System performance issues (likely due to the encryption process)
- Spikes in outbound network traffic
- Files with double extensions, like *.pdf.exe*

- Unusual use of PowerShell
- Anti-malware or EDR services disabled on an endpoint

If you see any of these, it's time to act.

Once ransomware is detected, figure out what you're dealing with. Which systems are compromised? What kind of ransomware is it? Encrypting, locking, or the double-extortion data-stealing kind? How fast is it moving? If you can figure these things out quickly, then you'll know how to better react.

First Moves

You need to decide *right now*, during planning, whether you'll try to grab forensic images before pulling the plug on infected systems. Then you need to put that decision in your plan. Why? Because when ransomware's actively encrypting your files at 2 a.m., you'll be under massive pressure to just shut everything down immediately. Make this call now, when you can think straight.

Your options when you've got an infected system:

Immediate power off
> The nuclear option. Safest and fastest way to stop the bleeding, but you're kissing any memory-based forensics goodbye. Everything in RAM gets wiped clean.

Pause VMs
> The sweet spot for virtual environments. Pausing stops the damage cold *and* preserves the memory image. Then you can copy the whole VM for analysis later. This is why we virtualize everything we can.

Isolate but leave running
> The high-wire act. You keep the system running but cut it off from talking to anything else—revoke its IP, firewall it off, block its C2 connections. This preserves the most evidence but it's also the riskiest. Only attempt this if you've got seasoned pros on your team who know what they're doing.

Containment and Evidence Preservation Procedures

Your IRP should establish your containment strategy and forensic evidence policies before an attack occurs. Document which systems will receive forensic treatment, what imaging methods apply to different scenarios, what resources and tools you'll need, and how evidence will be documented and preserved. These protocols ensure your team can simultaneously stop the attack from spreading while capturing the evidence you'll need for investigation, insurance claims, and regulatory compliance.

We cover this topic in detail in Chapters 13 and 14, but the purpose of this chapter is to talk about what should be in your plan. Let's start with an overview. Your focus at this point needs to be keeping it from getting worse.

Once an attack happens, you need to lock down or shut down the compromised systems as much (and as quickly) as possible. You need to do things like turn off remote access, make sure your backups are safe, and start blocking IP addresses and services at the firewall.

Attempt to determine how the ransomware is communicating to its C2 system. If you can't, then you have to consider killing the internet connection so it can't get further instructions or payloads. (As discussed in Chapter 5, this step should be preauthorized in case it's needed in the middle of the night. If you use a third-party resource, this authorization should be in the contract.)

Review all privileged account activities and consider resetting passwords, revoking MFA tokens, and all current sessions. (As you can see in the following case study, MFA can actually work against you.) If possible, shut down everything you can before they become infected. Remember, ransomware can't infect offline systems, and encryption doesn't work without power.

Case Study: Stolen MFA Token Facilitates Ransomware Infection

A mid-sized SaaS company became infected with ransomware, impacting all of its production systems and the majority of its employee workstations. The attackers demanded several million dollars in ransom, claiming that they had complete control of the company's network domain and access to its insurance and financial records.

How did this happen? The company's chief information security officer (CISO) was confident in their cybersecurity program, the layers of protection they'd implemented, and even the 24/7 monitoring they do around the clock… nothing tripped any alarms. The CISO reviewed all the firewall logs, anti-malware logs, and system configurations, looked for rogue devices, and tried to find patient zero. Nothing added up until an employee commented about something weird they experienced a few days prior.

User: I'm not sure if it's related to what's happening, but a few days ago, last Wednesday, I received an email from our company health insurance provider. The email looked OK to me; it looked like other emails from them. In the email, there was a link to a "new employee benefits portal" and a message that if I signed up for their fitness program, I would receive an Apple Watch. I tried clicking the link from my phone, but I got an error message about using my computer to access the site. I then logged into webmail and clicked the link from my computer. The insurance site looked familiar, and I registered for the program, but when I clicked "submit" nothing happened. So, it was the combination of the error message on my phone and the webpage that didn't do anything that made me feel like it was a scam.

CISO: Thank you, I'll check the email and webpage to see if it's related. You mentioned logging into webmail but didn't say if you had to use MFA.

User: It didn't ask me for MFA. In the past, I clicked "Remember this PC" or "Trust this PC," and I haven't had to enter the MFA again.

A review of the email determined that it was a cleverly crafted phishing email that avoided being filtered out by the email system. The link in the email led to a website that ran code to determine whether a user was connecting via mobile device or computer. If the connection was a computer, then the website attempted to steal the user's stored (remembered) MFA token from the internet browser. With the stolen MFA token, the attacker could log in to the company's network as if they were a legitimate user, without triggering any alarms or alerts. (Technically, they are not logging in, they are masquerading as an already logged in user and using that login to gain access.) The attackers then accessed the company's network and used this foothold to begin their attack.

Forensic Evidence Preservation

Before you start nuking systems and restoring from backups, we need to talk about preserving the crime scene. We know, we know—you just want to get everything back online. But those infected systems are sitting on gold: evidence about how the attack happened, what data they grabbed, and what the attackers were doing while they owned your network. You'll need this stuff for understanding the full scope, finding all the compromised systems, preventing round two, dealing with regulators, and filing insurance claims. Skipping this step costs you later.

While you are developing your IRP, make the call about which systems get the forensic treatment. Don't wing it at 3 a.m. when everything's on fire. Domain controllers? Always image those, they've got your authentication logs and show how attackers moved laterally. Database servers tell you what data got accessed. File servers might show what got stolen. Your backup systems? Critical for figuring out if the attackers poisoned your safety net. And if you can nail down patient zero, image that thing immediately. High-value targets like executive workstations often tell their own story about targeted attacks.

Forensic imaging methods

Your plan needs to spell out which imaging method you'll use for each system type. This connects back to the choices we talked about in "Containment and Evidence Preservation Procedures" on page 206.

Live imaging is what you do when you've isolated systems but kept them running. You're capturing memory, active processes, network connections—the whole nine yards. This requires specialized tools that won't mess up the evidence and people who actually know what they're doing to maintain chain of custody. It's complicated, but when you need systems online, it's your best shot at getting the complete picture.

Paused VM imaging is the easy button for virtual environments. Pause the VM and copy the files to safe storage. You get everything—memory, disk, the works—and you don't need fancy forensic tools. This is yet another reason why virtualizing everything makes your life easier.

Cold imaging is for when you've already pulled the plug. You're only getting storage at this point (memory's gone), but it's the safest way to stop the attack from spreading. Just be ready for the physical access requirements when you need to grab those drives.

Get your resources ready now

Your IRP needs to list out the forensic gear you'll need before you need it. Set up forensic workstations that have never touched your production network—this is non-negotiable for evidence integrity. Figure out how much storage you need for images (hint: a lot). Pick your forensic imaging tools now—we covered some good ones in Chapter 6. Prep your chain of custody templates so they're ready to go. And most importantly, get contracts signed with forensic vendors before the incident. We talked about this in "Teaming Up with Outside Help" on page 204—don't wait until you're desperate to start shopping around.

Document everything

For every system you image, you need to capture the basics: system name and what it does, when imaging started and finished, who did it, what tools they used (with version numbers), where the image is stored, and hash values proving the image hasn't been tampered with. Note anything weird that happened during imaging. This documentation isn't busywork—it tracks your progress, satisfies legal and regulatory requirements, and shows you knew what you were doing.

Forensic imaging

Let's get practical. Imaging big servers takes *hours*. Your recovery timeline needs to account for this. When people start pressuring you to skip imaging because "it takes too long," hold the line. The evidence you preserve now might be your only way to figure out what happened and stop it from happening again.

Keep your forensic gear on isolated networks. Never, ever plug forensic tools into your production network during an active incident—that's how you spread the infection to your evidence collection systems. Store your images on systems that weren't connected to production when the attack happened. This keeps your evidence clean and defensible.

Talk to legal counsel *now* about evidence retention requirements, especially if you're in a regulated industry. Some sectors have specific rules about how long you keep evidence and what chain of custody procedures you need. Figure this out during planning, not when you're in the middle of chaos.

For the detailed technical procedures on actually performing forensic imaging during an incident, check out Chapters 12 and 13.

Communication and Coordination Procedures

Your IRP should predefine all communication channels, notification sequences, and external partner engagement protocols. Document who communicates what to whom and when—from internal team coordination to external notifications for law enforcement, insurance carriers, regulators, and customers. Establish these communication paths and preapprove your messaging templates now so information flows smoothly during the chaos of an actual incident instead of creating bottlenecks while your team is under pressure. Here's an overview of what your communication and coordination procedures should address.

Notification, Communication, and Escalation Protocols

When ransomware attacks occur, you have to let the appropriate people know. Your IRT needs to loop in the right people, inside and out, without wasting time. Time is a recurring theme for effective response.

Inside scoop

The incident response leader declares the incident and gets it moving. They reach out to the IRT through approved methods, including alternate email (not your work email), text, phone calls, Teams (if it's available), or encrypted apps like Signal. Give your executive contact the rundown, including what's hit, how bad, what's next. Provide a similar briefing to the IRT and get the response rolling.

Outside calls

During the planning phase, confirm with your executive contact about connecting with insurance, outside legal counsel, and law enforcement. Someone other than the IRT leader is typically responsible for reaching out to these contacts. Depending on your organization's preference, contacting law enforcement is either pre-authorized for the IRT leader or determined by your executive or legal counsel. In either case and as soon as it's appropriate, reach out to your law enforcement contacts and get them looped in.

Contacting regulators is also typically not the responsibility of the IRT, and usually lies with legal or a compliance department and should be tracked as an IR activity.

You also typically have a period of time before these notifications are required (e.g., 48 to 72 hours after incident validation).

Notifications to customers, partners, etc., are not typically part of the IRT leader's role, but providing the necessary information is essential, such as who was affected, what type of data and how many records, etc.

Steer the story

A communications specialist should take point in handling any outside communications, like social media posts, phone inquiries, news media, etc. Have some "we're handling it" messaging ready and preapproved by legal for the press, but don't overshare. Stick to facts, no wild guesses, to keep your reputation intact and avoid legal headaches later.

Engaging External Response and Support

Sometimes, your IRT can't do it alone, and you need some pros to help with the heavy lifting.

Response firms

Keep a professional IR team on speed dial, and determine if you need a retainer to keep them at the ready. These guys eat ransomware for breakfast. Get to know them today, or more importantly, help them get to know your environment and what matters most. They can be a significant augmentation to your IRT, bringing resources for coaching, containment, cleanup, and forensic investigation and recovery.

Law enforcement

Federal agencies often have a lot of good intel on ransomware actors and sometimes some good recovery advice, tricks, and possibly a decryptor from previous cases. If you do pay the ransom, coordination between you, your insurance, and these cybercrime units can track the ransom payments or crypto trails.

Insurance carrier/broker

Your insurer has a list of approved go-to firms, including IRT, cybersecurity, digital forensics, technical remediation, and lawyers. In addition, if management decides to pay the ransom, it's your insurer that will typically negotiate and make the payment. Make sure you understand your policy and follow its guidance, specifically when you are required to inform them that there are indicators of an incident. Delaying can cause nonpayment!

Recovery and Investigation Procedures

Your IRP should outline your recovery priorities, backup restoration approach, and investigation procedures before you ever need them. Document what systems get restored in what order, how you'll validate backup integrity, your policy on ransom payment decisions, and what forensic investigation steps you'll take to understand how the attack happened. These frameworks ensure systematic recovery that prioritizes business-critical systems while capturing the lessons needed to prevent future incidents. Here's an overview of what your recovery and investigation procedures should address.

Data Recovery and Remediation: Assessing the Damage and Recovery Scope

The ransomware's out the door, it's contained and wiped out. Now comes the messy part: picking up the pieces. Recovery is no walk in the park. It's about getting your business back on its feet by restoring your systems to a usable state and ensuring this doesn't happen again. You've got to be smart about your recovery efforts, or the incident could get worse. The upside? With a solid plan, you can bounce back quicker, keep your data safe, and be more resilient for the next incident. Here are a few thoughts.

Before you start patching things up, you've got to know what was impacted or infected. It's like checking the wreckage after a crash. Your IRT needs to dig in and see how bad the damage is:

What got hit?
> Determine which systems and related data was infected. Then assess how the loss of these systems impacts the business. Can you still take orders, make product, provide services, or pay bills? Follow your agreed-upon prioritization schedule. Customer information and financials beat that random marketing folder most days.

Is it still good?
> Make sure that what doesn't appear to be infected is truly OK to keep. Whether it's an unaffected system or the data you are restoring to a rebuild server, it is imperative to use one or more anti-malware tools that are different from the one you were using before the attack. Bad actors love to sneak ransomware and the initial breach payloads into backups so that you self-infect during remediation.

> These safety checks should be done in a disconnected/air-gapped environment to ensure that any system that continues to be or becomes reinfected doesn't spread back onto the production network.

Are you ready?

Double-check your backups, and please say they were not encrypted by the attack. You should stress a strict rebuild policy and not a clean and restore approach. Once each system is rebuilt and data is restored to them, ensure each one is thoroughly tested before introducing them back into your production environment. Take this opportunity to start fresh, rolling back all rogue software, permissions, services, and privileges and limiting the environment to only what the business and users need.

Restoring Data from Backups

We'll cover this topic in more detail in Chapter 15, but if your backups are good, they are your golden ticket to getting back to normal. But don't just assume they are clean and complete or that this is a simple restore job:

Create recovery groups

A *recovery group* is a set of systems (e.g., servers/VMs) that depend on each other to work; therefore, you restore/recover them in a group. For example, you might need an authentication/authorization system, a DNS system, a database system, and a web server for a web-based application. That would be a recovery group. Create these recovery groups and assign them priorities based on the needs of the business.

Keep it offline

Make sure your pot of gold is untouchable until you are certain that the ransomware threat has been addressed. Even then, the first phase of recovery should be to limit access to your backup for only those systems or recovery network segments you are working with—not the whole network.

Pick your battles

Start with the essentials (prioritized from your earlier efforts), like internet access, email, your ERP (financial) system, or manufacturing and shipping. Verify management is still in agreement with the restore plan in the IRP, specifically what is expected to come back online and when.

Check your work

Make sure those backups are good, the restore is completed without errors or corruption, and the rebuilt systems are stable. Take notes on any issues and how they were addressed. Start to breathe easier, but don't pat yourself on the back (or ask for a raise) until you see it all working like it was before "the big one," which is how this will likely be referred to in the stories you tell your grandkids.

Build a recovery sandbox

In "Playing in a Sandbox" on page 225, we will cover the idea of using a sandbox for war games, but this sandbox serves a different purpose. Instead of creating a safe place to play war games, this will be used to restore your systems into a safe environment where they can be checked for malware before being released into production. Like many other parts of this plan, you should really learn how to do this as part of your IRP, and when testing your IRP, you should be testing this part as well.

Test an alternate boot method (if needed)

One of the things you're going to want to do when recovering into a sandbox is booting your server/VM from alternate media, such as a USB disk drive. This gives you a clean functional operating system through which you can restore your data and check it for malware—without allowing anything on that drive to execute. Read "Booting from alternate media" on page 426 for more details, but the point is to make sure this is part of your plan if you need it, and that you test it along with everything else.

Rebuilding and Restoring Systems

The data is flowing from your backups like a warm lazy river of comfort, so now is the time to tweak your system configurations, network restrictions, firewall rules, etc. Let's lock things down:

Start fresh

Don't trust anything ransomware touched. Wipe it and rebuild from scratch with clean installs and patch every gap before putting it back on the production network. We'll cover this in more detail in Chapter 15, but the best way to do this is via something called a golden image, which is an already-configured copy of the OS that you can use to re-image your OS drivers. Once you have a completely clean OS, you can restore the data.

Tighten things up

Take this opportunity to review and enhance your security posture. Review user access profiles and limit who has access to what. Review all remote access and restrict it to the extent possible. Reset everyone's passwords and enforce a strong policy for the new ones. There will be no more open doors.

Ease back in

Bring your fresh, newly built, and better-secured systems back online and watch for any hiccups. Monitor your "new" EDR solution (since the last one didn't help much) and run a vulnerability scanner to look for any remaining weak spots and keep an eye on your network traffic for anything weird.

Deciding on Ransom Payment

Paying the ransom should be your last resort, and you need to have this discussion during your planning phase. The IRT needs to ensure that executives have a clear and current understanding of the likelihood and timeline for recovery so they can make the best-informed decision possible. The decision to pay a ransom should not be made by the IRT, but there are several scenarios where the IRT may heavily suggest the need for a decryptor in order to recover. Think it over; it is not a comfortable decision to make. Things to consider:

Legal angle

Can you even do it, or is it against a regulation or illegal? (See "The Ransom Dilemma: Legal Landmines and Empty Promises" on page 275.)

Will it work?

Any chance they'll give you a legitimate decryptor, or just take your money? (You can assess based on prior behavior of the threat actor group via threat intel reports.)

Double-dip risk

Could they still leak your stuff after you pay? Or attack you again via some dormant backdoor, unpatched vulnerability, etc. A large percentage of those who pay the ransom will be attacked again within the same year.

Backup check

Can you dodge it and restore from the backups you have? Can you ensure that the restore doesn't also include the ransomware?

Evaluating Decryption Options (and Possibly Life Choices)

If you determined that the backups are compromised or, heaven forbid, you simply just didn't have any, now you need to start thinking about how to "decrypt" the mess this ransomware has made, initially focusing on how to accomplish this without paying the ransom.

Free tools first

Check the threat intel sites, like CISA or NoMoreRansom.org (or similar sites in your country), and reach out to professionals or law enforcement for available decryption keys. Ransomware experts could have some hacks too. While these experts may charge a premium, it's typically far less than the ransom itself.

Talking to the bad guys

Do not contact the ransomware actors directly on your own. If you are truly stuck without a recovery option and thinking of paying the ransom, the ideal next step is to work with your insurance provider. If you don't have insurance, then you should find an insurance carrier that will help you get through this. Insurance companies often have the resources and negotiators you need at this point. Alternatively and at a minimum, get your company's legal or outside counsel and law enforcement involved. You do not want to shoulder the risks associated with doing this on your own.

Much like real-life ransoms, you must ask for proof of life before paying anything. This requires the attacker to accept encrypted files you send to decrypt and prove that your money will be well spent. Make sure you send them examples of critical files, not just your resume. But remember that paying the ransom is a crapshoot, and they might ditch you or bail when you find out the decryptor doesn't work on everything.

Forensic Investigation and Root Cause Analysis

You can't forget to go back and figure out how this mess started. Digital forensic analysis and old-fashioned investigative curiosity can help look back at the facts, events, and data. Of course, your ability to do any digital forensics will be based on how much evidence you preserved during the containment phase. The more systems for which you were able to get a forensic image before you pulled the plug, the easier the forensic investigation will be. If you were unable to obtain any forensic images, you will be limited to log analysis. A few things you should be looking at and the insurance company will be interested in include:

How did the ransomware get in?
> Was it a phishing email? Was it stolen credentials that then led to compromised remote access (often due to scraped MFA tokens saved in a browser)? Or a network vulnerability we may have missed?

Preserve the evidence
> During your IR, make sure you grab all the logs, files, traffic, and anything requested by insurance or law enforcement. Make sure they are stored offline and secured from misplacement or damage.

Plug the holes
> Review your public/internet facing systems for any signs of abnormal activity, vulnerabilities, or other malware.

Post-Incident Review and Continuous Improvement

So, you survived a ransomware attack—nice work! Your T-shirt is in the mail! You locked it down, got your systems back, and hopefully did it all without paying the ransom. Solid moves, but don't book your cruise just yet.

The real win comes after the post-incident review. Think of it like a team huddle after a rough game. Get everyone together, review all details of what happened, compare notes, and figure out how to get better next time. Because there's always a next time.

Ransomware keeps evolving, and your IRP has to keep up. Here are a few things to consider for a post-incident review.

Conducting a Post-Incident Review

First up: get everyone involved in the response effort together, including your IRT, IT, experts, executives, legal, HR, and any outside help. This is typically an internal review and does not initially include insurance or outside counsel. A formal summary can be shared once your internal findings are organized.

Remember, this is not about pointing fingers or placing blame, it's about working together to put all the puzzle pieces together. Keep the review session casual and comfortable, order lunch, and maybe do it offsite. Determine the following, and connect it back to the metrics discussed in "Metrics of Effectiveness" on page 196:

Timeline
> Start compiling events and activities into a consolidated timeline. Try to determine when the attack started, how long it took until someone noticed, and everything else up until you stopped the attack.

Wins
> Capture all the strong points, like automated alerts, quarantines, solid procedures like employee notifications, and following the IRP, along with any impressive moves that someone did to improvise, innovate, or otherwise save the day.

Setbacks
> Were there any delays, gaps, or missteps? Issues with communications, contacts, configuration settings, or backups?

Ah-hah moments
> Were there any moments that came as a surprise (both good and bad) that need to be considered for improving the IRP, fill gaps in staffing, skills, or technical capabilities, etc.? Did anything blindside you?

Damage report
> How long were you down? What did it cost? What was the fall out (e.g., delayed orders, lost customers, penalties, etc.)?

People power
> Incident response is nothing without people. From the first person to observe or report the problem to every last contributor working to stop the attack. Everyone in the organization must be treated like part of the solution and given access to the resources to play their part. This means awareness training, understanding of procedures to follow, roles and responsibilities, etc. Were there any gaps in your people power?

Updating the Incident Response Plan

Time to remediate and look for ways to improve the IRP. Your review is going to find gaps, outdated information, and opportunities to improve the processes. Examples often include escalation delays or confusion, containment issues, or communications issues that include email, Teams, or phone outages. Here's how to shore it up:

Tune the steps
> Review the critical activities, including identification, impact analysis, containment, and recovery. Now that you've been through the fire, look for ways to improve timeliness, effectiveness, communication, and confidence.

Who's on first
> Review roles and responsibilities. Add new roles, responsibilities, and IRT members. Modify current roles and responsibilities by expanding where necessary and, in some cases, reducing what's expected from others. Create a RACI matrix to capture IRT role names with their respective Responsible, Accountable, Consulted, and Informed responsibilities.

Improve communications
> Communication can always improve. Consider what you and the organization could do better with regard to communications among the IRT, from the IRT to management and third parties, and from management to employees, contractors, and the media.

Remediation management
> All concerns identified during the incident must be remediated as soon as possible, and someone needs to take point on managing these to completion. Bad guys already know you are vulnerable and will try again and or tell others about it. This must include technical concerns, procedural improvement, staffing and skill gaps, agreements and contracts for future support, etc.

Conducting a Root Cause Analysis

If you haven't already done a root cause analysis during the attack, now is the time to do it. There will be many questions that you want the answers to, but do you have the time, resources, and management support to address them all? A root cause analysis can help answer the questions about what was affected, why things happened the way they did, what kind of ransom it was, and how the attackers were able to get in. Time to play detective:

Ingress point
> How did the ransomware get in? Phishing? Weak RDP? Compromised account? Exploited vulnerability in a perimeter system? A priority should be to find the

ingress point, patient zero, and anything else that would help you figure out how this started (e.g., weak passwords, unpatched software).

Blind spots
How did the attack sneak past your detection and defenses? Gaps in capabilities? Missed alert? Once you determine how they got in, you should be able to figure out why you weren't alerted sooner (i.e., before the ransomware activated). Document the gaps or deficiencies and start looking at tools, tech, skills, and services that will address any blind spots.

Attacker TTPs
What tools or tactics did they use? Any related IP addresses? Did you find the *dropper file* (i.e., the file that started the infection process)? These are a few pieces of the tools, tactics, and procedures (TTPs) that could help identify the attacker if they are incorporated into your alerting policies. Law enforcement would also benefit from this information in their pursuit of the criminals.

Training and Awareness Updates

You've figured out how they snuck in. Now it's time to make sure there's not a repeat performance. Review how you train your users and keep them current on attack trends, attacks, and what to keep an eye out for. Use this information to update your training procedures.

Testing and Refining the Plan

Updating the IRP should be done at least annually and after any incident, but don't forget to take it a step further and walk through it with your team. From an audit perspective, we consider design and operation to be two different activities.

Writing and updating the IRP is a design activity. It can be assessed as effective from a read-through for completeness. Actually testing the IRP is an operational assessment to ensure that it was designed well and it operates as intended. Operational testing is typically referred to as either a tabletop exercise or a war game:

Tabletop exercises (TTXs)
Run a moderated simulation of a ransomware attack to test your updated IRP. There are resources available online from CISA and other organizations to help you design and run these TTXs. (See "Cybersecurity Resources Around the World" on page 190.) There are also professional services firms that can custom build, moderate, and facilitate these for you. A quick internet search will get you started. The important outcome from the TTX is to determine if additional updates need to be made, or is the IRP good… for now?

Backup restore testing

As often as possible, backups should be tested for integrity, restore metrics, and variations of file, volume, and whole system recovery. Document these activities so you get credit in an audit or post-incident review, and address any issues you run into. Testing backup restoration will also help solidify your RTO and give you the information you need to set expectations during an IR.

Test your tools

Did you update your toolset, configurations, or capabilities after the breach? Make sure to test these as well. Ensure they are operating effectively, identifying threats faster, and providing the information you need to better respond to the next threat.

Cross-train

Switch up the roles and test the alternates on your IRT. Make sure everyone is comfortable and capable in their backup responsibilities.

Keep fine-tuning

Ransomware is always changing, and so are the TTPs of the attackers, so your IRP has to keep improving as well.

Planning an Annual Ransomware Tabletop Exercise

Once you have an IRP, an annual TTX is a great way to try it out. Planning an annual ransomware TTX might sound like a daunting task, but it's really about bringing people together to think through a messy, all-too-real scenario in a low-stress way. This section will walk you through the nuts and bolts of setting up the TTX, figuring out who needs to be there, what goals you're aiming for, and how to keep it practical and engaging. It's less about fancy tech and more about getting everyone on the same page.

Defining Exercise Goals and Objectives

OK, so you're setting up a ransomware TTX. Step one is to define your success criteria. This isn't just busywork; it's your chance to see how the IRT and other stakeholders will handle a ransomware scenario. Establish clear targets to keep the exercise on point. Here are a few to focus on:

Testing IRP effectiveness

How solid is your IIRP when it's go-time? Can your IRT grab the playbook, talk it through, and pull in the right resources and tools without fumbling?

Think of it as a practice game. Does your plan actually hold water, or is it just a fancy document created to check a box? Realize also that the TTX is often the first exposure most IRT members have to the plan. It is absolutely OK if it isn't perfect, that's one of the primary objectives of the exercise.

Spotting holes in the game plan

While you're at it, take note of things that weren't considered or documented in the IRP. Are there parts of the response that feel off or confusing? Maybe the team's stumped on something; dig into those and talk through it now. Better to address the weaknesses now than when ransomware's already tearing through your network.

Getting everyone in sync

Ransomware's not just IT's problem (I say this a lot). It will eventually involve management, internal legal, external legal, HR, PR, insurance and risk, compliance… pretty much everybody. This exercise is your shot to see if all the stakeholders can get through it.

Is the information flowing, can decisions be made, or are people tripping over each other? If the teams aren't on the same page, a real hit could turn into chaos. If you do expect there will be contention or political issues, then you should consider having a third party moderate and run the exercise.

Selecting Participants

Choosing the right participants for your ransomware TTX is important because you want to make sure all the key players are involved. This isn't just about the IT team, it's about bringing together all the different departments that will play a role during an actual ransomware attack.

By carefully selecting the right mix of participants, you'll ensure that the exercise covers all the bases and gives you a thorough test of how your response plan holds up under pressure. Some organizations have two exercises, with the first being a scrimmage among the tighter team that builds IRT confidence for the second exercise with broader participation.

Scenario Development

Creating a solid, realistic ransomware attack scenario is the heart of your TTX. You want to simulate a situation that could actually happen. This should be something that feels real and challenging, so your team can respond effectively when the time comes. Let's look at a few objectives:

Crafting realistic ransomware attack scenarios

When designing your scenario, think about the different types of ransomware you might face. It could be encryption ransomware that locks up critical files, or maybe something more complex like double extortion, where attackers not only encrypt data but threaten to release it publicly unless they get paid. You want to mix things up and consider all possibilities. A precursor to defining the scenario may be an exercise in determining the most likely threat vector and impacts specific to your organization.

Considering different attack vectors

Think about how the attack could enter your system. Maybe it's through a phishing email that tricks an employee into downloading malicious software. Or perhaps it's via an exposed RDP connection that gives attackers a way into your network. The attack vector sets the stage for how the incident unfolds and helps your team prepare for multiple types of entry points and what defensive controls and capabilities come into play.

Simulating business impact

It's critical to think about the real-world consequences to your business. What happens if systems are down for hours or days? How does a system outage impact your daily operations? For instance, consider how a disruption might affect order processing, manufacturing, customer service, or financial reporting. You want the exercise to reflect the chaos and the pressure of trying to keep things running while managing the attack.

Adding complexity and time pressure

A good scenario isn't just a straightforward "here's what happens, now respond" situation. You want to inject a bit of chaos by adding unexpected elements as the exercise goes on, like a second ransom demand, the absence of an IRT member, additional systems being compromised, or even fake media inquiries. Putting time pressure on participants can also help simulate the stress of a real attack, forcing them to make quick decisions and respond effectively under pressure. A third party moderator is good at throwing wrenches into the mix.

By creating a detailed and multifaceted scenario, you'll ensure that your team gets a true-to-life experience. They'll practice dealing with multiple layers of complexity and learn how to think on their feet. Consider ideas like the following:

- A second ransom demand
- Unavailability of a key IRT member
- Sudden system failure
- Fake news inquiry or social media leak

Facilitating the Exercise

Now that your scenario is ready, it's time to run the TTX. This is where your IRT puts the plan into action, and the goal is to create an environment where they can think critically and make decisions as if it's an actual ransomware attack. Here are some tips for facilitating the exercise:

Designate a moderator/facilitator

You'll need someone to lead the exercise and keep it on track, a moderator who understands ransomware, your ransomware response plan, and the scenario. Their job is to guide the discussion, ensure everyone stays involved, and introduce unexpected twists, when appropriate, to test how the team handles pressure. They're essential for keeping the exercise focused and productive. You should also designate a scribe who will observe, take notes, capture ah-hah moments and action items, and summarize the exercise from an observer's perspective.

Encourage active participation

The point here is to get everyone engaged; no one should be sitting quietly. From IT to executives to PR, every participant needs to take part in tackling the crisis. As the facilitator, prompt people to share their thoughts, offer solutions, and work together. It's about team building and making sure everyone's voice is heard in shaping the response.

Document key decisions and bottlenecks

As the exercise unfolds, keep track of what's happening. If you have a scribe, they will capture the decisions made, the steps taken, and any issues or delays that pop up. This could be uncertainty about roles or slow communication between teams. Recording these details is critical for the debrief afterward, giving you clear insights into what's working and what needs adjustment.

Keep the pressure on

To make it realistic, add some urgency. Ransomware attacks often come with deadlines for payment, but there is also a timeline for recovery so introduce surprises, like a change in ransom demand or a new system going down. Use these to push the team to act quickly. This helps represent the stress of a live incident, showing how well they adapt and stay focused when things get intense.

By facilitating the exercise with these steps, you'll turn it into a valuable learning opportunity. It's less about getting everything perfect and more about getting it out on the table and preparing your team to respond confidently when it counts.

Conducting a Ransomware War Game

Conducting a ransomware war game takes things up a notch from the planning you've already mapped out in your annual tabletop exercise. In this section, we'll walk through how to conduct a war game, including key players, the mock attack, and keeping it real without letting it get out of hand. It's your chance to pressure-test your IRT's reflexes.

When you're gearing up to handle a ransomware mess, you'll hear about two big ways to practice: tabletop exercises and war games. Both are super useful, but they're not the same thing: each has its own benefits and purpose. Let's break it down:

Tabletop exercises (strategic and procedural focus)
   A tabletop is like a group huddle with snacks. You grab your team, sit around, and talk through a ransomware attack step by step, following your IRP. It's all about hashing out what you'd do, who's handling what, and how you'd keep everyone in the loop. You're testing whether the plan actually works or if it's just fancy words on paper. It's less about doing stuff and more about nailing the strategy, ensuring it's comprehensive, and making sure you're all on the same page.

War games (tactical and operational focus)
   War games are next-level intensity. This is way more hands-on, like you're in the middle of an actual ransomware attack. Instead of just chatting, your team is at their keyboard and taking action, making decisions as the incident unfolds. It's fast, it's stressful, and it might even create some competition between the "red teams" (the pretend bad guys) and the "blue teams" (your defenders). This one's about seeing how your IRT holds up when the fire starts and how quickly they can put it out.

Setting Up the War Game Environment

Setting up a ransomware war game that actually works is all about making it feel real—like, *really* real.

Live attack simulation versus discussion-based

Here's where things get real. In a live war game, you're not just talking through scenarios—you're actually taking systems offline, making emergency calls, and watching the clock. It's the gut punch of a real attack without the actual damage. Systems might actually go offline, calls are made to administrators to react, and the stopwatch starts tracking your recovery efforts. It's about putting actual people in a pseudo-real situation and tracking the real response.

If that's too much, you can still run it discussion style by walking through each move step by step. Either way, the trick is to make it feel as close to the real deal as you can get.

Real-world consequences and time-based decision-making

Your war game needs teeth. Every decision should hurt a little. Time's running out, your options suck, and what you choose right now could sink the company or save it. That's the pressure your team needs to feel.

Picture this: a critical system just went down, and the clock's ticking. How fast does your team respond? Then, boom—ransom demand hits another system. How do they handle it when the fire's spreading? Can they think straight when everything's going sideways?

This isn't about making your team comfortable. It's about finding out if they can make the hard calls when the building's burning and every option looks terrible. Because that's exactly what real ransomware feels like.

Involving red team/blue team dynamics

Creating red and blue teams can be fun and competitive. The red team plays the bad guys, looking for ways to deploy their ransomware, while the blue team is your defenders, monitoring your systems, investigating anomalies, and putting out fires. The red team is there to poke holes and push the blue team into tough spots, adding some real-time tension you can't fake in a conversation-based exercise. It's a great way to spot weaknesses in your defenses that could be detrimental in a live attack.

Playing in a Sandbox

It's time to build your war game sandbox. Think of it as your own little digital doomsday playground—isolated from production, realistic enough to make people sweat, but contained so you can't accidentally torch your actual network. If you screw this up and let simulated ransomware escape into production, you're going to have a very bad day and a very awkward conversation with your CEO.

Building your mini disaster zone

Start with VMware or VirtualBox—both are solid for spinning up virtual machines fast. You're building a miniature version of your real environment, not a perfect replica. If your company runs on five servers, don't build fifty. That's just showing off and wasting time.

Mirror what actually matters. Spin up a couple Windows workstations, throw in a server or two (one running Active Directory if that's part of your environment), maybe add a Linux box if you use them. Keep it simple but make it *recognizable*. When your team logs in to this sandbox during the war game, they should think "Yeah, this looks like our stuff," not "What the hell is this?"

Load it with the software your team actually uses every day: Windows, Office apps, whatever tools run your business. The goal is familiarity. When the fake attack hits, you want your team thinking about the response, not fumbling around trying to figure out unfamiliar systems.

Making it dangerous (but not really)

Now comes the fun part: adding the ransomware element without actually nuking anything important. You need tools that *feel* like ransomware but won't jump the fence into your production network.

Check out KnowBe4's free tool called RanSim—it locks files and pops up ransom notes without actually destroying anything. Whatever you try—especially if using random tools from GitHub—just make sure you test anything inside the sandbox first. Run them, break them, see what they do. Don't find out during the war game that your "safe" simulation isn't so safe.

For network-level chaos, spin up Kali Linux on a separate VM. Use it to mimic attacker behavior—run hping3 to flood traffic, spoof some packets, make your monitoring tools light up. It's low tech, but it works for stress-testing whether your team actually notices when bad things are happening on the network. Figure 7-1 shows a basic sandbox configuration.

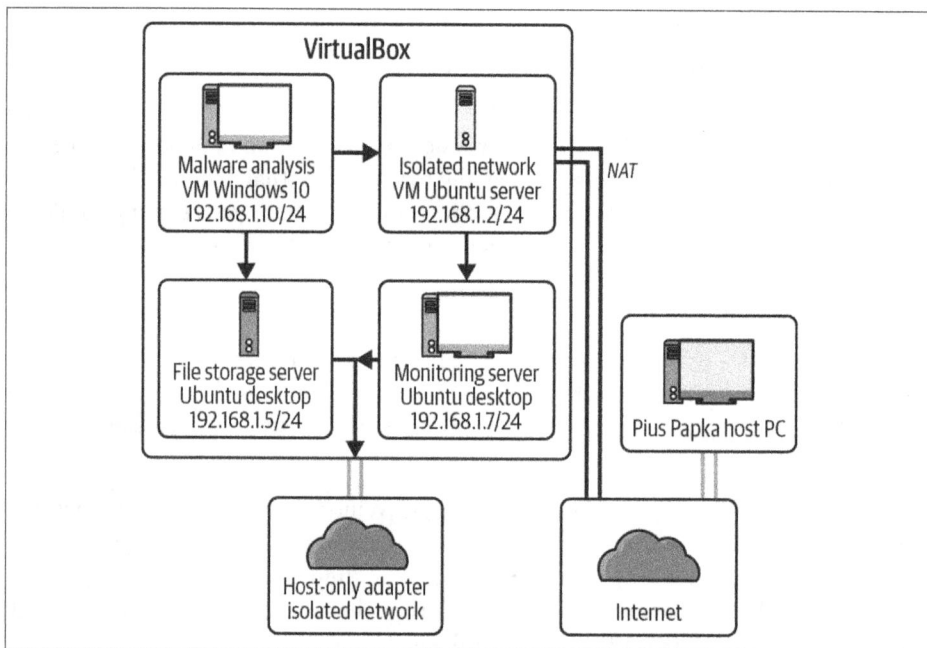

Figure 7-1. Basic sandbox configuration

Baiting the hook with fake data

Your sandbox needs data that feels real. Scatter some dummy files around—fake customer lists, mock financial spreadsheets, a pretend HR database. Tools like Mockaroo can generate realistic-looking datasets in minutes. Make it look legit enough that your team cares about protecting it during the exercise.

Got logs from real systems? Great. Anonymize them with a script and import them into a SIEM tool. Don't have a SIEM? Grab something lightweight like Graylog or the ELK Stack. Your defenders need to practice spotting bad stuff in actual log data, not just theory.

Free resources that aren't bad

Before you start throwing money at commercial platforms, grab the freebies. NIST has a nice framework profile (*https://oreil.ly/Lif05*) you should check out. CISA's #StopRansomware Guide (*https://oreil.ly/lSi1M*) has attack patterns like phishing emails and credential theft—replicate those.

If you do have a budget, platforms like AttackIQ or SafeBreach can automate chunks of your war game with preloaded ransomware behaviors. They're not cheap, but they're faster than building everything yourself.

Keeping it contained

Here's the non-negotiable part: keep this sandbox completely isolated from production. Use a dedicated VLAN, or better yet, air-gap the whole thing. The paranoia is justified here—you're literally practicing with tools designed to break stuff.

Test everything yourself first. Launch the "attack," watch it unfold, make sure it's challenging but not impossible. Your goal isn't to humiliate your team or prove how smart you are, it's to make them better. If your sandbox is too hard, people give up. Too easy, they learn nothing.

Once everything works and you've confirmed it can't escape, hand the keys to your red team and let the war game begin. Watch what happens. See how your team reacts when the pressure's on, when the tools are unfamiliar, when everything's going wrong at once. This is how you find out if your IRT can actually handle the real thing—or if you've got some serious work to do.

Evaluating Team Performance

The war game's over. Your team's catching their breath, maybe grabbing coffee, feeling pretty good about themselves. Now comes the uncomfortable part: figuring out what actually happened.

Don't skip this. Most organizations run the exercise, nod a bunch, say "good job everyone," and learn absolutely nothing. You just spent hours and resources on this war game—squeeze every lesson out of it.

Forget the generic performance review questions. Here's what you're really looking for:

Did they catch it fast enough?

Walk through the timeline. When did the first indicator show up? When did someone actually notice? If ransomware was spreading for 20 minutes before anyone raised an alarm, you've got a detection problem. Maybe your monitoring sucks. Maybe people aren't watching the dashboards. Maybe the alerts are going to an inbox nobody checks. Figure it out now.

Could they actually stop it?

Spotting the attack is step one. Containing it is where most teams fall apart. Did they know how to isolate infected systems? Did they have the access they needed, or did they waste a ton of time hunting down admin credentials? Did they accidentally make it worse by doing something that spread the infection? These are the hiccups that'll kill you in a real attack.

Did anyone know what they were doing?

Be honest. Was your team following the plan, or just winging it and hoping for the best? Did they go down dead-end paths? Make the same mistake twice? If the response looked like organized chaos, that's a training gap screaming at you.

Who talked to whom, and when?

Communication breakdowns are the silent killer in ransomware response. Did the IRT tell the CEO what was happening, or did executives find out from someone's panic email? Did legal get looped in before someone made a public statement or after? Did IT and security work together, or did they trip over each other?

One communication slip—one important person not getting critical information—can turn a contained incident into a PR disaster. Track every notification, every update, every call that should have happened but didn't.

What about the backups?

Here's the billion-dollar question: Could they actually restore from backups, or did they just assume the backups would work? Did they know where the backups were? How long it would take? Whether the backups were clean or potentially infected?

If your team stood there looking confused when someone asked about backup restoration, you just found your biggest gap. Fix that before the real thing hits.

The debrief that actually matters

Get everyone together while it's fresh. Not three weeks later when people have moved on. Within a day or two, max.

And look—this can't be a blame session. If people think they're getting in trouble for screwing up during a practice exercise, they'll clam up and you'll learn nothing. Make it safe to admit mistakes. That security analyst who accidentally isolated the wrong system? That's a learning moment, not a firing offense.

Ask simple questions: What went well? What went sideways? Where did you get stuck? What surprised you? What would you do differently?

Then dig into the specifics. Someone says "communication was bad"—OK, *specifically* what communication? Between who? What should have been said that wasn't? Get concrete answers, not vague feelings.

Document everything. Not just the wins and losses, but the ah-ha moments. The things people figured out on the fly. The workarounds they created when the plan didn't cover something. Sometimes the best improvements come from watching what your team does when the playbook doesn't have an answer.

Now do something about it

You've got a pile of findings. Great. They're worthless if you don't fix them.

Triage the problems. Some are quick wins—update a contact list, fix a broken process, add a missing step to the playbook. Do those immediately. Others need more work—maybe you need new tools, more training, or fundamental changes to how you operate. Those get added to a project plan with actual dates and owners.

And check on them. Put reminders in your calendar. Follow up. Because six months from now when you run the next war game, you don't want to be looking at the same damn problems you identified this time.

The war game showed you where you're weak. Now you know. So fix it, or don't complain when ransomware finds the same gaps you did.

Updating the Incident Response Plan

After the debrief, it's time to take all the insights you've gathered and update your IRP. The goal here is to make sure that your plan reflects the lessons learned during the exercise and is ready to handle real-life situations even better:

Adjusting response procedures based on findings
Based on the feedback and what you observed during the exercise, look for areas where your response procedures might need tweaking. Maybe certain steps were too slow or not as clear as they should have been. Adjust those steps to make them smoother and more efficient. It's all about making sure your team knows exactly what to do at each stage of a ransomware attack, without hesitation.

Closing security and operational gaps
Did the exercise reveal any gaps in your security infrastructure? Perhaps there were vulnerabilities that went unnoticed or weren't addressed quickly enough.

Take a hard look at where your security systems fell short and make a plan to patch those gaps. Also, assess your operational workflows to ensure that your business continuity can keep running smoothly if the worst happens.

Enhancing training and awareness programs
Sometimes, weaknesses are tied to knowledge gaps within the team. If you found areas where team members were unclear on their roles or the tools at their disposal, it's a good idea to beef up your training. Ensure that everyone is up to speed on the latest procedures, tools, and technologies to respond to a ransomware attack. Regular training sessions can help everyone feel more confident when the real deal happens.

Tracking Progress and Maturity

After the debrief and the updates to your IRP, there is still work to do. Now it's about keeping tabs on how things are shaping up over time, your IR maturity. This is how you know you're actually getting better and improving your readiness with every exercise or real-deal incident:

Key performance indicators
The metrics discussed in "Metrics of Effectiveness" on page 196 (also called key performance indicators, or KPIs) are your way of tracking if this plan's really doing its job. Think of them as your scorecard. You could track things like how fast your team spots a ransomware attack, how quickly you lock down systems, or the effectiveness of communications. These numbers give you hard proof of what's working and where you're still improving.

Monitoring incident response readiness over time
Wrapping up one exercise doesn't mean you're "all good." You've got to keep an eye on your team's readiness. Conduct regular check-ins on the status of remediated processes or capabilities and if they are working. If the same problems keep popping up, that's your cue to dig deeper in the next round of training or practice.

Looking for trends and patterns
As you keep at it, watch for any patterns that stick out. Is your team performing well every time, or are there still some stumbles? Spotting those trends lets you zero in on the stuff that needs more attention.

Summary

This chapter provided a comprehensive framework for building, testing, and maintaining an effective ransomware IRP that will be executed by your IRT:

Foundation and planning

Before writing your IRP, five prerequisites must be in place: executive sponsorship with decision-making authority, named team members with contact information, pre-approved communication templates, contracted external vendors, and identified tools and resources. Organizations should also leverage free resources from national cybersecurity agencies for frameworks, toolkits, and incident support. The plan must establish SMART goals, define clear scope covering ransomware types and systems, and align with business priorities.

Team assembly and response procedures

An effective IRT extends beyond IT to include legal, communications, HR, executive leadership, and pre-identified external partners. RACI matrices establish clear accountability for each role. The IRP should document strategic decision frameworks and procedures for four critical phases: detection and initial response (indicators and assessment criteria), containment and evidence preservation (forensic protocols and imaging methods), communication and coordination (notification sequences and engagement protocols), and recovery and investigation (restoration priorities and forensic steps). These documented frameworks ensure consistent decision-making under pressure rather than improvisation during crises.

Testing and continuous improvement

Organizations should test their plans through both TTXs (discussion-based strategic testing) and war games (hands-on tactical simulations in isolated sandbox environments). Post-incident reviews following either actual incidents or exercises capture lessons learned and drive plan improvements. Key metrics including mean time to detect, mean time to respond, mean time to restore, containment rates, and data recovery rates provide objective measures of capability and improvement over time. The chapter emphasized that effective IRPs document strategic decisions and procedural frameworks during planning (detailed technical execution procedures are covered in Chapters 9–16), and that ransomware preparedness requires ongoing testing, refinement, and cultural integration throughout the organization.

PART III

Detect

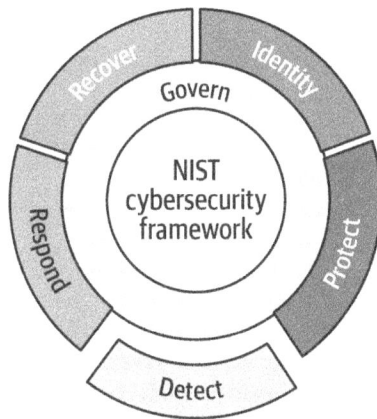

Spotting Ransomware Before It's Too Late

The NIST Cybersecurity Framework's *Detect* function is about developing and implementing activities to identify cybersecurity events in a timely manner. You can't stop or recover from an attack you don't know about, and the sooner you detect it, the better chance you have of containing the damage. Detection isn't about preventing attacks—it's about ensuring you find out within hours, not months.

Chapter 8, "Detection Tools", covers the essential systems that spot ransomware before catastrophe strikes. You'll understand EDR and XDR for real-time threat hunting across your environment, SIEM for comprehensive log analysis and compliance reporting, backup monitoring that serves as both early warning system and last line of defense, and logging practices that provide forensic evidence when incidents occur. We'll also discuss integrating these tools into a cohesive detection ecosystem and when managed security service providers make sense for organizations that need 24/7 monitoring without the expense of building in-house security operations center (SOC) capabilities.

By the end of this Detect section, you'll have visibility into ransomware activity from the moment it starts moving through your environment, not six months later when the damage is done.

CHAPTER 8

Detection Tools

You can't stop or recover from an attack you don't know about. And the sooner you detect an attack, the better chance you have of containing the damage and preventing total disaster. Detection tools aren't nice-to-have gadgets—they're your first line of defense when threat actors come knocking. And trust us, they are knocking.

This chapter covers the essential detection systems you need to spot ransomware before it's too late: extended detection and response (XDR) for real-time threat hunting across your environment, security information and event management (SIEM) for comprehensive log analysis and compliance reporting, backup system monitoring that serves as both early warning system and last line of defense, and logging practices that provide the forensic evidence you'll need when (not if) an incident occurs.

We'll also talk about integrating these tools into a cohesive detection ecosystem, because isolated tools create blind spots that attackers will exploit. And we'll discuss when it makes sense to bring in managed security service providers to handle detection for you—a decision that's less about budget and more about access to expertise and 24/7 monitoring that most organizations can't maintain in-house.

This chapter is a primer, not an encyclopedia. If detection is your primary focus or you're building a security operations center, you'll want to dive deeper into resources like *Cybersecurity Bible* by Shawn Walker (independently published), *Practical Threat Detection Engineering* by Megan Roddie, Jason Deyalsingh, and Gary J. Katz (Packt Publishing), or *Hunting Cyber Criminals* by Vinny Troia (Wiley). But if you're trying to build a ransomware defense strategy, this chapter will give you what you need to make informed decisions about detection capabilities.

Introduction to Detection Systems

Detection systems are like the smoke alarms of your data center. You hope they never go off, but you'd be a fool not to have them. They're what stands between you and finding out six months later that someone's been siphoning off your customer data since last winter.

But here's the thing about detection tools: they're only valuable if properly implemented and maintained. Companies sometimes spend tons of money on fancy detection systems that end up being nothing more than expensive paperweights and blinky lights because nobody bothered to configure them properly—or worse, nobody bothered to look at the alerts they generated. The latter is often caused by the former because a poorly configured detection system can create so many false alarms, everyone starts ignoring it.

Also understand that detection by itself is not prevention. Prevention is when you have an expensive car that has keys that cannot be duplicated, keyless entry systems that use biometrics, and immobilization systems that don't let the car go anywhere if someone tries to steal it. Detection is like having a car alarm that goes off once they're inside the car, perhaps notifies you via an alert, and even tracks the car after it's been stolen (e.g. LoJack). Both prevention and detection are essential—and there are tools that can do both—but it's important to understand that they serve different purposes, and confusing the two is a recipe for disaster.

Before we look at specific detection tools, let's talk about what makes a good detection system. First, it needs to be comprehensive. You can't just monitor your network perimeter and call it a day. You need visibility into your endpoints, your servers, your applications, your cloud environments, and yes, your backup systems. You wouldn't install an alarm system just on your front door.

Second, it needs to be timely. A detection system that tells you about an attack a week after it happened is about as useful as a weather forecast for yesterday. You need real-time or near-real-time alerting to have any hope of containing damage—which is becoming more critical in the world of cyber today.

Third, it needs to be accurate. False positives are the bane of every security team's existence. Too many, and people start ignoring alerts altogether, a phenomenon called "alert fatigue." It's like the boy who cried wolf—except in this case, when the wolf finally does show up, it devours your entire business.

Fourth, and perhaps most importantly, your detection systems need to be resilient. If an attacker can easily disable or blind your detection tools, they're not going to help very much. This means protecting your detection infrastructure, encrypting its communications, hardening its components, and ensuring it can operate even in degraded conditions.

With those principles in mind, let's explore what happens when you don't have adequate detection systems in place. It's not pretty, but it's important to understand the stakes.

Case Study: Accenture Quickly Stopped Attack

It was August 11, 2021, and Accenture—the massive global consulting firm that literally advises other companies on cybersecurity—gets hit by LockBit ransomware. The irony alone is enough to make you wince. The attackers wanted $50 million.

But here's where Accenture shows everyone how it's supposed to be done. Their security controls actually detected the attack. Not after the fact, not three weeks later when someone noticed something weird—during the attack. And the moment they detected it, they immediately contained and isolated the affected servers.

The bad guys still managed to compromise 2,500 computers and steal about 6 terabytes of data. They even published some of it on their leak site (mostly PowerPoints and case studies, nothing earth-shattering). But here's the thing: Accenture refused to pay the ransom and fully restored everything from backups.

Think about that for a second. They got hit by one of the most prolific ransomware gangs out there, the attackers made off with 6 TB of data and demanded $50 million, and Accenture basically said "nah, we're good" and recovered on their own. No massive costs, no business disruption lasting months, no paying criminals.

This is the gold standard, folks. They had:

1. Security controls that actually worked and were actively monitoring
2. A team that knew what to do when alerts fired
3. The authority to act immediately: shut it down, contain it, isolate it
4. Backups that actually worked and were tested

The only real damage? About 33,000 individuals had their data exposed, and Accenture took a bit of a reputation hit because, you know, they're the cybersecurity experts getting hacked. But operationally? They handled it perfectly. See Bisson, 2021 (*https://oreil.ly/rGAlC*).

An Undetected Attack

Let us paint you a picture of what happens when you've got no detection systems in place. It's not pretty.

Without detection tools, attacks just happen. They're kind of like the slow leak I, Curtis, had inside the wall in my kitchen that I didn't notice until I started to see mold in an odd place. Based on the amount of damage, it had been slowly growing inside my wall for months before I ever even knew it existed.

The typical *dwell time*—that's how long attackers hang out in your systems before you notice them—is measured in *months*, not days. I've seen companies where attackers had been lurking for over 200 days. Think about that.

Here's what typically happens. First, they get in through some mundane vector, maybe Bob in accounting clicked a phishing link because it promised photos of cute puppies. The attackers establish a foothold, escalate privileges, and start moving laterally through your network. They're mapping your resources, finding your crown jewels, and setting up camp.

And what are you doing during all this? Business as usual. That's the scary part.

Without detection tools, the first sign of trouble is when you get a ransomware demand. "Pay us $10 million or we delete all your data forever," or (even worse) "we expose your company's secrets to the world."

Let us walk you through an actual attack scenario at a midsized manufacturing company. They had basic perimeter security, just a firewall and antivirus, but no real detection systems. No SIEM, no XDR, no anomalous login alerts, no backup monitoring, nothing.

Day 1: An employee receives a targeted phishing email that appears to be from a supplier. It contains a Microsoft Word document infected with an embedded malicious macro. The employee opens it because it looks like an invoice they were expecting. The macro then deploys malware that will be the basis for the attack.

Days 2–5: The malware establishes persistence and begins reconnaissance. It maps the network and identifies domain controllers, file servers, and backup systems. The company's antivirus doesn't catch it because it's a zero-day exploit.

Days 6–14: The attackers move laterally through the network, compromising additional systems and elevating privileges. They're careful not to trigger any obvious alarms, working mostly during business hours to blend in with normal traffic.

Days 15–30: The attackers identify the company's most valuable intellectual property—design files for a next-generation product. They also locate and compromise the backup systems, subtly altering configurations so backups appear to succeed but are woefully incomplete. They also reduce the retention periods so that disk and cloud-based backups older than a few days are deleted.

Days 31–60: The attackers begin exfiltrating data, but they're smart about it. They do it slowly, encrypting the stolen files and sending them out through legitimate channels like email attachments or cloud storage services.

Day 61: The attackers have what they came for. They deploy ransomware across the network as a smokescreen, encrypting everything and demanding payment.

Now the company realizes they've been attacked. And when they try to restore from backups? They discover there are no backups older than a few days due to the retention change, and newer backups don't contain very much data. The company ends up paying millions in ransom, loses months of work, and suffers irreparable damage to their reputation.

This isn't a hypothetical scenario. This is what actually happens when you don't have proper detection systems in place. And it happens every single day to companies that thought, "It won't happen to us."

Case Study: CommonSpirit Health (When Detection Comes Too Late)

CommonSpirit Health—the second-largest nonprofit hospital chain in the US with 140+ hospitals across 21 states—detected "strange activity" on October 2, 2022. Sounds good, right? Except the attackers had already been inside their network since September 16. Two weeks of dwell time.

It gets worse. CommonSpirit didn't publicly confirm it was ransomware until October 12—10 days later. And they completely missed the scope. They initially thought only Washington, Tennessee, and Nebraska facilities were hit. Turns out? Over 100 facilities across 13 states.

The attackers didn't even need to breach the electronic health records (EHRs) directly; they just copied data from two file-share servers. It took CommonSpirit five months to figure out what was taken. Five months of going through files one by one.

Meanwhile, EHRs went down, ambulances got diverted, appointments were cancelled, they went back to paper records. Some hospitals were still struggling over a month later. At least 623,774 individuals had their data compromised, maybe up to a million.

The final bill? $160 million. They won't say if they paid the ransom. There's a class-action lawsuit. And in their annual report, they had to admit this could seriously affect their financial condition.

This is what failure looks like: they detected something but were already two weeks behind, took ten days to admit it was ransomware, took five months to understand the scope, and the whole thing cost $160 million. Read more here (Zivanov, 2025 (*https://oreil.ly/hcsLX*)).

The Numbers Are Scary

Here are some sobering statistics: according to various industry reports, the average time to detect a breach is still *over six months*. (IBM's 2025 "Cost of a Data Breach Report" (*https://oreil.ly/OB-LB*) found the average to be 181 days to detect and 40 days to contain.) That's more than six months of attackers having free rein in your systems. And the average cost of a data breach now exceeds $4 million ($4.44M according to the IBM report, also citing that industry specific averages vary widely —the average for healthcare, for example, was $7.42M). That's not counting the intangible costs, such as lost customer trust, regulatory penalties, damage to brand reputation.

But it gets worse. Without detection systems, you're not just vulnerable to external attackers. You're also blind to insider threats—employees or contractors who abuse their legitimate access for malicious purposes. These threats can be even more damaging because insiders already know where your valuable data is and how to access it.

The absence of detection also means you have no way to identify and remediate misconfigurations or vulnerabilities before they're exploited. It's like driving a car with no gauges. You won't know you're low on oil until the engine seizes.

And here's something many people don't consider: without proper detection, your forensic capabilities are also severely limited. When an incident does occur, you'll have little to no evidence to determine what happened, how it happened, who was responsible, and what was compromised. This hampers your ability to learn from the incident and prevent similar attacks in the future.

Now, you might be thinking, "But we have a firewall and antivirus software. Isn't that enough?" The short answer is: absolutely not. Those are prevention tools, not detection tools. They're designed to stop known threats at the perimeter. What about the threats that slip through? What about the threats that originate inside your perimeter? What about the novel threats your prevention tools have never seen before? That's why you need both prevention and detection.

Extended Detection and Response

Extended Detection and Response (XDR) is like having a team of security ninjas watching your environment 24/7, but without the expense of keeping them caffeinated. It collects and correlates data across multiple security layers—endpoints, networks, servers, cloud workloads, email—you name it.

What makes XDR special is that it doesn't just look at individual alerts like traditional systems. It connects the dots. That suspicious login followed by that unusual file access followed by that odd network connection? Each might seem innocent alone, but together they spell T-R-O-U-B-L-E.

The best XDR solutions use machine learning (ML), user and entity behavioral analytics (UEBA), and artificial intelligence (AI) to cut through the noise. Because let's be honest, your security team (or the few people whose part-time job is security) is already drowning in alerts. The last thing they need is more false positives. A good XDR system doesn't just find needles in haystacks; it will draw you a picture of who put it there, when it occurred, and—equally as important—it stops people from adding more hay.

When implementing XDR, start with your critical systems—the ones that, if compromised, would have you updating your resume. Then expand to include more data sources. XDR also isn't a "set it and forget it" technology. It needs tuning, updating, and regular maintenance. Let's take a closer look.

Traditional security tools operate in silos. Your endpoint protection platform (EPP) knows what's happening on your endpoints but has no visibility into network traffic. Your firewall sees network traffic but knows nothing about what's happening on your servers. Your email security gateway monitors messages but can't correlate them with endpoint activities.

XDR breaks down these silos by ingesting data from all these sources and more, then applying advanced analytics to identify patterns that indicate malicious activity. This holistic view is crucial because modern attacks don't confine themselves to a single domain. They move across endpoints, networks, cloud resources, and applications.

Here's a concrete example:

- An employee receives a phishing email (email domain).
- They click a malicious link (web domain).
- That downloads a dropper (endpoint domain).
- The dropper communicates with a C2 server (network domain).
- It receives instructions to exfiltrate data (data domain).

Traditional security tools might catch pieces of this attack chain, but they won't see the complete picture. XDR will.

The technical components of a typical XDR solution include:

Collectors/sensors
These gather telemetry from various sources, such as endpoint agents, network taps, log collectors, cloud APIs, etc.

Data lake
A centralized repository where all this telemetry is stored, normalized, and indexed for analysis.

Analytics engine

This is where the magic happens. The analytics engine applies a combination of rules, ML models, behavioral analysis, and threat intelligence to identify suspicious patterns. It's looking for anomalies, known indicators of compromise (IOCs), behaviors that match attack techniques documented in frameworks like MITRE ATT&CK, and any deviation from behavioral baselines at the user, device, and network layers.

Response automation

Once a threat is detected, XDR can trigger an automated response, such as isolating endpoints, blocking network connections, forcing password resets, or escalating to human analysts for further investigation. This is also referred to as security orchestration, automation, and response (SOAR).

Investigation interface

A dashboard or console that security analysts use to investigate alerts, hunt for threats, and manage incidents. The best interfaces provide clear visualizations of attack chains and tools for deep-dive investigations. Another huge value of an XDR platform is the "single-pane-of-glass" console for cybersecurity analysts to use instead of needing to log into the antivirus console, Active Directory console, firewall console, etc.; it's all in one place.

Most XDR platforms require sophisticated analysis by an analyst with the appropriate skills to decipher and make decisions. Many organizations lack the in-house expertise to maximize their XDR investment. This is where a managed security service provider (MSSP) or cybersecurity service provider (CSSP)—collectively referred to in this chapter as managed service providers (MSPs)—can help by providing the expert analysis and 24/7 monitoring many organizations can't maintain internally. We'll cover MSPs in "Managed Service Providers" on page 255.

Another challenge is data overload. XDR generates massive amounts of data, including telemetry from thousands of endpoints, network devices, servers, and cloud resources. Managing this data, ensuring it's properly ingested and normalized, and storing it cost-effectively and securely requires careful planning.

Despite these challenges, XDR represents a significant advancement in detection capabilities, and with the rapid evolution and integration of AI into XDR platforms like Stellar Cyber, XDR is becoming the most economical and effective detection and response solution. But it's not the only tool in your detection arsenal. Let's talk about another critical component: SIEM.

Security Information and Event Management

If XDR is your security ninja team, security information and event management (SIEM) is your security librarian, methodically cataloging everything that happens in your environment. SIEM systems collect logs from practically everything, including firewalls, servers, applications, you name it. They normalize this data, which makes apples-to-apples comparisons possible, and look for patterns that indicate something fishy is going on.

Similar to XDR, the power of a SIEM is in correlation. That failed login on your domain controller might not mean much, but when it happens alongside unusual database queries and after-hours VPN connections from overseas? Now you're looking at something worth investigating.

Like XDR systems, SIEMs also require work. They generate a lot of alerts, and tuning them is more art than science. You need skilled personnel who understand your environment well enough to separate the wheat from the chaff. A poorly tuned SIEM will very quickly get ignored.

Modern SIEMs are increasingly incorporating threat intelligence feeds, which is like giving your security team a cheat sheet of what the bad guys are up to. This context helps prioritize which fires to put out first.

While XDR is relatively new on the scene, SIEMs have been around for decades. They evolved from simple log management tools to sophisticated platforms that combine security information management (SIM) and security event management (SEM), hence the acronym SIEM.

Core Functions

The core functions of a SIEM include the following:

Log collection
SIEMs ingest logs from virtually every device, application, and system in your environment. This includes network devices, servers, endpoints, applications, cloud services, and security tools. The collection methods vary, but may include agents, agentless approaches, syslog, APIs, etc.; the goal is comprehensive visibility.

Normalization
Different systems produce logs in different formats. A Windows event log looks nothing like a Linux syslog or a Cisco firewall log. SIEMs normalize these disparate formats into a common schema, making it possible to correlate events across different sources.

Correlation
This is where SIEMs really shine. They apply rules and analytics to identify relationships between events that, when viewed in isolation, might seem benign but together indicate malicious activity. For example, a user logging in outside business hours (event 1), accessing systems they rarely use (event 2), and

downloading unusually large amounts of data (event 3) could indicate an account compromise.

Alerting

When correlation rules identify suspicious patterns, SIEMs generate alerts for security teams to investigate. These alerts should include context, like what happened, where it happened, when it happened, and why it's suspicious.

Compliance reporting

SIEMs help organizations demonstrate compliance with regulations like PCI DSS, HIPAA, SOX, and GDPR by generating reports that show security controls are in place and effective.

Forensic investigation

SIEMs store historical log data, providing a searchable repository for investigating security incidents. This historical data can be crucial for determining the scope and impact of a breach.

Typical SIEM Deployment

Here's what a typical SIEM deployment looks like:

Collectors/forwarders

These components gather logs from various sources and forward them to the SIEM. They may perform initial parsing and filtering to reduce the volume of data sent.

Indexers/processors

These ingest the raw logs, normalize them, and index them for efficient searching and analysis. In large environments, this processing layer might be distributed across multiple servers for scalability.

Data store

This is where normalized and indexed logs are stored. The data store needs to be optimized for both write-heavy operations (ingesting logs) and read-heavy operations (searching and analyzing logs).

Correlation engine

This applies rules and analytics to identify patterns across multiple log sources. Modern SIEMs use a combination of rule-based correlation and advanced analytics like ML.

Visualization and reporting

Dashboards, reports, and visualization tools that help security analysts understand what's happening in their environment and communicate findings to stakeholders.

Modern SIEMs are evolving beyond traditional log management and correlation. They're incorporating UEBA, SOAR, and advanced analytics powered by machine learning. These capabilities are blurring the lines between SIEMs and XDR, with some vendors offering platforms that combine elements of both.

One key advantage SIEMs have over XDR is their maturity in compliance reporting. If your organization is subject to regulations that require log retention and regular security assessments, a SIEM can be invaluable for demonstrating compliance.

XDR Versus SIEM

SIEM and XDR are actually complementary tools that serve different primary purposes in your detection strategy. Just so we're all on the same page, let's take a look at what makes them different in Table 8-1.

Table 8-1. XDR versus SIEM

Feature	SIEM	XDR
Primary focus	Primarily focuses on *log centralization and aggregation*, normalization, and correlation across your *entire IT environment*. It's designed to collect ALL the logs and make sense of them to detect threats and maintain visibility for audits.	Concentrates on *integrated threat detection, investigation, and response across multiple security layers* (endpoints, networks, cloud, etc.). Its goal is to provide a *proactive, holistic* approach to identifying and mitigating advanced threats.
Data sources	Ingests logs from *virtually everything*, including applications, infrastructure, security tools, business systems, etc. It's *comprehensive* but can be noisy.	More selective, primarily collecting security-relevant telemetry from *endpoints, networks, email, identity systems, and cloud workloads*. It prioritizes integration *within a specific ecosystem* (often vendor-specific) for deeper, cross-layered visibility.
Analysis approach	Primarily *rule-based correlation* with some behavioral analytics. Modern SIEMs incorporate ML, but they often require *significant tuning and customization* by analysts to reduce false positives.	Built from the ground up with *behavioral analysis and ML at its core* to detect sophisticated threats like zero-day exploits or lateral movement. It emphasizes *automated, context-aware analysis* across integrated data sources, *reducing manual effort*.
Historical focus	Strong emphasis on historical data for compliance, forensics, and investigations. Retention often measured in years. It retains logs long term for forensic investigations, compliance audits, and trend analysis, making it a go-to for retrospective insights into security incidents.	More focused on real-time and near-real-time detection and response. Retention is typically shorter (months rather than years). While it retains some data for investigation, its storage is typically tied to immediate threat hunting and remediation rather than long-term historical archiving.
Response capabilities	Limited native response capabilities; traditionally focuses on alerting humans to take action. It identifies threats but lacks native response automation. Analysts must use external tools or manual processes to contain or mitigate incidents, though integration with SOAR applications can enhance this.	Built-in automated response capabilities like endpoint isolation, process termination, and account lockout. It's designed to streamline and accelerate incident response by integrating detection and action within a single platform.

Feature	SIEM	XDR
Compliance orientation	Strong compliance reporting capabilities, often a primary driver for SIEM adoption, with robust features for log retention, audit trails, and reports for PCI, HIPAA, and GDPR.	Security-first approach with compliance as a secondary benefit. Its strength lies in threat mitigation rather than comprehensive log management for audits, making it a secondary tool for compliance needs.
Maturity and evolution	Mature technology with 20+ years of evolution, started as log management and evolved to add security capabilities, like real-time monitoring and advanced analytics. Next-gen SIEMs are integrating AI and cloud capabilities, but the core concept remains established and widely adopted.	Newer technology that evolved from EDR to include additional security domains, building on EDR to address siloed security tools. It is rapidly maturing with broader adoption, deeper integrations, and AI enhancements. All of this to position XDR as a forward-looking alternative or complement to SIEM.

Think of SIEM as your security librarian, methodically cataloging everything that happens across your environment. XDR is more like your security bodyguard—focused, action-oriented, and ready to intervene.

Case Study: Speed Saves $67 Million

Here's a story from January 2025 that shows what happens when you catch things fast and have people who know what they're doing ready to respond.

An UnderDefense client—they didn't name the company, but we know it's a financial entity—had an attacker get into their network through an unprotected user account on an internet-facing virtual desktop infrastructure (VDI) panel. No MFA. Just username and password. That's it. In 2025. I know, I know.

The attackers managed to encrypt 22 hypervisors. If you know anything about virtualization, you know that's really bad. One hypervisor can run dozens of virtual machines. Twenty-two hypervisors? That's potentially hundreds of systems offline. The estimated potential loss was $67 million. That's not the ransom demand; that's what it would have cost the business in downtime, recovery, lost revenue, and everything else.

But here's the key: UnderDefense caught it fast and responded immediately. Because they moved quickly, they were able to contain the damage before it spread further. The actual ransom paid? Zero. The actual loss? A fraction of what it could have been.

Now, don't get me wrong; the root cause here is inexcusable. Insecure onboarding, no MFA on an internet-facing VDI panel in 2025? That's IT malpractice. But once the breach happened, the speed of detection and response is what saved them from a $67 million disaster.

This is why you need monitoring, why you need an IRP, and why you need people who can move fast when things go sideways. The difference between catching an attack in the first few hours versus the first few days can literally be tens of millions of dollars. Read more at UnderDefense Cybersecurity, 2025 (*https://oreil.ly/RBMUv*).

Detection Tool Integration

Having all these fancy detection tools is great, but if they're not talking to each other, you're still vulnerable. It's like having guards posted around your building, but they're all wearing noise-canceling headphones listening to their favorite tunes.

Your SIEM should ingest alerts from your XDR, which should be aware of your backup system notifications, and so on. This gives you the full picture of what's happening.

The most effective SOCs I've seen use dashboards that consolidate data from all these systems in one place (see Figure 8-1). When something suspicious happens, they can move from system to system, tracking the evidence without needing to log in to a dozen different interfaces.

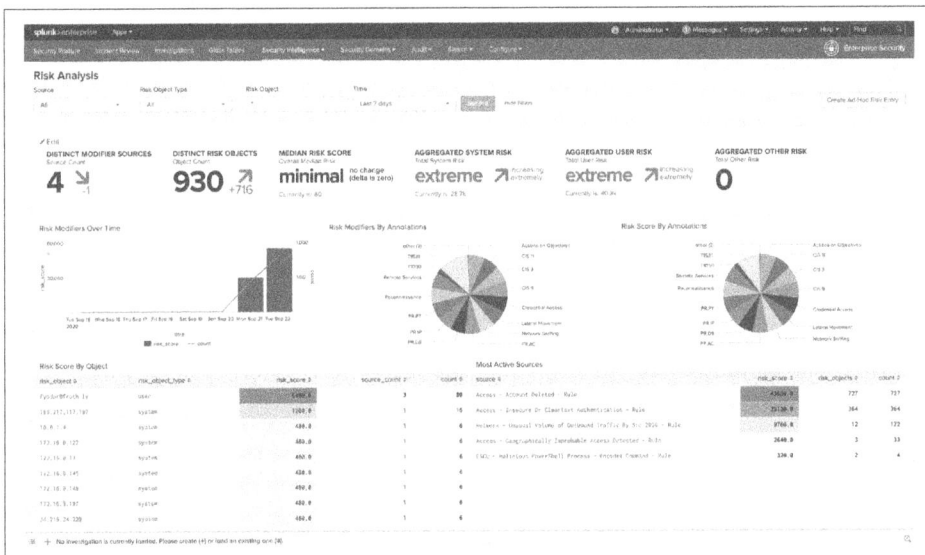

Figure 8-1. Dashboard that consolidates data in one place

This integration also helps reduce alert fatigue. Instead of getting five alerts about the same incident from five different systems, you get one comprehensive alert with all the relevant context.

Please also automate where you can. If your detection tools spot something that's definitely bad news—like ransomware encryption patterns or data exfiltration—they should be able to trigger automatic responses. Maybe that's isolating the affected systems, killing suspicious processes, or alerting the IRT. Every minute counts when you're under attack.

Let's examine what effective integration of detection tools actually looks like in practice. At the most basic level, integration means data sharing—ensuring that alerts and telemetry from one system can flow to others. But true integration goes beyond simple data flows to create a cohesive detection ecosystem that's greater than the sum of its parts.

Human Integration

One final aspect of integration that's often overlooked is human integration. Your detection tools should integrate not just with each other but with your human workflows, and the tools these humans use (e.g., Slack, Teams, Discord, etc.). This means:

Usable interfaces
Security analysts should have intuitive interfaces that present integrated data in ways that facilitate rapid understanding and decision-making.

Relevant alerting
Alerts should be routed to the right people with the right skills and authority to address them.

Contextual documentation
Alerts should include links to response playbooks, relevant policies, and contact information for subject matter experts.

Feedback mechanisms
Analysts should be able to easily provide feedback on alert quality, which feeds back into system tuning.

Elements of Integration

Here are some examples of what good integration can accomplish:

Centralized visibility
All detection data should flow into a central platform, typically a SIEM or security operations platform, that provides a unified view of your security posture. This eliminates blind spots and provides context for individual alerts.

Normalized taxonomy (i.e., terminology)
Different detection tools often use different terminology for the same concepts. Effective integration requires normalizing these taxonomies. For example, what one tool calls "malware detection" another might call "malicious code identification." Normalization ensures you're speaking a consistent language across tools.

Contextual enrichment

When an alert happens, it should be automatically enriched with relevant context from other systems. For example, an endpoint alert should be enriched with user information from your identity management system, asset information from your change management database, and vulnerability data from your scanning tools.

Cross-tool correlation

Look for patterns that span multiple detection domains, such as detecting lateral movement that correlates to VPN access. For example, correlate unusual account activity (identity domain) with abnormal network traffic (network domain) and suspicious process execution (endpoint domain).

Unified case management

When multiple detection tools identify aspects of the same incident, they should create or update a single case rather than generating multiple disconnected alerts. This gives analysts a comprehensive view of the incident.

Automated response workflows

Integration should enable automated response actions that span multiple tools. For example, when malware is detected on an endpoint, the system should automatically isolate the endpoint (endpoint tool), block related network traffic (network tool), scan for similar indicators elsewhere (SIEM/XDR), and check backup integrity (backup tool).

Feedback loops

Detection tools should learn from each other. For example, if your XDR identifies a new attack pattern, it should automatically update rules in your SIEM, firewall, and email security gateway to look for similar patterns.

Detecting Ransomware with Backups

While XDR and SIEM are powerful tools, they're primarily focused on your production environment. But how are you monitoring the integrity of your backup environment? As someone who's spent decades in the backup and recovery world, I, Curtis, can tell you that backup systems are both a last line of defense and a potential early warning system. Let's talk about how to leverage them for detection.

When ransomware hits, one of the first things it often does is go after your backups. That means that unusual backup system activity can be an early warning sign—a canary in the coal mine, so to speak. Configure your backup system to notify you when something's off—failed jobs, unexpected errors, abnormal backup sizes, or sudden performance changes. Don't just direct these alerts to the backup admin's inbox. Pipe them into your security monitoring systems too. And for heaven's sake, make sure your backup logs are being sent someplace where attackers can't tamper with them.

Backup systems have a unique vantage point in your infrastructure. They regularly scan your entire environment, looking at file metadata and content to identify what's changed since the last backup. This gives them visibility into patterns that other systems might miss.

Backup System Events and Anomalies

Here are specific backup system events and anomalies that can indicate a security incident:

Sudden increases in change rate
If your incremental backups suddenly grow much larger than normal, it could indicate mass file modifications—a telltale sign of encryption malware.

Deduplication ratio changes
Significant changes in deduplication ratios could indicate new types of data in your environment or mass file modifications.

Unexpected file extensions
New or unusual file extensions appearing in your backup selection could indicate ransomware activity. For example, if your backups start picking up files with extensions like *.encrypted*, *.locky*, or *.zepto*, you might have ransomware in your environment.

Changes to backup configurations
If your backup job configurations change unexpectedly—different selection lists, schedules, retention policies, or target locations—it could indicate an attacker trying to undermine your recovery capabilities.

Authentication failures
Repeated failed authentication attempts to your backup system might indicate an attacker trying to gain access to destroy or corrupt your backups.

Unusual access patterns
Backup administrators typically access the backup system during business hours and perform predictable actions. Unusual access times or activities could indicate compromised credentials.

Backup job failures
A sudden increase in backup job failures, especially across multiple systems, might indicate malware interference or system compromise.

Unusual restoration activities

Unexpected restore jobs or restoration of unusual data sets might indicate an attacker testing your recovery capabilities or attempting to replace legitimate files with malicious ones. Restores can also be used as an exfiltration method.

Changes to immutability settings

If your backup system supports immutable backups (those that cannot be altered or deleted until a specified retention period expires), any attempts to change these settings should be closely monitored.

Steps to Leverage Your Backup System

To leverage your backup system for detection, follow these steps:

1. Establish performance baselines

    Document normal backup performance metrics, like job duration, data transfer rates, backup sizes, change rates, verification times, etc. These baselines allow you to identify deviations that might indicate security issues.

2. Configure comprehensive alerting

    Most enterprise backup solutions include robust alerting capabilities. Configure alerts for job failures, configuration changes, performance anomalies, and authentication events.

3. Integrate with security monitoring

    Don't keep backup alerts in a silo. Forward them to your SIEM or XDR solution for correlation with other security events.

4. Implement role-based access control

    Limit who can access your backup system and what they can do. This helps prevent unauthorized changes and makes it easier to identify suspicious activities.

5. Enable detailed logging

    Configure your backup system to log all activities, including job operations, configuration changes, user actions, system events, etc. These logs are invaluable for detection and forensic analysis.

6. Regularly audit backup configurations

    Periodically review your backup configurations to ensure they haven't been maliciously altered. This includes selection lists, schedules, retention policies, and target locations.

7. Implement immutable backups

Where possible, use backup technologies that support immutability. This not only improves your recovery capabilities but also makes backup tampering more evident.

8. Monitor backup storage

   Make sure to monitor the immutable features in your storage, to make sure no one turns them off. Watch for unexpected activities in your backup storage, such as unauthorized access, unexpected deletions, or capacity anomalies.

Log Everything and Secure Your Logs

Logging is the foundation of effective detection, and even more crucial for forensic analysis, and the first thing any IRT will do is ask for your logs. They're the breadcrumbs that help you figure out what happened after the fact. But they're useless if they're compromised or unavailable.

First rule of logging: store copies of your logs outside the original environment. If your production environment is compromised, you need logs that the attackers can't touch. This might mean sending logs to a dedicated logging server or a cloud service.

The most sophisticated logging setups I've seen use write-once media or immutable storage for their logs. Once written, not even administrators can change them, which isn't very convenient for the attackers who want to cover their tracks.

And don't skimp on retention. Keep logs for at least a year, preferably longer. Some attacks are "low and slow," and you might need to look back months to see where they started.

Logs for Your Primary Environment

The following are logs to consider in your primary environment:

Operating system logs
   Configure Windows Event Logs, Linux syslog/journald, and other OS-level logging mechanisms to capture security-relevant events.

Application logs
   Ensure applications record authentication events, access to sensitive functions, configuration changes, and error conditions.

Network device logs
   Firewalls, routers, switches, and other network devices should log connection attempts, rule matches, configuration changes, and system events.

Security tool logs

Antivirus, endpoint detection and response (EDR), intrusion detection systems (IDS), intrusion prevention systems (IPS), and other security tools should log detection events, policy enforcement actions, and system status changes.

Cloud service logs

Enable comprehensive logging for all cloud services, including infrastructure (IaaS), platform (PaaS), and software (SaaS). Most cloud providers offer robust logging options, but they're rarely enabled by default.

Authentication system logs

Directory services (e.g., Active Directory), identity providers, and authentication systems should log all authentication attempts, account management actions, and policy changes.

Logs for Your Backup Environment

For your backup environment, pay particular attention to these logging areas:

Backup job logs

These should include detailed information about job execution, including start and end times, data processed, files backed up, verification results, and any errors or warnings.

Configuration change logs

Any change to backup configurations—job definitions, schedules, retention policies, storage targets, etc.—should be logged with details of what changed, when, and by whom.

Administrative access logs

All access to backup management interfaces should be logged, including authentication attempts (successful and failed), session activities, and logouts.

Storage system logs

The systems where backup data is stored should log access attempts, data writes, deletions, and capacity changes.

Replication logs

If your backup strategy includes replication to secondary sites or cloud services, log the replication activities, success/failure status, and any synchronization issues.

Recovery logs

All recovery operations, including file restores, system recoveries, and backup verifications, should be logged with details of what was recovered, when, where to, and by whom.

Where to Store Your Logs

Now, where and how should you store these logs? Before we talk about log storage, though, understand that regulatory requirements (e.g., HIPAA and GPDR) and contractual requirements (e.g., PCI) will often influence log storage decisions, often transforming them from operational preferences into legal mandates that dictate specific storage technologies, retention periods, and access controls. Here are some key examples of regulations that would affect your log choices:

HIPAA (healthcare)
> Requires 6+ year retention of audit logs containing personal health information (PHI), with tamperproof storage and strict access controls, often driving adoption of immutable storage solutions and geographically restricted cloud services

PCI DSS (payment card industry)
> Mandates one year online, three years total retention with real-time monitoring capabilities, typically necessitating SIEM solutions and centralized logging across the cardholder data environment

SOX (Sarbanes-Oxley)
> Demands seven-year retention of financial system logs with strong tamper-evidence controls, often requiring write once read many (WORM) storage or blockchain-based logging systems for audit trail integrity

GDPR (European privacy)
> Creates competing pressures by requiring data minimization and potential log deletion upon request, which may conflict with other retention requirements and necessitate sophisticated data classification in cloud logging services

FISMA (US federal information systems)
> Requires US government contractors to use approved storage solutions with specific security certifications, often limiting options to on-premises or FedRAMP-certified cloud providers

These regulatory frameworks will effectively determine your log storage architecture, where the cost of noncompliance far exceeds the investment in appropriate storage infrastructure.

Here are several approaches to log storage, each with its own advantages and considerations:

Centralized log servers
> Dedicated servers that collect, store, and manage logs from across your environment. These should be hardened, access-controlled, and regularly backed up offsite.

SIEM solutions

As discussed earlier, SIEMs provide not just log storage but also normalization, correlation, and analysis capabilities.

Cloud-based logging services

Services like AWS CloudWatch Logs, Azure Monitor Logs, or third-party offerings provide scalable, resilient log storage with built-in analysis tools. (Some SIEM solutions are cloud-based as well.)

Immutable storage solutions

Technologies that prevent modification or deletion of logs once they're written. These include WORM storage, blockchain-based logging systems, and cloud storage with immutability features.

> Please make sure your systems' clocks are synchronized! I, Mike, can't tell you how many incident investigations I've seen hampered by timestamp disparities across different systems. Use Network Time Protocol (NTP) to keep all your systems synchronized to the same time source.

Managed Service Providers

Let's be honest—this chapter might leave you feeling overwhelmed. Setting up comprehensive detection capabilities requires specialized expertise, significant resources, and ongoing commitment. It's a lot, especially for small and midsized organizations that don't have dedicated security teams.

This is where managed service providers (MSPs) and managed security service providers (MSSPs) come into the picture. They can be a lifeline for organizations that know they need detection capabilities but lack the internal resources to build and maintain them effectively.

Expertise Without the Hiring Headache

Good security analysts are expensive and hard to find. The cybersecurity skills gap is real; there are simply not enough qualified professionals to go around. An MSP gives you access to a team of experts without the hassle and expense of recruiting, hiring, and retaining them in-house.

I, Mike, consulted with a manufacturing company that spent eight months trying to hire a qualified security analyst. They cycled through three candidates who didn't work out before finally giving up and engaging an MSSP. Within two weeks, they had a fully functional detection capability monitored by experienced analysts. The cost was about 60% of what they would have spent on a single full-time employee, and they got 24/7 coverage to boot.

Faster Deployment

MSPs have done this before—many times. They've got tested deployment methodologies, pre-built detection rules, and established workflows. They've learned through trial and error what works and what doesn't.

While an in-house team might spend months figuring out how to deploy a SIEM or XDR solution effectively, a good MSP can have you up and running in weeks. They've already made the mistakes and learned the lessons so you don't have to.

24/7 Monitoring

Attackers don't work 9-to-5, and they're particularly fond of launching attacks on weekends and holidays when they know security staff will be thin. Providing round-the-clock monitoring with an in-house team requires at least five full-time employees just to cover all shifts (accounting for vacations, sick days, etc.).

MSPs spread this cost across multiple customers, making 24/7 monitoring affordable even for smaller organizations. One regional bank I, Mike, worked with calculated that building an in-house SOC with 24/7 coverage would cost them at least $750,000 annually in staff costs alone. They got comparable coverage from an MSSP for under $200,000 per year.

Tuning and Maintenance

As already mentioned, detection systems aren't "set it and forget it" technologies. They require constant maintenance, updates, and tuning. MSPs have dedicated staff for these operational tasks, ensuring your detection capabilities remain effective as threats evolve.

I've seen too many organizations invest hundreds of thousands in detection technology only to have it become gradually less effective because nobody had time to tune the rules, update the software, or adjust to changing environments. MSPs make these operational tasks their core business.

Multi-Client Intelligence

Here's a huge advantage of MSPs that's often overlooked: they see attacks across multiple clients and industries. This gives them visibility into threat trends that no single organization would have on its own.

> Be sure to discuss data privacy with your MSP, and to have it in your contract that they will not share information about your organization with any other organization.

If an MSP detects a new attack technique targeting one client, they can immediately update detection rules for all their clients. This cross-pollination of threat intelligence is invaluable. It's like having a neighborhood watch that spans the entire country.

Flexible Scaling

As your organization grows or your security needs evolve, an MSP can scale services up or down accordingly. Try doing that with an in-house team; it's much harder to scale human resources than it is to adjust a service contract.

Compliance Support

Many MSPs specialize in specific regulatory and contractual frameworks (HIPAA, PCI DSS, SOC 2, etc.) and can provide the documentation and evidence needed for compliance audits. This can save you significant time and reduce the stress of audit preparation.

Making the MSP Relationship Work

If you decide to work with an MSP for detection, here are some tips to make the relationship successful:

Treat them as partners, not vendors
> The most successful MSP relationships are true partnerships. Include your MSP in security planning discussions, share your business objectives, and treat them as an extension of your team rather than an external service provider.

Assign a clear internal owner
> Even with an MSP handling detection, you need an internal owner who understands what the MSP is doing and can act as a bridge between the MSP and your organization. This person doesn't need to be a security expert, but they do need to understand your business context and security goals.

Establish clear SLAs and expectations
> Document your expectations for detection and response in clear service level agreements (SLAs). What types of threats should they detect? How quickly should they respond to different types of alerts? What actions are they authorized to take without approval?

Conduct regular reviews
> Schedule regular service reviews to assess the MSP's performance against SLAs, discuss recent incidents, identify improvement opportunities, and adjust priorities based on evolving threats and business needs.

Test the relationship

Don't wait for a real incident to discover gaps in your MSP relationship. Conduct TTXs and simulated incidents to test communication flows, decision-making processes, and response actions. Also, integrate your MSP into your IRP, making sure they understand their roles and responsibilities during an incident.

Share context

Help your MSP understand your business context, critical assets, and unique risks. The more context they have, the more effective their detection will be. This isn't a one-time thing; keep them updated as your business evolves.

For many organizations, the question isn't whether they can afford managed detection services—it's whether they can afford not to have them. The combination of skilled staff shortages, escalating threats, and the potentially catastrophic costs of a successful attack makes a compelling case for leveraging MSPs to enhance your detection capabilities.

Just don't make the mistake of thinking you can completely outsource responsibility for security. The most successful approach is a partnership where you maintain oversight and strategic direction while leveraging the MSP's specialized expertise, technology, and 24/7 capabilities to execute effectively on your security strategy.

The Future of Detection

Let's finish our examination of detection tools by looking ahead at where the field is heading. Detection technologies are rapidly evolving, driven by both advancing threats and emerging technologies. Here are some key trends:

AI and ML maturity

Early ML-based detection often suffered from high false positive rates due to limited training data and lack of contextual awareness. Newer systems use more sophisticated models that can identify subtle patterns with less training data and fewer false positives. Be aware, however, of AI whitewashing. Not every vendor that puts the word AI on their literature is actually using AI.

Behavioral detection dominance

Signature-based detection is increasingly supplementary rather than primary. Modern detection systems focus on identifying abnormal behaviors rather than matching known patterns.

Identity-centric detection

As traditional boundaries fade in cloud and hybrid environments, identity has become the new security frontier. Detection systems are increasingly focusing on user and entity behavior analytics (UEBA) to identify compromised accounts and insider threats.

Cloud-native detection

Cloud environments require different detection approaches than on-premises infrastructure. Cloud-native detection tools should understand cloud architectures, APIs, and service interactions.

Supply chain focus

After high-profile supply chain attacks like SolarWinds, detection tools are evolving to better monitor vendor access, code integrity, and update processes.

Detection engineering as a discipline

Organizations are developing dedicated detection engineering teams that specialize in creating, testing, and refining detection rules and algorithms.

Collaborative detection

Industry information sharing and collective defense models are gaining traction, allowing organizations to benefit from each other's detection insights while maintaining privacy.

Deception technology integration

Honeypots, honeytokens, and other deception techniques are being integrated into mainstream detection platforms to identify attackers early in their reconnaissance phase.

These trends are creating a future where detection is more proactive, more accurate, and more tightly integrated with automated response capabilities. The distinction between detection and response will continue to fade as systems become capable of not just identifying threats but containing them without human intervention.

Detection tools are your early warning system in a world where breaches are a matter of "when," not "if." Without them, you're flying blind, and the first indication you'll have of an attack might be when your CEO is calling you at 3 a.m. asking why all the company data is encrypted.

Start with the basics: proper logging, backup system monitoring, and alerts for unusual behavior. Then layer on more sophisticated tools like SIEM and XDR as your security maturity grows.

Remember that no detection system is perfect. They all require tuning, maintenance, and skilled personnel to interpret their findings. But they're a heck of a lot better than the alternative—finding out you've been breached when it's too late to do anything about it.

We've spent decades helping companies recover from disasters, both natural and man-made. And we can tell you this with absolute certainty: detecting an attack early can mean the difference between a minor inconvenience and a company-ending catastrophe.

Summary

Detection systems are your early warning system in a world where the average breach goes undetected for over six months and costs exceed $4 million. Without proper detection, the first sign of trouble is often a ransom demand—after attackers have spent months mapping your network, stealing your data, and sabotaging your backups.

Effective detection requires four foundational elements: comprehensive coverage across all IT domains (not just the perimeter), real-time or near-real-time alerting capabilities, accuracy that minimizes false positives and alert fatigue, and resilience that prevents attackers from easily disabling your detection infrastructure.

XDR (extended detection and response) provides integrated threat detection across endpoints, networks, cloud workloads, and email. It excels at connecting the dots between isolated events to identify attack patterns and can trigger automated responses like endpoint isolation or process termination. XDR focuses on real-time threat hunting and automated response rather than long-term data retention.

SIEM (security information and event management) serves as your centralized log management and correlation platform. It collects logs from virtually everything in your environment, normalizes them for comparison, and applies rules to identify suspicious patterns. SIEMs excel at compliance reporting and forensic investigation with years of historical data retention but require significant tuning and skilled personnel to manage effectively.

These tools are complementary, not competing. SIEM provides the comprehensive log archive and compliance foundation; XDR delivers the real-time threat detection and automated response. They work best when integrated together, along with backup monitoring and comprehensive logging, to create a cohesive detection ecosystem.

Your backup systems serve double duty as both a last line of defense and early warning system. Ransomware frequently targets backups first, so monitoring for anomalies like sudden backup size increases, configuration changes, failed authentication attempts, or unexpected restore activities can alert you to attacks before encryption begins. Integrate backup alerts into your SIEM or XDR rather than keeping them isolated in the backup admin's inbox.

Logging is the foundation of both detection and forensic analysis. Store copies of logs outside your production environment using immutable storage where possible. Keep logs for at least a year, preferably longer for low-and-slow attacks. Regulatory requirements like HIPAA, PCI DSS, or SOX may mandate specific retention periods and storage technologies, effectively determining your log architecture, regardless of operational preferences.

Integration transforms individual detection tools into a cohesive defense system. This requires centralized visibility where all detection data flows to a single platform, normalized terminology across different tools, contextual enrichment that adds relevant information to each alert, automated response workflows that span multiple tools, and human integration that routes alerts to the right people with the right context and playbooks.

For organizations lacking internal expertise, managed security service providers offer 24/7 monitoring, threat intelligence, and specialized skills at significantly lower cost than building in-house capabilities. A regional bank calculated that in-house SOC coverage would cost $750,000 annually versus under $200,000 for comparable MSSP services. Just don't make the mistake of thinking you can completely outsource security responsibility—the most successful approach is a partnership where you maintain oversight while leveraging the MSSP's expertise and capabilities.

Start with comprehensive logging and backup monitoring, which provide immediate value with minimal complexity. Layer in SIEM for log correlation and compliance reporting, then add XDR for real-time threat detection and automated response as your security maturity grows. Test your detection capabilities regularly through simulated attacks to validate effectiveness before ransomware tests them for you.

The organizations that survive sophisticated ransomware attacks are those that detect threats within hours rather than months, respond automatically to contain damage before it spreads, and continuously adapt their detection capabilities to evolving threats. Detection tools aren't nice-to-have gadgets—they're the difference between a minor security incident and a company-ending catastrophe.

PART IV

Respond

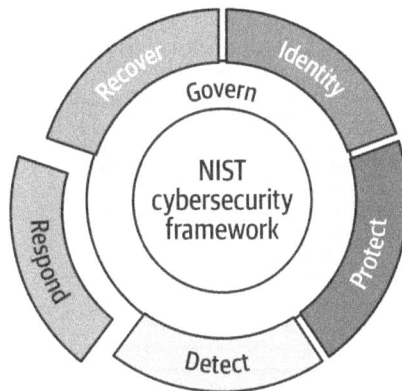

Fighting Through the Crisis When Ransomware Strikes

The NIST Cybersecurity Framework's *Respond* function is about taking action when a cybersecurity incident is detected. When ransomware breaches your perimeter, your ability to respond quickly and effectively determines whether you recover in days or struggle for months. This section walks you through the actual fight – hour by hour, decision by decision.

Chapter 9, "The First 12 Hours", throws you into the fog of war with ransomware actively spreading across your network. You'll navigate the impossible decisions about containment versus business continuity and ransom payment legality.

Chapter 10, "The Marathon", tackles the marathon phase after initial containment, balancing technical response with business operations. You'll learn degraded operations strategies, manage the human toll on your team, and handle the curveballs that no tabletop exercise prepared you for.

Chapter 11, "Analyzing the Breach", helps you methodically identify ransomware variants, map infection scope, and explore decryption options. You'll master essential analysis techniques from VirusTotal to sandboxing that work for organizations of any size.

Chapter 12, "Advanced Analysis and Forensics", covers specialist techniques for when basic analysis isn't enough—YARA rules, reverse engineering, memory forensics with Volatility, and comprehensive reporting that satisfies regulators and insurers.

Chapter 13, "Contain the Attack", guides you through building walls around the infection that it cannot breach, from network isolation to blocking C2 communications. You'll make critical decisions about forensics versus containment, then execute systematic isolation of every infected system.

Chapter 14, "Eradicate the Threat", ensures permanent removal of every ransomware trace through the clean-wipe-replace decision framework, hunting persistence mechanisms in boot sectors and firmware, and reinstalling from clean sources.

By the end of this Respond section, you'll have survived the worst days of your professional life with a systematic approach that stops the bleeding, preserves evidence, and permanently eliminates the threat without leaving backdoors for reinfection.

CHAPTER 9

The First 12 Hours

It's 8 a.m. on a Thursday, and your phone starts blowing up with calls from people: "All my files are locked! My computer is locked! And my files aren't working!" Moments later, a red skull flashes across your screen, demanding $500,000 in bitcoin. Your heart races, stomach sinks, eardrums begin pounding, the office erupts in chaos with employees panicking, and you're left wondering if your backups are safe. This is the gut-punch reality of a ransomware attack, a high-stakes marathon where every decision feels like it could save or sink the organization, and your job.

No playbook, not even the IRT framework you put together from Chapter 7, fully prepares you for the fog of war you've become immersed in. The miscommunications, ethical dilemmas, and surprises that test your fortitude and that neatly organized IRP. The plan where you prioritized critical systems, strategized on directions for isolating the infection, and communicated clearly. But in the heat of the attack, you're battling incomplete or outdated information, emotional overload, and a ticking clock. This chapter pushes you into the heart of a ransomware response, hour by hour, decision by decision, when you really feel the fog of war. Through real-world stories, practical lessons, and interactive exercises, you'll feel the chaos, learn to navigate tough calls, and discover how to keep you and your team afloat (Mike's PTSD got worked up just writing this intro).

Join with others dealing with the horrible problem of ransomware at *StopRansomware.com*, a companion site we developed with this book. We'd love to see you there!

This chapter focuses on surviving the immediate crisis while trying hard not to make things worse. The lessons taught are hard-won from guiding dozens of customers through real ransomware attacks and will prepare you for what comes next: the methodical work of analyzing what got you into this mess, which we'll tackle in Chapter 10.

Whether you're an IT professional rebuilding ransomware-encrypted servers, a CEO facing shareholder pressure, or a small business owner scrambling to save your livelihood, this is what it's like to fight ransomware in the trenches. We'll walk through the initial shock, the pressure-cooker decisions, the human toll, and the unexpected curveballs that no tabletop exercise can fully simulate. By the end, you'll have a survival guide to weather the storm and a few exercises to prepare your team for battle.

Throughout the rest of the book, we follow several organizations through their ransomware crises. Table 9-2 is a quick reference to details like ransomware variants, systems affected, and ransom amounts.

The Initial Shock: First Hours of the Attack

This chapter contains a play-by-play of one of the worst mornings of many people's lives, and Figure 9-1 is a timeline of the key events that are about to unfold.

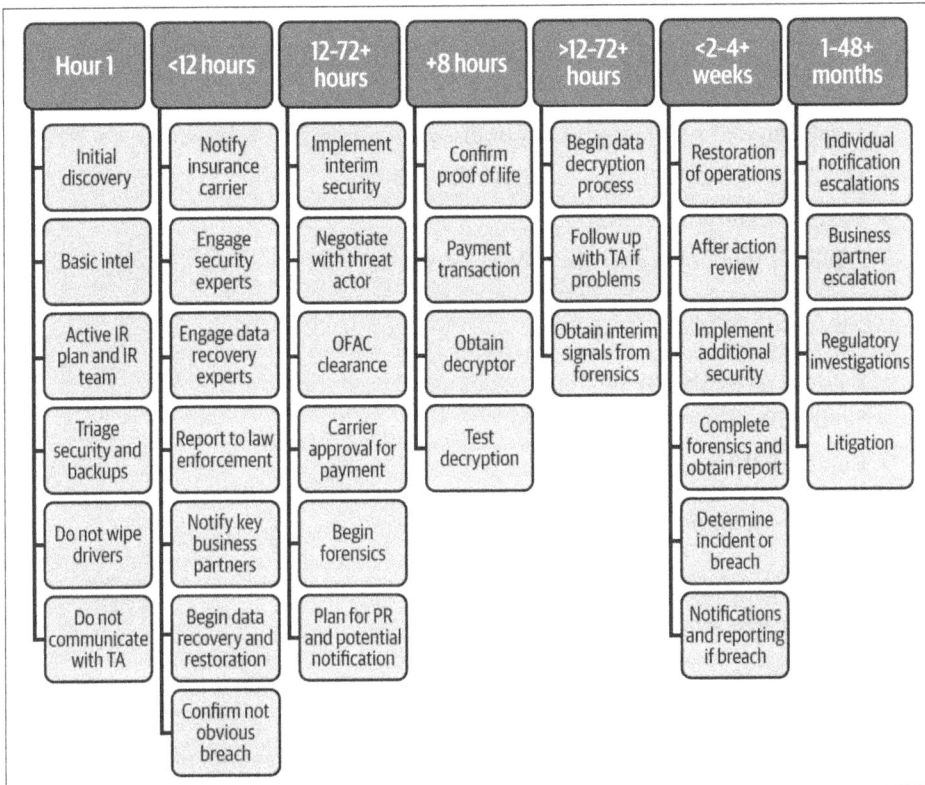

Figure 9-1. Ransomware timeline of key events (Tuma, 2024)

Crisis Response Quick Reference: First 60 Minutes

When your phone explodes with "my files are locked" calls, time is of the essence. This checklist covers the critical first hour. Follow it in order, then dig into the detailed guidance in the rest of the book:

Immediate (0–5 min):

- Breathe for 30 seconds.
- Activate IRT/designate incident leader.
- Start incident log (document everything).

Assess (5–15 min):

- Confirm ransomware (check for *.lock* files, ransom notes, EDR alerts).
- Identify which systems are hit.

- CHECK BACKUPS: are they accessible?

Contain (15–30 min):

- Isolate infected systems by VLAN or disconnect them.
- Disable nonessential remote access (VPN, RDP).
- Secure backups from infection.
- DO NOT shut down systems (preserve evidence?).

Get help (30–45 min):

- Call pre-vetted IR vendor.
- Notify CEO, legal, cyber insurance.
- Contact FBI/law enforcement.

Organize (45–60 min):

- Set up IRT communication channel.
- Schedule first status meeting.
- Cross-reference variant at NoMoreRansom.org.

Discovery and Panic

Thursday morning's attack hits like a lightning bolt, breaking the subtle white noise of people working on their computers and talking. For Sarah, the IT manager at a midsized retail company (which we'll call "ZapMart"), it began with a frantic call from the accounting department: "My spreadsheets are gone, and there's a weird file on my desktop that says '.*lock*.'" The EDR system, a cornerstone of the proactive defenses you built from Chapter 8, lights up with alerts. They include unauthorized processes spawning, files encrypting, and a ransom note from a ransomware gang demanding $500,000 in bitcoin within 72 hours. Sarah's first thought? *This can't be real. Not now.*

Panic spreads like wildfire throughout the office. Employees flood the helpdesk with calls for help, some confessing to clicking a suspicious email, others demanding to know why their files won't open. ZapMart's point-of-sale (POS) system, critical for processing millions in holiday sales, is down, and customers are lining up at registers, frustrated.

If you're unprepared, like the engineering firm we discussed in Chapter 1, to which we gave the fictional name of "Northforge," and where Lorenz Group locked 80% of their systems in a targeted attack, the instinct is to freeze. Disbelief turns to dread as you realize the scope of the incident. Customer databases, inventory systems, and payroll servers are encrypted and unavailable. Sarah's team at ZapMart, trained with war games from Chapter 7, knew to escalate to the IRT, but the sheer volume of alerts, currently including hundreds of endpoints reporting infections, create information and alert overload.

The chaos from this incident isn't just technical; it's human. ZapMart's email still works, so Sarah's inbox explodes with 50 unread messages, from the CFO demanding, "What's happening?" to a cashier asking, "Did I cause this?"

In Northforge's case from Chapter 1, the cybersecurity manager described a "sinking feeling" as executives gathered on a Teams call, their faces pale, realizing Lorenz Group's $10M ransom demand was no bluff. For small businesses without an IRT, the panic is even more paralyzing. Imagine being a small business owner staring at a ransom note, unsure who to call.

Case Study: 2024 Hospital Ransomware Crisis

In February 2024, a Midwest hospital chain (*https://oreil.ly/glQh9*) (Change Healthcare, a subsidiary of UnitedHealth Group) was crippled by ALPHV/BlackCat ransomware (*https://oreil.ly/aIjQg*), a sophisticated strain known for double extortion. Nurses discovered patient records were encrypted, and critical ventilators displayed error codes, threatening lives. The IT team, gutted by recent budget cuts, faced a deluge of panicked calls from doctors, administrators, and even patients' families. The CEO shared their despair online: "We thought we were ready, but the chaos was overwhelming." This mirrors Northforge's "hopeless" Teams call, where executives grappled with the loss of their proprietary data repository. Change Healthcare's understaffed response underscores the stakes for critical infrastructure, where delays can be deadly.

Survival tip

Activate your triage steps immediately. If you haven't already done so, designate your IRT's incident leader, your crisis quarterback, to centralize communication, coordination, and avoid duplicating efforts. Pull your asset inventory to identify critical systems, like POS or patient records, and prioritize their protection and appropriate prioritization. Take a deep breath, even for 30 seconds, because panic clouds judgment and leads to rash decisions. If you're a small business with no IRT, call your pre-vetted IR vendor or a local cybersecurity consultant now. *Don't try to go it alone.*

Exercise: Feel the chaos

Put yourself in Sarah's shoes. ZapMart's POS system is down, customers are angry, and your phone repeatedly dings with over 20 unread text messages from staff. Write down your first three actions (e.g., check EDR alerts, call IRT lead, notify CEO, take an antacid, update resume). Compare them to the checklist in "Crisis Response Quick Reference: First 60 Minutes" on page 267 (e.g., confirm attack, assess scope, activate IRT). What did you miss? Reflect on how panic influenced your choices and how you'd adjust under pressure.

Scrambling to Assess

The first few hours (1–6) are a desperate race to size up the attack, like triaging a patient in the emergency room. Sarah's team at Zapmart needed answers fast: Which systems were hit? Is the ransomware actively spreading? Is it a known variant with an available decryptor? Their EDR system flagged *.lock* file extensions, anomalous network traffic to lockbit.ru, and ransom notes in every department's shared drives. But this ransomware gang was cunning and disabled logging on most of the servers, creating blind spots that left ZapMart guessing. In Northforge's case from Chapter 1, the team didn't realize their proprietary data repository, a $7M intellectual property asset, was encrypted until six hours into the response, a devastating oversight that fueled their $10M ransom dilemma.

Assessing the situation is a battle against time and uncertainty. Sarah checked for indicators that would help determine what happened, including the *.lock* file extension appended to documents, ransom notes in Notepad files demanding bitcoin, and a *.onion* link for the gang's "customer support." They cross-referenced what they learned with the website NoMoreRansom.org, a free resource recommended in Chapter 7, and it confirms they are dealing with LockBit. Adding insult to injury, Sarah's network map and inventory, last updated six months ago, were useless for tracing the infection's spread across the environment. Change Healthcare faced similar hurdles. ALPHV's polymorphic code, described in "Polymorphism" on page 12, evaded signature-based detection, and its legacy systems lacked EDR coverage, forcing each system to be manually checked. For small businesses, the challenge can be even more difficult due to limited tools, a lack of dedicated cyber staff, and a ticking ransom deadline. Consider the following story of Maria, *who has no IT staff at all.*

Case Study: 2025 Small Business Nightmare

In March 2025, Maria's family-owned bakery in Seattle was hit by LockBit 3.0, a prolific RaaS strain. Maria discovered that their bakery's POS and inventory systems were encrypted when her cashier couldn't process orders, followed by a ransom note demanding $50,000. With no IT staff, she called her college-attending, tech-savvy nephew, who we will call "Keith," who struggled to identify the attack's scope using a free antivirus tool.

"I didn't even know what 'ransomware' meant," Maria told a local blog. Unlike Northforge's dedicated cyber team, Maria's lack of resources left her vulnerable, highlighting

---

the gap that Chapter 7's cyber hygiene training aims to close. Keith's attempt to find any event or log details to determine what happened to the POS system came up empty because the systems were not configured to capture events; it was a black box and a dead end. Maria also did not have cyber insurance to cover the revenue loss to her business or the expenses related to getting her systems back online.

Real-world hurdles pile up during an incident assessment, including outdated documentation, gaps in skills, tools, or resources, or an overwhelmed staff. Sarah's IRT team at ZapMart, despite having a good EDR, lost visibility when the ransomware gang deleted their system logs. (This is why we recommend offsite, immutable copies of such things.) Change Healthcare's understaffed IT team relied on manual folder checks, delaying their impact analysis by at least 12 hours. Keith, working alone, couldn't distinguish ransomware from a virus. The ransom note's daunting countdown (72 hours for Sarah at ZapMart, 48 hours for Change Healthcare, 96 hours for Maria) adds emotional stress similar to a bomb timer from a movie. If you're lucky, you spot indicators like the indicative C2 traffic. If not, you're flying blind, praying your backups are still safe.

Survival tip

Use the following Ransomware Symptoms Checklist to guide the incident assessment:

- Scan for ransomware file extensions (e.g., *.lock* or *.encrypted*).
- Check for C2 traffic in firewall logs.
- Review EDR alerts for unauthorized processes and other anomalous events.
- Cross-reference with NoMoreRansom.org or CISA's StopRansomware.gov[1] for known decryptors.
- Call your pre-vetted IR vendor—that is the whole point of having them on retainer.
- Document all findings in a shared incident log to avoid repeating work.
- If you're a small business like Maria's, lean on free tools like Malwarebytes, decryptor databases, or CISA's free Cyber Hygiene Services.

Speed is critical, but accuracy saves you from the bigger headaches later.

Use the decision tree in Figure 9-2 as a guide to your first-hour assessment, prioritizing actions to confirm the attack and assess its scope. Personalize it to your environment. It builds on Chapter 7's triage steps and Chapter 8's monitoring tools, helping you stay focused under pressure.

---

1 This is distinct from the companion site for this book, which is *StopRansomware.com*.

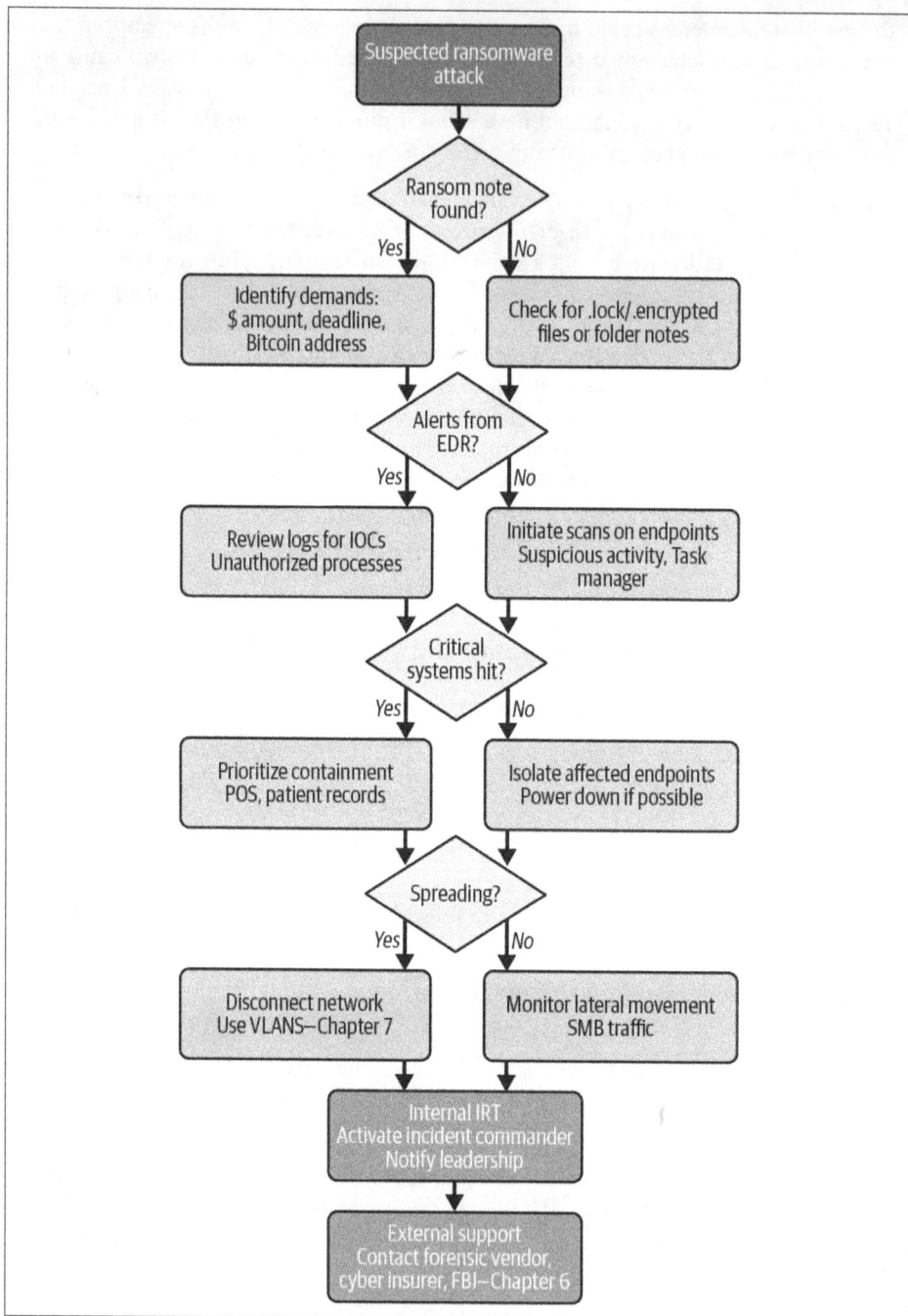

Figure 9-2. Ransomware detection decision tree

Exercise: Apply the decision tree

Apply this decision tree to Maria's bakery scenario. Which path do you take? If you find *.lock* files after 30 minutes, what's your next step? Write a 50-word action plan, referencing the tree's steps (e.g., "Check for *.lock* files, isolate POS"). Reflect on how the decision tree keeps you focused.

You've confirmed the attack and sized up the damage. Your EDR is lighting up, your backups are questionable, and your CEO is demanding answers. Now comes the hardest part: making decisions that could save your organization or sink it. You're about to face three impossible choices with incomplete information, conflicting pressures from every direction, and a countdown timer that won't stop. There's no perfect answer, no time to deliberate, and no room for error. Welcome to decision-making under fire.

Decision-Making Under Pressure

With the attack assessed, you now face the impossible choices that define whether your organization survives intact. These decisions hit fast (within hours of discovery) and each carries massive consequences. Should you shut down everything or isolate selectively? Do you pay the ransom or refuse? Who has authority when stakeholders are fighting? You're making these calls with incomplete information, conflicting pressures, and a ticking clock. There's no time to deliberate and no perfect answer.

Containment Dilemmas

With the attack confirmed, you face your first gut-wrenching decision: containment. Should you pull the plug on the entire network, taking a chance that it will stop the ransomware's spread while bringing the business to a halt? Or isolate systems incrementally, risking further infection if you miss a compromised endpoint? Sarah, ZapMart's IT manager, hesitated. Shutting down the POS system during peak holiday sales could cost the company $2 million a day, with angry customers flooding social media with complaints. But waiting too long can be bad as well, as Northforge from Chapter 1 found out, as it allowed Lorenz Group to encrypt their backups, forcing a $10M ransom demand they couldn't ignore.

The stakes vary by industry, but the pressure is universal. Change Healthcare faced an impossible choice: disconnect the network, potentially disrupting life-saving equipment and risking patient lives, or contain selectively, hoping to save critical systems. They chose selective isolation, but unsegmented legacy systems let the ransomware spread to billing and scheduling, costing 48 hours of recovery time. Maria's bakery had no network to disconnect. Her POS was a standalone system, and unplugging it meant turning away customers, a difficult choice for a small business already struggling.

Every containment decision balances speed, damage control, and business impact. Sarah's team at ZapMart opted to isolate POS servers using VLANs, a strategy from Chapter 7's network segmentation playbook, but a misconfigured firewall that was overlooked during a recent upgrade let the ransomware gang jump to HR systems. Their EDR system provided visibility for only 60% of endpoints, making every choice a gamble. Was the infection confined to accounting, or had it reached the cloud? Should they disable internet access entirely, risking supply chain coordination? For Change Healthcare, the question was even graver: could they isolate without shutting down life-support systems? Keith, lacking tools, powered off the POS. But without logs, he couldn't confirm if the ransomware had spread to Maria's laptop.

Case Study: Change Healthcare's Containment Failure

The attack on Change Healthcare illustrates containment's high stakes. CISA's post-incident report for the event (*https://oreil.ly/4djQa*) (Oasis Security, 2024) noted that unsegmented legacy systems, missed during a cost-cutting IT overhaul, allowed the ransomware to spread unchecked for 12 hours.

The IT team's decision to avoid a complete network shutdown, fearing patient harm, backfired when billing systems became infected, delaying care coordination. This echoes Chapter 5's network segmentation advice that VLANs and zero-trust architecture could have contained the attack faster, as they did for Sarah's POS environment at ZapMart (until the firewall failed). Change Healthcare's delay mirrors what happened at Northforge (when their backups were encrypted), where hesitation cost millions.

Containment dilemmas multiply across contexts. A manufacturing firm might hesitate to halt production lines, risking thousands in delayed orders. A school might avoid disabling Wi-Fi during exams, letting the ransomware spread to administrative servers. A wrong move could tank your business, or worse, endanger lives. And you're making these calls with incomplete data, as attackers like ALPHAV or LockBit disable monitoring tools to keep you in the dark.

Survival tip

Use the containment and isolation techniques discussed in Chapter 5 to guide you. Here's a summary of the list for your reference:

Isolate affected systems by VLAN
Segment infected devices from the rest of the network.

Secure your backups
Ensure backup systems are protected and inaccessible to attackers.

Block C2 IP addresses at the firewall
Prevent malware from communicating with the attacker.

Disable all nonessential remote access
> Shut down VPN, RDP, and other remote entry points that are not absolutely required.

Force all users to reauthenticate with MFA
> Invalidate existing sessions and require fresh multifactor authentication.

Disable compromised user accounts
> Immediately deactivate any accounts suspected of being breached to halt lateral movement.

Prioritize critical systems using "Know Your Environment" on page 87: POS for retailers, hospital patient records, factory production lines, etc. Accept that some downtime is inevitable; the cost of containment is lower than that of a full breach. Document every step in your incident log for post-incident review, as regulators and insurers will scrutinize your decisions. If you're a small business like Maria's bakery, focus on physical isolation (e.g., unplug devices) and call a vendor for IR and forensic support.

Exercise: Make the containment call

Imagine you're the incident response lead at a manufacturing factory. The production line is infected and stopping it delays $500K in orders. Selective isolation risks a spread to cloud backups. List the pros and cons of a full network shutdown or selective isolation of the production line. Choose one option and justify it in a writing exercise, referencing Chapter 5's containment steps (e.g., "Isolate by VLAN"). Reflect on how incomplete data (e.g., 60% EDR coverage) influences your choice.

The Ransom Dilemma: Legal Landmines and Empty Promises

Before considering any ransom payment, organizations must first determine whether such payments are even legal in their jurisdiction, as the penalties for violating these laws can be severe. Paying a ransom isn't just a financial choice; it's a legal tightrope that can haunt you long after the incident.

Many ransomware groups are designated as sanctioned entities, making payments to them illegal. In the United States, the Office of Foreign Assets Control (OFAC) designates which ransomware groups are sanctioned (*https://oreil.ly/fnC3J*), with penalties including fines up to $20 million or jail time for executives. OFAC sanctions explicitly prohibit payments to designated groups like ALPHV and LockBit. Organizations can be held liable even if they didn't know they were transacting with prohibited entities, as OFAC regulations operate on strict liability. The FBI's 2023 Internet Crime Report noted 2,825 ransomware cases, with 15% facing OFAC scrutiny post-payment.

In the UK, the Office of Financial Sanctions Implementation (OFSI) has similar sanctions and can impose penalties of up to £1 million per breach, even when the paying party was unaware of where the funds ended up. Since June 2022, this has been a strict liability offense, meaning OFSI can impose civil monetary penalties regardless of the payer's actual knowledge. Paying ransoms to sanctioned entities in the UK is a serious criminal offense and can carry a custodial sentence of up to seven years in prison and/or monetary penalties.

Australia takes an equally harsh stance, where making ransomware payments to sanctioned entities can result in up to 10 years in prison and substantial fines. The Minister for Foreign Affairs has the authority to designate sanctioned entities in Australia.

The legal landscape extends beyond sanctions violations. GDPR and US state laws, like California's CCPA, mandate breach notifications within 72 hours if data is leaked, with additional fines for delayed reporting. Cyber insurers add another layer of complexity: in 2024, a manufacturing company lost a $1 million insurance claim after paying the ransom without insurer approval, because their policy required pre-negotiation consent.

Several US states have gone further than federal sanctions, with North Carolina and Florida prohibiting certain state agencies from paying ransoms entirely. Other states like Pennsylvania, New York, Texas, Arizona, and New Jersey are considering similar legislation. The UK also is currently consulting on proposals to ban ransom payments by public sector bodies and critical infrastructure operators.

The legal landscape is rapidly evolving internationally, with 40 countries committing to never pay ransoms to ransomware gangs as part of the International Counter Ransomware Initiative. Even in jurisdictions where ransom payments aren't explicitly banned, significant legal risks remain. Both the EU and US prohibit making funds available to sanctioned individuals or entities.

Hiring a ransom negotiator, who can cut demands by 30%–50%, is an option, but it prolongs the crisis and risks scams from fake negotiators that are more common than you'd think on dark web forums. This is another decision that should be made beforehand; identify and secure a negotiator before you need one.

Legal counsel must be involved in every step. Organizations should consult with legal counsel familiar with their specific jurisdiction's laws, sanctions regimes, and anti-terrorism financing regulations before considering any payment, as the legal consequences of violation can far exceed the cost of the ransom itself. Be aware, however, that their advice often lags. This can often leave organizations under a ransom deadline to make critical decisions without complete legal guidance.

The boardroom debate

The ransom note will demand a huge amount of money in bitcoin within 72 hours: "Pay, or your data hits the dark web." This decision is a minefield, loaded with technical, financial, and ethical traps. Paying might seem like the fastest way to get the company back on its feet, but it's a gamble with poor odds: 8% of payers never receive decryption keys, and 80% are retargeted by the same or other gangs within six months. Refusing to pay risks permanent data loss, especially if backups are compromised, as they were for Northforge's $7 million proprietary engineering repository. Worse, it's double extortion, where attackers leak stolen data and add public humiliation and regulatory scrutiny to the equation.

The pressure was unbearable for Sarah, the IT manager at ZapMart. The ransomware gang's note threatened to leak customer credit card data to the internet if they didn't pay, which could trigger lawsuits and tank the company's stock. Pacing the board-room, her CEO argued, "Paying is cheaper than losing our customers." Legal counsel pushed back, warning that the gang might be on the OFAC sanctions list (or a similar list in your country), making payment a federal crime. The FBI was contacted and they urged against paying the ransom, citing no guarantee that decryption would work, in addition to possibly funding terrorism. Sarah's team at ZapMart confirmed that 50% of backups were intact, but restoring them would take 48 hours, time they didn't have with a 72-hour ransom deadline. Emotions will run high, including fear of losing your job, the financial impact of downtime, and a developing anger towards the attackers.

Change Healthcare faced a similar dilemma. With patient records encrypted and ventilators at risk, the board debated paying $1M to avoid fatalities. Their legal team flagged the 72-hour breach notification requirement for incidents where data was leaked. Regulatory fines could reach $20M. Change Healthcare's cyber insurer warned that paying without approval could void their $5M policy. In Maria's bakery, the $50,000 demand was a personal gut punch that caused her to dip into her personal savings or take out a loan, risking her family's financial security

Case Study: 2025 Cl0p/MOVEit Attack on Zellis's Customers

In May 2023, the Cl0p ransomware gang (*https://oreil.ly/6a5gF*) exploited a zero-day vulnerability (CVE-2023-34362 (*https://oreil.ly/UBsY_*)) in Progress Software's MOVEit Transfer managed file transfer application. Unlike traditional ransomware attacks, Cl0p focused solely on mass data theft (extortion) by exploiting the software's use across thousands of organizations worldwide.

One of the most notable victims was Zellis, a major UK-based payroll and HR software provider that used MOVEit to transfer client data. The compromise of a single third-party vendor immediately compromised the data of several massive, unrelated companies (*https://oreil.ly/AJUnS*):

Victims
> Zellis customers affected by the breach included British Airways (BA), the BBC, and the pharmacy chain Boots (*https://oreil.ly/zvcty*).

The threat

Cl0p did not encrypt files. Instead, they stole personal and payroll data and used their data leak site, "CL0P^_-LEAKS," to issue an ultimatum (*https://oreil.ly/cqcCM*): pay a ransom by a specific deadline or have the data publicly released.

Data compromised

The exposed data was highly sensitive, including employee names, addresses, dates of birth, and National Insurance numbers (*https://oreil.ly/zvcty*) (the UK equivalent of a US Social Security number).

The breach underscored the immediate and severe consequences of a supply-chain attack:

Regulatory scrutiny and fines

The exposure of vast amounts of UK citizen data triggered immediate investigation and potential punitive action by the UK Information Commissioner's Office (ICO), the primary regulator for GDPR compliance. GDPR fines can reach up to 4% of a company's global annual turnover (similar to revenue). British Airways, having faced a £20 million fine from the ICO after a 2018 data breach, was put under renewed pressure. The ICO also released a joint statement with the NCSC (*https://oreil.ly/9OCIT*) warning organizations against paying the ransom, stating that it is "a myth that paying the ransom makes the incident go away."

The inevitable leak

While Cl0p had historically claimed they would delete data upon payment, there was no way to verify this. Furthermore, even if a company like Zellis negotiated and paid, there was no guarantee that the criminals had not already sold the data to other groups. Cl0p's leak site confirmed the massive data theft, and for many affected companies, the information was publicly listed, forcing them into costly damage control, credit monitoring for millions of employees, and legal action (*https://oreil.ly/pIsTu*).

Echoing failure

The entire episode highlights the modern ransomware reality: paying a ransom to a financially motivated, often OFAC-sanctioned group like Cl0p (or its associated entities) does not guarantee data deletion and exposes the payer to potential regulatory penalties for transacting with sanctioned entities, in addition to the initial recovery and litigation costs.

Survival tip

Treat the ransom payment decision as a last resort, not a default. First, verify the status of your backups and test restores to confirm they're good. Consult your legal counsel and cyber insurer immediately to assess your options and policy terms. If you must negotiate, use a pre-vetted specialist (discussed in "Assembling Your Incident

Response Team" on page 198), often provided by the insurance carrier; they are trained to spot scams and haggle effectively.

Contact the FBI, US Secret Service, and/or CISA if you're in the US, or the appropriate law enforcement entities in your jurisdiction for guidance, but don't expect they have all the answers or access to the most recent decryptors. Assume any leaked data is gone forever and know that attackers rarely delete it, despite their promises.

Promptly notify regulators (e.g., 72 hours) to avoid fines. Document every decision for legal and insurance purposes. If you're a small business like Maria's, lean on free resources like CISA's StopRansomware.gov for tips and guidance.

Exercise: Payment dilemma

You're the CEO of a small business. Your backups are corrupted, and the ransom is $100,000. Your legal counsel warns you that the ransom gang is on the OFAC sanctions list, but your board demands that you make the payment to avoid them leaking company data. List three factors to consider (e.g., backup status, legal risks, retargeting odds). Role-play a phone call with the FBI: what do you say to seek guidance? Compare your approach to Chapter 7's payment considerations (e.g., "Verify backups first"). Reflect on how emotions (e.g., fear of leaks) sway your decision. (Estimated time: 10 minutes)

Stakeholder Conflicts

A ransomware response exposes fault lines across your organization, turning allies into obstacles. ZapMart's IT team pushed Sarah to rebuild from backups, arguing it was safer than paying the ransom. However, legal counsel argued that rebuilding from backups risked missing the regulatory-required 72-hour notification deadline if data was leaked, potentially costing the company $20M. The marketing team, desperate to control the narrative, drafted a social media post claiming "minimal impact," which Sarah vetoed because it wasn't accurate. The CEO, caught between factions, wavered and caused a slowdown in decision-making. (Executives often don't understand their roles during tabletops, so it's essential to focus on this during prep.)

In the 2024 Change Healthcare case, nurses clashed with IT, accusing techs of incompetence, especially when delays disrupted patient care. You can see example Reddit posts (*https://oreil.ly/hM5CS*) in Figures 9-3 and 9-4.

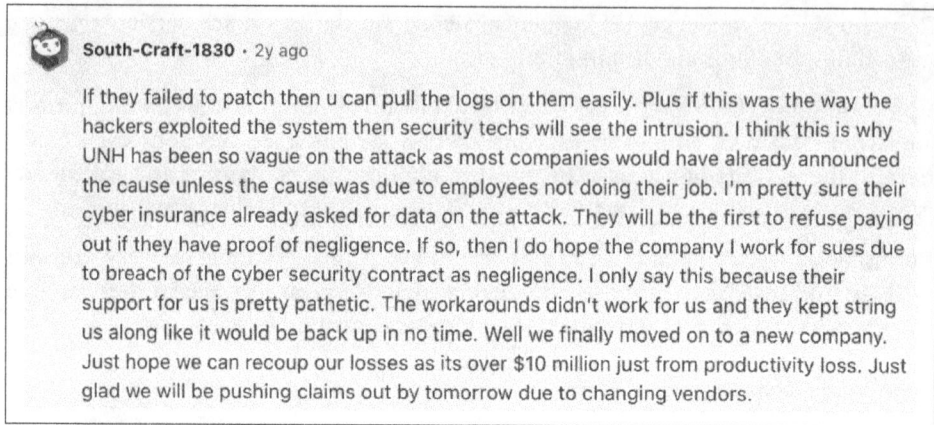

Figure 9-3. Change Healthcare customer complaining on Reddit

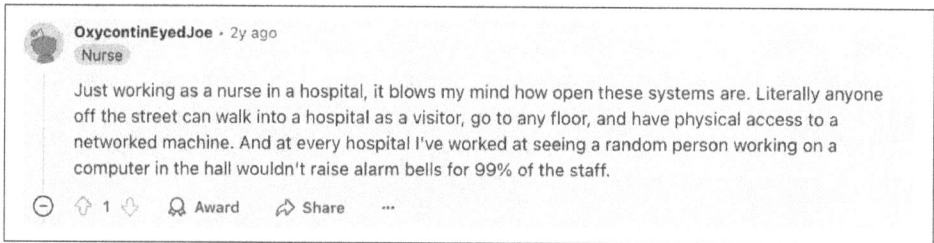

Figure 9-4. Nurses theorize on Reddit why Change Healthcare happened

Small businesses face unique situations, politics, and conflicts, often targeting individuals personally. At Maria's bakery, her family argued over whether or not to pay the $50,000 ransom. Her brother insisted on using personal savings, while her sister wanted to rebuild everything, fearing that they would be retargeted. Maria lost hours of possible recovery time to these debates, delaying containment of the malware. Customers added pressure, posting on social media: "Maria's bakery lost my order: hacked and hopeless!" Northforge's executives faced a similar conflict: the CFO demanded the ransom payment be made, IT pushed back with confidence for recovery, and the legal team warned of OFAC sanctions, leaving the CEO paralyzed on their "hopeless" conference calls.

These conflicts snowball without clear leadership and lines of authority and responsibility. ZapMart's CEO micromanaged the situation and second-guessed IT's containment plan. Change Healthcare's board demanded daily press conferences, diverting IT's focus from recovery. Maria's family debates turned emotional, with shouting amongst family members. Stakeholder misalignment isn't just annoying, it derails the response, prolonging downtime and amplifying damage.

Survival tip

The RACI matrix you learned about in Chapter 7 will help to clarify roles here: IT handles containment, legal manages compliance, and PR controls external messaging, for example. Set expectations for updates so stakeholders know when they will hear how things are going. Hold brief IRT meetings every 2 hours to align stakeholders. These can be 15 minutes or less and structured (e.g., status, blockers, decisions). Designate one external spokesperson, ideally from PR or leadership, that uses pre-approved templates (developed from guidance in Chapter 7) to avoid mixed signals or having to create them under pressure. For small businesses, you should assign roles even among family or limited staff (e.g., Maria handles customers and Keith manages the tech). Keep meetings short and focused to maintain momentum and brevity.

Exercise: Manage the chaos

You're Sarah's incident response lead at ZapMart. Draft a social media and PR response that lets people know what's going on, and what you are doing to contain things. Draft an internal memo to convey IT's need for more staff and resources to speed containment. Draft an internal memo that aligns teams with clearly assigned roles (e.g., "IT: containment, PR: messaging"). Compare your memo to the RACI matrix you created in Chapter 7: did you cover all stakeholders? Reflect on how you'd enforce the memo under pressure.

You Survived

You've survived the first terrible hours. The containment decisions are made, the ransom question is addressed, and your stakeholders know their roles. Your EDR is blocking the spread, your incident log is filled with entries, and law enforcement is engaged.

But take a breath, because what you've done so far is only the beginning. The immediate crisis is contained, but ransomware attacks aren't sprints. They're marathons. Your real challenge now isn't making split-second decisions under panic. It's sustaining operations, maintaining morale, and dealing with the endless curveballs that no tabletop exercise prepared you for.

The fog of war doesn't clear after six hours. It settles in for days, sometimes weeks. Welcome to the sustained battle.

Practical Exercises Summary

Table 9-1 summarizes the practice exercises in this chapter, so you can use it for tabletops and similar exercises. Each exercise builds specific skills your team will need during a real ransomware crisis.

Table 9-1. Exercises summary

Exercise name	Section	What you'll practice	Time
Feel the Chaos	Discovery and Panic	Making initial triage decisions under pressure; comparing your instincts to formal checklists	5 min
Apply the Decision Tree	Scrambling to Assess	Following systematic assessment procedures; using decision trees to stay focused during chaos	5 min
Make the Containment Call	Containment Dilemmas	Evaluating containment trade-offs; justifying decisions with incomplete data	10 min
Payment Dilemma	The Ransom Dilemma	Weighing legal, financial, and ethical factors in ransom decisions; role-playing FBI consultation	10 min
Manage the Chaos	Stakeholder Conflicts	Creating clear role assignments; drafting communication to align conflicting stakeholders	10 min

Case Study Review

We're using a lot of case studies in this chapter and the ones to come. Some are public stories that you can follow links to and learn more about; others are anonymized stories from my (Mike's) experiences in the field. A few are amalgams of multiple events. It's not important which is which; just focus on what you can learn from them.

Because it may be difficult to keep the details of these stories straight, we've put a table here to do just that. Table 9-2 lists all of the relevant details of these attacks. (Pseudonyms are shown with an asterisk.)

Table 9-2. Case study summary

Company name	Industry	Location	Ransomware variant	Ransom	Key systems affected	Data exfiltration	Key personnel
ZapMart*	Retail	US	LockBit 3.0	$500,000	POS, HR, Inventory	Credit card data	Sarah (IT Manager), CEO, CFO
Northforge*	Engineering	US	Lorenz	$10,000,000	Proprietary repository, 80% of systems	Unknown	Cybersecurity manager (resigned mid-crisis)
Change Healthcare	Healthcare	Midwest US	ALPHV/ BlackCat	$1,000,000 (paid)	Patient records, ventilators, billing, scheduling	2TB of data	CEO, nurses, IT team
Maria's bakery	Food service	Seattle, WA	LockBit 3.0	$50,000	POS, inventory systems, cloud invoices	Unknown	Maria (owner), Keith (nephew/IT support)

Company name	Industry	Location	Ransomware variant	Ransom	Key systems affected	Data exfiltration	Key personnel
BuyMore*	Retail	US	Cl0p	$2,000,000	Inventory files, ERP systems	1TB via missed SaaS account	IRT
Zellis (MOVEit)	Payroll/HR SaaS	UK	Cl0p	Unknown	Payroll data for British Airways, BBC, Boots	Employee names, addresses, DOB, National Insurance numbers	Unknown
Everline*	Retail	UK	Cl0p	$1,500,000 (paid)	Inventory systems	Unknown	Unknown
Chicago school	Education	Chicago, IL	Ryuk	$200,000	Servers (80%), cloud backups	Student data leaked	IRT
Techforge*	Manufacturing	Texas	AI-driven RaaS (LockBit derivative)	$1,000,000	Servers (50%), SaaS account	Via compromised SaaS account	IRT
California manufacturer	Manufacturing	California	ALPHV/ BlackCat	Unknown	ERP servers	1TB via Azure blob storage	IRT
Seattle logistics firm	Logistics	Seattle, WA	Conti	$1,000,000	60% of servers, AWS S3 buckets	500GB leaked to dark web	IRT
Willoughby's*	Retail	UK	LockBit 3.0	$2,000,000 (negotiated to $1M, blocked by sanctions)	Customer data systems	Customer data leaked despite negotiation	Legal team, negotiator, IRT

Summary

This chapter walks you through the brutal first hours of a live ransomware attack, from the panicked phone calls at 8 a.m. to the pressure-cooker decisions that determine whether your organization survives. When your systems start locking up and the ransom notes appear, the fog of war descends fast, but the lessons in this chapter can guide you through those critical first 12 hours.

The initial response sets the tone for everything that follows. You need to immediately activate your IRT and designate an incident leader to centralize communication, because without clear command and control, even small teams fragment under pressure. Use your ransomware symptoms checklist to quickly scan for encrypted files, check C2 traffic in firewall logs, and review EDR alerts, but don't forget to take 30 seconds to breathe. Panic clouds judgment and leads to rash decisions that cost precious time. Most importantly, call your pre-vetted IR vendor now instead of trying to go it alone.

The critical decisions under pressure will test every plan you've made. Containment becomes a balancing act between speed and business impact, where you must prioritize critical systems using your asset inventory while accepting that some downtime is inevitable. The ransom payment decision is a legal minefield where only 8% of payers receive fully working decryptors, 80% are retargeted within six months, and paying sanctioned groups like ALPHV or LockBit can trigger federal crimes with penalties up to $20 million. Sanctions regimes vary by country: OFAC in the US, OFSI in the UK, Australia's Foreign Affairs designations—but the consequences of violation are universally severe.

When stakeholder conflicts inevitably emerge, lean on RACI matrices to clarify roles so IT handles containment, legal manages compliance, and PR controls messaging. Set expectations for updates so stakeholders know when they'll hear status. Hold brief IRT meetings every 2 hours to align teams, designate one external spokesperson to avoid mixed messages, and for small businesses, assign roles even among family or limited staff.

The cases throughout this chapter, including ZapMart's holiday sales crisis, Change Healthcare's life-threatening system failures, Maria's bakery struggling without IT staff, and Northforge's paralyzed leadership, demonstrate that preparation separates chaos from control. Organizations with tested IRPs, practiced teams, and clear decision frameworks contain attacks faster, make better decisions under pressure, and position themselves for successful recovery.

You've now survived the initial shock and made the impossible decisions about containment, ransom payment, and organizational authority. Your systems are isolated, your stakeholders are aligned, and your incident log is documenting everything for regulators and insurers. The immediate crisis is contained.

But the battle is far from over. What you've done so far addresses the first 12 hours, the sprint phase of panic and critical decisions. Now you face a different challenge entirely: the marathon of sustained operations, where you must keep your business running, your team functional, and your recovery on track while the technical fight continues for days or even weeks. That's where we're headed in Chapter 10: sustaining operations, managing the human toll, and building resilience while the technical fight continues.

CHAPTER 10

The Marathon

This chapter continues the ransomware crisis from Chapter 9, following Sarah at ZapMart, Maria's bakery, Change Healthcare, and Northforge through days of sustained operations. (If you need to reference the details of these organizations, see Table 9-2.)

It's 12 hours into the attack. You've survived the worst morning of your professional life. The containment call is made: systems isolated, backups secured, stakeholders aligned. The ransom decision is documented (probably "hell no," maybe "we're thinking about it," definitely "get legal on the phone"). Your IRT knows who's doing what. The EDR alerts have slowed from a screaming flood to a tense trickle. You can almost breathe again.

Almost.

Because here's what your IRP didn't prepare you for, what every TTX glossed over, what Sarah at ZapMart is about to discover the hard way: the crisis doesn't end when you make the big decisions. It's just getting started. The initial adrenaline spike that carried you through those first brutal hours is gone. It's replaced by a grinding, exhausting realization that you're not fighting a sprint anymore. You're fighting a marathon, and you're already tired.

Sarah's store managers are calling every 20 minutes: "When can we sell again?" Maria's watching customers walk past her locked bakery doors, heading to the place down the street. Change Healthcare's nurses are handwriting medication charts on clipboards they haven't touched in a decade, and somewhere, a patient is waiting for a prescription that's stuck in an encrypted database. Your CEO wants updates every two hours. Your CFO is calculating revenue losses per minute. Your communications team drafted three different press releases and can't decide which version makes you look least incompetent.

The ransomware isn't actively spreading anymore because you've contained it. But your business is bleeding out anyway because nobody taught you how to sell products without a POS system, how to treat patients without electronic records, or how to keep a team functional when they've been awake for 36 hours straight and the person who clicked the phishing link is sobbing in the break room.

We're putting together a great companion site for this book at *StopRansomware.com*. If you like these case studies and exercises, we have even more over there!

This is the part where organizations either survive or collapse, not from the ransomware itself, but from failing to keep the basic things running while fighting the technical battle. Welcome to the sustained operation phase, where the fog of war doesn't clear. It just settles in and makes itself comfortable.

Keeping the Business Running During Crisis

The thing is that your business can't just stop while you fight ransomware. Customers don't care about your containment strategy. They're at ZapMart's registers with shopping carts full of holiday gifts, they're at Maria's bakery counter wanting their morning coffee and pastry, they're in Change Healthcare's emergency rooms needing their prescriptions filled. The clock is ticking not just on your 72-hour ransom deadline, but on every minute your business isn't generating revenue or serving customers.

This is where the technical crisis becomes a business crisis, and where your IRP collides headfirst with reality. You're making containment decisions that will shut down revenue-generating systems, and someone, probably a very angry CEO or board member, is going to demand: "How do we keep the business running?"

The Business Continuity Blind Spot

Most IRPs focus on the technical fight: isolate infected systems, preserve evidence, eradicate malware. What they miss is the operational nightmare happening simultaneously. While Sarah's IT team at ZapMart was isolating POS servers to contain the LockBit infection, the store managers were panicking about the line of frustrated customers wrapping around the building. While Change Healthcare's team was imaging infected servers, nurses were facing patients who couldn't get prescriptions, and administrators were fielding calls from insurance companies demanding claim updates.

Maria's situation at her bakery was even more direct and personal. When Keith powered off the infected POS system, she immediately faced a choice: turn away every customer at the counter, potentially losing them forever to the bakery down the street, or try to operate without any way to process payments or track inventory. For a small business operating on thin margins, every hour of lost sales could mean the difference between surviving and closing permanently.

Northforge from Chapter 1 discovered this gap the hard way. Their incident response plan had detailed technical procedures for containment and eradication, but nothing about how their engineering teams would continue working without access to the proprietary design repository that Lorenz Group had encrypted. Engineers sat idle for three days during the initial response, representing hundreds of thousands in lost productivity that the $10M ransom demand didn't even account for.

Now let's walk through what these organizations could have done differently if they'd planned for business continuity during a ransomware crisis.

ZapMart's Holiday Sales Crisis

Sarah's team shut down the POS systems at 9 a.m. on a Thursday during peak holiday shopping season. By 10 a.m., store managers were calling her cell phone in a panic as customers abandoned full carts and walked out. The CFO called at 10:30 a.m. demanding to know when sales would resume, mentioning that every hour of downtime cost the company approximately $200,000 in lost revenue.

What ZapMart could have done: If Sarah's IRP had included business continuity procedures, they could have immediately activated pre-planned workarounds. Store managers could have pulled out the manual credit card imprinters that were supposed to be stored in each location (but weren't, because nobody had checked in three years). They could have switched to a backup payment processing system that runs on tablets, separate from the main POS network. They could have activated the "manual operations" protocol they should have practiced during last year's TTX, where cashiers process sales on paper forms and enter them later.

Instead, stores remained closed for four hours while Sarah's team debated whether the backup payment system was safe to use, nobody could find the manual imprinters, and cashiers had no idea how to process a credit card without the POS system because they'd never been trained on it. Those four hours cost ZapMart approximately $800,000 in direct lost sales, plus immeasurable damage from customers posting angry reviews on social media and shopping at competitors instead.

The reality: ZapMart could have kept selling during the crisis, at reduced capacity, if they'd planned for it. Manual processing would have been slower, maybe 10 transactions per hour instead of 60, but slower sales beat no sales. A simple business continuity checklist, reviewed quarterly, would have revealed the missing imprinters and untrained staff before the crisis hit.

Change Healthcare's Patient Care Emergency

Change Healthcare's situation was even more critical because lives were at stake. When ALPHV encrypted patient records and billing systems, nurses couldn't access medication histories, doctors couldn't see lab results, and pharmacies couldn't verify prescriptions. The IT team made the right call isolating infected systems to prevent spread, but nobody had a plan for how patient care would continue during the outage.

What Change Healthcare could have done: healthcare organizations should have crisis-mode operating procedures that activate automatically when electronic systems fail. This isn't new. Hospitals have been planning for power outages and natural disasters for decades. The same principles apply to ransomware.

Change Healthcare could have immediately switched to paper-based workflows that were pre-designed and practiced. Nurses could have used printed medication lists that were supposed to be updated daily (but weren't). Doctors could have called pharmacies directly to verify prescriptions, using a pre-established priority hotline (that didn't exist). Administrators could have activated the manual billing process they'd theoretically documented in their business continuity plan (but never actually tested).

The hospital also could have prioritized system recovery based on patient impact rather than just infection spread. The ventilator management system should have been first priority for restoration, even if it meant taking risks with a potentially infected but critical system. Instead, IT followed the standard IR procedure of methodically clearing systems before restoration, which was technically correct but left critical care equipment offline for 24 hours.

Most critically, Change Healthcare needed someone making business continuity decisions in parallel with technical containment decisions. While the IT team focused on stopping the ransomware spread, a separate business continuity coordinator should have been activating manual procedures, prioritizing patient-critical systems, and coordinating with clinical staff. That role didn't exist in their IRP, so nobody filled it, and patient care suffered.

Maria's Bakery's Customer Service Challenge

Maria faced the most direct business continuity crisis: customers standing at her counter, ready to buy, while her POS system displayed a ransom note. Keith's immediate response was to shut down the infected system, which was technically correct but left Maria with no way to process sales.

What Maria could have done: small businesses often think business continuity planning is only for large corporations, but Maria needed it more than anyone. A simple business continuity plan would have given her immediate alternatives.

Maria could have accepted cash-only sales using a basic calculator and receipt book (which she should have kept on hand). She could have used her smartphone with a Square or PayPal reader for credit cards, completely separate from the infected POS system. She could have written down orders on paper with customer phone numbers, processing payments later when systems were restored—essentially running tabs for her regular customers who she'd known for years.

For inventory tracking, Maria could have used pen and paper or a simple spreadsheet on Keith's laptop (which wasn't infected because it wasn't connected to the same network). She could have communicated with customers via social media: "We're experiencing technical difficulties but still serving! Cash only today, and your patience is appreciated."

Instead, Maria closed the bakery completely for two days while Keith struggled to understand the attack. Those two days represented not just lost revenue but also lost customers who found other bakeries and might not come back. A $50 investment in a cash box, receipt book, and backup payment device would have kept her business operating at 70% capacity during the crisis.

The lesson: Maria didn't need an enterprise-grade disaster recovery system. She needed a one-page checklist titled "If The Computer Dies Tomorrow" with basic workarounds she could activate in five minutes. That's business continuity at its most essential.

Northforge's Engineering Productivity Crisis

Northforge's encrypted proprietary repository meant their engineering team couldn't access design files, CAD drawings, or project documentation. The CFO quickly calculated that 50 engineers sitting idle at an average cost of $100/hour meant the company was burning $5,000 per hour in unproductive salary costs, on top of the technical recovery expenses.

What Northforge could have done: engineering firms should maintain business continuity procedures that keep teams productive even when primary systems are down. Northforge could have immediately shifted engineers to work on other tasks that didn't require the data from the encrypted repository, tasks like updating documentation, customer site visits, training activities, or planning for upcoming projects.

More importantly, Northforge's business continuity plan should have identified which engineering data was absolutely critical and ensured it had recent, accessible backups in a separate location. Even if they couldn't prevent the repository encryption, they could have been restoring the most critical project files within hours instead of days. Their backup strategy focused on complete system recovery, which would take a week, rather than rapid restoration of the highest-priority data needed to keep engineers working.

Northforge also could have activated their relationships with vendors and partners. Some design files existed in emails to suppliers. Some CAD drawings were stored in their customers' systems as part of project deliverables. Instead of waiting for complete repository restoration, they could have been gathering these distributed copies to enable partial productivity.

ZapMart, Change Healthcare, Maria's bakery, and Northforge all made the same critical mistake: they treated incident response and business continuity as separate problems. They had technical playbooks for fighting ransomware but no operational playbooks for keeping their businesses alive during the fight. Store managers didn't know how to process sales without POS systems. Nurses couldn't access patient records. Maria turned away customers because she had no backup payment method. Engineers sat idle because nobody planned for how to work without the encrypted repository. Every one of them lost revenue, customers, and opportunities they'll never get back—losses that had nothing to do with the ransomware itself and everything to do with the gap in their planning. Those losses were preventable. The failures you just read weren't inevitable. They were predictable, avoidable consequences of missing a critical piece of the crisis response puzzle.

Business Continuity Strategies

So how do you avoid becoming another cautionary tale? How do you keep ZapMart's stores selling, Change Healthcare's patients receiving care, Maria's customers buying pastries, and Northforge's engineers working, all while your IT team is fighting the ransomware battle? The answer isn't hoping for the best or winging it during the crisis. It's making strategic decisions about business impact before the attack hits, building manual workarounds you can activate in minutes, and designating someone with business authority to make the hard calls about acceptable risk. Technical containment and business operations aren't competing priorities, they're two sides of the same crisis response. Let's build the strategies that keep both going simultaneously.

Business-Driven Prioritization

The technical containment decisions you make during the fog of war need to factor in business impact, not just infection spread. This is where your asset inventory from Chapter 7 needs a business impact column that you probably didn't include.

Sarah at ZapMart faced this decision when her EDR system showed both the POS network and the HR database were infected. The technical response would be to isolate both immediately. But the business impact was vastly different: isolating POS systems stopped all sales immediately ($200,000/hour impact), while the HR database outage only affected payroll processing (manageable for a few days). Sarah needed to make a business-informed decision: isolate POS first to contain the spread, but bring up a backup POS system within hours even if it carried some reinfection risk, while the HR database could stay offline for thorough cleaning.

Change Healthcare's priority decision was even starker: the billing system versus the patient records system. An encrypted billing system meant financial losses and administrative headaches. An encrypted patient records system meant potential patient harm. The technical team wanted to clear both systems thoroughly before restoration. The business continuity perspective demanded they take calculated risks to restore patient records faster, even if it meant a higher chance of reinfection that they'd have to fight again.

These business-driven prioritization decisions require someone with business authority making the calls alongside the technical IRT leader. Many organizations designate a "business continuity coordinator" role in their IRP who works parallel to the technical IRT, making decisions about:

- Which business functions must continue at all costs
- What degraded service levels are acceptable temporarily
- Which manual workarounds to activate
- How to communicate service limitations to customers
- When to take calculated risks with potentially infected systems to maintain critical operations

The business continuity coordinator at ZapMart would have been the person telling Sarah: "I know the backup POS system might be infected, but we need to take that risk because we can't keep stores closed. Bring it up in isolated test mode, process a few transactions, monitor like crazy, and if it looks clean, we're going live in one hour."

Degraded Operations and Manual Workarounds

Accept this reality: your business will operate in degraded mode during ransomware response. The question isn't whether you'll maintain full capacity (you won't), but rather how much capacity you can maintain with manual workarounds and backup systems.

ZapMart could have operated at 30%–40% capacity with manual credit card processing and paper receipts. It would have meant longer checkout lines, frustrated customers, and exhausted cashiers, but 30% of revenue beats 0% of revenue. Change Healthcare could have provided 60%–70% of normal patient services using paper records and phone calls, which would have been slow and painful but adequate for most non-emergency care. Maria's bakery could have run at 50% capacity with cash-only sales and manual order tracking.

The key is having these degraded operating procedures documented and practiced before the crisis. Your TTXs from Chapter 7 should include a scenario like this: "Your primary system is offline for 24 hours. Walk through how each department continues operating." The finance team needs to know how to process urgent payments without the accounting system. The customer service team needs to know how to help customers without access to the CRM. The warehouse needs to know how to ship orders without the inventory management system.

These procedures should be documented on paper or in a system completely separate from your primary infrastructure because during a ransomware attack, you might not have access to the online documentation you carefully prepared. Some organizations keep printed "Business Continuity Quick Start" guides in sealed envelopes in managers' offices. Others maintain a simple external website (like a Google site) with basic procedures that staff can access from their phones.

The procedures should be simple enough that stressed, exhausted staff can follow them during a crisis. "Use the green binder under the front counter" is better than "Refer to section 7.3.2 of the Business Continuity Management System documentation stored on SharePoint."

Communication: The Bridge Between Crisis and Customers

Your customers, partners, and vendors need to know what's happening and what to expect. This is where the communication templates you developed in Chapter 7 become critical, but with a business continuity twist.

Sarah at ZapMart needed to communicate multiple things simultaneously:

- To customers: "Our stores are open with limited payment options. We apologize for longer wait times and appreciate your patience."

- To vendors: "Our systems are experiencing issues. Deliveries should continue as scheduled but expect delays in order processing."

- To partners: "We're operating in manual mode. Please send orders via email rather than EDI until further notice."

- To employees: "Stores remain open. Follow manual processing procedures from the green binder."

Change Healthcare's communication was even more complex because it involved patient safety:

- To patients: "Our systems are affected by a cyber incident. We're working to restore services. If you need a prescription, call your pharmacy and they will contact us directly."
- To providers: "Switch to paper records and call our clinical team for patient histories. Use the emergency priority line for critical cases."
- To insurance companies: "Claims processing is delayed. We're maintaining a manual log and will resubmit once systems are restored."

Maria's communication was simpler but just as important:

- Sign on the door: "We're open! Cash only today while we work on our computer system. Thank you for your patience!"
- Social media: "Small technical hiccup today, but we're baking! Come get your favorite treats—cash or check only. We'll be back to normal soon!"
- Regular customers: Personal calls or texts: "Hey, just a heads up we're cash-only for a day or two. Still making your standing Friday order!"

The tone matters enormously. Don't say "We've been hit by ransomware and are negotiating with criminals." Say "We're experiencing technical difficulties and working with experts to resolve them." Don't overpromise ("We'll be back to normal tomorrow!") when you have no idea if that's true. Instead, set realistic expectations ("We expect limited operations for at least 24–48 hours") and then exceed them if possible.

Update these communications regularly. Even if there's no new information, telling stakeholders "No update yet, still working on it, expect another update in 4 hours" is better than radio silence. Silence makes people assume the worst.

The Revenue Versus Security Trade-Off

Here's the conversation that happens in every ransomware crisis, usually around hour 6:

CFO: "We're losing $200,000 per hour. Just bring the systems back online!"

Security: "If we rush this, we risk reinfection and starting over from scratch."

CFO: "We'll be bankrupt before you finish your perfect containment!"

Security: "They will be attacking again in two weeks if we don't do this right!"

Both are right. This is the fundamental tension of business continuity during a ransomware response. The business continuity perspective says: take calculated risks, accept some reinfection possibility, get critical revenue-generating systems back online fast. The security perspective says: don't rush, do it right, avoid reinfection at all costs.

The answer isn't one or the other, it's a negotiated middle ground that factors in:

The financial burn rate
How much is downtime actually costing? ZapMart's $200,000/hour was existential. A software company's downtime might cost much less if they're between product releases.

The reinfection risk
Is this a sophisticated attacker likely to have persistent backdoors? Or a relatively simple RaaS attack that you can contain with reasonable certainty?

The restoration timeline
Can you restore from clean backups in 24 hours? Or are you looking at a two-week rebuild? The longer the restoration, the more pressure to take shortcuts.

The business context
Is this peak season (like ZapMart's holiday sales) or slow season? Are there contractual obligations with financial penalties? Regulatory requirements?

Sarah at ZapMart ultimately made a calculated compromise: bring up one POS system in one store in heavily monitored mode, process transactions for two hours, and if it stays clean, bring up the rest. That two-hour test period represented $400,000 in lost sales, but it also gave her confidence that the restored systems wouldn't immediately reinfect.

Change Healthcare made a different calculation: patient records stayed offline until thoroughly cleaned (24 hours), but they activated a manual prescription verification hotline within 4 hours. It wasn't their normal system, it was slow and painful, but it kept patients from being unable to get medications.

These trade-off decisions need to happen in real time, with business and technical leaders in the room together. Having the business continuity coordinator role separate from the IRT leader makes this possible: two people with different perspectives collaborating on the decision rather than fighting over it.

Survival Tip

Build business continuity into your IRP before the crisis. For each critical system, document:

- What business function does it support?
- What's the financial impact per hour of downtime?
- What manual workarounds exist and how long can they sustain operations?
- What's the acceptable degraded service level?

- Who makes the call to activate workarounds?

Practice these workarounds quarterly, just like you practice your technical containment procedures. Run a tabletop exercise where POS systems are offline for four hours. Can your retail staff actually process sales manually? Do they know where the equipment is? Does the equipment actually work?

Designate a business continuity coordinator role in your IRP, separate from the technical IRT leader. This person focuses on keeping the business running while the technical team fights the ransomware. For small businesses like Maria's, this might be the owner or manager. For larger organizations, it's often someone from operations or business continuity management.

Create communication templates specifically for business continuity announcements, not just "we've been breached" messages, but "here's how we're continuing to serve you during the crisis" messages. Store these templates somewhere accessible when your primary systems are down.

Document acceptable risk thresholds for bringing systems back online. Under what conditions will you restore a potentially infected system to maintain critical operations? Who has the authority to make that call? Don't figure this out at 2 a.m. on day 3 of the crisis.

Exercise: Plan Your Degraded Operations

Pick one critical business system in your organization (POS, customer service system, manufacturing line, patient records, etc.). Write a one-page procedure for how your business continues operating if that system is offline for 24 hours. Include:

- What manual workaround you'll use (be specific—"use paper forms" requires forms to exist)
- What reduced capacity you'll achieve (50%? 30%?)
- How you'll communicate this to customers/users
- What equipment or supplies you need available
- Who trains staff on the manual procedure

Now test it. Actually try to execute the procedure. Can you find the paper forms? Do staff know how to use them? Does the backup payment processor actually work? Do you have contact information for the vendors you need to notify?

Document what you learned and update your business continuity procedures accordingly. Repeat this exercise for every critical system. (Estimated time: 30 minutes per system.)

The Bottom Line on Business Continuity

Technical incident response and business continuity aren't competing priorities, they're two sides of the same crisis. You can't just fight the ransomware and ignore the business impact, but you also can't just keep the business running and ignore the security risks. The organizations that survive ransomware best are those that do both simultaneously.

Sarah at ZapMart needed both a technical team stopping the infection spread and a business team keeping stores operational. Change Healthcare needed both IT restoring systems and clinical staff maintaining patient care. Maria needed both Keith fixing the POS and herself keeping customers served.

Build business continuity into your IRP now, before your worst Thursday morning. Practice it, test it, and make sure every stakeholder understands that "business continuity" and "incident response" are the same team working toward the same goal: getting your organization through the crisis intact.

Because when the ransom note appears and your systems start going down, you'll need answers to two questions simultaneously: "How do we stop this attack?" and "How do we keep our business running?" Chapter 7's IRP should give you both answers.

You've balanced technical containment with business operations, calculated acceptable risk thresholds, and activated your manual workarounds. On paper, you're managing the crisis. But there's another dimension to this nightmare that doesn't show up in your incident response playbook or business continuity plan: the human cost. Your IT team has been running on adrenaline and coffee for 48 hours. Your CEO is fielding angry board calls. That cashier who clicked the phishing link is terrified of being fired. Behind every technical decision and business calculation are exhausted, stressed, frightened people who are trying to hold it together while their world burns. Let's talk about what this crisis is actually doing to your team.

The Human Toll: Stress, Communication, and Morale

Let's dive into what the actual human toll looks like on the ground after a ransomware attack.

Emotional Rollercoaster

Responding to a ransomware incident is a psychological gauntlet that tests everyone, from IT analysts to CEOs. Sarah barely slept for three days, haunted by nightmares of layoffs if ZapMart couldn't recover. Her team felt scapegoated, especially the cashier who clicked the phishing link, a mistake echoing Chapter 1's employee email breach that sparked Northforge's Lorenz attack. "I thought I'd be fired," the cashier whispered, tears in her eyes. People started mocking Change Healthcare on X, as you can see in Figure 10-1.

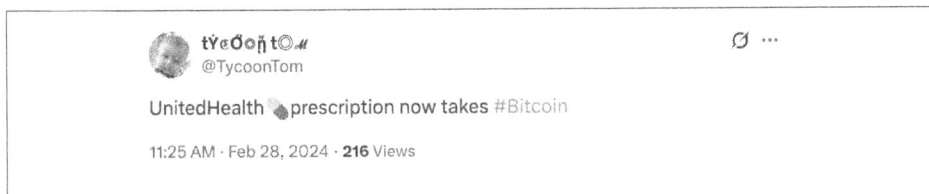

Figure 10-1. People mocking Change Healthcare's compromised prescription system

Maria, the bakery owner, cried alone in her office, terrified of losing her family's 30-year legacy to a $50,000 ransom she couldn't afford to pay.

Leaders face a unique burden. ZapMart's CEO fielded shareholder calls questioning, "How did you let this happen?" in response to social media posts labeling the retailer "incompetent." Change Healthcare faced patient families publicly voicing their outrage, like the X post in Figure 10-2.

Figure 10-2. Dark X post about Change Healthcare

Maria's neighbors asked, "Were you hacked?" at the counter, adding personal embarrassment. Northforge's executives felt "hopeless" on their conference calls, a despair that led their cybersecurity lead to quit mid-crisis, overwhelmed by the $7M loss of their data repository. Without support, burnout, resignations, or even long-term trauma can follow, turning a technical crisis into a human one.

Deep dive: Emotional toll

Chronic stress during a ransomware attack triggers cortisol spikes, impairing decision-making, memory, and emotional regulation (American Psychological Association, 2024 (*https://oreil.ly/3n5K7*)). IT staff, often blamed for breaches, report 30% higher burnout rates during incidents, with 10% leaving their jobs within a year. Small business owners like Maria face existential dread, with the fear of selling her home to pay the ransom sparking anxiety attacks. Post-crisis, 20% of responders show PTSD symptoms, including insomnia, hypervigilance, and intrusive thoughts, according to a 2025 Cybersecurity Deep Dive report. Mitigation strategies are critical but rare: scheduled breaks, peer support groups, and post-incident counseling can reduce burnout, yet only 15% of organizations budget for them. Leaders must model calm. Sarah's steady presence, despite her own fears, kept her team focused, while Change Healthcare's frantic CEO fueled panic.

For small businesses, the toll is deeply personal. Keith, Maria's only IT support, felt crushing guilt for failing to stop the ransomware threat. This is similar to Northforge's cyber lead who eventually resigned. Leaders like Maria or ZapMart's CEO must balance their own stress with supporting their teams, a tightrope act under a 72-hour ransom deadline.

Survival tip

Acknowledge the emotional toll openly and call it out in IRT meetings, like "I know this is brutal, and we're all stressing out." Schedule 10-minute breaks every 4 hours, even if it's just coffee or a quick walk; small pauses reduce cortisol spikes. Encourage staff to vent frustrations in a safe space, like a private office. As a leader, you must maintain calm, even if you're faking it—your team mirrors your energy. Post-crisis, offer counseling or paid time off to recover; small businesses can tap free mental health resources via local chambers of commerce. Don't ignore the human cost, it's as critical as the technical one.

Exercise: Build resilience

Draft a pep talk to your IRT after 48 hours of response. Highlight one small win (e.g., "We restored the email server in 45 minutes!"). Address their stress explicitly (e.g., "I know you're exhausted, and I'm proud of you"). How do you inspire them to keep going? Reflect on how your tone impacts morale and whether you'd deliver this in person or via email.

Communication Breakdowns

In the fog of a ransomware response, communication breakdowns turn allies into obstacles, amplifying the chaos, and fueling internal politics. Sarah's team misheard "isolate servers" as "reboot servers" during a frantic call, delaying containment by 4 hours and letting the ransomware encrypt 20% more systems. Her CEO leaked unverified details to a reporter, claiming "minimal impact," only to retract the comments when the company's HR systems later failed. This confusion sparked a social media storm, in tweets that have since been deleted or made private. Change Healthcare faced nurse–IT account clashes over ventilator reboots, with nurses assuming IT was "incompetent" when delays disrupted patient care. You can see these sentiments in the Reddit post in Figure 10-3.

A friend of mine worked for one of the companies that contributed to this mess. He was having panic attacks every Sunday at brunch because he'd be getting messages about shit breaking and their outsourced developers were unable to handle the issues. The complete and utter lack of security and competence in healthcare IT is astounding. I am an information security professional (and information warfare) and this has been a long time coming. We were doing our best to protect medical infrastructure during COVID with CTI League, but now we're all fighting other stuff and the medical infrastructure is seeing what happens when you don't take security seriously. It's a big case of "WE TOLD YOU SO".

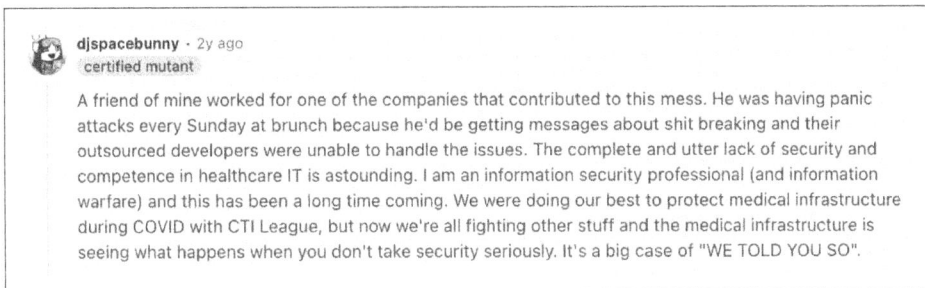

Figure 10-3. Reddit post blaming IT for Change Healthcare outage

Small businesses suffer intimate internal breakdowns. Keith misread the LockBit ransom note's bitcoin instructions, nearly sending $50,000 to a scam wallet, a mistake luckily caught by someone else before it was too late. Maria's sister emailed customers prematurely, admitting the breach without legal review, triggering panic and online complaints. Northforge's case saw similar woes: the CFO's offhand comment to staff about "paying the ransom" spread rumors, undermining IT's recovery efforts.

Survival tip

Lean on the communication templates you developed in Chapter 7 for internal updates, customer notifications, and media responses to ensure consistency. Set up a secure channel, like Signal or WhatsApp, or a dedicated Slack workspace (if it's working), for IRT chats to avoid email chaos or misheard calls. (Be sure to understand legal implications of out-of-band communications, such as discovery or document retention.) Update stakeholders hourly, even if it's just "no new information," to maintain trust and quell rumors. Monitor X (e.g., @ThreatIntel, @CyberSecNews) for public sentiment to gauge PR impact.

Exercise: Craft a message

Draft a customer email for Maria's bakery, admitting the breach without causing panic. Use the template you developed in Chapter 7 (e.g., "We're addressing a security issue and working with experts"). Ensure it's clear, empathetic, and reassuring. Compare it to a real breach notification, like Colonial Pipeline's 2021 statement (*https:// oreil.ly/PaG_a*). Reflect on how you'd tweak it for social media posting.

Maintaining Morale

A prolonged ransomware response can drain the spirit of even the most resilient team, turning exhaustion into despair. After 48 hours of dead ends, Sarah's IT crew at ZapMart was wearing down. One of her analysts commented, "We're never getting out of this." However, restoring the email server, a critical system, became a turning point. Sarah gathered her team, high-fived them, and said, "This is proof we're fighting back!" That small win, celebrated with a round of coffee, rekindled the team's drive. Keith at Maria's bakery, overwhelmed by LockBit's encryption of the POS, was ready to quit after a nonstop 36 hours. Maria baked his favorite chocolate chip cookies, a heartfelt gesture that lifted his spirits.

Change Healthcare's IT team hit a low when ventilators remained offline. Ordering pizza in the midst of battle will improve morale and provide a brief distraction (pro tip: plan for this before it gets too late in the evening—or hit a 24/7 taco/burger place). Contrast this with Northforge's situation, where the failure to celebrate small victories, like isolating 50% of infected servers, contributed to their cybersecurity lead's resignation. He walked out while the house was still on fire. Recognizing progress, however small, is a lifeline in the fog of war.

Small gestures matter immensely. Sarah's team played music during late-night shifts, boosting camaraderie. Change Healthcare's CEO sent handwritten thank-you notes post-crisis, a move that reduced turnover. Maria gave Keith a gift card for his unpaid hours, although it probably should have been more. Post-crisis recognition, including bonuses, public praise, or extra time off rebuilds trust and prevents burnout.

Survival tip

Celebrate small victories to keep your team going, like highlighting restored systems, containing infections, or even surviving another hour. Provide tangible pick-me-ups during long shifts: food, coffee, music, or a quick stretch break. Post-crisis, recognize efforts with public thanks, bonuses, or time off; small businesses like Maria's can offer personal gestures like gift cards or flexible hours. Schedule a team debrief to process the stress, using the post-incident review process you'll read about in Chapter 13. These actions aren't just nice, they're critical to retaining your team and continuing to grow together and prepare for the next fight.

Exercise: Boost morale

Plan a 10-minute team huddle for ZapMart's IRT after 24 hours of response. List one win to highlight (e.g., "We isolated the POS!") and one way to energize them (e.g., snacks, quick stretch). Write a script for your huddle, framing the win to inspire. Reflect on how this impacts team cohesion.

You're managing the technical response, keeping the business operational, and holding your team together. You've made the hard calls, activated your IRP and IRT, and followed your incident response procedures. Everything you've practiced in TTXs is working—mostly. But here's what no TTX can fully prepare you for: the surprises that punch you in the face when you least expect them. The decryptor that fails on 30% of your files. The IoT devices your EDR never saw. The FBI seizing your servers for evidence right when you need them most. Mike Tyson was right: everyone has a plan until they get punched in the face. Ransomware attackers thrive on those punches.

Unexpected Curveballs: What Plans Don't Prepare You For

Even if you think you're making an airtight plan, curveballs will always show up in real-life scenarios.

Technical Surprises

ZapMart had solid data backups stored offsite in immutable storage (as suggested in Chapter 7), but verifying them to be clean took 12 hours because of a slow network. This bottleneck wasn't previously considered or tested, delaying recovery efforts.

A common practice of ransomware groups is to provide a decryptor to demonstrate that it will work, often referred to as a proof-of-life tool. The proof-of-life decryptor given to ZapMart could not decrypt 20% of the files put through it. This is a common scam to extort more payments. The proof-of-life decryptor provided to Northforge completely failed at decrypting the company's proprietary data repository, leading to a complete loss. Change Healthcare found IoT thermometers infected, missed by their EDR system, requiring manual resets that diverted staff for 8 hours.

Other technical surprises were just waiting to be triggered, like ransomware re-encrypting files post-payment (e.g., Cl0p's double-dip tactics, Chapter 1), cloud misconfigurations exposing data, hidden/dormant backdoors, or variants exploiting zero-days like MOVEit. Maria's legacy POS system lacked logs, forcing Keith to guess how the attack occurred, whether it came from a phishing email, a website download, or a USB drive. Change Healthcare's ALPHV variant used anti-forensic techniques, wiping event logs as it moved from one host to another, a tactic described in Chapter 1's discussion of advanced malware. These curveballs test even the best defenses, like air-gapped backups or endpoint monitoring.

Case Study: 2025 Retail Supply Chain Attack

In January 2025, a UK retailer, which we'll call "Everline," was hit by Cl0p ransomware through a compromised supply chain vendor. This encrypted their inventory systems, disrupted deliveries for a week, and cost the company $3M in lost sales. The decryptor, provided after a $1.5M payment, failed on 30% of files due to a corrupted key, forcing a partial rebuild from backups. The vulnerabilities in their supply chain vendor's unpatched software were the entry point—an important reminder of Chapter 7's vendor vetting and due diligence advice. This also echoes the MOVEit breach, where third-party vulnerabilities triggered widespread attacks.

Survival tip

Backup and restoration failures are common, which is why testing both as often as possible is important—ideally on a quarterly basis, to avoid Sarah's 12-hour delay.

Maintain immutable backups or a secondary DR site to mitigate the risk that an attack will impact these. Engage your pre-vetted IR and forensics resources (discussed in Chapter 7) early to help with analyzing anomalies like IoT infections or failed decryptors. Update your ransomware playbook post-crisis with lessons learned, such as adding IoT scans or cloud audits. Small businesses can use free tools like CISA's Cyber Hygiene Scanner to spot misconfigurations.

Exercise: Plan for technical surprises

List three potential technical surprises (e.g., infected IoT devices, failed decryptor, legacy system with no logs). For each, propose a mitigation from Chapter 7 (e.g., network segmentation, immutable backups). Draft a plan to update your playbook with one lesson (e.g., "Add IoT scans"). Reflect on how you'd prioritize these mitigations with limited resources.

External Pressures

External forces turn a technical crisis into a public nightmare, complicating the response. The FBI seized Change Healthcare's servers for evidence, delaying recovery by 24 hours and frustrating staff. Maria's family pushed her to pay the $50,000 Lock-Bit ransom to cut costs, clashing with her no-pay stance and legal's OFAC concerns. Sarah's ransomware gang leaked ZapMart's customer data on a dark web "wall of shame," triggering the regulatory 72-hour notification requirement and a potential $20M fine. Maria faced a possible $10,000 Washington state fine for late reporting, which would be a crushing blow for her bakery. Social media posts amplified Change Healthcare's PR woes, with patients posting online that they haven't been able to fulfill prescriptions for over a week, as you can see in Figure 10-4.

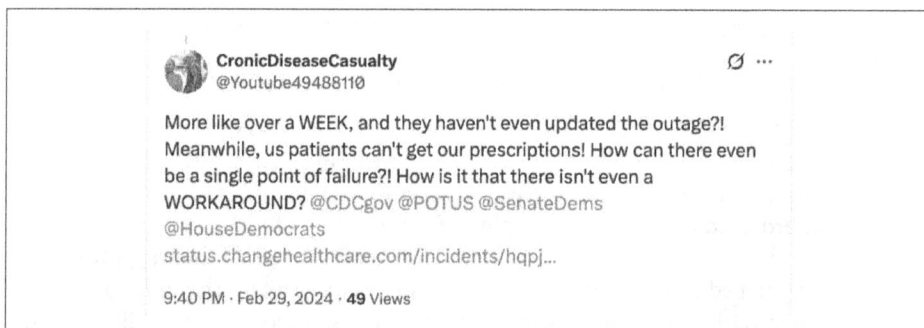

> **CronicDiseaseCasualty**
> @Youtube49488110
>
> More like over a WEEK, and they haven't even updated the outage?! Meanwhile, us patients can't get our prescriptions! How can there even be a single point of failure?! How is it that there isn't even a WORKAROUND? @CDCgov @POTUS @SenateDems @HouseDemocrats
> status.changehealthcare.com/incidents/hqpj...
>
> 9:40 PM · Feb 29, 2024 · **49** Views

Figure 10-4. Change Healthcare frustrations

Small businesses face uniquely personal pressures. Northforge's premature press release, claiming "contained breach," backfired when Lorenz Group leaked data, sparking a media backlash. Regulators, media, law enforcement, and even insurers demand conflicting actions, which cause confusion between notifying now, not paying, going public, or staying silent, leaving you caught in a crossfire and not knowing which way to go.

Exercise: Handle the press

Draft a social media post for Maria's bakery to address customer concerns about the ransomware attack and to respond to negative posts. Use the crisis communications template you developed in Chapter 7 (e.g., "We're resolving a security issue"). Ensure it's empathetic, clear, and proactive. Compare your draft to a real breach post. Reflect on how you'd monitor replies and continue to adjust or respond.

Resource Constraints

Understaffed teams often buckle under the weight and stress of a ransomware response. Sarah's three-person IT team juggled containment, forensics, and user complaints, working 18-hour shifts that led to human error and exhaustion-induced decision-making, like misconfiguring a firewall. Keith, Maria's only IT resource, was overwhelmed by LockBit, nearly bricking the POS with a bad patch. Northforge's two-person cyber team restored an infected backup by mistake, setting their recovery efforts back by 12 hours. Change Healthcare's budget cuts left them with one cybersecurity analyst, who quit mid-crisis.

Small businesses face dire circumstances. Maria couldn't afford an IR support vendor, relying on free tools like NoMoreRansom and Malwarebytes, which just weren't enough to help track down how the LockBit infection happened. Sarah had the budget to engage an IR vendor, but she didn't pre-negotiate a retainer, and when she needed one the most, they were all unavailable—Sarah's team was stuck. Even large firms struggle—insurers may cap vendor spending, and skilled staff are stretched thin. These limitations amplify every mistake, turning a manageable crisis into a marathon.

Survival tip

Prioritize tasks using your playbook: containment first, then recovery, then communication. Outsource IR support, forensics, and PR to the pre-vetted partners we discussed in Chapter 7. Post-crisis, invest in additional training to upskill on current or new technologies, build capacity by engaging resources to fill the IR gaps on your team, and conduct drills. Stretch limited staff by assigning clear roles, even if it's just "handle customers" or "monitor alerts."

Exercise: Allocate resources

You have an IT staff of two people and a $50,000 budget during a ransomware attack. List three priorities (e.g., IR vendor, EDR licenses, legal consulting). Justify your choices in a short narrative, referencing Chapter 7's priorities (e.g., "Containment first"). Reflect on how you'd stretch resources if the budget dropped to $20,000.

You've survived the initial shock, made impossible decisions under pressure, kept the business running, managed the human toll, and weathered the curveballs that no plan could predict. You're exhausted, your team is running on fumes, and you're probably wondering if you'll ever feel normal again. But here's what I've learned from walking dozens of organizations through their worst days: the ones who survive ransomware attacks don't just get lucky. They do specific things right, avoid specific mistakes, and learn specific lessons that make them stronger. After guiding companies through this nightmare again and again, I've seen clear patterns in what works, what breaks, and how to build real resilience. Let me share what I've learned in the trenches.

Lessons from the Trenches: Making It Through

I (Mike) have seen some things. I have been with many companies on their worst day, when they are currently being attacked with ransomware. Here are a few lessons I've learned along the way.

What Works

Preparation is the difference between chaos and control. We helped a healthcare company contain a Ryuk attack in hours, thanks to EDR alerts and a strategy to segment their networks. Their IRT, which continuously practiced TTXs and conducted war games, performed outstandingly, restoring 95% of systems in three days. Another organization (Everline), despite encountering several hurdles and setbacks, recovered 90% of their systems in a week, with the help of a ransomware playbook and the use of MFA to prevent reinfection. Sarah's incident response leadership role was also effective at keeping decisions focused. Tested backups, rapid containment, and a "see something, say something" culture turned a nightmare into a manageable situation.

What Breaks

The lack of preparation and unfamiliarity with roles, responsibilities, resources, and expectations will directly contribute to an ineffective response to significant incidents. A 2025 manufacturer paid $1M after untested backups failed, only to be retargeted within three months. Poor communication, like Sarah's "reboot" mix-up, often worsens the situation, adding hours to recovery. Over-reliance on making the payment as an effective response solution, as Colonial Pipeline learned in 2021, invites scrutiny and subsequent attacks; their $4.4M payment didn't prevent reputational damage. Maria's bakery lost customers due to delayed communication, a preventable PR issue that the templates you developed in Chapter 7 could have mitigated.

Building Resilience

Every attack exposes gaps and deficiencies, but they should also make you stronger. Everline adopted mandatory MFA, immutable backups, and quarterly war games as part of their post-incident remediation strategy. Maria sought the help of a consultant to implement a proactive cybersecurity culture, and more specifically, began to require training on email phishing and safe internet browsing. After analyzing how ALPHV's malware spread across the environment, Change Healthcare invested more heavily in network segmentation. Every organization must prepare and train on their response programs, run more war games, simulate difficult decisions (e.g., cut off the internet, pay the ransom, or rebuild everything), and offer stress management training to handle the emotional impact on those involved. Document lessons learned, capture new observations, inventory your critical assets and resources, and make friends with local IR professionals and law enforcement. Lastly, consider the things you don't know, like assets or devices you can't see or detect, and/or the skills and capabilities you don't have, then identify ways to address these gaps and build a roadmap for putting them in place.

Exercise: Reflect and Improve

List three gaps exposed by Sarah's response (e.g., slow backup verification, miscommunication). Propose fixes from Chapters 6 and 7 (e.g., quarterly restore tests, secure comms). Write a 50-word plan to update your IRT playbook with one fix (e.g., "Test backups monthly"). Reflect on how these strengthen your next response.

Practical Exercises Summary

Table 10-1 summarizes the practice exercises in this chapter, so you can use it for tabletops and similar exercises. (For Chapter 9 exercises, see Table 9-2.) Each exercise builds specific skills your team will need during a real ransomware crisis.

Table 10-1. Sustained operations exercises

Exercise name	Section	What you'll practice	Time
Plan Your Degraded Operations	Keeping the Business Running	Designing manual workarounds for critical systems; testing business continuity procedures	30 min
Build Resilience	Emotional Rollercoaster	Crafting motivational communication; addressing team stress and exhaustion	10 min
Craft a Message	Communication Breakdowns	Writing crisis communications; balancing transparency with reassurance	10 min
Boost Morale	Maintaining Morale	Planning team recognition; celebrating small wins to sustain momentum	5 min
Plan for Technical Surprises	Technical Surprises	Identifying potential failure points; proposing mitigations for unexpected problems	15 min

Exercise name	Section	What you'll practice	Time
Handle the Press	External Pressures	Drafting public statements; responding to negative social media during crisis	10 min
Allocate Resources	Resource Constraints	Prioritizing limited budgets; justifying resource decisions under constraints	20 min
Reflect and Improve	Lessons from the Trenches	Analyzing gaps in response; creating improvement plans for the IR playbook	10 min

Summary

You've survived some of the hardest decisions of your life. Systems are isolated, stakeholders are aligned, and the ransomware has stopped spreading. You can breathe again. Almost.

Because here's what nobody told you: the crisis doesn't end when you make the big decisions. It's just getting started. The sprint is over. Welcome to the marathon, and you're already exhausted.

This chapter walked you through the sustained battle: the days or weeks after containment when your business is bleeding out, your team is running on fumes, and customers don't care about your technical fight. They're at ZapMart's registers with full carts, at Maria's bakery wanting pastries, at Change Healthcare's emergency rooms needing prescriptions. Revenue losses pile up by the minute while your CFO calculates the burn rate and your communications team can't decide which press release makes you look least incompetent.

Business continuity and technical response aren't separate problems; they're two sides of the same crisis. ZapMart could have operated at 30%–40% capacity with manual credit card processing if they'd planned for it. Change Healthcare needed paper-based workflows they'd actually practiced, not theoretically documented. Maria needed a $50 cash box and backup payment device, not an enterprise DR system. Designate a business continuity coordinator who makes the hard calls about acceptable risk while your technical team fights the infection. Document degraded operations procedures before the crisis, practice them quarterly, and store them somewhere accessible when your primary systems are down.

The revenue versus security trade-off forces real-time negotiations between business and technical leaders. Sarah brought up one POS system in monitored mode, a $400,000 gamble that paid off. Change Healthcare activated a manual prescription hotline despite reinfection risks because patient care couldn't wait. Both made calculated compromises rather than choosing perfect security or unlimited risk. Document these thresholds before 2 a.m. on day 3.

Managing the human toll determines whether your team survives intact. Acknowledge exhaustion openly, schedule breaks every four hours, and celebrate small victories, even the victory of just surviving another hour. That cashier who clicked the phishing link is sobbing in the break room. Your IT analyst worked 36 hours straight and misconfigured a firewall from exhaustion. Twenty percent of responders show PTSD symptoms post-crisis. Order pizza, play music during late-night shifts, offer counseling afterward. These aren't nice-to-haves; they're what keeps your team from walking out mid-crisis like Northforge's cybersecurity lead did.

Communication breakdowns amplify chaos. Set up secure channels to avoid "isolate servers" being heard as "reboot servers." Designate one spokesperson. Update stakeholders hourly even when there's no news, because silence breeds panic. Use the templates from Chapter 7 to maintain consistency.

Expect curveballs that land square on your jaw. Backup verification takes 12 hours from slow networks. Decryptors fail on 30% of files. IoT devices your EDR never saw are infected. The FBI seizes servers for evidence right when you need them. Your family demands you pay the ransom. Social media explodes with angry customers. Understaffed teams work 18-hour shifts and make exhaustion-induced mistakes. Test backups quarterly, engage pre-vetted vendors early, and prepare for these punches before they land.

Building resilience means learning from every attack. Document lessons within 72 hours using the "Lessons Learned Template". Invest in MFA, network segmentation, and quarterly war games post-incident. The organizations that survive don't just get lucky; they prepare, practice, and learn from the trenches.

You've navigated the sustained battle, kept your business running during degraded operations, managed the psychological toll, and weathered the curveballs. Your team survived the marathon. Now you need to understand exactly what happened and how the attackers got in. That's next: the methodical work of analyzing the breach.

Lessons Learned Template

Here's a template you can use to capture information during the attack that will strengthen your defenses and response capabilities for next time. Fill it out during the incident and complete it within 72 hours of resolving the incident, then revisit it 30 days later to add insights that emerge with distance. (We will offer this as a downloadable asset on *StopRansomware.com*.)

RANSOMWARE INCIDENT LESSONS LEARNED

INCIDENT OVERVIEW

- Date/time of discovery: _____
- Ransomware variant: _____

- Systems affected: _____
- Estimated downtime: _____
- Ransom demand: _____ Payment decision: _____
- Total estimated cost (including lost revenue, IR vendors, ransom, etc.): _____

WHAT WORKED WELL

List 3–5 things your team did right that helped contain damage or speed recovery:

1. _____
2. _____
3. _____
4. _____
5. _____

Examples: "EDR alerts caught the infection within 15 minutes," "Pre-vetted IR vendor responded within 2 hours," "Manual backup payment system kept stores operating at 40% capacity"

WHAT DIDN'T WORK

List 3–5 things that failed, slowed response, or made the situation worse:

1. _____
2. _____
3. _____
4. _____
5. _____

Examples: "Network map was 6 months out of date," "Cashiers weren't trained on manual credit card processing," "Backup verification took 12 hours due to slow network"

ROOT CAUSE ANALYSIS

How did the attackers get in?

☐ Phishing email clicked by employee
☐ Compromised credentials (weak/reused passwords)
☐ Unpatched vulnerability in [system]: _____
☐ Third-party vendor compromise: _____
☐ Remote access left open (RDP, VPN)

□ Other: _____

Why wasn't it caught earlier?

_____

_____

What systemic gaps enabled this?

_____

_____

_____

DECISION-MAKING ANALYSIS

Containment decisions:

- What we did: _____
- Time to decision: _____
- Outcome: □ Effective □ Partially effective □ Ineffective
- What we'd do differently: _____

Ransom payment decision:

- What we did: _____
- Key factors: _____
- Outcome: □ Got decryptor □ Decryptor failed □ Didn't pay
- What we'd do differently: _____

Business continuity decisions:

- Manual workarounds activated: _____
- Time to activate: _____
- Effectiveness: □ Kept business running □ Partial operations □ Full shutdown
- What we'd do differently: _____

COMMUNICATION BREAKDOWN POINTS

Where did communication fail or cause delays?

Internal communication issues:

_____

_____

External communication issues (customers, vendors, media, regulators):

_____

_____

_____

PEOPLE, PROCESS, TECHNOLOGY GAPS

People gaps:

☐ Understaffed (needed ___ more people with _____ skills)
☐ Untrained on response procedures
☐ Key person unavailable/resigned
☐ Unclear roles and responsibilities
☐ Other: _____

Process gaps:

☐ No incident response plan
☐ Plan outdated or untested
☐ No business continuity procedures
☐ Missing communication templates
☐ Other: _____

Technology gaps:

☐ No EDR or inadequate coverage
☐ Backups corrupted/inaccessible
☐ Insufficient network segmentation
☐ Legacy systems without logging
☐ Other: _____

IMMEDIATE FIXES IMPLEMENTED (within 30 days)

1. _____

2. _____

3. _____

LONG-TERM IMPROVEMENTS NEEDED (30–90 days)

Improvement	Owner	Target date	Budget needed	Priority (H/M/L)

Improvement	Owner	Target date	Budget needed	Priority (H/M/L)

Examples: "Deploy MFA across all systems," "Quarterly backup restoration tests," "Update network inventory," "Hire additional security analyst"

HUMAN TOLL ASSESSMENT

How did this incident affect your team?

Burnout indicators:

- ☐ Staff worked 18+-hour shifts
- ☐ Team member(s) quit during or after incident
- ☐ Visible signs of stress/exhaustion
- ☐ Scapegoating or blame culture emerged

Support provided:

- ☐ Post-incident counseling offered
- ☐ Paid time off for recovery
- ☐ Team recognition/bonuses
- ☐ Stress management training

What we'll do differently to support our team:

_____

_____

_____

FINANCIAL IMPACT

Cost Category	Amount
Ransom payment (if paid)	$
IR vendor/consultants	$
Legal fees	$
Forensics	$
Lost revenue	$
System restoration	$
Regulatory fines	$
Credit monitoring/PR	$
Insurance deductible	$
TOTAL	$

Insurance recovery: $_____ Net cost: $_____

KEY TAKEAWAYS (3–5 sentences)

What are the 2–3 most important lessons from this incident?

_____

_____

_____

_____

_____

_____

NEXT STEPS

    ☐ Share this lessons learned doc with executive leadership by [date]
    ☐ Update incident response plan based on these findings by [date]
    ☐ Schedule tabletop exercise to test improvements by [date]
    ☐ Present findings to board/stakeholders by [date]
    ☐ Conduct 30-day follow-up review on [date]
    ☐ Archive this document in [location] for future reference

Document completed by: _____ **Date:** _____

Reviewed by: _____ **Date:** _____

CHAPTER 11

Analyzing the Breach

This chapter builds on the story started in Chapters 9 and 10. You're still in the fog of war, but you've stopped the initial bleeding and are moving to analysis. We will cut through the fog of a ransomware attack, hour by hour. We'll walk you through identifying the ransomware variant, assessing its scope, and hunting for decryption or remediation options with each step building on your incident response plan (IRP) and detection tools. We'll dig deeper into Maria's bakery, Sarah at ZapMart, and Change Healthcare stories, along with a few others, and we'll share with you a few free tools like VirusTotal and NoMoreRansom.org, plus practical techniques like sandboxing that work for organizations of any size. For those needing advanced forensics like memory analysis or reverse engineering, we'll cover those specialist techniques in Chapter 12. Survival tips will keep you clear of pitfalls, like scam decryptors or premature containment. Interactive exercises will put you in the Incident Response Team's shoes, whether you're an IT manager like Sarah, a small business owner like Maria, or a hospital admin fighting for patient safety.

By the end of this chapter, you'll have a battle-tested playbook for ransomware attacks and be ready for the next phase, containment and eradication. With ransomware losses projected to hit $57 billion globally in 2025 (according to CyberSecurity Ventures (*https://oreil.ly/nK5qH*)), and AI-driven emerging ransomware strains, this isn't just a technical exercise, it's a survival skill. Let's start the detective work by naming your enemy.

Beginning the Investigation

The ransomware attack hit hard, but working through the cloud of debris (e.g., ransom notes flashing on screens, systems getting bricked, and management demanding answers) has developed a tense, focused determination to fight and recover. Your Incident Response Team (IRT) has isolated critical systems. You've also got a ransom note demanding $500,000 in bitcoin, complete with a 72-hour countdown and a *.onion* link to a "support" portal. (*.onion* is a special type of website address used on the Tor, or The Onion Router, network to access anonymous onion services.)

The stakes are sky-high: Maria's bakery was losing $2,000 a day with its POS down; Sarah's retail chain (which we are calling "ZapMart") faced a PR nightmare as customer data leaks surfaced on X (in tweets that have since been deleted or made private); Change Healthcare was risking patient lives with encrypted ventilators. Before you can contain, negotiate, or recover, you need to answer three burning questions: *What ransomware is this? How far has it spread? Can we decrypt it without paying?*

This is the analysis phase—a high-stakes investigation where every clue you can collect will shape your response. Think of it as a crime scene: the ransomware is the suspect, your network is the victim, and you're the detective piecing together evidence to tell the story. Get it right, and you save time, money, or even lives. Get it wrong, and you may end up going down the rabbit hole of despair, wasting precious time and resources while the ransom clock runs out. In Chapter 9, Sarah at ZapMart and Maria at the bakery both spent quite a bit of time identifying if they were infected with LockBit 3.0. Change Healthcare's ALPHV/BlackCat attack, with its polymorphic code, evaded detection, resulting in 12 hours of manual patient checks.

Why Analysis Matters

Ransomware thrives on chaos, but analysis brings clarity. Identifying the variant, such as LockBit, ALPHV, Cl0p, or some strain developed since this book was released, unlocks critical intelligence. Intelligence about your particular ransomware infection can be extremely valuable, like the variant's encryption strength, indicators of compromise (IOCs), techniques and tactics (e.g., exfiltration), and whether a decryptor exists.

In Chapter 1, we explored how polymorphic code lets ALPHV dodge antivirus scans, while double extortion (encrypt + leak) pressures victims to pay. Knowing the variant enables you to anticipate these moves. For example, Sarah's team at ZapMart confirmed a *.lock* variant via VirusTotal, revealing it was LockBit 3.0 with a known RSA-2048 encryption—no decryptor available. This saved them from wasting time on futile decryption attempts, focusing instead on backups.

Assessing the scope of the attack includes determining how many systems are affected, whether the malware is still spreading, and if data was stolen. All of this will determine your containment strategy. Maria's bakery thought only her POS was encrypted, but a missed laptop infection let LockBit spread to her cloud-based accounting files, doubling her recovery time. Change Healthcare's unsegmented network let ALPHV encrypt the billing system and patient ventilators, a scope failure that effective network segmentation (VLANs) could have prevented. Exploring decryption options, which we will cover in this chapter, is often a long shot. But decryption can also save millions. A 2023 engineering firm paid $7M for a proprietary decryptor that failed, while a free NoMoreRansom.org tool unlocked an older CryptoLocker strain for a school district that would not otherwise have recovered.

Analysis isn't just technical, it's strategic. It enables your decision tree: isolate now or wait? Pay the ransom or restore from backups? Notify regulators or hold off? It also feeds into your eradication plan and being confident that you don't miss lingering malware or dormant backdoors. For small businesses, it's a lifeline: Maria's nephew (who we are calling "Keith") used free tools to confirm LockBit, avoiding a scam decryptor that could have bankrupted the bakery. For enterprises, it's a force multiplier: in "Case Study: 2025 Cl0p Supply Chain Attack" on page 325 you'll read of a CISO that leveraged EDR logs to determine Cl0p's spread, saving 10 hours of manual log and data analysis. With 80% of 2024 attacks involving data exfiltration, and AI-driven phishing rising in 2025, analysis is your first step to reclaiming control.

Guidance for Small and Medium-Sized Businesses

Small and medium-sized businesses (SMBs) face unique obstacles during ransomware analysis that larger enterprises don't encounter. Limited budgets, small IT teams, and lack of specialized expertise create barriers that can delay response and amplify damage. However, understanding these challenges and leveraging available resources can level the playing field.

Resource Constraints

Most SMBs operate with minimal IT staff, often a single technician or outsourced support, who lack training in advanced forensic tools like Volatility, Ghidra, or enterprise EDR platforms. Maria's bakery relied on Keith, who missed critical C2 traffic because he'd never used Wireshark. Without dedicated security personnel, SMBs struggle to interpret EDR alerts, analyze memory dumps, or conduct reverse engineering during the chaos of an active attack.

Leverage external expertise rather than attempting complex analysis in-house. CISA offers vendor referrals for forensic analysis through its Incident Response program (*report@cisa.dhs.gov* or 888-282-0870). The UK's NCSC provides guidance on selecting incident response providers and can offer referrals through their incident management team. Australia's ACSC maintains relationships with trusted cybersecurity providers and can provide recommendations when contacted at 1300 CYBER1. EU organizations can consult their national cybersecurity agencies or ENISA for vetted incident response partner recommendations. Forensic firms like Mandiant, CrowdStrike, or Blackswan Cybersecurity can provide professional memory analysis, variant identification, and scope assessment. Many cyber insurance policies include incident response services, so be sure to verify coverage before an attack. For ongoing support, consider managed security service providers (MSSPs) who monitor systems and provide 24/7 expert response at predictable monthly costs.

Limited Tooling and Visibility

Enterprise-grade tools like comprehensive EDR solutions, SIEM platforms, or threat intelligence feeds often exceed SMB budgets. Maria's POS system wasn't configured for logging, leaving Keith blind to how LockBit spread. Without cloud monitoring, SMBs miss infections in Google Drive, AWS S3 buckets, or SaaS applications. Free tools like Wireshark or Volatility require significant training to use effectively, and misconfigurations can corrupt evidence or miss critical IOCs.

Start with free, SMB-friendly tools and services. CISA's Cyber Hygiene Scanner (request via 888-863-8656) identifies vulnerabilities and infections in AWS, Azure, or Google Cloud environments. Use VirusTotal for variant identification instead of attempting YARA rules. NoMoreRansom.org catalogs free decryptors for over 100 ransomware variants. Malwarebytes offers free scanning for endpoints. AWS GuardDuty provides a free tier for basic threat detection. Focus on enabling basic logging across all systems, including Windows Event Logs, firewall logs, and cloud audit logs (CloudTrail, Azure Activity Logs), which cost nothing but provide forensic value. Retain logs for 90 days minimum.

Knowledge Gaps

SMB staff often lack cybersecurity training, making it difficult to distinguish ransomware variants, interpret IOCs, or assess attack scope. Keith misidentified LockBit as WannaCry when attempting to use Ghidra, wasting 12 hours. Without understanding of threat intelligence feeds, cloud security, or memory forensics, SMBs risk making critical errors, like Keith nearly paying a fraudulent negotiator or clicking a fake leak site that installed spyware.

Invest in targeted, practical training before an incident occurs. Free resources include CISA's ransomware training modules, YouTube tutorials for tools like Nmap or PowerShell, and vendor-provided webinars from companies like CrowdStrike or Malwarebytes. Join your sector's Information Sharing and Analysis Center (ISAC) for peer support and threat intelligence, such as K12-SIX for schools, Auto-ISAC for dealerships, etc. Conduct quarterly tabletop exercises (TTXs) using scenarios from this chapter to practice response procedures. Most importantly, establish relationships with managed service providers (MSPs) or forensic vendors now, when you're not under a ransom deadline, so you have expert support on speed dial during an actual attack.

Tool Complexity

Advanced forensic platforms require specialized skills that SMBs rarely possess. Commands like `volatility -f memdump.raw --profile=Win10x64 pslist` or reverse engineering with Ghidra are beyond most small business IT capabilities. Even well-intentioned staff can cause harm, and improper evidence handling can frustrate forensic investigations and create legal liability.

Use automated, user-friendly alternatives when available. Platforms like Magnet AXIOM or FireEye's Redline simplify memory analysis with graphical interfaces, though they require licensing. For malware analysis, upload suspicious files to cloud-based sandboxes like Hybrid Analysis or submit them to CISA's Malware Analysis Submission portal for professional reports. Focus your internal efforts on simpler but high-value activities: running PowerShell scripts to find encrypted files (`Get-ChildItem -Path C:\ -Recurse -Include *.lock`), using Nmap for network scans (`nmap -p 445,3389 192.168.1.0/24`), and checking VirusTotal for variant identification. Leave complex memory forensics, reverse engineering, and advanced threat hunting to experts.

Budget Limitations

Cyber insurance, forensic vendors, enterprise tools, and MSPs all cost money that SMBs often don't budget for cybersecurity until after an attack. Maria faced a $50,000 ransom with no insurance coverage for revenue loss or incident response costs. Many SMBs delay investing in preventive measures, then face catastrophic expenses during recovery.

Prioritize cyber insurance that covers incident response costs, forensic analysis, legal fees, and business interruption, not just ransom payments. Policies typically cost $1,000–$5,000 annually for SMBs, far less than a single incident. Negotiate preapproved vendor relationships through your insurer to avoid delays during a crisis. For tools, leverage free tiers: AWS GuardDuty, CISA scanners, Malwarebytes, VirusTotal. Invest minimally in basics that deliver maximum protection: enable MFA (free), configure logging (free), implement offline backups ($100–500 for external drives), and segment your network using existing router/firewall capabilities (often free). Consider shared services, offered by some MSPs in a "community SOC" model, where small businesses share monitoring costs.

Lack of Preparation

SMBs typically lack IRPs, asset inventories, or pre-vetted vendor relationships. When ransomware hits, they waste critical hours determining who to call, what systems are affected, and what data was stolen. Maria didn't know her asset list included cloud storage until LockBit encrypted her Google Drive invoices.

Complete Chapter 7's preparation work now: create an asset inventory including all cloud services, develop a basic IRP with contact information for CISA, agencies in other countries, as well as local forensic vendors, and run one TTX annually. Document your critical systems and prioritize them for protection. Test backup restoration quarterly. Maria could have avoided negotiation entirely with verified, clean backups. Join local business groups or chambers of commerce that offer free cybersecurity resources and peer support. The Small Business Administration (SBA) provides templates for incident response and reporting that Maria successfully adapted.

Remember: SMBs aren't expected to match enterprise capabilities. Success means knowing your limitations, preparing reasonable defenses, and having expert help on standby when sophisticated attacks occur. The goal isn't perfect analysis but a fast, effective response that minimizes damage and enables recovery.

Whether you're a small business owner like Maria working with limited resources, or an IT professional at an enterprise like ZapMart with a full security stack, there's one analysis technique that everyone should understand and use: sandboxing. It's the great equalizer of ransomware analysis, a way to safely examine suspicious files and malware behavior without risking further infection. Free cloud-based platforms like Hybrid Analysis and ANY.RUN put enterprise-grade analysis capabilities within reach of any organization, regardless of budget or technical expertise. Before we dive into the step-by-step process of identifying variants, assessing scope, and exploring decryption options, let's cover this foundational technique that you'll rely on throughout your analysis.

Sandboxing for Behavior Analysis

Sandboxing is a critical technique in cybersecurity that involves executing ransomware or other malicious software in a controlled, isolated virtual environment. This allows security personnel to observe and analyze its behavior without risking harm to live systems. By running the malware in a sandbox, security researchers and analysts can study key characteristics such as encryption methods, command-and-control (C2) communication patterns, persistence mechanisms, and other malicious activities. This controlled environment mimics real-world systems, allowing for detailed behavioral analysis while ensuring the malware cannot escape to cause actual damage.

Real-World Applications of Sandboxing

Everline, discussed in Chapter 9, was infected by Cl0p, the ransomware that appended *.cl0p* file extensions to their encrypted files. Everline's security team utilized Cuckoo Sandbox, an open source automated malware analysis tool, to analyze the ransomware's behavior. The sandbox revealed that the ransomware specifically targeted Everline's enterprise resource planning (ERP) systems, attempting to encrypt critical business data and disrupt operations. This insight allowed Everline to prioritize containment strategies and focus recovery efforts on their ERP infrastructure.

Similarly, ZapMart's cybersecurity team encountered a LockBit ransomware variant. By sandboxing the ransom note dropped by the malware, the team uncovered an embedded spyware installer designed to exfiltrate sensitive data even after the ransom was paid. This discovery enabled ZapMart to implement additional network monitoring to block the spyware's communication with its C2 servers, mitigating further damage.

Practical Sandboxing Tools and Techniques

Organizations of all sizes can leverage sandboxing to enhance their ransomware defenses. Free and accessible sandboxing platforms, such as Hybrid Analysis, provide robust environments for analyzing suspicious files. For example, Change Healthcare uploaded both the ransom note and the associated executable (dropper file) to Hybrid Analysis. The platform's analysis flagged the files for their use of Tor-based C2 traffic, confirming the ransomware's affiliation with ALPHV and providing actionable intelligence to block the associated network activity.

For organizations seeking greater control, setting up isolated virtual machines (VMs) offers a customizable sandboxing solution. These VMs can be configured to replicate specific operating systems and network environments, allowing analysts to observe how ransomware interacts with targeted systems. Tools like VMware Workstation, VirtualBox, or Microsoft Hyper-V can be used to create these isolated environments. Best practices include ensuring the VM is disconnected from production networks, using snapshots to revert to a clean state after each test, and monitoring network traffic with tools like Wireshark to capture C2 communications.

SMBs with limited resources can turn to government-supported initiatives for assistance. CISA offers sandboxing support through its Automated Indicator Sharing (AIS) program and partnerships with cybersecurity vendors. SMBs can upload suspicious files to CISA's Malware Analysis Submission portal, which provides detailed reports on malware behavior, including ransomware-specific actions like file encryption or lateral movement attempts. Similarly, the UK's National Cyber Security Centre provides its Early Warning service and Exercise in a Box toolkit for free incident response training, Australia's ACSC offers tailored support through its Small Business Cyber Resilience Service for businesses with fewer than 20 employees along with 24/7 technical assistance via their hotline (1300 CYBER1), and the European Union's ENISA provides free assessment tools and awareness program toolkits specifically designed for resource-limited organizations.

Advanced Sandboxing Considerations

Modern ransomware often employs anti-analysis techniques to evade detection in sandbox environments. For instance, some variants delay execution, check for virtualized environments, or use obfuscated code to complicate analysis. To counter these tactics, you will have to go beyond the basic sandbox we discussed in "Playing in a Sandbox" on page 225 with advanced sandboxing platforms that incorporate dynamic analysis features, such as simulating user interactions or running the malware for extended periods to trigger its full behavior. Tools like Joe Sandbox and ANY.RUN offer cloud-based, interactive sandboxing with advanced reporting capabilities, making them suitable for analyzing sophisticated ransomware strains.

Additionally, organizations can combine sandboxing with other threat intelligence tools to enhance their understanding of ransomware campaigns. For example, integrating sandbox results with threat feeds from platforms like VirusTotal or Recorded Future can provide context about the ransomware's origins, targeted industries, or associated threat actors. This holistic approach enables organizations to anticipate and prepare for emerging ransomware threats.

Best Practices for Effective Sandboxing

Effective sandboxing requires a strategic approach that balances security isolation with operational efficiency, ensuring suspicious files and potential ransomware can be safely analyzed without compromising production systems:

Use reputable platforms
Leverage trusted sandboxing tools like Hybrid Analysis, Cuckoo Sandbox, or commercial solutions to ensure reliable and safe analysis.

Isolate environments
Ensure sandboxes are fully isolated from production systems to prevent accidental malware execution or lateral movement.

Monitor network activity
Capture and analyze network traffic to identify C2 servers, data exfiltration attempts, or other malicious communications.

Combine with threat intelligence
Correlate sandbox findings with external threat intelligence to gain deeper insights into the ransomware's tactics, techniques, and procedures (TTPs).

Leverage free resources
SMBs and under-resourced organizations should take advantage of free or government-supported sandboxing services, such as those provided by CISA.

By incorporating sandboxing into their cybersecurity strategy, organizations can gain critical insights into ransomware behavior, enabling faster detection, response, and recovery. Whether using free tools like Hybrid Analysis or advanced platforms for in-depth analysis, sandboxing remains a cornerstone of modern ransomware defense.

Survival tip

Start analysis within the first hour of detection. Think of it like an accident victim arriving at the emergency room; they must be quickly assessed and triaged to prioritize care and resources. Use the RACI matrix from Chapter 7 to assign roles (e.g., forensic lead, log analyst) and your IRP to select tools (e.g., VirusTotal). Document every finding in your incident log, including dates, times, IOCs (covered later in this chapter), contacts, and communications to avoid missing details and rework and to support third-party requests from regulators, insurance, and legal. Small businesses in the US can call CISA's 24/7 hotline (888-282-0870) for free guidance. In the UK, small businesses can contact the NCSC for free guidance and access resources tailored for small organizations, while Australian small businesses can call the ACSC's 24/7 hotline at 1300 CYBER1 (1300 292 371) for immediate technical assistance, and EU small businesses can access free support through their national cybersecurity agencies or ENISA's online resources and toolkits.

Exercise: Why analysis saves you

Imagine you are a small business owner struck by ransomware. In 50 words, articulate why identifying the variant and scoping the attack are crucial. Consider how your IRP could accelerate this process, enhancing your ability to respond effectively and mitigate damage.

Identifying the Ransomware Variant

Putting a name to your ransomware attacker is the first move in the analysis game. Is it LockBit 3.0, ALPHV/BlackCat, Cl0p, or a new AI-driven strain cooked up by a RaaS service? The variant dictates everything, including encryption strength, exfiltration risk, negotiation tactics, and decryption odds. In Chapter 9, Sarah and Maria both knew pretty quickly they were infected with LockBit 3.0. Change Healthcare's ALPHV attack used polymorphic code, delaying its identification by 12 hours until VirusTotal flagged it.

Why is variant identification so critical? It's like diagnosing a disease: the right diagnosis unlocks the right treatment. LockBit 3.0's RSA-2048 encryption has no public decryptor, pushing you toward focusing on recovering from backups. ALPHV's double extortion means stolen data is likely on a leak site, triggering regulatory requirements for 72-hour notification. Cl0p's supply chain tactics, seen in BuyMore's attack later in this chapter, required the victim to contact all of their vendors to determine if their infection spread. Misidentifying the variant could mean chasing the wrong fix. Northforge mistook Lorenz for WannaCry, wasting 24 hours on a useless decryptor.

Step 1: Examine the Ransom Note

The ransom note is your first clue, often a text file (e.g., *READ_ME.txt*), desktop pop-up, or email. Read the note carefully but don't click on any links—they may install more malware or track your IP address. Save a copy in a secure, isolated system (e.g., a sandboxed VM, see "Playing in a Sandbox" on page 225). Note specific phrases, file extensions (e.g., *.lock*, *.encrypted*, *.sz40* for Lorenz), or bitcoin wallet addresses. These are IOCs that tools like VirusTotal can analyze. Unfortunately for Change Healthcare, the ALPHV ransom note scored on only 40 out of the 70 antivirus engines, requiring them to conduct manual analysis.

> Small businesses may lack the ability to analyze the ransom note or other ransomware artifacts, which is why we encourage the use of MSPs/MSSPs, as discussed in Chapter 7. Please know that there are fake ransomware analysis tools that serve only to further infect you. Keith used NoMoreRansom.org to confirm LockBit but unfortunately clicked the *.onion* link, resulting in a spyware infection.

Online tools

Several online tools allow users to upload ransom notes or encrypted files to determine the ransomware strain. (Uploading encrypted files to these known tools poses little data loss risk, as the only thing they can see is filenames and not the data inside the files.) Popular ransomware identification tools include:

- No More Ransom ID Ransomware (*nomoreransom.org*)
- MalwareHunterTeam's ID Ransomware (*id-ransomware.malwarehunterteam.com*)
- VirusTotal (*virustotal.com* for analyzing ransomware executables)

Group-IB compiled a list (*https://oreil.ly/TbyEJ*) of many common ransomware notes. A few examples include:

- Ryuk uses plain-text ransom notes with an email contact (see Figure 11-1).
- DarkSide provides a unique victim ID and an extortion message (see Figure 11-2).
- REvil uses a structured ransom note with a Tor link for negotiations (see Figure 11-3).

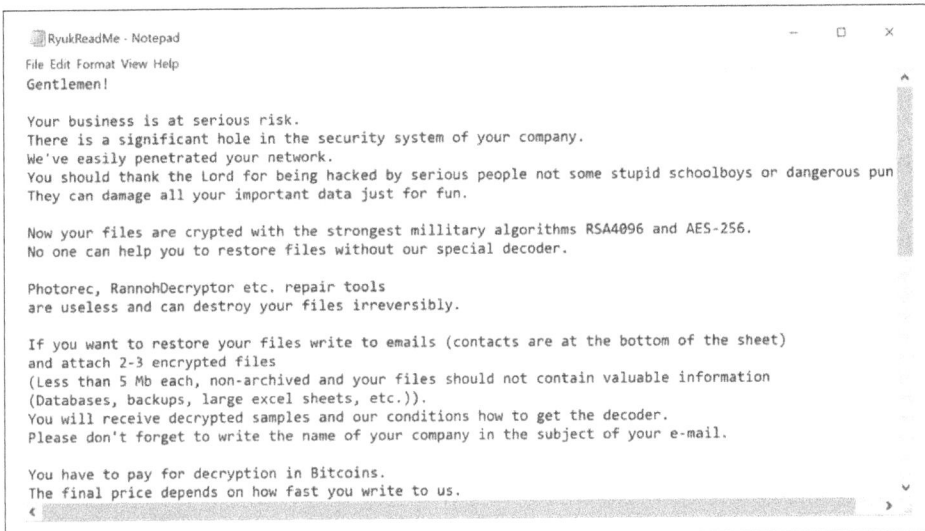

Figure 11-1. Ryuk ransomware note

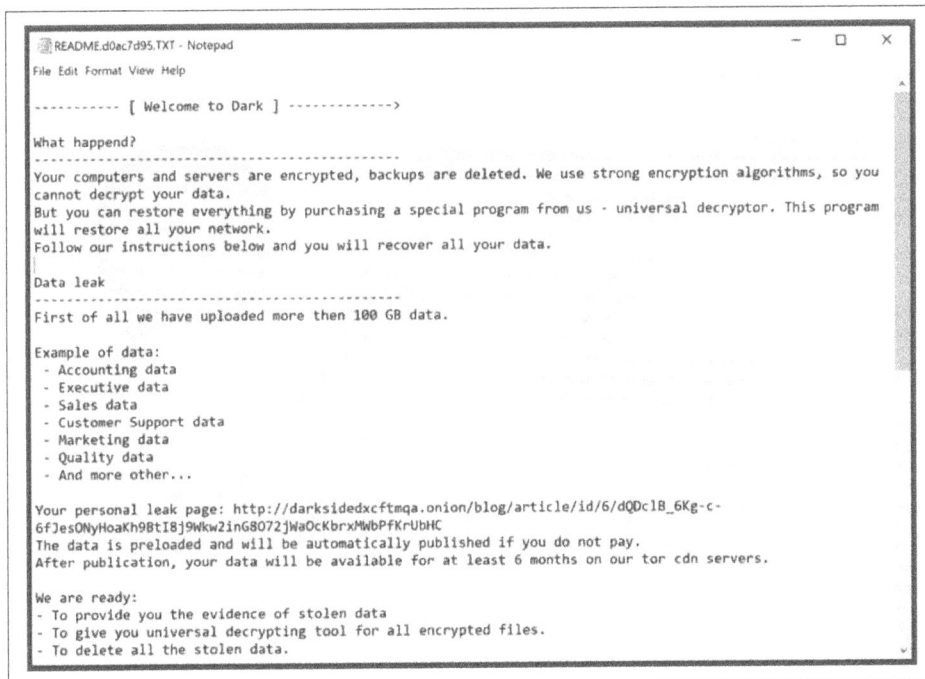

Figure 11-2. DarkSide Ransomware Note

```
=== Welcome. Again. ===

>> Whats Happen?

Your files are encrypted, and currently unavailable. You can check it: all files on your system has
extension 1G7753. ◄━━━━
By the way, everything is possible to recover (restore), but you need to follow our instructions.
Otherwise, you cant return your data (NEVER).

>> What guarantees?

Its just a business. We absolutely do not care about you and your deals, except getting benefits. If we do
not do our work and liabilities - nobody will not cooperate with us. Its not in our interests.
To check the ability of returning files, You should go to our website. There you can decrypt one file for
free. That is our guarantee.
If you will not cooperate with our service - for us, its does not matter. But you will lose your time and
data, cause just we have the private key. In practice - time is much more valuable than money.

>> Sensitive Data

Sensitive data on your network was DOWNLOADED.
If you DON'T WANT your sensitive data to be PUBLISHED in our blog - you have to act quickly.

!!! You should check our blog, using Tor Browser, your data could already be published !!!
http://blogxxu/<redacted.onion> ◄━━━━

Data includes:
- Employees personal data.
- Complete network map including credentials for local and remote services.
- Private financial information
- Manufacturing documents
- And more...

>> How to get access to the website?

Using a TOR browser!
  1) Download and install TOR browser from this site: https://torproject.org/
  2) Open our website: http://lqndxxea<redacted.onion> ◄━━━━
  3) When you open our website, put the following data in the input form:

Key:

<redacted> ◄━━━━
_____
!!! DANGER !!!
DON'T try to change files by yourself, DON'T use any third party software for restoring your data or
antivirus solutions - its may entail damage of the private key and, as result, The Loss all data. !!! !!!
!!!
ONE MORE TIME: Its in your interests to get your files back. From our side, we (the best specialists) make
everything for restoring, but please should not interfere. !!! !!! !!!
```

Figure 11-3. REvil ransomware note

Survival tip

Save the ransom note as evidence, but don't interact with it. Use your forensic toolkit
(e.g., sandboxed VM, digital forensics imaging software, etc.) to analyze the file safely.
Upload the text from the note or screenshots to VirusTotal or NoMoreRansom.org
to identify the variant. Google Image Search can help here as well. Be sure to investigate the resources available to you in your country, discussed in "Cybersecurity
Resources Around the World" on page 190, especially if you're an SMB. Log all IOCs
(extensions, wallets) for use in the next phase.

Step 2: Check File Extensions and System Artifacts

File extensions are a dead giveaway for many variants. LockBit uses *.lock*, ALPHV uses *.encrypted*, Cl0p uses *.cl0p*, and Lorenz uses *.sz40*. We saw in Chapter 9 that files on Sarah's POS system at ZapMart were renamed *data.xls.lock*, confirming encryption by LockBit. Maria's bakery also saw a LockBit extension added to their files (*order.pdf.lock*). Change Healthcare's infected patient records had *.encrypted* extensions, but legacy systems made it difficult to determine the full extent of ALPHV's propagation, requiring manual folder checks across all their devices.

Manually inspect critical folders (e.g., *c:\Users*, shared drives) for renamed files. Use your asset inventory to prioritize systems, like POS for retailers, core processing systems for banks, and patient record systems for healthcare. If you have endpoint detection and response (EDR), check alerts for encryption processes (e.g., *ransomware.exe*). Sarah's EDR flagged a process named "svc32.exe," a known LockBit IOC. Without an EDR, companies can use the Windows Task Manager or Activity Monitor (Mac) to manually spot suspicious processes, but be careful—terminating them may corrupt files.

System artifacts like registry changes or scheduled tasks can also point to the variant. LockBit often creates a registry key (HKEY_CURRENT_USER\Software\LockBit). ALPHV schedules tasks to run the encryptors after a reboot. Use free tools like Autoruns (Sysinternals) to inspect tasks, as Sarah's team did, confirming LockBit's persistence. Small businesses can use Malwarebytes' free scanner to flag artifacts, though it missed Maria's cloud invoice infection due to the lack of cloud support in the free tool.

If possible, security teams can also analyze the ransomware executable itself using a sandbox environment and malware analysis tools. Tools for malware analysis include:

- ANY.RUN (interactive malware sandbox, *any.run* is the website)
- Hybrid Analysis (*hybrid-analysis.com*)
- Cuckoo Sandbox (*cuckoo.cert.ee*)

Case Study: 2025 Cl0p Supply Chain Attack

In 2025, a US retailer (which we'll call "BuyMore") was hit by Cl0p via a vendor's unpatched ERP software. The ransom note demanded $2M, with *.cl0p* extensions added to affected inventory files. The IRT uploaded the note to VirusTotal, which provided confirmation of Cl0p and an indication that the attack will likely involve double extortion. NoMoreRansom.org did not have a decryptor, but CISA noted Cl0p was sanctioned by the US Office of Foreign Assets Control (OFAC), ruling out paying the ransom. BuyMore's EDR logs showed a C2 domain (*cl0p[.]ru*), but their system inventory was missing one SaaS account, which meant no one noticed it had been infected with Cl0p, allowing it to exfiltrate 1TB of data before anyone noticed. Once the data breach was identified, it activated a regulatory mandate requiring notification within 72 hours. Vendor audits could have caught the vendor's unpatched ERP software.

Survival tip

Compare infected file extensions against a variant list, for example, *.lock*, indicating LockBit. Prioritize system assessments using your asset inventory. Execute Autoruns or Malwarebytes to uncover ransomware artifacts. Engage forensic vendors for intricate artifacts. Document findings, such as ".cl0p on ERP, 1/8/25," for regulatory purposes.

Exercise: Spot the Variant

Assume the role of Sarah's IRT lead at ZapMart. A ransom note demands $500,000, and *.lock* files appear on the point-of-sale system. In 100 words, draft a plan to confirm the variant using VirusTotal and NoMoreRansom.org, incorporating your forensic toolkit. Inspect one artifact, such as a registry key, with Autoruns. Reflect on alternatives if endpoint detection and response tools are unavailable, ensuring a robust identification strategy.

Step 3: Analyze Logs and Network Traffic

Logs are one of the first places you should look when things go bad. If your log sources are configured well, protected, and cover more than 30 days, you have a potential goldmine of information and a good chance at variant identification.

EDR tools like CrowdStrike, SentinelOne, or Huntress will log unauthorized processes, C2 traffic, or file encryption activities. OpenXDR platforms, like Stellar Cyber, can also ingest event data from multiple sources, like EDR, NDR, firewalls, etc., and establish baselines from which any behavioral deviations can be alerted on.

Zapmart's EDR showed Sarah's CISO that *svc32.exe* was contacting a Russian IP, a LockBit IOC. Firewall logs can reveal C2 domains (e.g., cl0p[.]ru) or Tor traffic, as Change Healthcare's ALPHV attack showed. If the malware wipes your log files, a common anti-forensic tactic, then you're stuck doing manual system reviews, as Keith learned when he discovered that Maria's POS system wasn't configured for logging.

Take a look at the log analysis process laid out in Figure 11-4. First start with EDR alerts for suspicious processes or network connections. Cross-reference IP addresses or domains with threat intelligence feeds like Abuse.ch or CISA's Known Exploited Vulnerabilities (KEV) catalog. Sarah's team matched a C2 IP address to LockBit's known infrastructure, further confirming the variant. If you don't have an EDR, check the Windows Event Logs, Event ID 4688 for processes, and firewall logs for outbound traffic. Change Healthcare's ALPHV attack showed 2TB of outbound traffic to a Tor node, a solid clue of exfiltration.

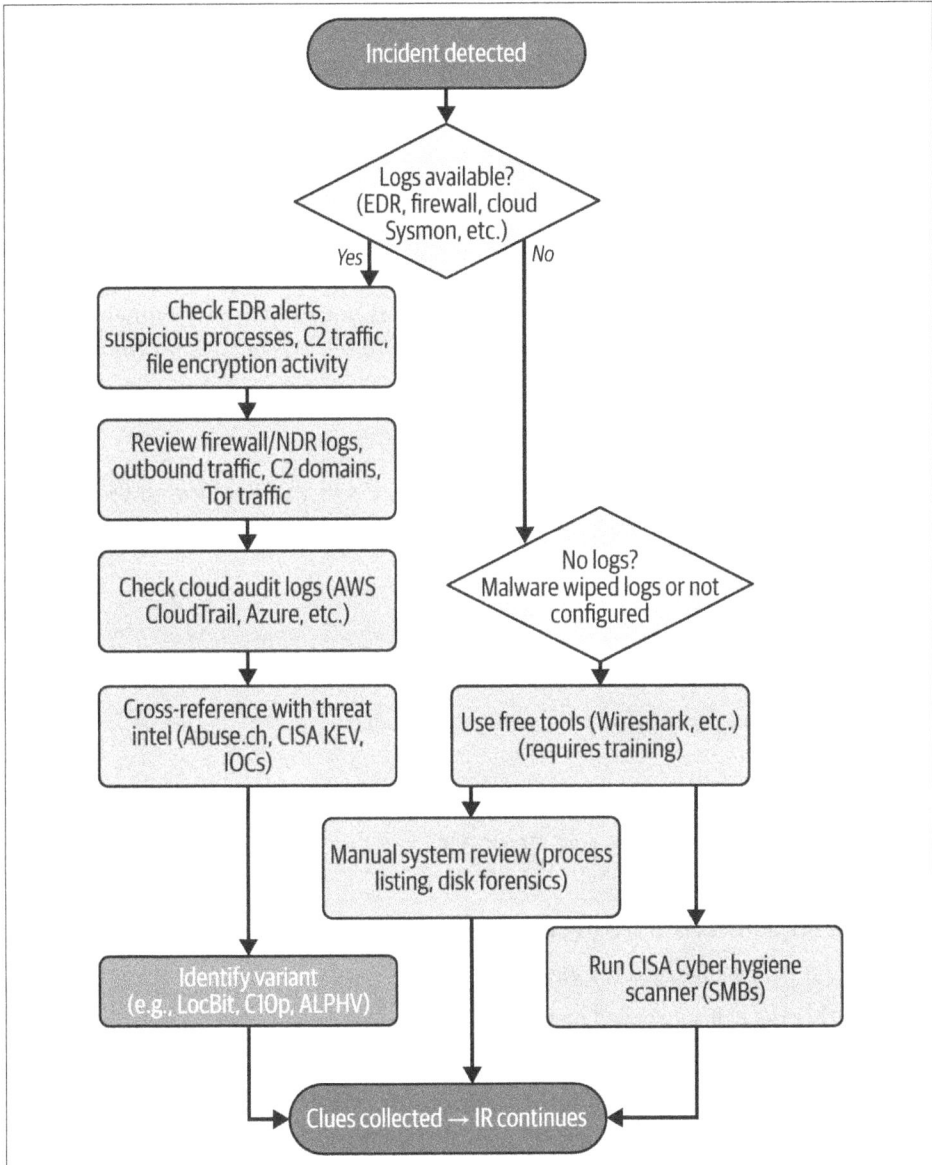

Figure 11-4. A flowchart of the log analysis process

Small businesses or environments without logging capabilities can use free tools like Wireshark to capture network traffic during the IR. However, most of these tools do require training to be effective, although YouTube can be quite helpful if you have time. Keith wasn't aware of the tools available to help him collect data during the IR. (We will again point out the value of a professional at a time such as this.) As a result, he missed LockBit's C2 traffic and delayed his variant identification by several hours. CISA's Cyber Hygiene Scanner, free for SMBs, can be downloaded and run during an IR to identify IOCs. For cloud systems, check audit logs (e.g., AWS CloudTrail) for unauthorized access, as Cl0p exploited in the 2025 retailer case, as well as suspicious logins and login locations.

What is AWS CloudTrail?

AWS CloudTrail is Amazon's audit logging service that records API calls and activities across your AWS infrastructure. Think of it as a comprehensive activity log that tracks "who did what, when, and from where" in your AWS environment. Events are delivered to S3 buckets and can also be sent to CloudWatch Logs for real-time monitoring and alerting.

How CloudTrail works

Event capture: CloudTrail automatically logs every API call made to AWS services, whether through:

- AWS Management Console (web interface)
- AWS command-line interface (CLI)
- AWS SDKs and APIs
- Other AWS services making calls on your behalf

Event details recorded:

- Identity of the caller (user, role, or service)
- Time and date of the call
- Source IP address and geographic location
- Request parameters and response elements
- Whether the call succeeded or failed

Why CloudTrail is critical for security

Visibility: Without CloudTrail, you're essentially blind to what's happening in your AWS environment. It's like having security cameras for your cloud infrastructure.

Forensics: When a security incident occurs, CloudTrail provides the timeline and evidence needed to understand:

- How attackers gained access

- What they did once inside

- What data or systems were compromised

- When the breach occurred

Compliance: Many regulatory and contractual frameworks require audit trails, making CloudTrail essential for compliance with standards like SOC 2, PCI DSS, and HIPAA.

Case Study: 2025 AI-Driven RaaS Attack

In February 2025, a Texas manufacturer, which we'll call "Techforge," was hit by a new RaaS strain using AI-crafted phishing emails to bypass filters. Once the systems were infected, the ransom note, with *.aienc* extensions, demanded $1M. The ransom note was uploaded to VirusTotal, which identified the ransomware as a LockBit derivative, from which a subsequent investigation determined there was no decryptor for it.

EDR logs were the initial focus of Techforge's IRT and showed a large volume of C2 traffic to a Bulgarian IP address. The IRT's focus on network traffic distracted them from other data sources, like their AWS CloudTrail logs, which would have shown a compromised SaaS account. The IRT's failure to identify and review all possible log sources in a timely manner allowed the ransomware to spread to over 50% of their servers, ultimately costing $3M in downtime. In addition to updating their log review procedures in the IR playbook, the company could have implemented cloud monitoring to catch the SaaS account compromise, saving almost an entire day of IR activities and a lot of money. The following is a sample of an EDR log:

```
Timestamp: 2025-06-07T14:32:17Z
Host: WKSTN-014
Event Type: Network Connection
Source IP: 192.168.1.45
Destination IP: 185.220.101.123
Destination Port: 443
Protocol: TCP
Process Name: svchost.exe
Process Path: C:\Windows\System32\svchost.exe
SHA256 Hash: 8f9a2b1c4d6e7f8901a2b3c4d5e6f7a8b9c0d1e2f3a4b5c6d7e8f9a0b1c2d3e4
Action Taken: Connection blocked, process quarantined.

Timestamp: 2025-06-07T14:33:05Z
Host: WKSTN-014
Event Type: File Creation
File Path: C:\Users\Public\ransom_note.txt
SHA256 Hash: a1b2c3d4e5f6a7b8c9d0e1f2a3b4c5d6e7f8a9b0c1d2e3f4a5b6c7d8e9f0a1b
Action Taken: File quarantined.

Timestamp: 2025-06-07T14:34:22Z
```

```
Host: SRV-003
Event Type: Process Execution
Process Name: encryptor.exe
Process Path: C:\ProgramData\encryptor.exe
SHA256 Hash: b2c3d4e5f6a7b8c9d0e1f2a3b4c5d6e7f8a9b0c1d2e3f4a5b6c7d8e9f0a1b2c
Action Taken: Process terminated, system isolated.
```

Survival tip

To enhance your ransomware response, regularly analyze your EDR logs against free threat intelligence feeds like Abuse.ch's URLhaus. Here is what that process looks like:

- Extract IP addresses, domains, or file hashes from your EDR alerts.

- Cross-reference them with URLhaus to identify matches with known ransomware C2 servers or payloads, such as LockBit or Cl0p.

- Use automated scripts or SIEM integrations to streamline this process, ensuring rapid confirmation of variants.

- Always validate findings with additional sources like CISA's KEV catalog to avoid false positives.

Exercise: Dig through logs

Practice identifying ransomware IOCs using threat intelligence feeds.

1. Use the simulated EDR log above and extract the destination IP addresses, bitcoin wallet, and file hashes from the log entries.

2. Use Abuse.ch's URLhaus (*https://urlhaus.abuse.ch*) and AlienVault's Open Threat Exchange (OTX) (*https://otx.alienvault.com*) websites to search for these IOCs and document any matches, noting the ransomware variant and any associated campaign details.

3. Verify any findings using CISA's Known Exploited Vulnerabilities catalog (*https://www.cisa.gov/known-exploited-vulnerabilities-catalog*).

4. Write a brief report (100–150 words) summarizing your findings, including the matched IOC, ransomware variant, and confidence level based on source reliability.

Challenge: If no matches are found, propose an alternative approach to confirm the IOCs using a social media source like @ThreatIntel on X, and describe how you would validate the information to avoid misinformation.

Step 4: Leverage Threat Intelligence Feeds

Threat intelligence feeds (e.g., URLhaus, OTX, FirEye, or CISA's AIS) aggregate real-time data on ransomware IOCs, including IP addresses, domains, file hashes, and tactics. They're like a global wanted list for cybercrime, helping you confirm variants when tools like VirusTotal fall short. The 2025 Cl0p supply chain attack on BuyMore was flagged by CISA's KEV catalog, linking *.cl0p* files to a vendor exploit.

Free threat intel feeds like Abuse.ch's URLhaus or AlienVault's OTX track ransomware C2 domains and hashes. Figure 11-5 shows you an example from URLhaus.

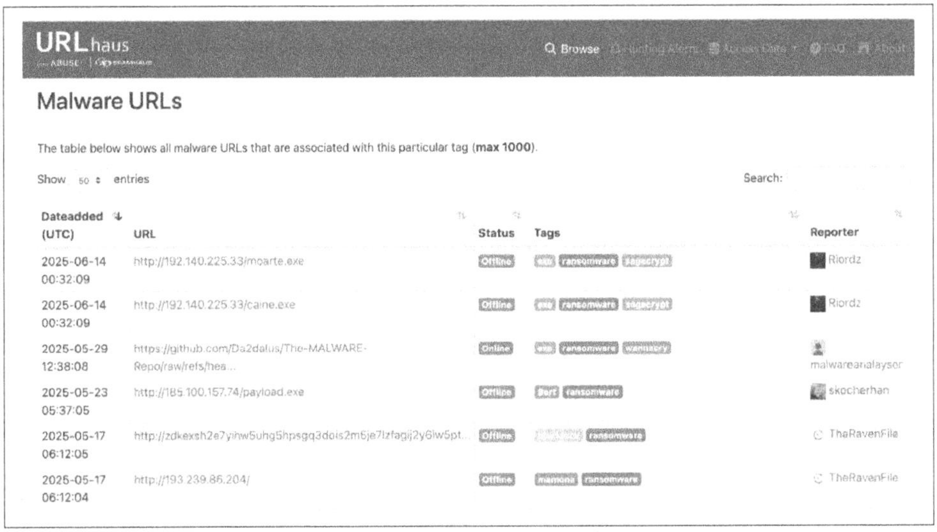

Figure 11-5. URLhaus screenshot

Sarah's IRT queried OTX for the ransom note's bitcoin wallet, tying it to LockBit 3.0's 2024 campaign. Paid feeds like Recorded Future or FireEye offer deeper insights, catching ALPHV's Tor nodes in the Change Healthcare case. Small businesses can access CISA's AIS for free, which flagged Cl0p's ERP exploit in the 2025 retailer case. Similarly, the UK's NCSC offers free Early Warning alerts that notify organizations of potential threats, Australia's ACSC provides free Alert Service notifications about emerging ransomware campaigns, and ENISA offers threat intelligence resources accessible to all EU member state organizations.

If your organization is classified as part of United States critical infrastructure, then you are eligible for access to the Multi-State Information Sharing and Analysis Center (MS-ISAC), as well as your sector's specific ISAC (e.g., FS-ISAC for financial services, CU-ISAO for credit unions, K12-SIX for K12 education, Auto-ISAC for auto dealerships, etc.). Check feeds against your EDR logs and alerts, or firewall traffic to confirm matches.

Social media posts, such as X and Reddit, are a goldmine for real-time intel. Monitor handles like @ThreatIntel or @RansomWatch for variant updates. A 2025 post linked an AI-driven RaaS strain's *.aienc* files to a Bulgarian C2, helping Techforge identify their attacker. But always verify your intel with primary sources (e.g., CISA, VirusTotal) because misinformation spreads fast and can derail your response, as Keith learned when a fake X post led him to a scam site.

Survival tip

Query logs against Abuse.ch or CISA's AIS for IOC matches. Monitor X (@ThreatIntel) but cross-check with VirusTotal. Engage a forensic vendor for paid feeds if budget allows. SMBs can email CISA (*report@cisa.dhs.gov*) for free AIS access. Similar resources may be available in other countries (e.g., NCSC in the UK, ACSC in Australia, etc). Log feed findings for the eradication phase.

Exercise: Hunt with Intel

You lead Techforge's incident response team. A "*.aienc*" ransom note suggests an AI-driven strain. In 100 words, outline a plan to confirm the variant using Open Threat Exchange and CISA's KEV catalog, referencing endpoint logs. Reflect on verifying an X post's credibility to ensure reliable intelligence.

Assessing the Attack's Scope

With the variant identified (e.g., LockBit for ZapMart and Maria's bakery or ALPHV for Change Healthcare), you need to map out the damage. Which systems were hit? Is the ransomware still spreading? Was any data exfiltrated? Scoping the attack defines your containment strategy and avoids surprises, like the previously mentioned engineering firm's $7M repository loss from a missed infection. Remember that Maria underestimated the scope of her attack.

Scoping requires precision. Use your asset inventory to identify critical systems, such as the POS systems for retailers, patient records for hospitals, and the ERP system for manufacturers. EDR alerts and logs can be very telling and often reveal infection patterns. Without tools, you're manually checking folders, which can be both a distraction and a setback. BuyMore's attack discussed earlier in this chapter missed an infection of a SaaS vendor, letting 1TB leak to the dark net. Let's break this down further.

Step 1: Inventory Infected Systems

Start with your asset inventory to determine critical systems to be checked. For Sarah, this meant ZapMart's POS terminals, billing servers, and HR databases. For Change Healthcare, it was patient records, ventilators, and imaging systems. Maria prioritized her POS and inventory PC. Use your EDR to scan endpoints for IOCs (e.g., *.lock* files, *encryptor.exe*). ZapMart's EDR showed Sarah that 50 out of 100 endpoints were infected with LockBit, helping them focus their containment efforts and resources.

Without an EDR solution, you can manually search folders for ransom notes or extensions. Change Healthcare ran a PowerShell module called *Get-ChildItem* to find *.encrypted* files:

```
Get-ChildItem -Path C:\ -Recurse -Include *.encrypted,*.txt -ErrorAction
SilentlyContinue | Select-Object FullName
```

This found 5,000 affected files, confirming the spread of ALPHV in the environment. SMBs like Maria's can use Windows Search function to look for "*.lock" but they risk missing hidden files. Free tools like Malwarebytes scan endpoints but don't look at cloud data. This is why Maria's scan missed her cloud sync folder. Cloud systems (e.g., Google Drive, AWS) must have logging configured to be of any use, and the timely review of the logs is critical during this phase. BuyMore's Cl0p attack missed a SaaS account, resulting in compromised backups.

IoT devices can be a blind spot. Change Healthcare's IoT thermometers lacked EDR coverage, hiding ALPHV's foothold. A network scanner like Nmap can detect such infections. Log your findings, for example, "POS encrypted, 3/10/2025, 50 files," for containment planning.

Survival tip

Cross-reference your inventory with endpoint scans or manual checks. Use Power-Shell for hidden files. Review cloud logs for SaaS breaches. Scan IoT devices with Nmap. Small businesses may use Malwarebytes or CISA's scanner (888-863-8656). Update logs hourly. We'll talk about some of these tools in Step 2.

Exercise: Map infected systems

You are Keith, Maria's nephew at her bakery. The point-of-sale system displays *.lock* files, and you suspect cloud involvement via the laptop. In 150 words, outline a plan to inventory infections using your asset list and PowerShell, scanning cloud logs. Reflect on addressing potential IoT oversights.

Step 2: Detect Lateral Movement

Lateral movement is a hallmark of ransomware attacks, enabling malware to spread across networks and compromise critical systems. Attackers exploit vulnerabilities in protocols like SMB, RDP, or unpatched systems to propagate ransomware from an initial foothold to high-value targets such as servers, backups, or ERP systems. Detecting and disrupting lateral movement is essential to contain ransomware and minimize damage. This section explores techniques, tools, and real-world examples to help organizations identify and mitigate lateral movement effectively.

Understanding lateral movement in ransomware

Common techniques of lateral movement include exploiting misconfigured protocols like SMB (port 445) or RDP (port 3389), abusing stolen credentials, or utilizing tools like PsExec for remote execution. Sarah, ZapMart's IT administrator, discovered that a misconfigured firewall allowed ransomware to spread to human resources systems via SMB. Firewall logs revealed unusual traffic on port 445, which could have been flagged earlier with proper monitoring.

Similarly, Change Healthcare traced the attack's spread to SMB exploitation. Windows Event Logs showed Event ID 4450, pointing to the use of SMB to facilitate the ransomware's propagation to billing systems. The Chicago school district identified open SMB ports on multiple servers using a simple Nmap scan (`nmap -p 445,3389 192.168.1.0/24`). This scan revealed vulnerabilities that explained the ransomware's rapid spread across their network.

From Government Weapon to Global Catastrophe

The dangers of undeterred lateral movement are well illustrated by the story of EternalBlue and WannaCry. EternalBlue was a cyber weapon developed by the NSA to exploit a critical vulnerability in Windows file-sharing protocols, allowing remote code execution without user interaction. In 2017, hackers stole and publicly released this tool, making it available to cybercriminals worldwide.

WannaCry ransomware weaponized EternalBlue in May 2017 to create a "wormable" attack that could automatically spread across networks without requiring users to click malicious links or open attachments. Unlike typical ransomware that infects individual computers, WannaCry used the EternalBlue exploit to autonomously scan for and infect every vulnerable Windows machine it could reach. Within 72 hours, it infected over 300,000 computers across 150 countries, crippling hospitals, government agencies, and businesses worldwide.

The relationship between EternalBlue and WannaCry illustrates a critical cybersecurity lesson: vulnerabilities initially developed for government surveillance can quickly become weapons in the hands of criminals. While Microsoft had released a patch for the EternalBlue vulnerability months earlier, the widespread failure to apply this patch created a global crisis, highlighting how lateral movement capabilities can transform a localized infection into a worldwide catastrophe and making patch management and network segmentation absolutely critical for defending against modern ransomware threats.

Tools and techniques for detecting lateral movement

This section covers many of the same tools we discussed in Chapter 5 when we were talking about how to minimize lateral movement. However, this is a different

---

discussion now. You have been attacked and we are using these tools to assess the level of damage. To detect lateral movement, organizations must actively monitor network traffic, system logs, and endpoint activity. Following are key methods and tools to identify suspicious behavior:

Network scanning with Nmap

Nmap is a powerful, open source tool for discovering open ports and services that ransomware may exploit. Devices with open SMB or RDP ports are common entry ports for ransomware. These vulnerable devices can be detected by running this nmap command: `nmap -p 445,3389 192.168.1.0/24`. For example, the school district discussed in Chapter 12 used Nmap to pinpoint servers with exposed SMB ports, enabling them to close these vulnerabilities and halt further spread.

Firewall and system log analysis

Reviewing firewall logs for unexpected SMB (port 445) or RDP (port 3389) traffic is critical. Windows Event Logs can also reveal lateral movement indicators, such as Event ID 4450 for SMB connections or Event ID 4624 for successful logons via RDP. Organizations should configure logging to capture these events and use SIEM systems to centralize and analyze logs in real time.

EDR

EDR solutions, such as CrowdStrike or SentinelOne, can detect IOCs associated with lateral movement, such as the use of *PsExec.exe* or unusual process execution. In the absence of comprehensive logs, EDR alerts can provide visibility into suspicious activities, like unauthorized access to administrative shares or remote command execution.

Network traffic analysis with Wireshark

Wireshark is a free tool for capturing and analyzing network traffic, allowing organizations to identify anomalous SMB or RDP activity. However, its complexity can be a barrier for less experienced teams. For instance, Keith attempted to use Wireshark to monitor LockBit's spread but missed critical traffic patterns due to unfamiliarity with the tool. SMBs with limited expertise should consider simpler alternatives or seek external support.

CISA's free scanning tools

CISA offers free scanning tools through its Cyber Hygiene Services, which can detect open ports and vulnerabilities like exposed SMB or RDP services. Small and medium-sized businesses can request a scan via CISA's portal, receiving actionable reports to secure their networks. Similar resources may be available in other countries.

Table 11-1 gives you a more complete list of log analysis tools, the level of skill required to use them, and what kind of output you should expect from them.

Table 11-1. Log analysis tools

Tool	Use case	Skill level needed	Output type
VirusTotal	Ransomware variant identification, IOC verification	Beginner	Detection scores, threat intelligence reports
NoMoreRansom.org	Finding free decryptors for ransomware variants	Beginner	Available decryptors, variant identification
Nmap	Network scanning for open ports, lateral movement detection	Intermediate	Port scan results, service enumeration
Wireshark	Network traffic analysis, C2 communication detection	Advanced	Packet captures, traffic analysis
EDR solutions (CrowdStrike, SentinelOne)	Real-time threat detection, behavioral monitoring	Intermediate	Alerts, process logs, threat reports
SIEM platforms (Splunk, QRadar)	Log aggregation, correlation, anomaly detection	Advanced	Centralized logs, correlation reports, alerts
Volatility Framework	Memory forensics, extracting encryption keys	Advanced	Process lists, network connections, memory artifacts
DumpIt	Memory dump capture for forensic analysis	Beginner	Raw memory dump files
Ghidra	Reverse engineering ransomware samples	Expert	Disassembled code, function analysis, IOCs
IDA Pro	Advanced reverse engineering, malware analysis	Expert	Code analysis, encryption algorithms, C2 infrastructure
YARA rules	Custom malware signature creation and detection	Intermediate	Pattern matches, malware classification
Cuckoo Sandbox	Safe malware behavior analysis	Intermediate	Behavioral reports, network activity logs
Hybrid Analysis	Cloud-based malware sandboxing	Beginner	Automated analysis reports, IOC extraction
AWS CloudTrail	Cloud activity monitoring, breach detection	Intermediate	API call logs, user activity records
Azure Activity Logs	Azure resource monitoring, unauthorized access detection	Intermediate	Resource access logs, security events
PowerShell Scripts	File enumeration, system analysis	Intermediate	File lists, system information
Malwarebytes	Basic malware scanning for SMBs	Beginner	Scan results, quarantine reports
Autoruns	Startup program analysis, persistence detection	Beginner	Startup program lists, registry entries
Recuva/PhotoRec	File recovery from encrypted systems	Beginner	Recovered file listings
EnCase/FTK	Enterprise forensic analysis	Expert	Comprehensive forensic reports, evidence preservation
CISA Cyber Hygiene Scanner	Free vulnerability scanning for SMBs	Beginner	Vulnerability reports, remediation guidance

Case Study: 2024 Manufacturer Breach

In February 2024, a California-based manufacturer suffered a devastating ALPHV ransomware attack. The attackers gained initial access through a compromised API key from a third-party SaaS vendor, which allowed them to infiltrate the manufacturer's cloud environment. The ransomware appended *.encrypted* extensions to files on ERP servers, and SMB logs later revealed that 1TB of sensitive data had been exfiltrated before encryption.

The manufacturer's EDR system failed to detect lateral movement within the cloud environment, as it was not configured to monitor cloud-based API calls. Many organizations overlook cloud monitoring because they assume their traditional endpoint security tools provide adequate coverage, not realizing that cloud environments require separate monitoring of API calls, service-to-service communications, and identity-based access patterns. However, AWS CloudTrail logs later revealed unauthorized API calls, indicating the attacker's movement from the compromised SaaS vendor to the ERP systems. A delayed scope scan allowed ALPHV to encrypt critical backups, resulting in a $2 million loss from ransom payments and downtime.

Here are some lessons learned:

Cloud monitoring is critical
> Organizations using cloud services must enable and review logs like AWS CloudTrail or Azure Activity Logs to detect unauthorized access or lateral movement.

Third-party risk management
> Regularly audit and secure API keys and access controls for third-party vendors to prevent supply chain attacks.

Proactive scanning
> Conducting real-time scope scans and monitoring could have identified the compromised API key earlier, potentially preventing the encryption of backups.

Backup protection
> Implement air-gapped or immutable backups to ensure ransomware cannot compromise recovery options.

By adopting robust detection strategies and leveraging tools like Nmap, Wireshark, and CISA's services, organizations can identify and disrupt lateral movement before ransomware causes catastrophic damage. The 2024 manufacturer breach underscores the importance of proactive monitoring, especially in cloud environments, to contain ransomware and protect critical assets.

Survival tip

Examine logs for ports 445 and 3389. Use Nmap or endpoint tools for lateral movement. Check cloud logs for API misuse. Log findings for eradication.

Exercise: Track lateral movement

You're the manufacturer's IT lead. ALPHV has spread via SMB. In 100 words, devise a plan to detect movement using Nmap and logs, checking CloudTrail. Reflect on gaps in SMB tools that could hinder detection. (Estimated time: 10 minutes)

Step 3: Confirm Data Exfiltration

Double extortion has become a hallmark of modern ransomware attacks, where attackers not only encrypt data but also exfiltrate sensitive information to pressure victims into paying ransoms. Confirming data exfiltration is critical to assess the scope of a breach, mitigate further damage, and comply with regulatory requirements like GDPR or CCPA. This step involves analyzing network traffic, endpoint activity, and external intelligence to identify stolen data and prepare for potential public leaks. Below, we explore methods, tools, and real-world examples to guide organizations in confirming data exfiltration effectively.

For advanced techniques on safely monitoring dark web leak sites directly, see "Step 6: Monitor Dark Web Leak Sites" on page 351.

The threat of double extortion

In a double extortion attack, attackers steal sensitive data before deploying ransomware, threatening to leak it on dark web marketplaces or leak sites if the ransom is not paid. The Change Healthcare breach discussed in Chapter 9 is a perfect example of this.

Similarly, a school district hit by the Ryuk ransomware in 2025 failed to detect cloud-based exfiltration, only discovering the breach after stolen student data appeared on a leak site. The lack of cloud monitoring delayed their response, resulting in GDPR fines and reputational damage. These cases underscore the need for proactive exfiltration detection to mitigate financial, legal, and public relations risks.

Techniques for confirming data exfiltration

Like the section on lateral movement, this section will discuss tools and techniques already discussed in this book; however, the purpose of these tools will be different. The key here is to use these tools to determine if data has been exfiltrated.

Organizations can use a combination of network analysis, endpoint monitoring, and external intelligence to confirm data exfiltration. Below are key approaches and tools:

Firewall log analysis

Firewall logs are a primary source for detecting large or unusual outbound data transfers. Look for spikes in traffic to unfamiliar IP addresses, especially those associated with Tor or known C2 servers. In Change Healthcare's ALPHV case, logs showed sustained transfers to a Tor IP, indicating exfiltration. Configure firewalls to log outbound traffic details, including destination IPs, ports, and data volumes, and use SIEM systems to automate anomaly detection.

Network traffic analysis with Wireshark

Wireshark, a free packet analysis tool, allows organizations to capture and inspect network traffic for exfiltration indicators, such as FTP, SFTP, or HTTP/HTTPS uploads to C2 servers. Analysts can filter for specific protocols or IP addresses to identify suspicious activity. However, Wireshark requires technical expertise, and misconfigurations can lead to missed detections, as seen in the Ryuk school case, where cloud traffic went unnoticed.

Endpoint detection tools

EDR solutions, such as Microsoft Defender, Huntress, or CrowdStrike, can detect exfiltration behaviors, such as unauthorized file compression, mass file access, or connections to external servers. Look for indicators like processes initiating FTP sessions or accessing cloud storage services (e.g., Dropbox, Mega) without authorization. EDR tools provide detailed telemetry to trace exfiltration attempts back to specific devices or users.

External threat intelligence

Services like DarkOwl or Recorded Future monitor dark web marketplaces and leak sites for stolen data. By consulting these platforms, organizations can confirm if their data has been exposed or offered for sale. For example, Change Healthcare cross-referenced their breach with DarkOwl, confirming ALPHV's leak before it became public, allowing them to prepare a response.

Cloud monitoring

In cloud environments, exfiltration often occurs via unauthorized API calls or cloud storage services. Tools like AWS CloudTrail, Azure Monitor, or Google Cloud Audit Logs can detect suspicious data transfers. The Ryuk school's failure to monitor cloud activity delayed their detection, emphasizing the need for cloud-specific visibility.

CISA and forensic support

SMBs with limited resources can engage forensic vendors or request assistance from CISA, if you're in the US. CISA's Incident Response services include exfiltration analysis, helping SMBs identify stolen data and assess breach scope.

Forensic vendors use advanced tools to reconstruct attack timelines and confirm data theft. If you're in the UK, the NCSC offers incident response support and guidance for organizations affected by ransomware, while Australian SMBs can access free tailored incident response assistance through the ACSC's Small Business Cyber Resilience Service and 24/7 technical support at 1300 CYBER1, and EU organizations can contact their national cybersecurity agencies for forensic assistance and breach analysis support.

> Organizations should determine now, not after an incident, whether CISA (or equivalent government) resources are available to them. These resources are great, but they're not helpful if you can't get their attention.

Regulatory and public relations considerations

Identifying data exfiltration activates compliance requirements under regulations such as GDPR, CCPA, or HIPAA, all of which demand prompt breach notifications. Make sure to involve legal and compliance in the discussion, so you can remain compliant. For example, GDPR requires organizations to notify authorities within 72 hours of discovering a breach involving personal data. Failure to comply, as seen in the Ryuk school district case, can result in significant fines.

Documenting exfiltration findings, including the types of data stolen (e.g., personal, financial, or health records), is essential for crafting accurate notifications and managing public relations. Engage legal counsel to ensure compliance and prepare public statements to maintain stakeholder trust.

Exercise: Find the leak

You are the IT lead for a school district potentially compromised by Ryuk ransomware. There is concern that student and staff data may have been exfiltrated. In 150 words, draft a plan to confirm exfiltration. Use firewall logs and Wireshark and consult DarkOwl for external intelligence. Reflect on GDPR steps if exfiltration is confirmed, ensuring regulatory adherence. (Estimated time: 10 minutes.)

Exploring Decryption and Remediation Options

At this point in the attack, you now know the exact ransomware that has infected your systems and scoped its damage, like Maria's infected POS or Techforge's SaaS breach.

As a reminder, here is the ransomware that infected the examples we have been following:

- Maria's bakery, Sarah at ZapMart, and Techforge: LockBit 3.0
- CA manufacturer: ALPHV/BlackCat
- BuyMore: Cl0p
- Change Healthcare: ALPHV/BlackCat
- 2025 Chicago school: Ryuk

Now, the million-dollar question (literally): *Can you decrypt the files without paying the ransom?*

The odds are slim, especially for modern strains like LockBit and ALPHV, which use RSA-2048 encryption that is virtually unbreakable without the private key. Yet, exploring decryption and remediation options is a critical step. A free decryptor saved a college thousands of dollars in 2023, while you learned in Chapter 9 of a scam decryptor that bricked 10% of Maria's files. This section guides you through evaluating decryptors, using forensic tools, and avoiding traps, ensuring you make informed decisions before pivoting to containment. This is just another reminder that any tools you use should come from trusted sources. It can be very easy to grasp at straws when you are desperate for a solution.

Step 1: Check for Public Decryptors

Some ransomware variants, especially older or poorly coded ones, have public decryptors (tools reverse-engineered by researchers to unlock files without payment). Earlier examples noted that CryptoLocker's 2014 strain was cracked by NoMoreRansom.org, saving thousands of victims. Newer variants like LockBit 3.0 or ALPHV, with their robust encryption, rarely have decryptors due to complex key management in RaaS models. Still, checking is your first move.

Start with NoMoreRansom.org, a Europol-backed site offering 100+ free decryptors. Upload a ransom note or encrypted file to match the variant. Sarah's team tried this for LockBit's *.lock* files but found no solution and had to refocus on recovering from backups. Change Healthcare's ALPHV *.encrypted* files had no decryptor, confirmed by NoMoreRansom's database. Emsisoft's free decryptor tool supports strains like STOP/Djvu but requires exact variant matches.

CISA's StopRansomware.gov provides decryptor lists and guidance. One college recovered 80% of files using CISA's CryptoLocker tool, avoiding payment. Test decryptors in a sandboxed VM to safeguard production systems; Sarah's CISO skipped this step, losing 5% of their test files to a defective tool. If no decryptor exists, backups or forensic analysis offer the next avenues.

Law enforcement can also be valuable resources for decryption. The FBI and US Secret Service maintain ransomware investigation teams who have worked numerous cases. In some instances, they have obtained decryptors from other victims or through their own investigations that may work on your encrypted systems. Contact the FBI's Internet Crime Complaint Center (IC3.gov) or your local FBI field office. While there's no guarantee they'll have a decryptor for your specific variant, it costs nothing to ask, and they can provide valuable guidance on your response.

Survival tip

Check NoMoreRansom.org and StopRansomware.gov for decryptors matching your variant's ID (e.g., *lock* = LockBit). Always conduct your testing in a sandbox. Avoid unverified decryptors; 80% are fraudulent, and some even contain more malware. Log all of your activities for insurance purposes.

Exercise: Hunt for a decryptor

You're Change Healthcare's IT lead. NoMoreRansom.org's site doesn't list a decryptor for ALPHV's *.encrypted* files. Draft a 100-word plan to explore Emsisoft's tool and CISA's site, using a sandbox. Reflect on the next steps if no decryptor exists, considering backup restores and other potential options.

Step 2: Use Forensic Tools for Remediation

If public decryptors fail, forensic tools can analyze encrypted files, recover partial data, or uncover attacker artifacts for remediation. Tools like EnCase or FTK are enterprise grade, used by Sarah's CISO to extract LockBit's encryption logs, salvaging 20% of their files, and a small portion of that were partially recoverable. (These tools are expensive and require significant training to be effective. This is another time to be thinking about an MSP.) Free alternatives like Recuva or PhotoRec recover unencrypted file fragments; Keith used Recuva to recover 10% of Maria's bakery's invoices, though proprietary POS files were lost.

For IT professionals, forensic analysis can clarify the extent of the encryption. The 2025 Ryuk victim school used FTK to confirm *.ryk* files used AES-256 encryption, ruling out any brute-force decryption. If exfiltration occurred, assume your data is compromised; decryptors won't help. Engage a forensic vendor for complex systems; Change Healthcare's ALPHV attack required EnCase to analyze ventilator firmware but luckily resulted in the recovery of 50% of their devices. SMBs can use CISA's Cyber Hygiene Scanner to flag recoverable files, though it does not search cloud data.

Decryptor scams are a minefield on the dark web, typically falling short of successful file recovery and often installing spyware in the process. Keith downloaded a fake LockBit tool, which then locked up Maria's laptop. Fake ransomware negotiators are a growing business on *.onion* sites, demanding up-front fees. Another company learned this the hard way in 2023, losing $50,000 to a scammer. Verify tools with pre-vetted vendors, CISA, or similar resources in other countries. Cyber insurers may cover forensic costs, but pre-approval from your insurance provider is a great first step.

Cybersecurity firms, insurance companies, and law firms often have dark net contacts that are capable of decrypting your files through brute force, coding their own decryptor, negotiating with the threat actors, or hacking the threat actors to get the decryptor. These resources often charge between 35% and 50% of the ransom, paid up front. But even these "known" dark net resources can turn on you anytime.

Step 3: Evaluate Payment Risks (Last Resort)

Paying the ransom is a last resort and is full of risks. Maria's family pushed her to pay LockBit's $50,000, but OFAC sanctions blocked it. Change Healthcare's ALPHV payment of $1M yielded a faulty decryptor, bricking 15% of their systems. And there are countless situations where IT and the IRT are confident in their recovery capabilities, and the business decided to pay the ransom anyway. Some went well, and others resulted in getting attacked again within six months. According to the FBI, only 30% of ransom payers recover all data, and 80% are retargeted within a year.

Payment considerations

If your organization is considering payment, consult your legal counsel and insurance provider for compliance with OFAC in the US, or organizations such as the UK's OFSI or Australia's Minister for Foreign Affairs sanctions designations. See "The Ransom Dilemma: Legal Landmines and Empty Promises" on page 275. (FYI, LockBit and ALPHV are sanctioned by OFAC, which means it's illegal to pay them.)

Your insurance provider will use a negotiator to verify "proof-of-life" for decryptors, testing one or more files (ideally one of each critical file type), because the only thing worse than paying a ransom is paying one and not being able to decrypt your files. Maria's bakery recovered 50% of their files from backups instead of paying the ransom, saving her small business $50,000.

Remember, everything you do and all the decisions you make must be documented, including the five w's of Who, What, When. Where, and hoW. This documentation will be crucial in your post-mortem analysis, explaining to upper management what happened, and defending your organization against any lawsuits that may result from the event.

For the legal and ethical framework around ransom payments, see "The Ransom Dilemma: Legal Landmines and Empty Promises" on page 275. For detailed negotiation tactics if payment becomes necessary, see "Expanding Decryption: Negotiating with Attackers" on page 358.

Survival tip

The ability to recover from backups is a godsend, but you must make sure you are restoring "clean" data and not facilitating a reinfection. Then, once you've confirmed the recovered environment is clean and your data integrity is solid, you can stop communicating with the threat actors. Also, if your backups do fail or they are dirty, make sure you ensure your legal team checks for any OFAC sanctions (or similar ones in your country) before paying a ransom. Finally, always request "proof-of-life" from threat actors to prove their decryptor works on the files you care about.

Summary

You've cut through the fog. The ransomware variant is identified, whether it's LockBit, ALPHV, Cl0p, or some AI-driven strain that didn't exist when this book was written. You've scoped the damage: which systems are encrypted, how far the infection spread, whether data was exfiltrated. You've checked for public decryptors (probably found nothing, but you looked). You've continued to fill out your incident log documenting every IOC, every finding, every timestamp for the regulators and insurers who'll come asking questions later.

This chapter equipped you with the essential analysis playbook: examining ransom notes, checking file extensions, analyzing logs and network traffic, leveraging threat intelligence feeds, using sandboxing to observe malware behavior safely, inventorying infected systems, detecting lateral movement, confirming data exfiltration, and exploring decryption options. These are the fundamentals every organization needs, whether you're Maria's bakery using VirusTotal and NoMoreRansom.org, or Sarah's retail chain cross-referencing EDR alerts with threat intel feeds.

For many organizations, this is enough. You've got the intelligence to guide your containment decisions, inform your stakeholders, report to regulators, and begin remediation and recovery. The techniques in this chapter, accessible tools, free resources from CISA and similar agencies worldwide, and practical survival tips all provide the foundation for effective ransomware response without requiring specialist expertise or enterprise budgets.

But if you're a security analyst or incident responder who needs to go deeper, like a sophisticated attack that demands advanced forensics, custom YARA rules, monitoring dark web leak sites, performing memory forensics, or conducting reverse engineering, Chapter 12 will cover those topics. These advanced techniques are for when basic analysis isn't enough, when regulators demand comprehensive forensic reports, or when you're hunting for hidden artifacts that could prevent the next attack.

You've survived the essential analysis. Now you're ready to either begin remediation and recovery with what you've learned, or dive into the advanced forensics that separate good incident response from great incident response.

CHAPTER 12

Advanced Analysis and Forensics

You've identified the variant, scoped the damage, and checked for decryptors. Chapter 11's essential analysis gave you what most organizations need: enough intelligence to guide containment, report to regulators, and start recovery. Sarah at ZapMart confirmed LockBit 3.0 via VirusTotal. Maria used NoMoreRansom.org. Keith checked file extensions and called it a day. For many incidents, that's enough.

But some attacks require way more than basic analysis.

ALPHV's polymorphic code dodged Change Healthcare's signature-based detection for a long time. A Seattle logistics firm's Conti infection (discussed later in this chapter) wiped every log file, leaving the IRT blind to how it spread. BuyMore's Cl0p attack hid in a SaaS account that wasn't even on their asset inventory, exfiltrating 1TB before anyone noticed. The California manufacturer's ALPHV breach moved laterally through cloud APIs that their EDR never monitored. These attacks demand techniques that go beyond "upload the ransom note to VirusTotal." This is where advanced forensics come in:

- Writing custom YARA rules to detect variants that evade commercial tools
- Monitoring dark web leak sites to confirm what data was stolen
- Extracting encryption keys from memory dumps using Volatility
- Reverse-engineering ransomware executables to understand how they work
- Analyzing cloud-specific logs that traditional tools miss
- Building comprehensive forensic reports that satisfy regulators and auditors

These techniques aren't quick. Sarah's CISO spent 40 hours learning Volatility before successfully extracting LockBit's encryption key. The logistics firm hired a specialist with IDA Pro expertise because none of their staff could reverse-engineer Conti's executable. This isn't "Google it and try" territory; it's specialized work that requires training, experience, and tools that cost real money.

Advanced means advanced. The techniques in this chapter, including memory forensics, reverse engineering, YARA rules, and dark web monitoring, require specialized expertise. Don't experiment with them during a live incident unless you're already trained. Mishandling evidence or misconfiguring tools wastes precious time and can make things worse.

Want to learn these skills? We (the authors) built *StopRansomware.com* specifically for readers of this book, with training resources and safe practice environments where you can learn these techniques without the pressure of a ransom deadline.

Need help now? Call the forensic vendors you pre-vetted in Chapter 7. They do this daily, have the right tools, and your insurance probably covers it.

Here's the reality: most organizations outsource this stuff. Forensic vendors like Mandiant, CrowdStrike, and Blackswan Cybersecurity do this work daily. Your cyber insurance probably covers it. CISA (or your country's equivalent) can help or make referrals. If you're a small business like Maria's bakery, you definitely don't need to master Volatility; you need to call in someone who already has.

But understanding these techniques helps even if you never personally use them. You'll know when to escalate to specialists. You'll ask better questions of forensic vendors. You'll understand what's actually in those expensive reports they send. And if you're an IT professional or security analyst building your career in incident response, this is the deep stuff that separates good responders from great ones.

Although the tools in this chapter are not meant for the casual user, we are going to have videos and other resources on the companion site for this book. Check them out at *StopRansomware.com*.

This chapter covers the advanced techniques for when Chapter 11's basics aren't enough. Use what fits your situation, outsource what exceeds your expertise, and don't feel bad about calling in the experts. That's what they're there for.

Advanced Analysis Techniques

Chapter 11 answered three critical questions:

- *What ransomware is this?*

- *How far has it spread?*
- *Can we decrypt it?*

Those answers drive 80% of your response decisions. But advanced analysis answers the questions that come next:

- *How did they get in?*
- *Where are they hiding?*
- *What did they actually take?*
- *How do we prove all this to regulators?*

The difference between basic and advanced analysis isn't just tool complexity, it's investigative depth. Basic analysis identifies LockBit via file extensions and VirusTotal. Advanced analysis writes a YARA rule that catches LockBit variants that morphed to evade detection. Basic analysis checks firewall logs for suspicious outbound traffic. Advanced analysis runs Volatility against a memory dump to extract the exact C2 domains and encryption keys the ransomware used. Basic analysis infers cloud infections based on user reports. Advanced analysis digs through AWS CloudTrail to prove exactly which API calls the attacker made and when.

These deeper investigations matter in specific situations. When regulators demand forensic proof of your breach scope (GDPR's 72-hour clock doesn't care about "we think"). When your cyber insurer needs documentation before paying a $2M claim. When you're hunting for persistent backdoors that could let attackers waltz back in next week. When the variant is so new that threat intelligence feeds have nothing. When logs are wiped and you need memory forensics to reconstruct what happened.

Sarah's team at ZapMart used basic analysis successfully; VirusTotal confirmed Lock-Bit, EDR showed 50 infected endpoints, and backups were clean. Done. But Change Healthcare's ALPHV attack required Volatility because the ransomware wiped their logs. The California manufacturer needed cloud-specific analysis because the breach happened entirely through AWS APIs that their EDR never saw. Northforge paid a forensic vendor $50,000 for reverse engineering after their initial analysis failed to explain how Lorenz encrypted their proprietary repository so thoroughly.

The techniques and tools discussed in this chapter—YARA rules, dark web monitoring, reverse engineering, memory forensics, cloud investigation, comprehensive reporting—aren't everyday tools. They're specialized, time-intensive, and often better handled by experts. But knowing they exist, when they're needed, and what they can reveal makes you a better incident responder even if you never personally write a single line of YARA.

Let's dig into the advanced stuff.

Step 5 is not a typo. We're picking up where we left off in Chapter 11, which was "Step 4: Leverage Threat Intelligence Feeds" on page 331.

Step 5: Craft YARA Rules (Advanced)

IT pros should consider YARA, which is a pattern-matching engine designed to help malware researchers and security professionals identify and classify malware samples. Think of it as a Swiss Army knife for creating custom detection rules that can hunt for specific malware characteristics across files, processes, or network traffic.

YARA operates by allowing you to write rules that describe malware families or specific threats. These rules are a powerful way to identify ransomware by matching file patterns or behaviors. Think of YARA as a custom antivirus signature you write to catch variants that evade VirusTotal. Change Healthcare's ALPHV attack dodged EDR until a YARA rule flagged its encryptor's mutex, ALPHV_MTX. (A *mutex* is a synchronization object in the OS that ensures only one instance of the process, thread, or program can access shared resources at a time.) Sarah's CISO wrote a YARA rule for LockBit's *.lock* files, catching 90% of infected endpoints (about 50 of them).

The following is a simple YARA rule for LockBit's ransom note, based on its *READ_ME.txt* format:

```
rule LockBit_Ransom_Note {
  meta:
    description = "Detects LockBit 3.0 ransom note"
    author = "YourOrg"
    date = "2025-03-10"
  strings:
    $a = "LockBit 3.0" nocase
    $b = ".lock" nocase
    $c = "Tor Browser" nocase
  condition:
    all of them
}
```

Free YARA repositories like Neo23x0's signatures offer pre-built rules for ALPHV, Cl0p, and Ryuk. The BuyMore Cl0p case used a Neo23x0 rule to flag *.cl0p* files, saving four hours.

Small and medium-sized businesses (SMBs) without YARA expertise should hire a forensic vendor to help them with YARA. Keith tried a GitHub YARA rule but misconfigured it, missing LockBit's cloud infection. If you're new at this kind of work, test rules in a sandbox to avoid false positives. IT pros can integrate YARA with EDR for real-time detection, as Sarah's CISO did.

Download Neo23x0's YARA rules from GitHub (*https://github.com/Neo23x0/signature-base*) for common variants. Test in a sandbox before deploying. Engage forensic vendors for complex rules. Log YARA hits (e.g., "ALPHV_MTX, 3/10/25") for the next phase. SMBs can rely on VirusTotal instead.

Exercise: Write a YARA rule

You are Sarah's CISO at ZapMart. LockBit's ransom note references ".lock" and "Tor Browser." In 50 words, draft a YARA rule to detect it, using the example provided. Test it in a sandbox. Reflect on adapting it for ALPHV's *.encrypted* files to broaden its utility. (Estimated time: 15 minutes)

Step 6: Monitor Dark Web Leak Sites

Ransomware gangs like LockBit and ALPHV use dark web "wall of shame" sites to leak exfiltrated data, a double extortion tactic. Checking these sites confirms the variant and exfiltration risk. Maria's LockBit note linked to a *.onion* leak site, which @RansomWatch tied to LockBit 3.0. Change Healthcare's ALPHV site listed stolen patient records, triggering GDPR's 72-hour notification.

This chapter talks about using Tor for ransomware research. This isn't as simple as downloading Tor and using it. There may be laws and policies against its use, so make sure you are aware of any of these prior to using it.

Use a secure Tor browser in a sandbox to visit *.onion* links from the ransom note—never use a corporate network. Search for your organization's name or data samples (e.g., "Maria's Bakery orders"). Free services like DarkOwl or X posts (@RansomWatch) monitor leak sites. BuyMore found their inventory data on a leak site via DarkOwl, confirming exfiltration. If data is posted, assume it's public, as Change Healthcare learned when ALPHV leaked 2TB.

As discussed in the previous warning, you should avoid dark web access without expertise. Instead, use a forensic vendor to check sites. Log findings (e.g., "Leak site lists customer data, 3/10/25") for use in your PR response.

Case Study: 2025 Ryuk School Attack

In March 2025, a Chicago school was hit by Ryuk, with *.ryk* files and a $200,000 demand. The ransom note linked to an *.onion* leak site, which DarkOwl tied to Ryuk's RaaS. A YARA rule from Neo23x0 flagged the encryptor, but the absence of an EDR let Ryuk spread to 80% of servers. CISA's AIS confirmed a C2 domain, but a missed cloud backup infection delayed recovery by 48 hours. An EDR solution could've caught the spread, significantly reducing recovery time and costs.

Survival tip

Check leak sites from a sandboxed Tor browser or DarkOwl. Monitor @Ransom-Watch for leak updates. Log findings for GDPR/CCPA notifications. SMBs can call CISA (888-282-0870) for dark web checks. In the UK, the NCSC provides guidance on monitoring for data exposure and can assist with threat assessments, while Australian organizations can contact the ACSC's 24/7 hotline at 1300 CYBER1 for assistance with dark web monitoring, and EU organizations can leverage resources from their national cybersecurity agencies or ENISA for breach assessment support.

Exercise: Check the dark web

You're the school's IT lead. Ryuk's note links to a *.onion* site. Draft a 100-word plan to verify exfiltration using a sandbox and DarkOwl, referencing double extortion. Reflect on how you'd proceed without Tor access, using CISA. (Estimated time: 10 minutes.)

Expanding Identification: Reverse-Engineering Ransomware Samples

Identifying the ransomware variant, like LockBit 3.0, ALPHV/BlackCat, Ryuk, or a new 2025 strain, is the foundation of your response. While tools like VirusTotal and YARA rules pinpoint variants through indicators of compromise (IOCs) (e.g., *.lock* files, C2 IPs), reverse-engineering ransomware samples offers deeper insights into the malware's behavior, encryption, and potential weaknesses. This advanced technique, ideal for IT pros like Sarah's CISO, uncovers hidden payloads or decryption clues missed by automated tools. Reverse engineering is like decoding a criminal's playbook. It is time-intensive but can reveal game-changing details, such as their exact attack sequences, backup communication channels, and the specific vulnerabilities they target first.

Reverse engineering is an advanced process that should only be attempted by experts. This section should therefore be considered for informational purposes only.

Why Reverse Engineering Matters

Reverse engineering involves analyzing a ransomware executable's code to map its functions—encryption algorithms, C2 communications, or persistence mechanisms. In Chapter 1, we noted that ALPHV's polymorphic code morphs to evade detection, requiring manual analysis. Reverse engineering proves invaluable in confirming malware variants when VirusTotal's 60–70 detections yield inconclusive results, such as in Sarah's LockBit incident. It also becomes essential when logs have been erased, as seen in the case of Maria's bakery. Reverse engineering also uncovers proprietary encryption, like Change Healthcare's ALPHV attack on ventilator firmware, which standard tools missed. For IT veterans, tools like IDA Pro or Ghidra dissect executables, revealing code strings or mutexes (e.g., ALPHV_MTX).

How to Reverse-Engineer Safely

Reverse-engineering ransomware is a critical but high-risk process that involves analyzing malicious code to uncover its functionality, such as encryption algorithms, C2 infrastructure, or mutexes. Performing this analysis in a secure, isolated environment is essential to prevent accidental execution or reinfection. This section outlines safe reverse-engineering practices, tools, and real-world examples, emphasizing the importance of using a sandboxed VM and leveraging expert resources for SMBs.

The importance of safe reverse engineering

Reverse engineering provides deep insights into ransomware behavior, enabling organizations to confirm variants, identify C2 servers, or assess decryption feasibility. However, analyzing live malware on production systems risks further infection or data loss. This is why you need a sandboxed environment, as discussed in Chapter 7 and earlier in this chapter.

For example, in 2025, Sarah's CISO used Ghidra, a free reverse-engineering tool, to analyze LockBit's *svc32.exe* in a sandboxed VM. The analysis revealed a hardcoded C2 domain (lockbit[.]ru), confirming the LockBit 3.0 variant and guiding containment efforts. Similarly, the IT team at the school district hit by Ryuk in 2025 used IDA Pro, a paid tool, to identify Ryuk's AES-256 encryption algorithm. This confirmed that decryption without the private key was infeasible, prompting a focus on backups for recovery.

Tools and workflow for reverse engineering

Reverse engineering requires specialized tools and a disciplined approach. Following is a detailed workflow using free and paid tools, along with practical guidance:

Set up a sandboxed environment

- Copy the ransomware into a sandbox that follows the guidelines covered in Chapter 7, and in "Advanced Sandboxing Considerations" on page 320.
- Use snapshots to revert the VM to a clean state after analysis.

Choose a reverse-engineering tool

Ghidra
> A free, open source tool from the NSA, suitable for analyzing ransomware binaries. It supports disassembling and decompiling code to reveal strings, functions, and network calls.

IDA Pro
> A paid, industry-standard tool with advanced features for complex malware analysis, ideal for identifying encryption algorithms or C2 infrastructure.

Radare2
> Another free alternative, though less user-friendly than Ghidra for beginners.

Follow a Ghidra workflow
Follow these steps to analyze a ransomware sample like *encryptor.exe*:

Load the sample
> Import the executable into Ghidra's CodeBrowser and create a new project.

Analyze code
> Run Ghidra's auto-analysis to disassemble the binary. Search for strings like ransomware names (e.g., "LockBit 3.0"), *.onion* URLs, or C2 domains (e.g., lockbit[.]ru). A simple ransomware executable might finish in under 10 minutes, while complex packed malware could take an hour or more.

Trace functions
> Identify encryption functions (e.g., RSA-2048, AES-256) or network calls to C2 servers. Look for mutexes (e.g., ALPHV_MTX) that indicate the ransomware's presence.

Export findings
> Document IOCs, such as mutexes, IP addresses, or domains, in your incident log for containment and reporting.

Cross-reference with threat intelligence
Validate findings using platforms like VirusTotal or DarkOwl. For instance, Sarah's CISO confirmed the lockbit[.]ru domain by checking VirusTotal, which flagged it as a known LockBit C2.

Be sure to Monitor @RansomWatcher on X for real-time updates on ransomware variants like Conti or Ryuk.

Case Study: 2025 Conti Logistics Attack

In April 2025, a Seattle logistics firm was hit by a Conti ransomware variant, appending *.conti* to files and demanding $1 million. Initial VirusTotal scans showed 50/70 detection hits but were inconclusive due to obfuscation, and attackers wiped local logs, complicating analysis. The IRT used IDA Pro in a sandboxed VM to analyze Conti's *encryptor.exe*. They identified a mutex (CONTI_MTX) and a Russian C2 IP, confirming the variant. However, a missed infection in an AWS S3 bucket allowed Conti to spread to 60% of servers, exacerbating the breach.

CISA's vendor analysis later uncovered Conti's deployment of double extortion tactics (Chapter 1), involving the exfiltration of 500GB of data, which was subsequently published on a leak site. This triggered GDPR's 72-hour notification requirement, costing the firm $500,000 in fines and recovery efforts. Had the IRT monitored their cloud logs (e.g., AWS CloudTrail), they could have detected unauthorized S3 access earlier, potentially saving significant costs.

Lessons learned in this section:

Sandboxing is non-negotiable
Using a sandbox prevented further spread during IDA Pro analysis.

Cloud monitoring is critical
Integrating cloud log analysis from Chapter 7 could have caught the S3 breach.

Expert support saves time
CISA's vendor analysis provided faster, more accurate results than internal efforts.

Regulatory compliance
Documenting IOCs (e.g., CONTI_MTX, C2 IPs) ensured GDPR-compliant notifications.

Survival tip

Reverse-engineer in a sandbox with Ghidra or IDA Pro, logging strings (e.g., CONTI_MTX, 4/5/25) for your incident report. SMBs should use CISA, a similar organization in their country, or vendors to avoid errors. Never analyze live systems; this is to prevent reinfection. Monitor @RansomWatch for Conti or other variant updates.

You're the IT lead for the Seattle logistics firm hit by Conti ransomware. The *encryptor.exe* sample is isolated in a sandbox. Draft a 150-word plan to reverse-engineer it with Ghidra, targeting mutexes, referencing Chapter 9's IOCs. Reflect on using CISA if Ghidra fails. (Estimated time: 15 minutes)

Expanding Scope Assessment: Cloud-Specific Analysis

Cloud environments, such as AWS, Azure, and Google Cloud, introduce unique challenges in ransomware incident response due to their distributed nature, complex permissions, and reliance on APIs. Examples of the unique challenges include the shared responsibility mode and concerns around multitenancy. Assessing the attack's scope in cloud systems involves identifying infected assets, tracing lateral movement, and detecting data exfiltration. Ransomware can remain dormant or spread undetected without proper cloud scoping, as seen in several 2025 incidents. This section provides a detailed guide for auditing cloud infections, leveraging cloud-native tools for IT professionals and accessible alternatives for SMBs.

Why Cloud Scoping Matters

Cloud systems are prime targets for ransomware due to permissions that are often misconfigured, stolen credentials, or vulnerabilities exploited by initial access brokers (revisit Chapter 1 for more info).

For instance, in BuyMore's case, the CISO missed a Cl0p infection in a SaaS account because it wasn't on the system inventory, allowing the ransomware to lay dormant before encrypting and exfiltrating critical data. The 2025 Ryuk attack on a school district overlooked cloud-based backups in Google Cloud, delaying recovery by weeks.

Change Healthcare suffered 2TB of data exfiltration via compromised Azure blob storage. The breach went undetected by endpoint detection and response (EDR) tools, which lacked visibility into cloud activity. Maria's bakery lost cloud-stored invoices to LockBit's sync folder in Google Drive due to unmonitored cloud logs. These cases highlight that cloud scoping is critical to identify infected buckets, VMs, or SaaS applications, prevent scope creep, and support more informed containment strategies, such as isolating AWS instances.

How to Scope Cloud Infections

Effective cloud scoping starts with a comprehensive inventory of cloud assets, as outlined in "Know Your Environment" on page 87. This includes S3 buckets, Azure VMs, Google Drive folders, and SaaS applications. Following are detailed steps and tools for auditing cloud infections, tailored for IT professionals and SMBs:

1. Compile a cloud asset inventory.

Reference your asset inventory to list all cloud resources, including AWS S3 buckets, Azure VMs, Google Cloud Storage, and SaaS platforms like Salesforce or Google Workspace. Categorize assets by sensitivity (e.g., customer data, financial records) to prioritize scoping efforts. For example, BuyMore identified critical S3 buckets containing ERP data, which were targeted for exfiltration.

2. Analyze cloud audit logs.

Cloud-native logging tools provide visibility into unauthorized access, API calls, or file modifications:

AWS CloudTrail

Review logs for suspicious API calls, such as `s3:PutObject` or `s3:GetObject`, indicating data modification or exfiltration. BuyMore found 1TB of S3 exfiltration via unauthorized `s3:GetObject` calls.

Azure activity logs

Check for VM encryption, credential abuse, or blob storage access. The 2024 hospital's ALPHV attack showed 500 unauthorized logins to Azure resources, flagged in activity logs.

Google Cloud audit logs

Detect changes to Google Drive files, such as new *.lock* extensions. Maria's bakery identified *.lock* files in Drive, indicating LockBit's infection.

3. Use cloud CLI commands for targeted checks.

For AWS, use the AWS CLI to identify infected S3 objects:

```
aws s3api list-objects --bucket my-bucket --query
"Contents[?contains(Key, '.lock')]"
```

This command lists S3 objects with ransomware extensions (e.g., *.lock*, *.encrypted*). Similar commands exist for Azure (`az storage blob list`) and Google Cloud (`gcloud storage ls`).

4. Leverage cloud-native security tools.

IT professionals can use advanced tools to correlate logs and detect anomalies:

AWS GuardDuty

A threat detection service with a free tier that flags unauthorized S3 access or API calls

Azure Sentinel

A SIEM solution for correlating cloud and on-premises logs. Sarah's CISO used Sentinel to identify LockBit's SaaS breach via anomalous API activity.

Google Security Command Center

Detects misconfigurations or file changes in Google Cloud environments.

5. Cross-reference with threat intelligence.

Use platforms like VirusTotal, DarkOwl, or @ThreatIntel on X to validate cloud IOCs, such as suspicious IP addresses or API keys. BuyMore cross-referenced CloudTrail findings with DarkOwl, confirming the exfiltration destination.

Survival Tip

Audit your cloud assets with CloudTrail, GuardDuty, or Azure Sentinel. Use CLI commands like `aws s3api list-objects` to check for ransomware extensions. SMBs can contact CISA's Cloud Hygiene Scanner (888-863-8656) for free support. In the UK, organizations can use the NCSC's Check Your Email Security tool and request free cyber assessments, while Australian SMBs can access the ACSC's Cyber Health Check tool and receive expert guidance through their Small Business Cyber Resilience Service, and EU organizations can utilize ENISA's free web-based assessment tools for cloud security maturity evaluations. Remember when you are in the middle of the attack (Chapter 9) to log anything you find (e.g., "S3 .encrypted, 2/5/25") for use in the containment phase. Monitor @ThreatIntel for cloud attack trends.

Expanding Decryption: Negotiating with Attackers

Negotiating with ransomware attackers is a high-stakes, last-resort option explored only after decryption alternatives like public decryptors and forensics have been exhausted, as we talked about in Chapter 9. While negotiation may seem like a path to recovery, it carries significant risks, including unreliable decryptors, retargeting, and legal consequences. In addition, it's important to understand that even if you do negotiate and pay a ransom, only 30% of those who pay recover all data and 80% face subsequent attacks, according to the latest FBI data. Negotiation is therefore best left up to professionals, and this section is therefore for informational purposes only. It outlines tactics, risks, and ethical considerations, emphasizing the priority of backup restoration for SMBs and larger organizations.

> Before considering negotiation, review Chapter 9's discussion of the legal landmines and ethical considerations around paying ransoms, and Chapter 11's guidance on evaluating payment risks.

Why Negotiation Is Risky

Negotiating with attackers involves contacting them through "support" portals on the dark web or via email, typically to reduce ransom demands or verify decryption tools. However, outcomes are unreliable. One company in 2024 paid $1 million to ALPHV (BlackCat) but received a faulty decryptor that corrupted 40% of files.

Ethical and legal dilemmas complicate negotiation. Paying ransoms funds cyber-crime, enabling further attacks. As mentioned in "The Ransom Dilemma: Legal Landmines and Empty Promises" on page 275 in Chapter 9, many countries prohibit payments to designated groups like LockBit, Conti, or ALPHV. Violating sanctions can result in fines or legal action. The tactics seen in "Double Extortion" on page 20 mean stolen data often remains public, even after payment, as seen in the 2025 Ryuk school attack, where leaked student data triggered GDPR notifications despite negotiations.

How to Negotiate (If You Must)

If negotiation is unavoidable, follow a structured, secure approach to minimize risks. Following are key steps for engaging attackers:

1. *Engage a professional negotiator.*

   Use a vetted negotiator provided by your cyber insurance or recommended by incident response vendors. Negotiators are trained to interact with attackers, assess decryptor viability, and ensure OFAC compliance. Insurance companies often have established relationships with specific ransomware groups and under-stand their negotiation patterns, typical ransom reductions, and decryptor relia-bility. For example, Sarah's CISO used a negotiator to reduce LockBit's $500,000 demand to $300,000, though OFAC sanctions ultimately blocked payment. SMBs should avoid direct contact, as Keith nearly paid a fraudulent LockBit negotiator impersonating the real group.

2. *Access the dark web portal safely.*

   Have a professional that is familiar with the dark web connect to the attacker's portal using a Tor browser in a sandboxed VM, disconnected from business networks. This prevents malware embedded in portals from infecting systems. Never use production environments, as attackers may exploit connections to deploy additional payloads.

3. *Request a "proof-of-life" decryptor.*

   Ask attackers to decrypt a sample of critical file types (e.g., ERP databases, finan-cial records) as proof their decryptor works. Test the decryptor in a sandboxed VM to verify functionality and ensure it does not contain additional malware. In the Willoughby's case discussed later in this chapter, the "proof-of-life" decryptor failed in testing, revealing LockBit's unreliability. Willoughby's wasted time test-ing a decryptor that appeared functional but failed on large datasets.

4. *Negotiate ransom reductions.*

   Cite budget constraints or partial backup recovery as a basis for reducing demands. For instance, Willoughby's negotiated a $2 million ransom to $1 mil-lion by claiming limited funds, though the decryptor wasn't fully functional. Be cautious, as attackers may raise demands or leak data in retaliation, as Ryuk did to the 2025 school when negotiations stalled.

Make sure that your cyber policy docs are protected! We have seen attackers tell the negotiator that their offer is too low because they have accessed the unsecured insurance policy and know the limits!

5. *Ensure you're not breaking the law.*

Consult your legal team to verify the attacker group (e.g., LockBit, ALPHV) is not on OFAC's sanctions list, or a similar list in your country. Tools like Chainalysis or TRM Labs can trace cryptocurrency wallets to sanctioned entities. If payment is blocked, as in Sarah's case, pivot to restoration or decryption options.

6. *Consult CISA and legal counsel.*

Before engaging attackers, contact CISA (US)/NCSC (UK)/ACSC (AU)/CCCS (CA)/ENISA (EU) for guidance on sanctions and negotiation risks. (See Chapter 7 for more info on these organizations.) Notify law enforcement (e.g., FBI/Europol) and legal counsel to align with regulatory requirements, such as GDPR or CCPA, especially if data was exfiltrated.

Risks of Negotiation

Here are some risks you run into with negotiation:

Unreliable decryptors

Attackers often provide faulty or incomplete decryptors, as seen in Change Healthcare's ALPHV case.

Retargeting

80% of those who pay are attacked again, per FBI 2024 data, as groups exploit known vulnerabilities.

Data leaks

Double extortion ensures stolen data may be leaked regardless of payment, as in the Ryuk school case.

Sanctions violations

Paying sanctioned groups risks hefty fines, as OFAC warned in 2025.

Fraudulent negotiators

Scammers posing as attackers can trick victims, as nearly happened to Keith.

Escalated demands

Aggressive negotiation may lead to higher ransoms or immediate data leaks, as Ryuk demonstrated.

Best Practices for Negotiation

In addition to the best practices covered in the preceding, be sure to follow these practices when negotiating:

Prioritize backups

Use Chapter 6 to fortify your backup system so that you never need to consider negotiation, just like Maria's bakery did successfully.

Use professionals

Rely on vetted negotiators (see "Assembling Your Incident Response Team" on page 198) to handle *.onion* communications and OFAC checks.

Case Study: 2025 Retail Negotiation Failure

In early 2025, another UK retail chain was hit by LockBit 3.0, demanding £2 million. We'll call this company "Willoughby's." A negotiator, approved by their insurer, used a secure Tor browser in a sandboxed environment to access the *.onion* portal and successfully negotiated the demand down to £1 million. The legal team, with the assistance of TRM Labs, confirmed that sanctions against LockBit would prevent the payment to LockBit. The "proof-of-life" decryptor, tested in a sandbox, failed to decrypt 20% of sample files, indicating its unreliability. LockBit leaked customer data on a dark website, triggering GDPR's 72-hour notification requirement and €5 million in fines. Fortunately, Willoughby's restored 70% of their systems from backups, keeping them from having to pay the ransom. If the retailer had conducted more rigorous testing of their backups beforehand, they could have avoided the need for negotiation altogether.

Lessons learned:

Backup reliance

Robust, tested backups reduce negotiation dependency.

Sanctions awareness

Sanction checks are critical to avoid legal risks.

Sandbox testing

Verifying decryptors in a sandbox prevents false hope.

Regulatory compliance

Documenting leaks ensures GDPR adherence, though fines remain costly.

Exercise: Plan a Negotiation

You're the IRT lead for Willoughby's facing LockBit's $2 million demand. Draft a 100-word plan to negotiate via a negotiator, testing a decryptor, referencing OFAC risks. Reflect on avoiding negotiation with solid backups. (Estimated time: 10 minutes)

Expanding Advanced Analysis: Volatility Tutorial

Memory forensics and comprehensive reporting are critical components of ransomware incident response. The Volatility Framework is a powerful tool for uncovering hidden ransomware artifacts. Its clear, structured reporting ensures stakeholders, regulators, and insurers are informed, which facilitates compliance and recovery. This section provides a detailed Volatility tutorial for IT professionals, vendor alternatives for SMBs, and guidance on crafting post-analysis reports to close the analysis phase effectively.

Volatility Tutorial

Memory forensics is essential for identifying ransomware artifacts like processes, encryption keys, or C2 connections that may evade EDR tools. The Volatility Framework, an open source tool, enables analysts to examine memory dumps for IOCs. For example, Sarah's CISO used Volatility to extract LockBit's encryption key from a POS terminal's memory dump, recovering 30% of encrypted files. This tutorial deepens Chapter 9's advanced techniques, offering a step-by-step guide for IT professionals and vendor alternatives for SMBs.

Best Practices for Volatility Analysis

In addition to the best practices for analysis mentioned previously in this chapter, be sure to follow these best practices for analysis using Volatility:

Verify profiles
Confirm the correct OS profile with imageinfo to avoid errors

Target IOCs
Focus on ransomware processes (e.g., *ryuk.exe*), mutexes (e.g., LOCKBIT_MTX), and C2 IPs

Volatility Workflow

Below is a detailed workflow for using Volatility to analyze a ransomware-infected system's memory dump, with practical examples from 2025 incidents:

1. Capture a memory dump.

Use a tool like DumpIt (free for Windows) to capture a memory dump from the infected system. Run DumpIt with administrative privileges to create a raw memory file:

```
DumpIt.exe /O memdump.raw
```

The dump size matches the system's RAM (e.g., 32GB RAM = 32GB dump). Transfer the file to a secure, isolated analysis machine to prevent accidental malware execution. In the 2025 Ryuk school attack, IT staff used DumpIt to capture a server's memory, enabling Volatility analysis.

2. Identify the OS profile.

Determine the operating system profile to ensure accurate analysis. Run the `imageinfo` plug-in:

```
volatility -f memdump.raw imageinfo
```

This outputs profiles like Win10x64 or Win2016x64. Sarah's team identified Win10x64 for their POS terminal, ensuring compatibility with subsequent commands. Incorrect profiles lead to analysis errors, so verify the system's OS version (Chapter 7's asset inventory).

3. List running processes.

Use the `pslist` plug-in to identify active processes, including ransomware executables:

```
volatility -f memdump.raw --profile=Win10x64 pslist
```

Look for suspicious processes, such as *svc32.exe* (LockBit) or *ryuk.exe*. The 2025 Ryuk school found *ryuk.exe* in their server's memory, confirming the variant. Cross-reference process names with Chapter 9's IOCs from VirusTotal or DarkOwl.

4. Extract artifacts.

Use additional Volatility plug-ins to uncover ransomware artifacts:

netscan

Identifies network connections, including C2 IPs. Run:

```
volatility -f memdump.raw --profile=Win10x64 netscan
```

The Ryuk school discovered a Bulgarian C2 IP, guiding containment by blocking the address.

malfind

Detects injected or malicious code, including mutexes. Run:

```
volatility -f memdump.raw --profile=Win10x64 malfind
```

Sarah's team found LockBit's mutex (LOCKBIT_MTX), confirming the variant.

`mimikatz`
Extracts credentials or encryption keys from memory:

```
volatility -f memdump.raw --profile=Win10x64 mimikatz
```

This helped Sarah's CISO recover 30% of files by extracting LockBit's key.

5. *Cross-reference with threat intelligence.*
Validate findings using platforms like VirusTotal, DarkOwl, or @ThreatIntel on X. For example, the Ryuk school confirmed their C2 IP matched known Ryuk infrastructure on DarkOwl, enhancing containment accuracy.

Case Study: 2025 School Ryuk Recovery

The Chicago school district hit by Ryuk ransomware used DumpIt to help the IT team capture a memory dump and ran Volatility's `pslist`, identifying *ryuk.exe* as the primary process. The `netscan` plug-in revealed a Bulgarian C2 IP, enabling firewall rules to block communication. A vendor extracted encryption keys from memory, recovering 20% of files.

However, the absence of EDR allowed Ryuk to reinfect cloud backups, costing $100,000 in downtime. Implementing EDR monitoring could have detected lateral movement earlier, preventing reinfection.

Lessons learned:

Memory forensics impact
Volatility's `pslist` and `netscan` provided actionable IOCs.

Vendor support
Vendors supplemented the school's limited expertise.

EDR importance
EDR could have prevented reinfection.

Backup protection
Immutable backups would have reduced recovery costs.

Survival Tip

Run Volatility in a sandbox, targeting IOCs like processes or C2 IPs. SMBs should use CISA (US)/NCSC (UK)/ACSC (AU)/CCCS (CA)/ENISA (EU) or vendors for

---

support. Log artifacts (e.g., "ryuk.exe, 3/5/25") for Chapter 13's containment. Monitor @ThreatIntel for memory attack trends.

Exercise: Use Volatility

You're the IT lead for the Chicago school district with a Ryuk-infected server's memory dump. Draft a 150-word plan to use Volatility's `pslist` and `netscan`, referencing C2 IPs. Reflect on vendor needs if Volatility fails. (Estimated time: 15 minutes)

Post-Analysis Reporting

Completing the analysis phase requires documenting findings in clear, structured reports for stakeholders—executives, regulators, insurers, and public relations teams. Reports built from your incident response plan (IRP) templates justify actions, support recovery, and ensure compliance with regulations like GDPR's 72-hour notification requirement. This subsection guides IT professionals and SMBs in creating effective post-analysis reports.

Building a Report

Use IRP templates to structure reports, summarizing key findings from the analysis phase. A comprehensive report includes the following, which can be added to the AI prompt "Create an Incident Response After Action Report with the following attributes:"

Ransomware variant
> Identify the strain, e.g., "LockBit 3.0, confirmed via VirusTotal." ZapMart used VirusTotal's 60/70 detection hits to confirm LockBit.

Scope of infection
> Detail affected systems and data, e.g., "50 POS devices, 1TB exfiltrated."

Decryption efforts
> Note outcomes, e.g., "No public decryptor; 30% recovered via Volatility's key extraction."

Actions taken
> List response steps, e.g., "Isolated systems, engaged vendors."

Next steps
> Outline containment plans, such as firewall updates or backup restoration.

Sample Report

The following is an AI-generated Incident Response After Action Report based on the ZapMart story. Please note that from a Privacy and Governance perspective, you should not use any identifiable, sensitive, or confidential details in your prompt. Replace each with a token or generic word/phrase that you can then find/replace in your final draft report.

Executive Summary

On [insert date of incident, e.g., September 15, 2025], ZapMart experienced a ransomware attack identified as LockBit 3.0. The infection impacted 50 Point-of-Sale (POS) devices and resulted in the exfiltration of approximately 1TB of sensitive data, including customer payment information and internal records. Immediate response actions included isolating affected systems and engaging external cybersecurity vendors for forensic analysis. Decryption efforts yielded partial success, with 30% of encrypted data recovered using advanced memory forensics tools. No ransom was paid, and no public decryptor was available. This report summarizes the incident details, actions taken, and recommended next steps to enhance future resilience. Key lessons include the need for improved endpoint detection and regular backup testing.

Incident Overview

Ransomware variant

The ransomware strain was identified as LockBit 3.0. Confirmation was achieved through analysis on VirusTotal, where the malware sample received 60 out of 70 detection hits from various antivirus engines. Indicators of compromise (IOCs) matched known LockBit signatures, including file encryption patterns (e.g., appending ".lockbit" extensions) and ransom note contents demanding cryptocurrency payment.

Scope of infection

The attack compromised a total of 50 POS devices across 10 retail locations. These systems were primarily running outdated Windows OS versions with unpatched vulnerabilities. Approximately 1TB of data was exfiltrated, including:

- Customer data: Payment card details, transaction logs.
- Internal data: Employee records, inventory databases.
- No evidence of lateral movement to core servers or cloud infrastructure was found, limiting the breach to edge devices.

The infection likely originated from a phishing email or exploited remote desktop protocol (RDP) vulnerability, though root cause analysis is ongoing.

Response Actions

Timeline of Key Events

- Detection (T+0 hours): Anomalous behavior detected via endpoint security alerts on POS devices.
- Initial containment (T+2 hours): Affected systems isolated from the network to prevent further spread.
- Forensic analysis (T+4 hours): Engaged third-party vendors (e.g., cybersecurity firm) for malware reverse engineering and data recovery.
- Recovery phase (T+24 hours): Attempted decryption and system restoration initiated.

Actions Taken

The incident response team followed ZapMart's IR playbook with the following steps:

1. Isolation: Immediately disconnected infected POS devices from the network and disabled remote access protocols.
2. Vendor engagement: Contracted external experts for advanced forensics, including memory dumping and analysis using tools like Volatility.
3. Notification: Informed internal stakeholders (IT, legal, executive leadership) and prepared for potential regulatory reporting (e.g., GDPR/PCI-DSS compliance).
4. Monitoring: Enhanced monitoring on unaffected systems to detect any residual threats.
5. Communication: Maintained a command center for real-time updates; no external communications were issued pending full assessment.

No ransom was paid, aligning with organizational policy against funding criminal activities.

Decryption Efforts

No publicly available decryptor exists for LockBit 3.0 at the time of the incident. Recovery efforts focused on forensic techniques:

- Utilized Volatility framework to extract encryption keys from memory dumps of infected systems.
- Achieved 30% data recovery, primarily non-critical files; the remaining 70% remains encrypted pending further analysis or potential law enforcement assistance.

- Backups were partially effective but revealed gaps in coverage for POS-specific data.

Lessons Learned

- Strengths: Rapid isolation prevented broader network compromise. Vendor partnerships accelerated forensics.
- Weaknesses: Outdated POS software and insufficient multifactor authentication (MFA) on RDP ports contributed to initial access. Backup integrity checks were not performed recently, leading to incomplete restores.
- Opportunities: Implement automated threat hunting and regular penetration testing to identify vulnerabilities proactively.

Next Steps and Recommendations

To contain residual risks and prevent recurrence, the following actions are recommended:

1. Containment and recovery:
   - Restore remaining data from verified backups within 72 hours.
   - Conduct full system wipes and rebuilds on all 50 affected POS devices.
2. Security enhancements:
   - Update firewalls to block known LockBit C2 domains and implement zero-trust network segmentation.
   - Enforce MFA across all remote access points and patch management for POS systems.
3. Monitoring and training:
   - Deploy advanced endpoint detection and response (EDR) tools on all devices.
   - Conduct organization-wide phishing awareness training within 30 days.
4. Follow-up:
   - Schedule a full IR playbook review and tabletop exercise in Q4 2025.
   - Engage law enforcement (e.g., FBI) for potential decryption support or threat actor attribution.

This report will be updated as additional forensic findings emerge. All questions should be directed to the Incident Response Lead.

If you are in the US, submit a report to CISA (report@cisa.dhs.gov) with IOCs like process names, mutexes, or C2 IPs. If you are in the UK, report to the NCSC through their incident reporting service and notify the Information Commissioner's

Office within 72 hours for GDPR compliance, while Australian organizations should contact the ACSC via ReportCyber or call 1300 CYBER1, and EU organizations must report to their national cybersecurity agency and relevant data protection authority within the GDPR's 72-hour notification requirement. ZapMart (Sarah) filed a GDPR-compliant report within 72 hours, avoiding fines.

For executives, use plain language: "LockBit encrypted 50 systems; we're restoring backups, no ransom paid." SMBs can use the SBA templates, which simplify reporting. Maria's bakery adapted an SBA template to document LockBit's impact, streamlining insurer communication.

Regulatory and Stakeholder Considerations

Here are some regulatory considerations:

GDPR/CCPA compliance
Document data exfiltration (e.g., "2TB patient data leaked") and file reports within 72 hours to avoid fines.

Insurer requirements
Provide detailed IOCs and recovery steps to support claims, as ZapMart did for their cyber insurance.

Public relations
Align reports with Chapter 7's PR plan to manage stakeholder trust.

Legal documentation
Log findings to support potential litigation or law enforcement investigations.

Summary

This chapter went deep. YARA rules to catch variants that morph past VirusTotal. Dark web monitoring to confirm what data leaked. Using Volatility to pull encryption keys from memory dumps. Reverse-engineering ransomware executables with Ghidra or IDA Pro. Cloud-specific forensics digging through AWS CloudTrail and Azure Activity Logs. Negotiation tactics for the worst-case scenario. Comprehensive reporting that satisfies regulators, insurers, and executives.

These aren't techniques you learn in an afternoon. Sarah's CISO spent 40 hours mastering Volatility before successfully extracting LockBit's encryption key. The Seattle logistics firm paid a specialist because none of their staff could reverse-engineer Conti's executable. The Chicago school district needed vendor support to run memory forensics on their Ryuk-infected servers. This is specialized work that requires training, expensive tools, and experience you typically don't build during a live ransomware attack.

Here's what matters: you now know these techniques exist, when they're needed, and what they can reveal. You know when basic analysis from Chapter 11 isn't enough, like when logs are wiped, when regulators demand forensic proof, when you're hunting persistent backdoors, and when the variant is too new for threat intelligence feeds. You know when to call the forensic vendors you pre-vetted in Chapter 7 instead of experimenting with Volatility while the ransom clock ticks down.

Most organizations outsource this advanced work, and that's the smart play—not defeat. Your cyber insurance probably covers it. CISA, NCSC, ACSC, or ENISA can make referrals. Forensic vendors like Mandiant, CrowdStrike, or Blackswan Cybersecurity do this daily. Maria's bakery didn't need to master YARA rules; they needed a phone number. That's the reality.

But if you're an IT professional or security analyst building your incident response career, these advanced techniques separate competent responders from exceptional ones. You'll ask better questions when vendors present findings. You'll understand what's actually in those expensive forensic reports. You'll know when a $50,000 reverse-engineering engagement is justified versus when basic log analysis would suffice. You'll spot the gaps in analysis that could let attackers maintain persistence.

You've completed the analysis phase, both essential and advanced. You've identified the variant, scoped the damage, explored every decryption option, and documented everything for regulators, insurers, and stakeholders. Your incident log is complete with IOCs, timestamps, C2 domains, and lessons learned. You've got the intelligence you need.

Now it's time to act on it. The next phase is containment and eradication. You'll be isolating remaining threats, closing the doors attackers used, hunting for backdoors, and ensuring they can't waltz back in next week. The analysis told you what happened. Containment and eradication ensure it stops happening. Let's finish this fight.

CHAPTER 13

Contain the Attack

You've survived the worst 48 hours of your professional life. Your hands still shake when you think about those early panicked calls, the red skull flashing across screens, and the impossible choice between shutting down the network or watching the infection spread. Chapter 9 helped you make it through the fog of war, clouded by the stakeholder conflicts, the exhausted team working 18-hour shifts, and the gut-wrenching decision about whether to pay the ransom.

In Chapters 11 and 12, we shifted gears. You became a detective, methodically identifying the ransomware variant you were dealing with, mapping infections across all systems, confirming that important data was (or was not) exfiltrated, and ruling out any magic decryption solution. You know exactly what hit you and how bad it is.

Now comes the fight that determines everything: stopping this thing from spreading.

Welcome to the *containment* phase. Get it right, and you can move forward to safely eradicate the threat and recover. Get it wrong, and the ransomware spreads to every corner of your network while you scramble to catch up. Proper containment is what separates organizations that recover in days from those that struggle for months.

Change Healthcare thought they'd contained ALPHV. Three days later, a missed cloud storage infection spread to the backup systems they were counting on for recovery. Northforge contained what they thought was all of Lorenz, only to watch it spread from a system they'd overlooked. Sarah at ZapMart isolated the POS systems perfectly but missed a persistence mechanism lurking in the HR database that kept the infection alive.

One overlooked system. One infected endpoint you didn't isolate. One connection you didn't sever. That's all it takes to turn contained chaos into uncontrolled disaster.

While this chapter is designed to be your guide to the steps you should be doing, it will be woefully inadequate if you have never done these things before. We therefore want to once again stress the importance of professional help in such a situation. Hopefully you followed our advice and you are not doing this on your own. We will have some tools on our companion site, *StopRansomware.com*, that will help you evaluate and select such professionals. We also have a full glossary and list of all tools we discuss in the book.

What Is Containment and Eradication?

Containment means building walls around the infection to prevent further spread while you prepare for recovery. It's the difference between losing 50 systems and losing 500. It requires network segmentation, access controls, and constant verification that your walls are actually holding.

Eradication means hunting down every trace of the ransomware: every component, every backdoor, every persistence mechanism the attackers planted. You'll search registry keys, scheduled tasks, startup folders, cloud storage, and forgotten IoT devices. You'll verify, reverify, and verify again before you dare to bring systems back online.

These are two distinct phases of incident response. Containment stops the bleeding. It prevents the ransomware from spreading another inch while you catch your breath and plan your next moves. Eradication removes the cancer; it permanently eliminates every trace of the infection so you can safely restore operations without fear of reinfection.

This chapter focuses exclusively on containment. By the end of this chapter, you'll know how to stop ransomware from spreading, isolate infected systems, preserve forensic evidence, and safely shut everything down. You'll have built walls around the infection that it cannot breach. Chapter 14 will then cover eradication, which is the process of permanently removing the ransomware from every infected system.

Miss anything during containment, and the ransomware spreads to systems you thought were safe. Miss anything during eradication, and you're starting over. But let's not let either of those happen, shall we?

Whether you're fighting to protect customer data like Sarah, save a family business like Maria, or ensure patient safety at a hospital, this chapter will help you transform your analysis into decisive containment action. By the end, the ransomware will be stopped, isolated, and ready for the eradication phase that follows.

The Importance of Containment

Solid containment (this chapter) sets the stage for eradication (Chapter 14), which sets the stage for recovery (Chapter 15). In my (Curtis's) consulting business, I've seen organizations make catastrophic mistakes during containment. I've watched companies isolate the obviously infected systems while missing the quietly infected ones that became patient zero for a second wave. I've seen teams preserve forensic evidence so carefully that the ransomware had hours to spread while they worked. I've watched organizations accidentally isolate critical infrastructure that shut down their entire business instead of just the infected parts. The containment phase is where panic meets precision, and precision must win. Remember to follow your IRP and do what you've already decided to do; don't let panic win the day.

Let me be clear about something right from the start: containment is not about getting back online as quickly as possible. That's what your executives will be screaming for, but speed without strategy during containment just spreads the infection faster. Containment is about stopping the bleeding, building walls around the infection that it cannot breach, preserving the evidence you'll need later, and buying yourself the time to plan a proper eradication and recovery. Rush containment, and you'll spend the next week watching ransomware pop up in systems you thought were clean. Take the time to do containment right, and you set yourself up for a smooth eradication and recovery process. (This is another thing you might want to explain to executives *before* you have an incident.)

Suits Get in the Way

Thinking about suits encouraging you to just move on reminds me of a data restore many years ago, where we had someone in the NOC (network operations center) managing the incident (Joe), and someone in the data center actually doing the restore (Ron). Joe was on speaker phone as Ron asked him where he was.

"In the NOC," said Joe.

"It must be pretty stressful over there. Let me guess; you've got Tom and Tom on your left and right shoulder?" said Ron.

Tom T and the other Tom T took a step back from where they were standing, on Joe's left and right shoulder.

"You're on speaker phone, Ron," said Joe.

"%&#(%$*%$((%!!!!"

The Containment Versus Forensics Dilemma

Before you take any action, you face a critical decision that will shape your entire response: *Do you prioritize stopping ongoing damage or preserving forensic evidence?* This isn't a theoretical question. Every containment action you take alters or destroys evidence:

- Disabling user accounts changes Active Directory state and authentication logs
- Killing ransomware processes destroys volatile memory containing encryption keys, C2 addresses, and attack artifacts
- Disconnecting networks terminates active C2 communications you could be monitoring
- Shutting down systems loses all memory contents forever

At the same time, every minute you spend carefully preserving evidence is another minute ransomware is:

- Encrypting additional files
- Exfiltrating sensitive data
- Spreading to more systems
- Potentially destroying backups

You cannot fully optimize for both. You must choose your priority.

> If you are a cloud-centric or virtualization-centric environment, you get to skip this whole debate! For more information, skip to "The cloud/virtualization approach" on page 376 or "Snapshot, Suspend, or Pause All Infected VMs" on page 382.

Three Approaches

There are typically three ways to handle the containment versus forensics dilemma, and there is a fourth way if you are cloud-centric or virtualization-centric. The *containment-first* approach prioritizes stopping ongoing damage immediately, even if it means destroying some forensic evidence in the process. The *forensics-first* approach prioritizes preserving comprehensive evidence before taking containment actions, accepting some additional damage while you carefully capture memory dumps and disk images. The *hybrid* approach takes a middle path: quickly capture volatile memory from a few key infected systems, then immediately shift to aggressive containment. The *cloud/virtualization* approach applies only if you are fully virtualized or running in the cloud, and it involves freezing, suspending, or snapshotting your infected VMs before you do anything else.

Containment-first approach

The *containment-first* approach is recommended for most organizations, as it's less complicated and requires less experience. It prioritizes stopping ongoing damage over preserving perfect forensic evidence. It's especially the right choice for small to medium businesses without dedicated forensic capabilities, where systems are actively encrypting and you're losing critical data in real time. Organizations whose cyber insurance doesn't require detailed forensics for claims processing will also find this approach more practical and less risky than attempting complex evidence preservation during crisis conditions.

The sequence of the containment-first approach is as follows:

1. Start with your infected inventory (know what's infected).
2. Immediate containment actions (stop the bleeding).
3. Forensic disk preservation (image disks that you can).
4. Pull the plug (shut everything down).
5. Clean, wipe, or replace (Chapter 14).

The trade-off of the containment-first approach is that you will have less detailed forensic information about exactly how the attack happened, but you'll stop damage faster and recover more quickly.

Forensics-first approach

The *forensics-first* approach is recommended only for those organizations with advanced cyber capabilities, or immediate access to cyber professionals with such experience. It prioritizes comprehensive forensic evidence collection, even if it means accepting some additional damage while you work. It's the right choice when you have experienced forensic professionals on staff or immediately available to execute the effort. Organizations facing potential litigation, regulatory action, or law enforcement involvement often need this detailed forensic record to support their case. Critical infrastructure organizations that need to understand attack attribution (who attacked them, how, and why) require this level of analysis. This approach only makes sense if you have robust offline backups and can tolerate additional files being encrypted while you carefully collect evidence, knowing you can recover from clean backups after the forensic work is complete.

The sequence of the forensics-first approach is as follows:

1. Start with your infected inventory.

2. Immediate system isolation.

3. Dump the RAM to an external USB.

4. Pull the plug.

5. Generate a digital forensic image of the storage drive(s) (HDD, SDD).

6. Clean, wipe, or replace the storage drive(s) (Chapter 14).

The trade-off of this approach is that additional files may be encrypted and more data may be exfiltrated during forensic imaging, but you'll have complete evidence for investigation, prosecution, and preventing future attacks.

The hybrid approach

In practice, most organizations take a hybrid approach, which involves a quick memory capture on a few representative infected systems (5–10 minutes per system), followed by immediate containment of everything else. Then they perform imaging of infected disks after achieving containment. This balances stopping damage with preserving the most volatile evidence (memory) that would be lost anyway during containment.

The sequence of the hybrid approach is as follows:

1. Start with your infected inventory.

2. Identify critical systems.

3. Dump the RAM to external USB.

4. Rapid live forensic imaging of *critical* infected systems.

5. Immediate containment actions.

6. Pull the plug.

7. Generate a digital forensic image of the storage drive(s) (HDD, SDD).

8. Clean, wipe, or replace the storage drive(s) (Chapter 14).

The cloud/virtualization approach

If you're running a virtualization-first or cloud-first environment, you've got what amounts to a cheat code for the forensics versus containment dilemma. Virtualized systems let you have your cake and eat it too; you can preserve perfect forensic evidence *and* achieve immediate containment, all in one action that takes seconds instead of minutes.

Here's the magic: when you suspend a virtual machine, the hypervisor freezes the VM in its exact current state and writes everything, both the virtual disk contents and the complete memory state, to files on the host system. The ransomware can't execute another instruction. It can't encrypt another file. It can't communicate with C2 servers. It's completely frozen in time. And unlike shutting down a physical system where memory contents vanish, everything is preserved exactly as it was at the moment of suspension.

This gives you the best of both approaches simultaneously. You get immediate containment, stopping the ransomware dead in its tracks. But you also get comprehensive evidence preservation, like perfect memory dumps and disk images captured at the exact moment of the attack, with zero evidence degradation. You don't have to choose between stopping damage and preserving evidence because suspension does both. If you're in a virtualized environment, this capability fundamentally changes your incident response strategy and is one of the strongest arguments for virtualization if you haven't already made the move.

The sequence of the cloud/virtualization approach is as follows:

1. Start with your infected inventory.
2. Snapshot, suspend, or pause all infected VMs.
3. Immediate containment actions.
4. Forensic disk preservation.
5. Pull the plug.
6. Clean, wipe, or replace (Chapter 14).

Containment decision tree

We know this is a complicated process. So we've prepared a flowchart to lay it all out. You can see it in Figure 13-1. Please refer to this as you follow this chapter.

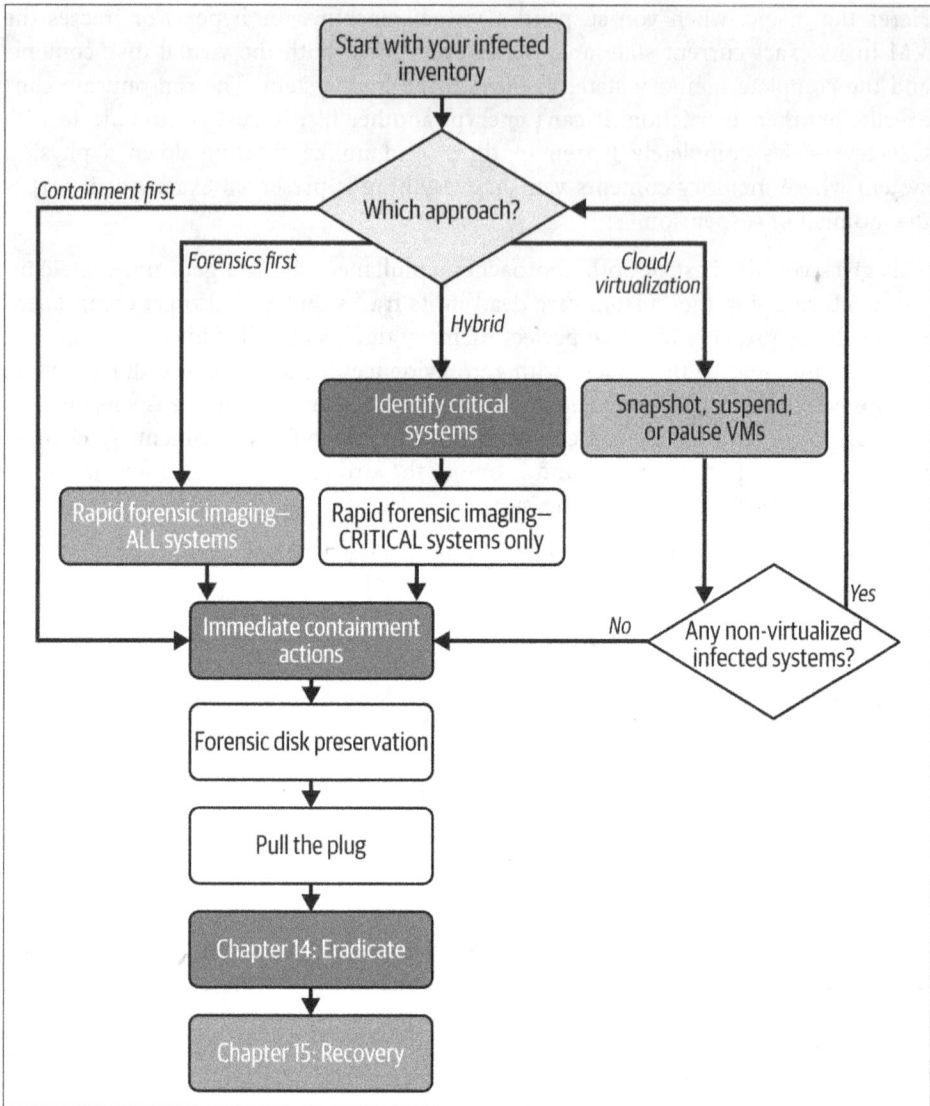

Figure 13-1. Containment decision tree

Make the Decision

This decision should be made in advance and documented in your IRP (see Chapter 7). An active attack is the worst time to debate philosophy. Consider these factors:

Legal/regulatory environment

Are you in a highly regulated industry (healthcare, finance) or jurisdiction that might require detailed forensics? Do you face potential lawsuits where evidence quality matters?

Business impact tolerance

Can your business survive additional hours of encryption while you collect evidence? What's the cost of downtime?

Available expertise

Do you have forensic professionals immediately available who can work quickly and competently under pressure? If you're calling someone who needs to drive/fly to your location, you probably can't afford forensics-first.

Attack velocity

Is the ransomware spreading rapidly, or does it appear contained? Fast-moving attacks demand containment-first.

Insurance requirements

What does your cyber insurance policy require? Some policies require forensic evidence for claims processing.

Data sensitivity

Are you protecting personal health information, financial data, or national security information? Higher sensitivity might justify forensics-first despite the cost.

Where to Start Containment

Before you shut down a single system, start wiping drives, or do anything else, you need to understand exactly what you're dealing with. That is the importance of the activities from Chapters 9–12. You must start with an accurate inventory of systems that are infected and, just as important, clean systems that you don't have to worry about. Beginning the containment phase is like building the foundation of a house; get this wrong, and everything else is pointless. Get this wrong, and you'll likely have to do everything else all over again—after you pour the foundation again.

This may sound straightforward, but it's not. The chaos of an active ransomware attack colors everything and makes it very hard to properly conduct this step, especially if you're being asked every hour how things are going. You're operating with limited information while critical, often revenue-driving systems are shutting down. Pressure is high, and everyone is demanding immediate answers. If you've never met senior management before, you will now.

Do not make assumptions. Too many organizations assume that because a server isn't showing obvious signs of infection, it is clean. Later they find out it has the ransomware payload; it just wasn't executed yet.

You should, of course, start with the obviously infected systems: those that have shut down, are displaying ransomware screens, or have encrypted files. But don't stop there. Just because a system doesn't look infected doesn't mean it isn't. Ransomware often spreads laterally through networks before executing, which means you might have dozens of systems that are infected that haven't yet shown any symptoms.

The network monitoring tools discussed in Chapter 8 will be your best friends in this phase. Look for unusual network traffic patterns, suspicious process executions, and any indicators that suggest lateral movement. If you've deployed EDR, SIEM, and SOAR tools, now is their time to shine. Please remember, however, these tools aren't perfect, and malware is designed to evade detection. It's a constant arms race between detection tools and the malware trying to hide from them. They actually use detection tools while developing their malware to see if their new variant can be detected!

Use the inventory you developed in the previous chapters to track your progress as you begin this phase. My favorite method of doing this would be an online spreadsheet that many people can access, such as Google Sheets or a Microsoft 365 spreadsheet, although it is important to have a backup plan if those systems are not available. You can also use a whiteboard, although this is difficult to scale if it's a large attack, and it's also difficult to share with anyone not physically there. But, of course, use whatever works for your team.

Track every single system in your environment and its status. Mark systems as *confirmed infected*, *suspected infected*, or *presumed clean*. Being conservative is the key. When in doubt, list it as suspected infected.

Pay special attention to your domain controllers, backup systems, and any infrastructure that could be used for persistence or lateral movement. As we discussed in Chapter 2, these systems are prime targets for attackers, and they can be the key to understanding how widespread the infection really is. If your domain controllers are compromised, you're looking at a much more complex remediation than if the attack was contained to user workstations. If your backup system is compromised, you may be looking at a total loss. Hopefully at least one copy of your system backups is on immutable storage. This is why we focused so much in previous chapters in making sure that this is prevented at all costs— within reason, of course.

Don't forget about your cloud infrastructure either. Many organizations make the mistake of focusing solely on their on-premises systems during the initial assessment, only to find out later that their cloud environments were also compromised. Check your cloud instances, storage accounts, and any hybrid connections between your on-premises and cloud environments.

Finally, don't forget about any mobile devices, tablets, and other nonstandard endpoints that might not be part of your standard server infrastructure. If they are connected to your network, they should be in the inventory. Remember that attacks often target these devices as entry points or use them for data exfiltration, so they need to be included in your inventory.

The inventory process should be collaborative but controlled. You need multiple sets of eyes looking at different parts of your environment, but you also need someone coordinating the effort to avoid duplication and confusion. Assign specific team members to specific network segments or system types and have them report back to a central coordinator who maintains the master inventory.

Remember that this inventory is a living document. As you gather more information and conduct deeper analysis, you'll need to update the status of various systems. A system that initially appeared clean might later reveal signs of infection, or forensic analysis might reveal that a system you thought was infected was actually clean.

What happens now will be based on your environment and approach:

1. If you are a cloud or virtualization environment, start with "Snapshot, Suspend, or Pause All Infected VMs" on page 382.

2. If you are adopting the forensics first approach, go to "Rapid Forensic Imaging" on page 387.

3. If you are adopting the hybrid approach, go to "Identify Critical Systems" on page 385.

4. If you are adopting the containment-first approach, go to "Immediate Containment Actions" on page 388.

Case Study: Quick Containment by UVM Health Network

On October 28, 2020, and in the middle of the COVID-19 pandemic, a University of Vermont Health Network employee took their work laptop on vacation. They opened a personal email from what looked like their local homeowners association, and boom: malware installed. When they got back from vacation and plugged the laptop into the work network via VPN, the attackers were ready.

But here's what UVM did right: when their IT staff realized they'd been breached on October 28, they immediately shut down the internet and took the Epic health records system offline. Within hours, they ran a scan of the entire system and found a folder with a link to contact the attackers—a ransom note.

Now, they considered paying for about five seconds. Literally. "We considered it for about five seconds," said Doug Gentile, their senior VP of network IT. They realized that even if they paid, they'd still need to wipe everything and rebuild to make sure the malware was gone. Paying wouldn't save them any time or effort.

So they called the FBI immediately, brought in Cisco Talos (they kept them on retainer like we talk about in Chapter 7), and Governor Phil Scott even deployed the Vermont National Guard to help. They refused to pay and had to rebuild and restore everything.

It still cost them $65 million. The EHR was down for 28 days, which meant paper records, no phones, and seriously disrupted patient care for over two weeks. Their cyber insurance only covered $30 million, so they ate $35 million in losses. And this happened during the height of COVID: talk about bad timing!

But here's the thing: it could have been so much worse. By shutting everything down immediately when they detected the breach, they prevented the attackers from spreading further into affiliate hospitals and other systems. They minimized the blast radius.

The entry point? An employee opening a personal email on a work computer. The malware was from a legitimate local business that had itself been hacked. Could have happened to anyone. But the quick response is what kept it from being even more catastrophic.

Oh, and justice was eventually served: in 2024, Ukrainian national Vyacheslav Penchukov pleaded guilty. He's looking at up to 20 years. See Jickling, 2020 (*https://oreil.ly/n6JMW*).

Snapshot, Suspend, or Pause All Infected VMs

This section explains the practical workflow for using virtualization to simultaneously contain and preserve evidence.

Step 1: Suspend VMs Immediately

Access your hypervisor management console (vCenter for VMware, Hyper-V Manager for Microsoft, or your cloud provider's console). Select the infected VMs and choose "Suspend" from the power options menu. Do not choose "Shutdown" or "Power Off"; those options lose all memory contents. You must use "Suspend" to preserve both disk and memory state.

For cloud environments, create snapshots of suspended instances. Like suspending a VM, this will immediately create a full disk image of the VM and its memory. Once the snapshot has been completed, you can then pause or stop the VM.

Check your hypervisor or cloud account: either might be compromised. If attackers gained access to your virtualization or cloud infrastructure, they could have infected the hypervisor, modified VM files, or planted backdoors in your templates and snapshots. Before you trust suspended VMs or use them for recovery:

- Check hypervisor logs for unauthorized access or unusual administrative actions
- Verify that management credentials (vCenter, Hyper-V admin, cloud IAM roles) haven't been compromised
- Review changes to VM templates and base images
- Confirm that your hypervisor software itself is running a clean, updated version
- For VMware ESXi, check for modifications to the hypervisor's boot partition or persistence mechanisms

If you find evidence of hypervisor compromise, you may need to shut down or suspend the hypervisor hosts themselves and consider them part of your infected inventory requiring full eradication.

Step 2: Copy VM Files to Isolated Forensic Storage

Once you've suspended or made a snapshot of the VM, the VM exists as files on your hypervisor's storage or in the same cloud account. You need to immediately protect that image from being tampered with.

For on-premises environments, copy these files to isolated storage that's not connected to your production network:

VMware
    Copy the *.vmdk* disk files and *.vmem* or *.vmsn* memory/snapshot files

Hyper-V
    Copy the *.vhd* or *.vhdx* disk files and *.bin* or *.vsv* memory files

KVM/QEMU
    Copy the *.qcow2* disk files and any associated memory dump files

For cloud environments, create snapshots of suspended instances and copy them to isolated storage accounts or buckets that use separate credentials from your production environment. In AWS, create EBS snapshots and AMIs. In Azure, create managed disk snapshots. In Google Cloud, create persistent disk snapshots. Store these in separate projects or accounts if possible.

Step 3: Document Everything

Record which VMs were suspended or snapshotted, at what time, by whom, and where the files were copied. This documentation is critical for the forensic chain of custody and for understanding your incident timeline.

Also be forewarned that suspended VMs consume significant disk space. A VM with 32GB of RAM and 500GB of virtual disk will create suspended state files totaling over 500GB. Before suspending large numbers of VMs:

- Check available storage on your hypervisor datastores or cloud storage accounts
- Calculate how much space you'll need (sum of memory + disk for each VM)
- Ensure you have at least 50% more space than your calculation to avoid running out mid-operation
- Consider suspending VMs in stages if storage is limited

Running out of storage during suspension can corrupt VMs or lose evidence, so this planning step is critical.

Create a Panic Button Script

If you're in a heavily virtualized or cloud environment, create and test a script or runbook that can suspend multiple VMs based on criteria like cluster membership, tags, or network segment.

For VMware environments using PowerCLI:

```
Get-VM -Tag "Infected" | Suspend-VM -Confirm:$false
```

For Azure using Azure CLI:

```
az vm list --query "[?tags.Status=='Infected'].name" -o tsv | xargs -I {} az vm
deallocate --name {}
```

Test these scripts during tabletop exercises to ensure they work correctly and suspend the right VMs without accidentally affecting clean systems.

The Suspend Versus Shutdown Distinction

Make absolutely certain your team understands that "Suspend" and "Shutdown" are completely different operations with opposite forensic consequences. Create documentation, add warnings to runbooks, and emphasize during training that:

- Suspend = Preserves memory and disk state (forensically valuable)
- Shutdown = Loses all memory contents (destroys volatile evidence)

- Power Off = Same as shutdown (loses memory)

Put visual warnings in your hypervisor consoles if possible or create custom roles that only allow suspension operations during incidents.

Testing Your Suspension Process

During non-incident times, practice suspending VMs, copying their files, and verifying that you can later mount the virtual disks and analyze the memory dumps. This ensures:

- Your team knows the correct procedures.
- Your storage systems have adequate capacity and performance.
- Your forensic tools can actually read the suspended VM files.
- Your documentation is accurate and complete.
- The process works as quickly as you expect during a real incident.

Run through this at least once per quarter so the procedures stay fresh and you catch any environmental changes that might affect the process.

If you have any infected systems that are not virtualized or in the cloud, then go to "Identify Critical Systems" on page 385 (hybrid approach), "Rapid Forensic Imaging" on page 387 (forensics-first approach), or "Immediate Containment Actions" on page 388 (containment-first approach).

If you don't have any non-virtualized infected systems, then move on to "Immediate Containment Actions" on page 388.

Identify Critical Systems

You only need to do this step if you are adopting the hybrid approach mentioned earlier. If not, you can skip it.

If you've chosen the hybrid approach mentioned earlier in the section of this chapter called "The Containment Versus Forensics Dilemma" on page 374, you need to identify which handful of systems will receive quick memory captures before you move to full containment mode. You can't image everything before containing the threat, so you need to be strategic about which systems will give you the most valuable forensic evidence in those critical first minutes.

Start with your domain controllers. These systems are gold mines for forensic evidence because they contain authentication logs, credential hashes, and evidence of lateral movement across your entire network. If attackers compromised your domain controllers, the memory dump will show you exactly how they escalated privileges and spread through your environment. Spend five minutes capturing memory from your primary domain controller before you do anything else.

Next, prioritize any file servers or database servers that show signs of active encryption. If you can catch the ransomware process in the act of encrypting files, the memory dump might contain encryption keys, C2 server addresses, and other artifacts that disappear the moment you kill the process or shut down the system. This is your only chance to capture this volatile data.

Look for systems showing unusual network activity in your monitoring tools. If a workstation or server is communicating with suspicious external IP addresses or making an abnormal number of outbound connections, that system's memory likely contains active C2 communications. Capturing this before you block the traffic preserves evidence of exactly how the attackers were controlling the ransomware.

If you've identified the initial infection point, the first system that got compromised, prioritize that system for memory capture. It will contain evidence of the initial attack vector, whether that was a phishing email, an exploited vulnerability, or stolen credentials. This information is critical for understanding how to prevent the next attack.

We would add to your list any infected systems that store very important data. It might be very important to figure out how they were compromised, so capturing their memory image right now would be a good idea.

Finally, if your backup systems were compromised, capture memory from the backup server before you do anything else. This will show you exactly how the attackers accessed your backups and what tools they used to compromise your recovery capabilities. This evidence is essential for proving to regulators and insurers that your backup systems were adequately protected.

Don't let perfect be the enemy of good here. If you spend an hour deciding which systems to image, you've lost an hour of containment time. Pick the obvious high-value targets (domain controllers, actively encrypting systems, and the initial infection point), capture their memory, and move on. You're not trying to preserve every piece of evidence; you're trying to capture the most critical evidence that won't survive containment actions. Once you're done with this step, you can move immediately to the "Rapid Forensic Imaging" on page 387 section that follows this one.

Rapid Forensic Imaging

You only need to do this step if you are adopting either the forensics-first or hybrid approach mentioned earlier. If you are doing the hybrid approach, you should have already completed the steps in "Identify Critical Systems" on page 385.

We're calling this *rapid forensic imaging* to distinguish it from the comprehensive forensic imaging you might be familiar with. Traditional forensic imaging is a meticulous, time-consuming process where you create bit-for-bit copies of entire hard drives (operations that can take hours or days for multi-terabyte systems). That's important work, but it's not what you're doing in the first critical minutes of a ransomware response.

Rapid forensic imaging focuses exclusively on capturing volatile memory (the contents of RAM) from a small number of critical systems (i.e., memory dump). It's *rapid* because modern tools can dump 32GB or 64GB of RAM to a file in 5 to 10 minutes, and because we're only doing this on a few systems. It's *forensic* because you're preserving evidence in a forensically sound way that can be analyzed later or even used in legal proceedings. It's *imaging* because you're creating a complete snapshot of memory at a specific point in time.

Why is memory so valuable that it's worth these precious first minutes? Because it's where active processes live. When ransomware is running on a system, everything it's doing right now, including its encryption keys, command-and-control server addresses, credential hashes, attack tools, and network connections, is being loaded into RAM. The moment you kill the ransomware process, shut down the system, or even just wait too long, all of that evidence vanishes forever. RAM is volatile. Once power is lost or processes are terminated, the data is gone and you can never get it back.

This volatility is exactly why we emphasize rapid. Every minute you wait, the evidence degrades. Windows and Linux constantly overwrite RAM as processes run. The ransomware might detect your defensive actions and purge its memory artifacts. The attackers might kill their tools and clean up. The clock is ticking from the moment you decide to do this.

Tools like DumpIt (free for Windows) or FTK Imager (free from AccessData) are designed specifically for rapid memory capture. You run the tool with administrative privileges, it creates a file the size of your system's RAM, and you're done. No complex configuration, no lengthy setup, no difficult technical decisions. Point it at a USB drive or network share, hit Enter, wait a few minutes, and you have a forensically sound memory dump.

The memory dump file is just raw data at this point. You don't analyze it during the crisis; that's work for after you've contained the attack. You just need to capture it and store it somewhere safe and isolated from your network. Copy it to an external drive, upload it to isolated storage, or transfer it to your forensic analysis workstation. The goal right now is preservation, not investigation.

This is why you only do rapid forensic imaging on a handful of critical systems before shifting to full containment. You're not trying to preserve perfect evidence from every infected machine. You're making a calculated trade-off: spend 10 minutes per system capturing the most valuable volatile evidence from the most important systems, then immediately shift to stopping the ransomware from spreading further. The comprehensive forensic imaging of hard drives can wait until after containment when you have time to do it properly and the ransomware can't cause more damage while you work.

Immediate Containment Actions

The actions in this section will alter or destroy forensic evidence. If you've chosen the forensics-first, hybrid, or cloud approach, be sure that you have done what you need to do to collect forensic evidence before you move to this step. If you've chosen the containment-first approach, proceed immediately with the following actions.

Once you've identified which systems are infected through your inventory process, you need to act immediately to stop the ransomware from spreading further. These containment actions must happen quickly, but they must also be systematic. Think of this as building a firewall around the infection.

The goal of immediate containment is not recovery; it is to stop the bleeding. Every minute that ransomware remains active on your network is another minute it can encrypt files, steal data, or spread to additional systems. But rushing through containment without a plan can be just as dangerous as moving too slowly. You need to balance speed with precision.

The time sensitivity of this step becomes much less critical if you are in a virtualized or cloud environment and are able to pause/snapshot all infected VMs.

Step 1: Isolate Infected Devices

Network isolation is your first and most critical containment action. An infected device that remains connected to your network is like a contagious patient wandering through a hospital. The infection will continue to spread until you quarantine the source. Start with your inventory and identify the characteristics of each infected system that will inform your containment strategy:

Device purpose and criticality
> Is this a workstation, server, or critical infrastructure like a domain controller?

Data sensitivity
> What data does this system contain? Customer information? Financial records? Intellectual property?

User profile
> What type of user operates this system? Do they have administrative privileges? Access to sensitive systems?

Network access
> What can this system reach on your network? Does it have access to file servers, databases, or backup systems?

Dependencies
> What other systems rely on this device? What will break if you isolate it?

This information will help you prioritize which systems need immediate isolation versus which ones you can address in a staged approach. A compromised domain controller requires immediate action. An infected workstation with limited network access might get a lower priority.

Disable compromised user accounts

Before you even touch the infected devices themselves, disable the user accounts associated with those systems. This is a critical step that many organizations miss in their rush to isolate hardware. This is because ransomware often steals credentials before executing. Even if you isolate the infected hardware, attackers might still be able to access your network using stolen usernames and passwords. Disabling accounts cuts off this access vector. Here is a list of things to consider when disabling user accounts:

- Immediately disable the primary account associated with each infected system.
- Force revocation of all authenticated sessions for those users across your entire environment.
- Revoke or reset MFA tokens to prevent attackers from using stolen authentication credentials.

- Reset passwords for all affected accounts (don't just disable them).
- Check for service accounts that might have been running on infected systems and disable those as well.

Use your Active Directory or identity management system to disable these accounts. If you have a SIEM or SOAR platform, you might be able to automate this process. But don't let perfect automation prevent good manual action. If you need to manually disable accounts, do it.

Document which accounts you've disabled and why. You'll need this information later when you're restoring services and re-enabling access for legitimate users.

Disconnect from network

With user accounts disabled, now focus on isolating the infected hardware itself:

Physical disconnection
If possible and safe to do so, physically unplug network cables from infected devices. This is the most certain way to prevent network communication. For wireless devices, disable the wireless adapter through management tools or physically remove wireless cards if you can.

Network-based isolation
If physical disconnection isn't practical (e.g., remote systems or devices you can't physically access), use your network infrastructure to isolate the devices:

- Disable the switch port the infected device is connected to.
- Use access control lists (ACLs) to block all traffic to/from the infected device.
- Remove the infected device from all VLANs.

Quarantine VLANs
If your network supports it, create a dedicated quarantine VLAN, a separate network segment designed specifically for compromised systems. Move infected devices to this VLAN where they can't communicate with production systems but where you can still monitor and analyze them if needed. Configure this VLAN to:

- Block all outbound internet access.
- Block all communication with other VLANs.
- Allow only monitoring traffic from your security tools.
- Log all attempted communications.

The quarantine VLAN approach is particularly useful if you need to keep systems powered on for forensic analysis or if you're performing staged isolation and need to monitor systems before final shutdown.

Be sure to document every isolation action: which systems were isolated, when, how (physical versus network), and who performed the action. This documentation is critical for understanding the timeline of your response and for any post-incident analysis.

Step 2: Disable Attack Vectors

Now that you have isolated any infected devices, you need to close the pathways ransomware uses to spread laterally through your network. Even if you've isolated the known infected systems, other systems might already be compromised but not yet showing symptoms. Shutting down these attack vectors prevents further propagation.

Disable network shares

Ransomware loves network shares. Shared drives, mapped network folders, and file servers are prime targets because they allow ransomware to encrypt data across multiple systems without needing to compromise each individual device. Therefore, you need to take immediate action on network shares:

Identify what any infected users have access to.
> Review the permissions for accounts associated with infected systems. What file shares can they access? What network drives were mapped?

Unmount or disable those shares immediately.
> Don't wait to assess whether they're infected. If a compromised account had access, treat those shares as potentially compromised and disable access.

Temporarily restrict SMB protocol.
> SMB is the most common file-sharing protocol and a favorite target for ransomware. Consider temporarily disabling SMB on critical systems or blocking SMB traffic at your firewall (port 445) between network segments.

Permanently disable SMBv1.
> If you're still running SMBv1 anywhere in your environment, now is the time to permanently disable it. SMBv1 has well-known vulnerabilities that ransomware actively exploits. Modern systems don't need it. (Windows 10 and newer versions use SMBv3 by default.)

For immediate response, you might need to take the drastic step of temporarily disabling all file sharing across your environment. Yes, this will impact business operations. But continued ransomware spread will be worse. Work with your business leadership to make this decision but err on the side of aggressive containment.

Document which shares were disabled, when, and the business justification. You'll need this for your incident timeline and for explaining decisions to stakeholders.

Terminate malicious processes

Ransomware running on infected systems consists of active processes that are encrypting files, communicating with C2 servers, or preparing to spread. Terminating these processes can stop ongoing damage.

To identify and kill malicious processes:

Use any EDR tools you have.
Modern EDR platforms can identify ransomware processes and automatically terminate them. Check your EDR console for alerts about suspicious process execution, unusual file access patterns, or processes with known ransomware signatures.

Manual process inspection.
Use Task Manager on Windows or command-line utilities like ps and top on Linux. Look for:

- Processes with suspicious names (e.g., svc32.exe, encryptor.exe, or random character strings)
- Processes consuming unusual amounts of CPU or disk I/O
- Processes making large numbers of file operations
- Processes with network connections to suspicious IP addresses

Kill identified processes immediately.
On Windows: `taskkill /F /IM processname.exe`. On Linux: `kill -9 [PID]`. Be aware that some ransomware monitors for termination attempts and may respond by immediately encrypting remaining files or wiping data.

Monitor for process restart.
Some ransomware includes persistence mechanisms that automatically restart killed processes. If you kill a process and it immediately restarts, you have a persistence problem that needs to be addressed (we'll cover this in Chapter 14).

Enforce application whitelisting policies.
If you have them configured, they will be very helpful. This prevents unauthorized executables from running, even if ransomware tries to launch additional processes.

Terminating processes can sometimes trigger defensive behaviors in sophisticated ransomware. Some variants are programmed to detect defensive actions and respond by immediately encrypting all remaining files or wiping data. This is another reason why having cybersecurity professionals guide this process is so important. They understand which ransomware families have these defensive capabilities and how to handle them safely.

Document which processes were terminated, on which systems, and what happened afterward. (Did they restart? Did the system behavior change?). This information helps with forensic analysis and eradication planning.

Step 3: Block External Communication

Ransomware doesn't operate in isolation. Most modern ransomware families communicate with external C2 servers to receive instructions, download additional payloads, upload stolen data, or negotiate encryption keys. Blocking this external communication is critical to preventing the attack from progressing further. Your firewall is the gatekeeper between your network and the internet. Use it to block ransomware from communicating with its operators:

Identify known malicious IPs and domains.
Use the threat intelligence you gathered during analysis (Chapters 11 and 12) to identify C2 servers associated with your specific ransomware variant. This might include IP addresses, domain names, or Tor endpoints.

Create block rules immediately.
Update your firewall to explicitly deny all traffic to/from these malicious destinations. Don't just block outbound traffic, also block inbound traffic in case attackers are trying to remotely control infected systems.

Block traffic from infected systems.
Even if you don't know all the C2 addresses, you can block all outbound internet traffic from known infected systems. This prevents data exfiltration and prevents the ransomware from downloading additional tools.

Monitor your firewall vendor's threat feeds.
Many next-generation firewalls receive regular updates of known malicious IPs and domains from threat intelligence services. Ensure these feeds are enabled and updating. Some provide specific ransomware C2 lists that are updated multiple times per day.

The challenge with firewall rules is that ransomware operators frequently change their C2 infrastructure. They rotate IP addresses, register new domains, and use techniques like domain generation algorithms to evade blocking. This is why you need multiple layers of defense, not just firewall rules. Let's now take a look at DNS filtering and network monitoring.

Deploy DNS filtering

DNS filtering blocks malicious domain name lookups before connections are even established:

Configure DNS filtering services.
> Tools like Cisco Umbrella, Cloudflare for Teams, or OpenDNS can block access to domains known to be associated with ransomware campaigns. If you don't already have these deployed, now is the time to implement them.

Block newly registered domains.
> Many ransomware campaigns use freshly registered domains for C2 servers. Configure your DNS filtering to block or flag domains registered within the last 30–90 days (adjusting for false positives based on your environment).

Monitor DNS queries.
> Look for suspicious DNS query patterns such as:
>
> - High volumes of queries to random-looking domains (possible domain generation algorithm activity)
> - Queries to known malicious domains
> - Queries to Tor node addresses
> - DNS tunneling attempts (unusually long or frequent DNS queries)

Use web proxies.
> Configure web proxies to intercept and inspect HTTP/HTTPS traffic. Block access to suspicious URLs and known malicious sites. Log all blocked attempts for forensic analysis.

Network monitoring and IDS/SIEM

Even with firewall rules and DNS filtering in place, sophisticated ransomware might find ways to communicate. Active monitoring helps catch these attempts:

Deploy or activate IDS (intrusion detection systems).
> Configure IDS to alert on the following:
>
> - Connections to known C2 infrastructure
> - Unusual volumes of outbound traffic
> - Data exfiltration patterns (large uploads to external sites)
> - Tor network connections

- Encrypted traffic to suspicious destinations

Leverage your SIEM platform.
If you have SIEM deployed (see Chapter 8), configure alerts for:

- Firewall blocks to known ransomware C2 servers
- Repeated connection attempts to blocked destinations
- Unusual protocols or ports being used
- Network traffic patterns that deviate from baseline behavior

Monitor for beaconing.
Ransomware often "phones home" to C2 servers at regular intervals. Look for periodic outbound connections that might indicate beaconing behavior (connections that happen every few minutes or hours to the same destination).

The key is to layer these controls. Firewall blocks prevent most communication. DNS filtering catches domain-based connections that slip through. IDS and SIEM monitoring alert you to evasion attempts. Together, they make it very difficult for ransomware to successfully communicate with its operators.

Blocking C2 communication can also prevent ransomware from receiving encryption keys. In some cases, ransomware cannot execute its encryption phase without communicating with C2 servers first. This is why blocking external communication quickly can sometimes prevent encryption of systems that are infected but not yet encrypted.

Step 4: Automate Containment

If your organization has invested in SOAR platforms or similar automation tools, this is their moment to shine. Automation allows you to execute containment actions faster and more consistently than manual processes.

SOAR platform capabilities

Modern SOAR platforms can integrate with your existing security tools to automate containment:

Automated device isolation
Configure SOAR playbooks to automatically isolate devices as soon as your EDR or SIEM detects ransomware indicators. The playbook can:

- Disable user accounts in Active Directory.
- Disable switch ports via your network management system.
- Move devices to quarantine VLANs.
- Update firewall rules to block traffic from infected systems.

All of this happens in seconds rather than the minutes or hours manual processes require.

Automated process termination
SOAR can trigger EDR systems to automatically kill processes matching ransomware signatures or behaviors, without waiting for analyst approval.

Automated share disabling
Playbooks can disable network shares, unmount drives, and block SMB traffic across multiple systems simultaneously.

Automated firewall updates
As your threat intelligence feeds identify new C2 infrastructure, SOAR can automatically update firewall rules across your entire infrastructure.

Consistent execution
Humans under stress make mistakes. Automation ensures every containment action follows the same process every time.

SOAR playbook design

If you have SOAR capabilities, ensure your ransomware playbooks include:

Trigger conditions
What events trigger the playbook? EDR alerts? SIEM correlation rules? Manual activation?

Automated actions
What does the playbook do automatically without human approval? Usually time-critical actions like isolation and process termination.

Human approval gates
What actions require human approval before executing? Usually this includes actions that might impact business operations like disabling critical services.

Rollback procedures
If the playbook makes a mistake, how do you undo the actions?

Documentation
The playbook should automatically document all actions taken, creating an audit trail for incident response.

Notification
Who gets notified when the playbook executes? Ensure your IRT receives real-time alerts.

Real-time alerts and reporting

Automation isn't just about executing actions—it's also about keeping your team informed:

- Generate real-time alerts when containment actions are executed, whether automatic or manual.
- Produce detailed reports showing:
  — Which systems were isolated and when
  — Which user accounts were disabled
  — Which firewall rules were updated
  — Which processes were terminated
  — Any errors or failures in containment actions
- Provide dashboards showing the current containment status across your entire environment.
- Feed data back into your SIEM for correlation with other security events and to maintain your incident timeline.

For organizations without SOAR

If you don't have SOAR platforms, don't despair. You can still achieve significant automation benefits:

Scripting
Create PowerShell, Python, or bash scripts that execute multiple containment actions with a single command (for example, a script that disables a user account, blocks their IP address at the firewall, and sends alerts to your security team).

Network automation
Many network devices support automation through tools like Ansible or even simple CLI scripts. Pre-create scripts that can quickly isolate devices or block traffic.

EDR automation
Most EDR platforms include some automation capabilities, even without full SOAR integration. Enable automatic isolation features for high-confidence detections.

Runbooks
Even without automation, detailed runbooks that document step-by-step containment procedures allow team members to execute consistently and rapidly.

The key principle is this: anything you do manually during an incident, you'll do more slowly and with more errors than if you had prepared automated responses in advance. Every minute you spend during an incident deciding what to do next is a minute the ransomware is still spreading.

Verification and Monitoring

After executing immediate containment actions, you need to verify that they're working.

Confirm device isolation.
   Attempt to ping or connect to isolated devices from other network segments. They should be unreachable.

Verify account disabling.
   Attempt to authenticate with disabled accounts. Authentication should fail.

Check firewall logs.
   Confirm that traffic to C2 servers is being blocked and logged.

Monitor for containment bypass.
   Sophisticated attackers might try to work around your containment measures. Watch for:

   - New user accounts being created
   - Different C2 infrastructure being contacted
   - Lateral movement through paths you didn't isolate
   - Data exfiltration through alternative channels

Update your inventory.
   As containment actions reveal additional infected systems or confirm that suspected systems are clean, update your master inventory.

Containment isn't a one-time action, it's an ongoing process that continues until you're certain the threat is fully contained and you've moved into eradication. Continue monitoring and adjusting your containment measures throughout the incident response process.

With containment actions verified and monitoring in place, you've built walls around the infection that it cannot breach. The ransomware is boxed in, unable to spread to new systems. Now you can shift focus from stopping the spread to preserving the evidence you'll need to understand how this happened and prove you responded appropriately. If you haven't already captured forensic images of infected systems, now is the time.

Forensic Disk Preservation

With immediate containment actions in place and the ransomware's ability to spread significantly limited, you can now focus on preserving forensic evidence on disk.

If you followed the forensics-first or hybrid approaches, you've already captured volatile memory from infected systems. This section covers capturing complete forensic disk images: bit-for-bit copies of entire hard drives, including unallocated space and hidden areas. If you followed the containment-first approach, this is your first opportunity to preserve forensic evidence now that the threat is contained.

Have you ever watched a crime drama and seen detectives get angry because some uniformed policemen had "trampled all over their crime scene"? Once this is all over, you may want to do an even more detailed analysis than you did in Chapters 11 and 12. If that's the case, you're going to want to use digital forensics to preserve the crime scene as best as you can before tampering with the evidence by cleaning things up.

This is your crime scene. Just like in criminal investigations, preserving evidence is paramount. The information contained in these infected systems might be the only way you'll ever understand how the attack happened and what data was accessed; both of which are key to preventing it from happening again.

This is another area where many organizations falter. They see infected systems as problems to be solved rather than evidence to be preserved. They want to start cleaning systems right away. This urgency is totally understandable, but it's also dangerous. Once you've altered the state of an infected system, that evidence becomes "muddy," much like walking through a crime scene, and it can't be undone.

Forensic imaging isn't as simple as making a backup. You need bit-for-bit copies of the entire system, including unallocated space, temporary files, and metadata that normal backup processes would ignore. If possible, you also need an image of what's in memory. (This is why you needed to decide to do this earlier if you were using the forensic-first approach.) This requires using specialized forensic tools that can create these copies without altering the original data. We discussed identifying and procuring these tools in Chapter 8.

Start by identifying which systems need to be imaged. The confirmed infected are obviously first on the list, followed by those you suspect have been infected. Once those are taken care of, you should also consider imaging systems that might have been part of the attack path even if you believe they are clean. Any firewalls and domain controllers, for example, might contain logs or artifacts that show how the attackers got in or moved around in your network.

For each system you plan to image, you will need to decide whether to image it live or after shutdown. Live imaging allows you to capture the current state of memory, running processes, and open network connections information that would be lost if you shut the system down. Live imaging requires more specialized tools and is riskier, because it risks allowing the malware to continue executing and potentially causing more damage. Cold imaging, where you shut down the system and image the storage devices offline, prevents further malware execution but loses any data that is in memory (which is why many grab just the memory image at the very beginning of their IRP). As already mentioned, an exception to this would be virtualized or cloud systems that can be easily paused and imaged without losing what is in memory or risking further attacks.

Use dedicated forensic workstations that are isolated from your network, and never connect forensic equipment directly to your production network. The last thing you want is for your forensic tools to become infected and spread the malware to other systems.

The imaging process itself can take quite a bit of time, especially for systems with large storage volumes. A server with multiple terabytes of storage might take many hours to create a complete image. This is where having multiple forensic technicians and multiple sets of equipment becomes important. Being able to image multiple systems at one time will greatly speed up the process. You also might consider imaging only the primary system drive and memory, rather than imaging the secondary drives.

Continue to document everything during the imaging process. This information will be useful for the post-mortem discussion in Chapter 16 and for any legal discussions you find yourself in, especially for those in highly regulated or litigious industries (you know who you are). Record which systems have been imaged, when the imaging started and completed, who performed the imaging, and what tools were used. This documentation will become part of your evidence for legal and insurance purposes, which means it might be scrutinized by external investigators or auditors. This data (e.g., date, time, who, and how) will be very valuable, and storing it contemporaneously is the best way to ensure its accuracy.

Finally, be sure to consider all the legal implications of your imaging efforts. Be sure to consult with counsel throughout this process. If there's any possibility that this attack will result in litigation, regulatory action, or conversations with law enforcement, your forensic images need to meet legal standards for evidence preservation, which would also include documenting the entire chain of custody. Once again, you should learn how to do this well before you need to do this.

The Final Shutdown Decision

At this point, you've completed your inventory, taken immediate containment actions to limit the ransomware's spread, and preserved any forensic evidence you wanted to preserve. Now you face the final shutdown decision: should isolated systems remain powered on for additional analysis, or should you shut them down completely?

Be aware that some ransomware variants monitor for shutdown signals or defensive tools and respond by immediately encrypting critical system files that would normally be encrypted later in the attack timeline. Others include wiping the entire hard drive. To avoid triggering a scorched earth response that destroys data that could have otherwise been saved, ensure that whatever you do, *do it quickly*.

Pull the Plug

Actually powering off systems has the best chance of triggering a response. If you are in a fully virtualized environment, however, it should be quite easy to pause all VMs. That would stop further damage, while not giving the ransomware very much time for a defensive response. As mentioned earlier in "The cloud/virtualization approach" on page 376, consider creating a "panic button" script that would pause all VMs in your entire environment. Once all VMs on a given hypervisor are paused, you can then power off the hypervisor. Remember that the hypervisor can be infected.

Leaving infected systems running is very dangerous! Active malware can continue to spread laterally, encrypt additional files, exfiltrate sensitive data, and establish additional persistence mechanisms.

The key is making informed shutdown decisions based on your analysis from Chapters 11 and 12. You already know which ransomware family you're facing and its specific behaviors. Now is the time to use that knowledge.

For example, if you're dealing with a ransomware variant that's known to fully wipe drives or encrypt everything if they detect any defensive measures, you might need to shut down systems more aggressively (i.e., pulling the plug instead of pushing the power button). If you're facing malware that focuses primarily on encryption and doesn't include advanced anti-forensic capabilities, you might have more flexibility in your timing.

Your inventory already identified business criticality and system dependencies. Use that information to prioritize shutdown decisions. Systems already isolated and fully encrypted are lower priority for shutdown. Systems still functional with critical data need immediate shutdown to prevent further encryption.

Consider implementing a staged shutdown approach where you shut down systems in groups rather than all at once. This allows you to monitor for any unexpected behaviors or responses from the malware and adjust your approach accordingly.

Whatever order you choose, be sure to do it systematically. Start with systems that pose the greatest risk for lateral movement, such as domain controllers, file servers, and other critical infrastructure. Then you should move to systems that contain the most sensitive data, followed by systems that are most critical to business operations.

Remember that a shutdown isn't always permanent. In some cases, you might need to temporarily power on infected systems, perhaps in a sandbox, to gather additional evidence or to facilitate specific recovery procedures. Plan for this possibility by ensuring you can safely restart systems in an isolated environment if you need to.

Continue to meticulously document your shutdown timeline. Record which systems were shut down, when they were shut down, who made the decision, and what factors influenced the decision.

Case Study: Quick Action by Norsk Hydro

So picture this: it's March 19, 2019, and Hilde Merete Aasheim is about to have her first day as CEO of Norsk Hydro, a massive Norwegian aluminum manufacturer with 35,000 employees across 40 countries. She's probably got her first day planned out: meetings, press interviews, the usual new CEO stuff.

Then her phone rings at four in the morning.

"That's normally not when you get a phone call," she said later. And the message on the other end? "We are under a severe cyber attack, you have to come to work." Welcome to the C-suite, right?

What hit them was LockerGoga ransomware, and it was nasty. All 171 of their sites got hammered. The ransomware encrypted files across the company and then, this is the evil genius part, it disabled the network adapters, changed all the passwords, and logged everyone off. So victims couldn't even see the ransom note anymore. They might not even realize they'd been hit with ransomware.

But here's where Norsk Hydro shows everyone how it's supposed to be done. IT immediately shut down the network and servers to stop it from spreading further. No hesitation, no "let's wait and see," no "maybe it's not that bad." Just boom; shut it down.

And when they found the ransom note? "There was never the option to pay any ransom," Aasheim said. Not "we considered it," not "we thought about it." Never an option. They decided they were going to restore from backups and do this the right way.

Now, it wasn't easy. They had to switch to manual operations across all 171 sites. Manufacturing facilities that normally run on computers were suddenly back to doing things by hand. But you know what? Most operations were running normally within a week. A week!

The whole thing still cost them somewhere between $60 and $75 million and their profits fell 82% that quarter, but law enforcement and the infosec industry called their response the "gold standard." They did everything right: immediate shutdown, no ransom payment, transparent communication with the public throughout the crisis, and recovery from backups.

The entry point? Classic stuff: weaponized email attachment from what looked like a trusted customer back in December 2018 (three months earlier—this is why we want at least 90 days of logs). By the time they detected it, it was already too late. But once they knew, they moved fast.

Oh, and here's the kicker: Norsk Hydro had cyber insurance, but it only covered a fraction of the costs. Even with insurance, they still took a massive financial hit. But they made the right call; paying the ransom wouldn't have helped them rebuild all those servers, all those PCs, or all of those networks anyway.

Law enforcement loves this case because Norsk Hydro refused to pay and proved it could be done. The transparency was refreshing too; they kept updating everyone on what was happening instead of going radio silent like so many companies do.

This is your model, folks. When ransomware hits, shut it down immediately, don't pay, restore from backups, and be honest about what happened. It's not cheap, it's not fun, but it's the right way to do it. And let's be honest, that T-shirt reads a lot better than the one you paid for. See Briggs, 2019 (*https://oreil.ly/iWbOQ*).

Summary

You've done it. The ransomware is contained. Every infected system is isolated and shut down. The attack cannot spread any further. Your forensic evidence is preserved for the investigation that will follow. Your team can finally come up for air, at least for a moment.

But don't mistake containment for victory. Those shut-down systems sitting in your data center or suspended in your hypervisor are still infected. They're dormant, not dead. The ransomware is still there, lurking in boot sectors, registry keys, scheduled tasks, and places you haven't even thought to look. Put those systems back on the network without thorough eradication, and you're right back where you started. The ransomware will roar back to life and you'll watch in horror as systems you thought were safe start encrypting files all over again.

Containment stops the bleeding. Eradication removes the cancer. You've applied the tourniquet, now let's surgically remove the infection.

The decisions you make during containment set the foundation for everything that follows. Get containment right, and eradication becomes straightforward. Get it wrong, and you'll be fighting containment battles for weeks while the ransomware keeps finding new paths to spread. The documentation you created, the forensic images you preserved, the systematic approach you followed; all of this makes the eradication phase possible.

Remember that containment isn't just about technical actions. It's about building confidence. Your employees, customers, partners, and regulators all need to believe that you've stopped the threat from spreading. The professionalism and thoroughness you demonstrated during containment will carry forward into eradication and recovery.

Communication matters enormously during this transition. Keep your stakeholders informed that containment is complete but the work isn't finished. Explain that the next phase of eradication is about permanently removing the threat so you can safely restore operations. Set expectations that eradication will take time and cannot be rushed. The worst thing you could do right now is declare victory prematurely and bring systems back online before you've thoroughly eradicated every trace of the ransomware.

Take a moment to acknowledge what your team has accomplished. Containing an active ransomware attack is intense, stressful work. Your people have been working around the clock under enormous pressure. Before you move into the eradication phase, make sure your team is adequately rested, fed, and mentally prepared for the work ahead. Eradication requires just as much precision as containment, but without the same time pressure. Use this breathing room wisely.

Chapter 14 will walk you through the eradication process: deciding whether to clean, wipe, or replace each infected system, reinstalling operating systems from clean sources, and ensuring your data is truly clean before you restore it. The thoroughness you demonstrated during containment needs to carry through to eradication. One missed persistence mechanism, one overlooked backdoor, one infected system you didn't properly clean; that's all it takes to face reinfection and start this entire process over again.

The threat is contained. Now let's make sure it's gone for good.

CHAPTER 14

Eradicate the Threat

You've contained the attack. Infected systems are isolated and shut down. The ransomware can't spread another inch. Your forensic evidence is preserved. The walls you built around the infection are holding strong. Chapters 9–13 got you to this point. The threat is boxed in, dormant but dangerous.

Now comes the hard part: erasing it from existence.

> The steps in this chapter are remarkably easy; what's not easy is deciding which steps to take. We have some further thoughts on that on our companion site, *StopRansomware.com*.

Welcome to the *eradication* phase. This is where you hunt down and permanently remove every trace of the ransomware from every infected system. Every component. Every backdoor. Every persistence mechanism the attackers planted. You'll make decisions about cleaning, wiping, or replacing hardware. You'll reinstall operating systems from clean sources. You'll scrutinize data to ensure it's truly clean before you dare restore it.

This is where 80% of reinfection happens. Organizations rush through eradication because the pressure to get back online is enormous. They do a quick antivirus scan, see no immediate threats, and declare victory. Three days later, sometimes three weeks later, the ransomware resurfaces. All that containment work was for nothing.

Northforge thought they'd eradicated Lorenz completely. They wiped the obviously infected drives, reinstalled Windows, and brought systems back online. Forty-eight hours later, a scheduled task they'd missed redeployed the malware and they were starting over from scratch.

Sarah's team at ZapMart wiped the POS systems but didn't check the boot sectors. LockBit came roaring back during their busiest sales weekend. A hospital cleaned what they could see in the filesystem but missed malware hiding in bad sector remapping areas. The reinfection happened during a critical surgery scheduling period.

One overlooked registry key. One infected boot sector. One persistence mechanism you didn't find. That's all it takes to waste everything you've accomplished so far.

Eradication isn't optional. It's not something you can do halfway. Either you remove every trace of the ransomware, or you're setting yourself up for reinfection. This chapter will show you how to do it right. It will show you how to make decisions about cleaning versus wiping versus replacing hardware, how to reinstall operating systems properly, and how to ensure your data is truly clean before you restore it.

Whether you're protecting customer data like Sarah, saving a family business like Maria, or ensuring patient safety at a hospital, this chapter will help you permanently eliminate the threat. By the end, you'll know how to bring systems back online with confidence that the ransomware is truly gone.

Let's finish this fight.

Clean, Wipe, or Replace

Once you've completed your forensic imaging and have shut down your infected systems, you face another important decision. You need to decide how to handle each infected system, and this decision can have long-term implications. You have three options, and they exist in what I like to call the good/better/best spectrum in terms of certainty that you've eliminated the threat. Your choices include cleaning the infection, completely wiping the system, or replacing the hardware entirely. Each approach represents a different balance between speed and certainty.

Let me be clear about the hierarchy here: cleaning is good when it works, wiping is better because it's more foolproof, and replacement is best because it guarantees complete eradication. But "best" doesn't always mean "right for your situation." The choice depends on your specific circumstances, time constraints, and tolerance for risk.

Cleaning

The *cleaning* method for removing malware focuses on identifying and removing all malware components while preserving the existing operating system installation, applications, and data. It may seem like a quick path to victory, but most experts advise against it as a method of preparing your environment for a restore after a cyber attack.

Having said that, even though it is risky, it is important that you know how to clean a system of malware. Even if you completely wipe a system or buy all-new hardware, you will still likely need to restore data at some point, as you'll see in "Clean Data Disks" on page 417. That restored data should be checked for ransomware and its associated tools before being declared ready for production.

The big concern with the cleaning method is that you will miss something. Either you will fail to find and delete one of the many companion tools your threat actor installed to get the job done, or you will miss something they secretly stored outside the filesystem. First let's talk about the tools they install to deploy ransomware, stay persistent, and avoid detection.

Ransomware companion tools

As we discussed in previous chapters, "ransomware" is not a monolithic piece of software. It is actually a set of tools designed to do a variety of things. Some help to gain entry, others spread laterally in your environment, and others perform privilege escalation. Only one of the various tools that may have been copied to your systems is the one encrypting and demanding a ransom. You may be able to identify the variant of ransomware you have been attacked with, after which you can get rid of that malware. But if you leave its companion tools in place, you will get infected again.

The following is a list of some of the companion tools commonly used in ransomware attacks. It is far from exhaustive, and this list will change with time. This is why, as with many other tasks in this book, you must engage a specialist in this area, who will know the latest things to look for.

Primary loaders.   First, there are tools that cybercriminals will use as the initial infection vector to gain access to your systems. They typically arrive through phishing emails containing malicious attachments or links, making employee security awareness training a critical defense layer. They will then serve as stepping stones to deploy the actual ransomware. They can also be used for persistence, meaning that they help to reinfect you if you recover. These tools can be difficult to detect, as they can remain dormant once the ransomware is deployed, meaning that you will have to directly seek them out to find and delete them:

TrickBot
> This is an information stealing trojan that has been a constant partner-in-crime with ransomware. It often serves as the initial infection vector that then downloads and deploys the rest of the payload.

BazarLoader
> This is a malware loader delivered by TrickBot that serves as another pathway for ransomware deployment.

Emotet

Emotet is a botnet malware that has been used by many ransomware groups as an initial entry point.

Data exfiltration.   These tools are specifically designed to steal your sensitive data before encryption occurs, enabling double extortion attacks, as we discussed in previous chapters. They will target backup credentials, business documents, and other valuable information that can be used for additional leverage against their victims. This typical attack chain is illustrated in Figure 14-1.

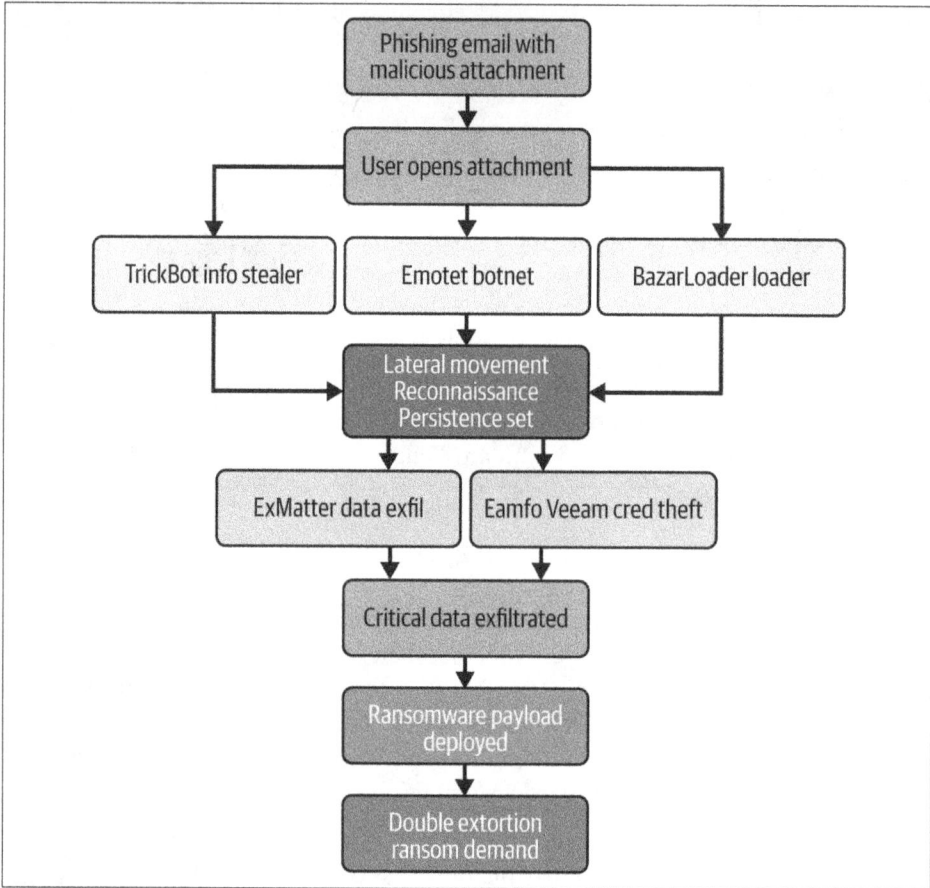

Figure 14-1. Typical attack chain

ExMatter

ExMatter is a data exfiltration tool used by many ransomware groups for double extortion.

Eamfo

Eamfo is specialized malware designed to steal credentials stored by Veeam backup software. This can enable the threat actor to use Veeam to exfiltrate data by restoring it to a location they control. We feel it's important to note here that we are not implying that Veeam is inherently insecure—quite the contrary. They have done quite a lot of work in the last few years beefing up their security. However, their popularity has led to the development of this specialized tool designed specifically to attack Veeam. But you can see in Figure 14-2 how easy it is to stop this attack.

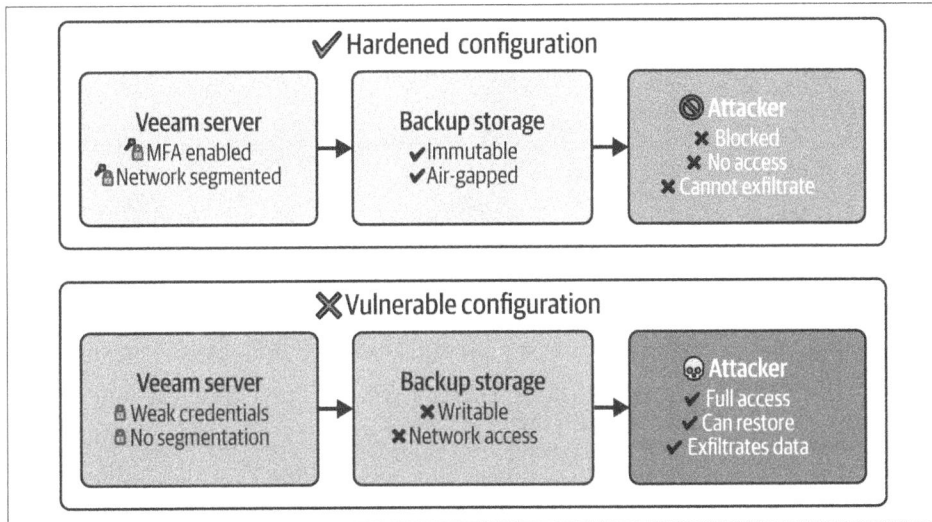

Figure 14-2. Stopping the Veeam attack

Command-and-control (C2) frameworks. This group of tools is easy to find, but you might not be looking for them. They started out as legitimate penetration testing and red team tools but have been weaponized by ransomware groups. They use them for remote access work and lateral movement. Using legitimate tools for illegitimate purposes allows them to maintain persistent access to compromised networks while avoiding detection by security systems:

Cobalt Strike

Originally designed as a legitimate penetration testing tool, it has been widely weaponized by attackers. It deploys an agent called *Beacon* on victim machines, which provides command execution, keylogging, file transfer, and lateral movement capabilities.

Metasploit

Metasploit is a penetration testing tool designed for reconnaissance and exploitation of target systems. It has many exploit modules that are used for legitimate security testing, but once an exploit has been found, it can also be used for illegitimate means. Threat actors use it to move laterally and deliver ransomware payloads.

PowerShell Empire

PowerShell Empire is a framework similar to Metasploit but is specific to Power-Shell. It's a post-exploit tool that allows the attacker to run PowerShell scripts in memory and establishes stealthy connections back to the attacker's systems.

All of these tools work together in a multistage attack. Loaders like TrickBot or Emo-tet gain initial access, data exfiltration tools like ExMatter steal sensitive information, and then the actual ransomware payload encrypts systems for the final extortion demand. The C2 tools help to orchestrate all this using legitimate tools you might not even look for.

Hidden tools

In addition to the many installations of malware you can find in the filesystem, malware can also be found in numerous hidden locations that would not be found in a filesystem scan. This is perhaps the number one reason that the clean method should not be your primary method of ridding your environment of ransomware. Cleaning the places that malware can hide outside of the filesystem will often wipe the entire drive, forcing you to do a restore. And without that you might leave malware that will redeploy itself on the next reboot.

For example, advanced malware can embed itself in all of the following places, which we will cover in more detail later in this chapter:

- Boot sectors and master boot records
- Storage device firmware
- Hidden partitions and unallocated disk space
- Bad sector remapping areas disguised as failed disk regions
- Extensible Firmware Interface (EFI) system partitions containing infected boot managers
- Hypervisor layers that virtualize the entire system
- Network card and peripheral firmware
- SSD overprovisioning areas

Each of these hiding places requires specific cleaning procedures—from low-level formatting and SECURE ERASE commands to firmware flashing and complete hard-ware replacement. This makes thorough eradication without a complete reformat extremely unlikely. It is why many people consider compromised storage devices still compromised even after aggressive cleaning attempts. These two reasons are why most cyber professionals will lean more towards total reformatting (i.e., wiping) over a filesystem clean.

Wiping

The wiping process requires a complete system wipe that includes every sector of every storage device, including the boot sector, partition tables, as well as any unallocated space and bad sectors. You need a full overwrite of the entire drive to guarantee that no malware components survive in hidden areas. Threat actors can be very sneaky, so once again you must work with a cyber professional to make sure you are wiping everywhere ransomware tools can hide. Here's a quick list of the kinds of areas where ransomware can hide, and ideas of how to clean those areas:

Boot sectors and boot managers

Malware can infect the boot record (e.g., master boot record [MBR], GUID Partition Table, EFI system partition), which means it loads even before your OS does. A quick format doesn't touch these areas at all, and even a full format might miss infected boot sectors. This is why some ransomware can seemingly resurrect itself even after what you thought was a complete system rebuild.

Use tools like DBAN (Darik's Boot and Nuke, available at *https://dban.org* and seen in Figure 14-3), its commercial equivalent Blancco Drive Eraser (available at *https://blancco.com/enterprise-free-trial*), or even dd to perform a complete zero-fill of the entire drive, including all boot sectors.

```
Darik's Boot and Nuke
=======================

Warning: This software irrecoverably destroys data.

This software is provided without any warranty; without even the implied
warranty of merchantability or fitness for a particular purpose. In no event
shall the software authors or contributors be liable for any damages arising
from the use of this software. This software is provided "as is".

http://www.dban.org/

  • Press the F2 key to learn about DBAN.
  • Press the F3 key for a list of quick commands.
  • Press the F4 key for troubleshooting hints.
  • Press the ENTER key to start DBAN in interactive mode.
  • Enter autonuke at this prompt to start DBAN in automatic mode.
boot: _
```

Figure 14-3. DBN screenshot

> Using these tools improperly can result in accidental data loss. Please do not let this be the first time you have used such a tool.

For MBR infections, use the `fdisk /mbr` or `bootrec /fixmbr` commands, and follow with a full disk wipe. You can also use commercial tools like WipeDrive or Blancco to specifically target and overwrite boot sector areas multiple times with different patterns. You can delete the EFI system partition (ESP) using `diskpart` or similar tools, then re-create it during the installation of the OS. Be sure to also use firmware settings to clear the boot order and trusted boot databases. Tools like `bcdedit` can also be used to rebuild boot configuration data, but completely re-creating the ESP is safer. These are all skills you should, of course, practice doing well in advance of needing them.

Firmware-level infections

This is where things get really nasty. Computing devices have their own mini computers with their own firmware. Some advanced persistent threats have learned to hide in the firmware of storage controllers, network interface cards, and even USB devices. When malware lives at this level, it's completely invisible to the operating system and survives any software-based cleaning attempt (although this is rare and would typically be done via a supply chain attack).

Software cleaning is often impossible with firmware infections. Firmware flashing (if available from the manufacturer) can help, using professional data recovery services with specialized equipment, or physical destruction. Some enterprise drives support secure firmware updates, but this requires manufacturer tools and may void warranties. All of this is why many people lean towards storage system replacement.

Hidden partitions and unallocated space

Storage devices often contain hidden partitions that don't show up in normal disk management tools. Recovery partitions, OEM diagnostic partitions, and other manufacturer-specific areas can harbor malicious code. Some malware can even create its own hidden partition or hide in unallocated space between partitions. Standard formatting operations typically only affect the main user partitions, leaving these hidden areas completely untouched.

Use disk partitioning tools like `GParted`, `diskpart`, or `fdisk` to view all partitions including hidden ones. Delete *all* partitions, not just the main ones, then re-create the partition table from scratch. Tools like TestDisk can reveal hidden partitions that standard utilities miss. Follow partition deletion with a full disk zero-fill using dd or specialized wiping software to clear unallocated space between partitions.

Bad sector remapping areas

This one is particularly clever. All storage devices maintain tables of *bad sectors*, or areas of the disk that have failed and been remapped to protect your data. Some malware can mark good sectors as bad and hide its code in these "quarantined" areas. The storage device's firmware thinks these sectors are unusable, so they're not touched by formatting operations or normal disk activities. It's like hiding in a condemned building that everyone avoids.

Use low-level formatting tools provided by drive manufacturers (like Western Digital's Data Lifeguard or Seagate's SeaTools) to perform a low-level format that rebuilds the bad sector tables. For SSDs, use the manufacturer's secure erase utility or the ATA SECURE ERASE command, which instructs the drive's firmware to cryptographically erase all data including remapped sectors. Some enterprise drives support sanitize commands that specifically target these hidden areas.

Hypervisor and virtualization layers

Very advanced threats install themselves as hypervisors, essentially creating a virtual machine environment where your original operating system runs as a guest. If you logged into your original system, you can scan all you want—you will not see any malware. The malware has complete visibility and control over everything the OS does and presents to you. That's why it's completely invisible to software running within the virtualized environment. Even formatting what you think is the physical drive wouldn't help.

You will have to find where the hypervisor is loading to clean it, which means starting with the boot sectors, BIOS, UEFI settings, etc. You're looking for a strange boot setup. Look for unauthorized virtualization features or hypervisor installations. Temporarily disable Intel VT-x or AMD-V features during cleaning, then re-enable after confirming clean installation. In severe cases, you may need to flash the motherboard or completely replace the hardware.

Network interface card and peripheral firmware

Your network card, graphics card, and other peripherals all have their own firmware, and some of these can be reprogrammed to include malicious code. Once infected, these peripherals can reinfect a clean system as soon as they're connected. This is why some organizations replace not just the storage devices but all the peripheral hardware when dealing with advanced persistent threats.

Reflash all such equipment with the original manufacturer's firmware by downloading it from the manufacturers. Use the firmware update utility from the manufacturer, rather than third-party tools. For critical systems, consider replacing such peripheral equipment. Also, be sure to disconnect all nonessential peripherals during a system rebuild and reintroduce them one at a time after firmware verification.

SSD overprovisioning areas

Solid-state drives maintain hidden overprovisioning areas, which is extra storage space used for wear leveling and performance optimization. These areas are managed entirely by the SSD's controller firmware and are completely inaccessible to the operating system. Malware that manages to hide in overprovisioning areas is essentially untouchable by any software-based cleaning method.

The `ATA SECURE ERASE` command is your friend. It instructs the SSD's controller to cryptographically erase all data including overprovisioned areas. Many SSD manufacturers also provide secure erase utilities (like Samsung Magician or Intel SSD Toolbox) that can do this for you. For enterprise SSDs, use the `SANITIZE` command, which provides even more thorough clearing. If these commands are not available or fail, physical destruction may be the only reliable option.

Case Study: UVM Health Network Wiped Clean

Remember when we talked about the UVM Healthcare attack in Chapter 13? The one where an employee opened a personal email on vacation and brought the malware back into the network? Well, let's talk about what they did after they refused to pay, because this is the part that really matters.

Doug Gentile, their senior VP of network IT, made something very clear when they decided not to pay the ransom: "It wasn't going to save us any time." Think about that. Even if the attackers gave them a working decryptor, and that's a big if, UVM felt it would be quicker to do what they did.

They wiped the servers clean and rebuilt them. Not patched them, not "cleaned" them with antivirus, *wiped them*. Then they wiped and reimaged 5,000 laptops and computers. Every single one. They rebuilt 1,300 servers from scratch. Restored 600 applications. And they had to scan and clean 5,000 malware-ridden machines to make absolutely sure nothing was left behind.

"For an organization of our size, that is just a huge undertaking," Gentile said. And he's not wrong. This was Vermont's largest hospital during COVID, and they're basically rebuilding their entire IT infrastructure from the ground up in the midst of a global pandemic.

The whole process took 28 days to get their EHR back online. Twenty-eight days of paper records. No phones. No email. Radiologists couldn't get imaging results. Labs couldn't deliver test results electronically. It was like practicing medicine in 1990.

But here's why they did it this way: because paying for a decryptor doesn't remove the malware. It doesn't close the backdoors the attackers opened. It doesn't eliminate the tools they left behind for future access. Even if you decrypt your files, you're still compromised. The only way to be sure you've removed the threat is to wipe everything and start over.

It cost them $65 million total, and their insurance only covered $30 million of it. But you know what they didn't have? A second ransomware attack six months later using the same backdoor. That's because they actually cleaned house.

This is the reality nobody wants to talk about: removing ransomware isn't about decryption. It's about forensically cleaning your entire environment, which means wiping and rebuilding. Whether you pay the ransom or not, you're doing this work anyway. So why pay? Read more here (Jickling, 2020 (*https://oreil.ly/n6JMW*)).

Replacing

Entirely replacing infected hardware might seem extreme, but sometimes extreme situations call for extreme measures. If you have the budget and time, completely replacing infected systems with new hardware is a really safe option. It's expensive, but it's safe.

The fundamental problem with cleaning or wiping is that you can only remove malware that you can find. As we've already discussed, this stuff can be really good at hiding. There might be components buried so deep you cannot find them. Miss even one component, and the entire cleaning effort was worthless.

The best thing about the replacement option is its simplicity. Simply throw out the infected gear and put in new gear. This would be a much better use for your cyber insurance money than using it to pay the ransom.

Making the Decision

Choosing between wiping, cleaning, and replacement for each infected system may not be easy. There's no one-size-fits-all answer, and different systems in your environment might require different approaches based on their specific characteristics and importance to your business. All of this should be agreed upon in advance of an attack and documented in the IRP created in Chapter 7.

You should have already documented the criticality of each system to your business operations and agreed to a recovery order (prioritization) back during the planning stages mentioned in Chapter 7. Systems that are critical to revenue generation, customer service, or regulatory compliance should generally receive more aggressive treatment. You can't afford to take risks with these systems, so wiping or replacement might be more appropriate than attempting to clean them.

Consider also the complexity and uniqueness of each system's configuration as well. Systems that you cannot automatically rebuild because they have complex, custom configurations *might* be better candidates for cleaning attempts, even though this approach carries more risk. Systems with easily rebuilt standard configurations might be better candidates for wiping or replacing. Consider this a chance to update your build process to more modern, cleaner methods to better facilitate such a rebuild.

Think about the specific malware family you're dealing with and its characteristics. Some ransomware families are notorious for being difficult to completely clean, making wiping or replacement more attractive. Others have well-established cleaning procedures that make the cleaning approach more viable.

We cannot overemphasize the use of a cybersecurity professional during this decision-making process. Like many other areas of IT, cybersecurity has become very specialized, and for good reasons. You should have a cybersecurity expert or specialist by your side during this process. You also should be doing as much of the decision-making in advance as you can. If you decide in advance which systems will get replaced, which will get wiped, and which will get cleaned, things will go much smoother.

Reinstall the Operating System

Once each system is completely clean, you may reinstall the operating system and begin your restore. How well this goes will depend on how well you prepared for this eventuality. If you have an automated process that will install the operating system, and configure it to your standards, this will go much easier. Boot from external media, run your automated rebuild process, and you end up with a clean, properly configured system.

If you don't have these processes prepared in advance, reinstalling can take a really long time. It can mean the difference between a rebuild that takes a few minutes or hours, and one that can take days. You'll be scrambling to find installation media, tracking down device drivers, re-creating configurations from memory or incomplete documentation, and trying to remember all the customizations and settings that made each system work properly in your environment.

This is where virtualized environments have a huge advantage. In a virtual environment, reinstalling often just means deleting the virtual disk files and re-creating them from templates or base images. You can have a clean, configured VM running in minutes rather than hours or days. If you're running physical servers, this is a compelling argument for accelerating your virtualization efforts.

User workstations, standard servers with common roles, and systems that can be easily rebuilt from automation tools are excellent candidates for automated OS installs. Complex systems with unique configurations, extensive customizations, or applications that are difficult to reinstall might be better candidates for more manual efforts.

Clean Data Disks

This chapter focused mainly on operating system disks. With system disks you have both the luxury and the requirement to wipe or replace them. Operating systems, applications, and configurations can all be reinstalled from clean sources. You don't need to preserve the existing installation because you can re-create it. It's relatively easy to "restore" your environment to before the attack—without actually doing what backup folk think of as a restore.

Data disks present an entirely different challenge. You can't reinstall data; you can only restore it—and your backup might be contaminated. Even if you have backups from before the attack began, you might have been infected for weeks or months before the attack was detected. Your "clean" backups might actually contain dormant malware waiting for the right conditions to activate.

This is why earlier in this chapter we talked about making sure you learn how to clean after an attack, because you're inevitably going to have to do it for your data disks. This is why we recommend a hybrid approach for most organizations: be aggressive with operating system disks by wiping or replacing them but acknowledge that you'll need excellent cleaning capabilities for data disks regardless. Practice and perfect malware cleaning techniques because you're going to need them.

Summary

You've made the hardest decisions of the entire incident response process. You've chosen which systems to clean, which to wipe, and which to replace entirely. You've reinstalled operating systems from clean sources. You've scrutinized your data to ensure it's free from malware before restoration. Every infected system in your environment has been thoroughly eradicated and rebuilt from the ground up.

This is where organizations either succeed or fail at recovery. The thoroughness you demonstrated during eradication will determine whether you recover cleanly or face reinfection in the coming days and weeks. The companies that cut corners here by skipping the deep cleaning, missing persistence mechanisms, and not properly verifying their work are the ones calling back a month later to start the whole process over again.

But you didn't cut corners. You followed the principles in this chapter. You were aggressive with operating system disks, wiping or replacing them rather than trying to clean malware that might be hiding in places you can't see. You acknowledged that data disks present different challenges and approached them with appropriate care. You documented your decisions and your work so you can prove to regulators, insurers, and stakeholders that you did this properly.

Remember that eradication isn't just about removing malware. It's about building confidence that your systems are truly clean, confidence that it's safe to restore operations, confidence that you won't be doing this all over again next month. The decisions you made and the diligence you demonstrated during this phase will carry forward into recovery and beyond.

The distinction between cleaning, wiping, and replacing isn't arbitrary. It reflects different levels of certainty about threat elimination. Cleaning is appropriate for data that can't be re-created, but it carries risk. Wiping provides a higher level of certainty for operating systems and applications, but the gold standard is replacement. Replacement guarantees complete eradication but costs more money and time. Understanding these trade-offs and making informed decisions for each system in your environment is what separates successful eradication from reinfection disasters.

Don't forget the lessons about where malware hides. Boot sectors, firmware, hidden partitions, bad sector remapping areas, EFI system partitions, even hypervisor layers. Ransomware can lurk in places that survive standard formatting and reinstallation. This is why we emphasized working with cybersecurity professionals who understand these hiding places and know how to properly eradicate them. This isn't work you want to learn during an active incident.

Take a moment to acknowledge what your team has accomplished. Eradication is painstaking, detailed work that requires precision and patience. Your people have been working under pressure for days, making decisions that will impact your organization for months to come. The thoroughness they demonstrated during eradication sets the stage for a successful recovery.

But the work isn't finished. Eradication removed the cancer, but now you need to restore operations. Chapter 15 will walk you through the recovery process. We're going to be restoring data from clean backups, bringing systems back online systematically, validating that everything works properly, and ensuring you don't face reinfection. The foundation you built during containment and eradication makes recovery possible. Now let's get your organization back to business.

One missed persistence mechanism, one infected boot sector, one contaminated backup is all it takes to face reinfection and start this entire process over again. But you've been thorough. You've been systematic. You've eliminated every trace of the ransomware from your environment.

The threat is eradicated. Now let's bring your systems back to life.

PART V

Recover

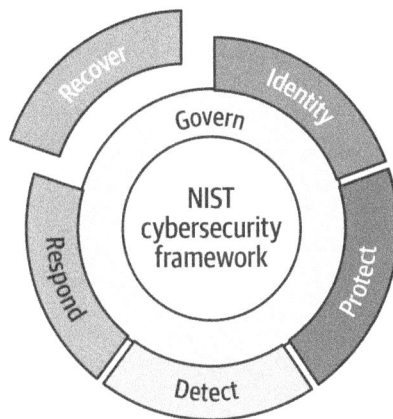

Rising from the Ashes Stronger Than Before

The NIST Cybersecurity Framework's Recover function is about restoring capabilities and services impaired by a cybersecurity incident, and implementing improvements based on lessons learned. The containment walls are holding, the threat is eradicated, and now comes the part everyone's been waiting for: getting back to business. But recovery isn't just about speed—it's about doing it right so you don't end up right back where you started and coming back stronger than you were before.

Chapter 15, "Restore and Recover", tackles the methodical process of bringing your organization back to life. You'll prioritize critical systems, make informed decisions about restore points, and leverage sandbox environments to verify everything is clean before going to production. We'll cover operating system restoration options (from full reinstalls to golden images), data restoration challenges (including curated restore techniques), and cloud-based recovery strategies. The chapter emphasizes that recovery is a marathon, not a sprint—rushing this phase is how 80% of reinfections happen.

Chapter 16, "Post-Mortem Analysis", transforms your painful experience into organizational strength. You'll conduct structured post-mortem meetings with clear documentation, identify root causes through methodical analysis, and turn mistakes into actionable improvements. We'll show you how to update your incident response plan (IRP) based on real-world lessons, implement enhanced monitoring to catch threats earlier, and share intelligence with the broader community. This chapter ensures you don't just recover; you evolve into a more resilient organization that's better prepared for whatever comes next.

By the end of this Recover section, you'll have safely restored operations using proven methodologies that prevent reinfection, documented comprehensive lessons learned that strengthen your security posture, and built organizational resilience that transforms a disaster into a catalyst for long-term improvement.

CHAPTER 15

Restore and Recover

Congratulations. You've made it through the containment and eradication phase, which hopefully will be the hardest part. The threat actors have been kicked out, the malware has been cleaned up, and you've wiped or replaced all infected systems. Now comes the part that everyone has been waiting for: getting your organization back to normal operations. This is where all that preparation we talked about in earlier chapters pays off.

We will once again mention the slight difference between the words *restore* and *recover*. To many people, they mean the same thing, and this book is guilty of sometimes saying the word "recover" when we meant "restore." But technically, a restore is simply the act of copying the data from a backup of any kind to the system to be restored. A recovery is a more holistic process that includes the restore and all the various actions around it to get your environment back to a good state.

The Goals of Recovery

The obvious goal is getting your organization operational again. Users need to work, customers need to be served, business needs to continue. Speed matters. Everyone from the CEO down is going to be asking when things will be back to normal.

But if speed is your only goal, you're going to make mistakes. Here's what you should actually be focused on: getting critical systems back first, not getting infected again, and coming back stronger than you were before.

That second goal—not getting infected again—is the one that keeps me up at night during recoveries. I've seen organizations go through the entire incident response process twice because they were in such a hurry to restore that they brought the malware right back into their environment along with their data.

Think about what you just went through. You methodically identified every infected system. You carefully cleaned up malware and closed vulnerabilities. You kicked the threat actors out. All of that work can be undone in an instant if you restore from a backup that was taken after the initial compromise.

Here's the problem with backups in a ransomware situation: they're supposed to be your safety net, but they can also be your reinfection vector. If the attackers had access to your environment for weeks or months before launching their ransomware—and they usually do—then your backup systems were faithfully backing up infected systems that whole time. Your backups might contain the very malware you just spent days or weeks cleaning up.

This is why you can't just restore everything and call it done. Just like you were methodical during containment and eradication, you need to be just as careful putting things back together. Every system needs to be verified clean before it goes back into production. Everything needs to be tested. You need to watch for signs of reinfection. We'll cover how to do this in "Scanning After Restore" on page 436.

Comparatively speaking, this should be easier than the containment and eradication phase. But it's not going to be easy. Recovery from a ransomware attack is still methodical, careful work. You need to restore systems in the right order, verify they're clean, and make sure they stay that way. Rush this phase and you might find yourself right back where you started, except now the attackers know exactly how you respond to their attacks.

This is where all that preparation we talked about in earlier chapters pays off.

Prioritize Your Restores

Before you restore a single system, pull out your incident response plan (IRP) from Chapter 7. Remember when you sat down and categorized all your systems by business priority? When you figured out which systems were absolutely critical to operations and which ones could wait? This is where that planning pays off.

Start with your highest-priority systems first. In most organizations, that means domain controllers and authentication systems, because nobody can do anything without being able to log in. Then you move on to core business applications—the systems that directly generate revenue or provide critical services to customers. Communication systems like email and messaging usually come next, followed by financial systems and the supporting infrastructure that everything else depends on.

But here's the reality I've seen play out in actual recoveries: your carefully planned priorities from Chapter 7 might need some adjustment when you're in the thick of it. You might discover that a system you thought was lower priority is actually a dependency for something critical. Or you might find that a high-priority system has no clean backup going back far enough, forcing you to skip it temporarily and come back to it later with a different strategy.

The key is to be flexible while keeping your overall priority framework in mind. I've watched teams get distracted during recovery, restoring "just one more system" that isn't really critical because it seemed easy or because someone asked nicely. Don't fall into that trap. Every system you restore is another system you need to secure, monitor, and maintain. Focus on getting core business operations running first, then expand from there.

One more thing to consider: dependencies matter just as much as priority. A database server doesn't do you much good without the application server that uses it. This is why we create recovery groups and test them together: domain controllers, database servers, application servers, and web servers that all serve a common application. Restore them as a group in your sandbox, test them individually, then test them together before moving them to production.

If you didn't create a prioritized list in Chapter 7, or if you're reading this in the middle of an actual incident and didn't have the luxury of advance preparation, stop and take an hour right now to create one. Get your leadership team together and hammer out what needs to come back first, second, and third. I know it seems like you don't have time for this when you're under pressure, but trust me, this hour of planning will save you from making reactive, emotional decisions about what to restore next when you're exhausted at 2 a.m. three days from now.

We've put together the flowchart you can see in Figure 15-1 to help you navigate this process.

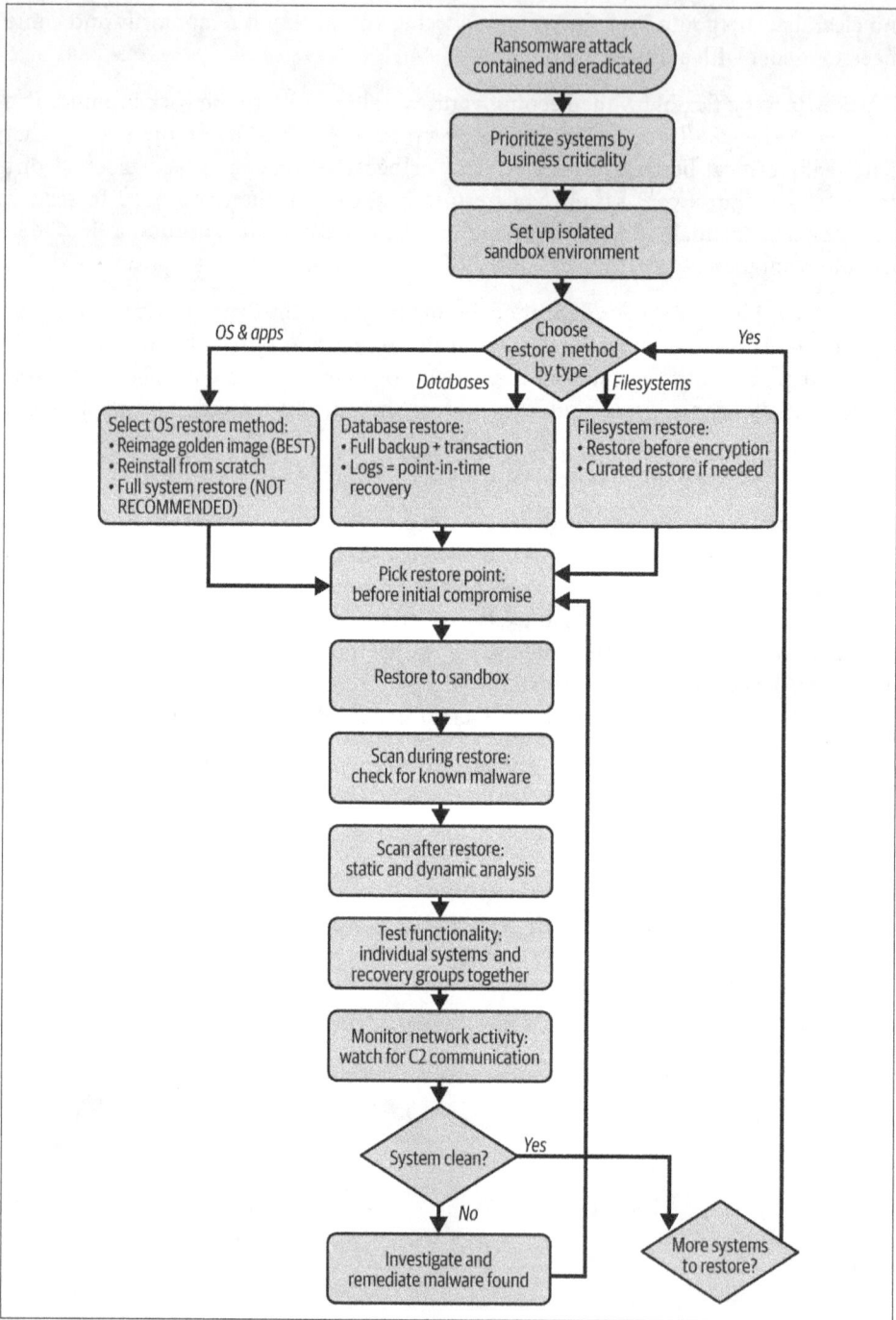

Figure 15-1. Restore process

Choose a Restore Method for OS and Apps

First let's talk about the different ways you can restore the operating system and applications. We will then have a different discussion about how to restore filesystems and databases, and another one about SaaS apps. Each approach of restoring the OS and application drives has its advantages and disadvantages, and the right choice depends on your environment, your backup system, and your tolerance for risk. These choices are in order of our preference, with the best option listed last.

Full System Restore

One approach is to restore the entire system from a backup of that system, including the operating system, applications, and configuration. Then (hopefully) you restore just the application data from more recent backups. (See the following section about the importance of separating these drives.)

This approach can work well if you have good full system restore capabilities and can trust your system-level backups. (It would be best if these backups were from before the earliest evidence of infection.) But you need to be careful about the restore point you choose. If the attackers had access to your environment for months before launching their attack, even your "clean" system backups might be compromised.

We do not recommend the full system restore option. It is described here only for completeness and so you know what *not* to do.

Separating OS/application and data disks

Please don't use the full system restore option. If you are, you may need to reexamine the design of your drives and virtual disk images. It's very common to run an entire server/VM from one disk (or virtual disk image). That might mean you will be forced to restore the entire disk and boot it before you can access your database or other important files.

Therefore we strongly recommend following the practice of separating your OS and application virtual or physical disks from your data disks. You can put the OS and application executables on one disk, but do not put any data on that disk. Put all data on one or more other disks. That way you can recover just the data disks after you have a functioning and clean operating system—whichever of these three restore options you choose.

Booting from alternate media

If you are going to use the full system restore option, which we do not recommend, you will need to thoroughly scan any media you plan on booting from before booting from it. This would include a bare OS drive or a VM image that you are planning on booting after restoring it.

Like everything else in this book, the time to learn how to do this (and what tools you will use) is before an attack happens. For each OS you are running, learn how to create a bootable USB drive, and be sure to document any of these procedures as you develop them, *and make them part of your IRP*. Either create these drives in advance and have them at the ready or create them using an isolated environment that did not touch your production network. One tool we've found particularly useful is Rufus, which you can find on GitHub (*https://oreil.ly/OAGUT*). It is a Windows executable, but it can create a bootable OS from Windows or Linux. There are ways to do this without Rufus, but it just makes it easier.

Create or retrieve your bootable USB drives, boot into your preferred operating system, then run your favorite malware scanning tool. Use multiple scanning engines if you can. What one misses, another might catch. This is another area where a professional who specializes in disaster recovery will be very helpful.

This method is really only necessary if you're using the full system restore option, which we don't recommend. The OS drive should really only be "restored" by rebuilding it from a golden image, or through a complete reinstall and reconfiguration of the OS from its original media. It's simply too easy for malware to hide in bootable areas of the disk.

Reinstall and Reconfigure

Another approach is to fully reinstall the operating system from scratch, configure it to your environment's standards, restore your applications, and then configure them to your environment's standards. (Do not confuse this with reimaging your operating system, which is restoring the OS from a golden copy. In this method, you are literally pulling out your operating system discs or images of them and restoring and configuring your OS the old-school way.) Then, of course, you restore the data drives.

This approach gives you high confidence that you're starting with a clean system. The operating system and applications come from known-good sources, not from potentially compromised backups. You're only restoring the data, which is easier to scan for malware.

While this runs no risk of reinfection like the previous method, the downside is that this approach takes a long time. You need to rebuild every system from the ground up, which means reinstalling and reconfiguring everything. If you have complex application configurations or custom software, this can be a major undertaking. If you can find a way to fully automate this process, then this is a perfectly fine way to bring your world back to life.

Reimage

Let's talk about the best practice—but also the one that requires the most prep work. You will use a *golden image* that represents the operating system configured the way you want it, along with the appropriate applications installed and properly configured as well. This requires creating a separate golden image for each type of server—prior to the attack, of course—and then keeping it offline, or storing it on immutable media (e.g., CD or DVD). This represents the easiest, quickest, and safest method to a clean OS and ready-to-use application. You will still then need to restore the data drives (e.g., the actual database or file server drives) once the system is operational.

The only downside to this method is that you have to prepare for it in advance. It is technically possible to create a golden image after an attack, but it is riskier and will cost you valuable time. However, perhaps you can use the time that others are spending during the containment and eradication phase to create your golden image. Just make sure you are doing it from clean install media, not backups of possibly infected systems.

Choose a Restore Method for Databases

Database restores are somewhat unique in the backup world because they can restore right up to the point of failure. In the case of ransomware, this means you can restore right up to the moment before encryption started. This capability exists because of how database applications handle their data.

Most database systems write every change to what's called a *transaction log* (also called a redo log or write-ahead log, depending on the database). Think of it as a detailed journal of everything that happens to the database. When you insert a row, update a field, or delete a record, the database writes that change to the transaction log before it writes it to the actual database files. This way, if the database crashes mid-operation, it can replay the transaction log to recover any changes that didn't make it to the main database files.

From a backup perspective, this is incredibly powerful. Here's how it works:

First, you restore a full backup of the database. This might be from last night, last week, or whenever your most recent full backup was taken. At this point, your database is in the state it was when that backup completed.

But you're not done. Next, you apply the transaction logs that were created since that full backup. The database replays every transaction in order, bringing the database forward in time. You can stop this process at any point—including the exact moment before the ransomware encryption started.

Let's say your full backup was taken Sunday night, and the ransomware hit Wednesday afternoon at 3:47 p.m. You can restore Sunday night's backup, then apply all the transaction logs through Wednesday at 3:46 p.m. You lose one minute of data instead of days or weeks. This is far better than having to go back to your last known good backup from before the attackers got in, which might be months old.

The key requirement is that your backup system must be backing up those transaction logs regularly—ideally every few minutes or hours, depending on your recovery point objective. If you're only backing up the database files themselves during your nightly backup, you won't have this capability.

The specifics of how this works vary significantly by database platform. Oracle, SQL Server, PostgreSQL, MySQL, and other databases all handle transaction logs differently. They have different file formats, different application procedures, and different considerations for things like point-in-time recovery. Some databases also support incremental backups that can reduce the number of transaction logs you need to apply.

It is also possible to use snapshots and replication as a means to accomplish the same thing. Instead of a restore followed by applying transaction logs, you would simply restore the database to the most recent snapshot that was taken prior to the ransomware event.

These details are far too complex and platform-specific for this chapter. If you need to understand the mechanics of database backup and recovery for your specific platform, I recommend checking out my (Curtis's) other O'Reilly books: *Modern Data Protection* provides comprehensive coverage of database protection strategies, and *Backup & Recovery* goes deep on the technical implementation details for various database platforms.

For the purposes of ransomware recovery, the important thing to understand is that databases give you options. You can restore to the last full backup, you can restore to the last transaction log you have, or you can restore to any point in between. This flexibility makes database recovery one of the less stressful parts of the entire ransomware recovery process—assuming your backup system was properly protecting those transaction logs.

Choose a Restore Method for SaaS Applications

SaaS applications like Microsoft 365, Salesforce, Google Workspace, and others present a completely different recovery challenge than traditional infrastructure. The good news is that you don't need to worry about rebuilding operating systems or reinstalling applications; the vendor handles all of that. The bad news is that you're entirely dependent on the vendor's infrastructure, their recovery capabilities, and their API limitations.

This is where the third-party backup strategy we discussed in Chapter 6 becomes absolutely critical. If you've been relying solely on the SaaS vendor's built-in recovery features, you may discover during a ransomware attack that those features aren't sufficient for your needs. Vendor retention policies might not go back far enough. Their recovery tools might not let you selectively restore clean data while excluding compromised content. And in some cases, ransomware actors specifically target the vendor's recycle bins and version history to eliminate your recovery options.

The SaaS Recovery Challenge

Unlike traditional infrastructure where you control the environment, SaaS recovery has some unique constraints:

- *API throttling* is probably your biggest operational challenge. SaaS vendors limit how quickly you can read or write data through their APIs. This means a restore that would take hours with traditional infrastructure might take days or even weeks for a large SaaS environment. There's no way around this; the vendor controls the throttling limits, and they're not going to lift them just because you're having an emergency.

- *Limited environment isolation* is another challenge. You can't just spin up a parallel "sandbox" version of your SaaS environment the way you would with traditional infrastructure. Most SaaS applications tie your data to a specific tenant or organization, and you can't easily create a duplicate environment for testing. Some vendors offer trial or development environments, but these typically have data size limits that make them impractical for full-scale recovery testing.

- *Vendor-dependent recovery capabilities* mean you're limited to whatever tools and features the vendor provides. If the vendor's restore functionality doesn't support the granular recovery you need, you're out of luck, even when you have a third-party backup solution. For example, as of this writing, Microsoft 365 gives you no way to restore Teams conversations.

The Delete-and-Restore Approach

The safest approach to SaaS recovery after ransomware is similar to the reimage approach we recommended for traditional infrastructure: completely delete the compromised content and restore from a known-good third-party backup.

Here's how this typically works:

1. Identify the scope of compromise. In a SaaS environment, this might mean an entire SharePoint site, a Salesforce org, specific mailboxes in M365, or particular workspaces in collaboration tools. Treat each logical section of your SaaS application as you would treat a system in traditional infrastructure.

2. Pick your restore point just like you would with traditional systems. Go back to before the attack started. With SaaS applications, this is even more critical because you often can't scan for malware in the same way you would with traditional files. The vendor's infrastructure is opaque to you; you can't boot a SharePoint site from alternate media and scan it for malware. Your main defense is restoring from a point in time before the compromise.

3. Completely delete the compromised section. Don't try to selectively clean it. Don't rely on the vendor's recycle bin. Actually delete it. This is the SaaS equivalent of wiping a disk before restoring. Yes, this feels scary, but it's the cleanest way to ensure you're not reintroducing malware. (Investigate if there is a way to delete it from your recycle bin as well.)

4. Restore from your third-party backup that's stored in different, immutable infrastructure. This is why we emphasized in Chapter 6 that SaaS backups must be stored separately from the SaaS platform itself. If your M365 backup is stored in OneDrive, or your Salesforce backup is stored in Salesforce, you haven't actually protected yourself. It's a basic violation of the 3-2-1 rule we discussed in Chapter 3.

5. Verify permissions and access controls after the restore. Ransomware actors often modify permissions to maintain access or to spread their attack. Don't assume that restoring the data also restored secure permissions. Review and reset access controls as part of your recovery process.

SaaS Recovery Timeline Expectations

Be realistic about recovery timeframes. Due to API throttling, SaaS recovery takes longer than traditional infrastructure recovery. Much longer.

A terabyte of data that you could restore from traditional backups in hours might take days or weeks to restore to a SaaS platform. The vendor's API limits are typically measured in requests per minute or gigabytes per hour, and they're non-negotiable.

Factor this into your recovery planning. If your critical business processes depend on SaaS applications, understand that you might be operating at reduced capacity for an extended period. Plan for this in your incident response procedures.

Some organizations keep local copies of critical SaaS data (spreadsheets, documents, reports) specifically to maintain business continuity during an extended SaaS recovery. This isn't a substitute for proper backups, but it can help keep critical operations running while the full recovery proceeds.

Application-Specific Considerations

Every SaaS application has its own quirks and challenges for recovery:

- Microsoft 365 has complex interdependencies between Exchange, SharePoint, OneDrive, and Teams. A file shared in Teams might be stored in SharePoint, referenced in an email in Exchange, and synchronized to multiple OneDrive accounts. Restoring one component might break references in others. You need to understand these relationships and restore them in the correct order.

- Google Workspace has similar sharing and collaboration challenges as M365, with the added complexity of Google's specific approach to file ownership and sharing permissions.

- Salesforce has extensive customizations, integrations, and workflows that might not be captured in basic backups. Your third-party backup needs to capture not just the data, but also the metadata, custom objects, and configuration that makes your Salesforce environment functional.

We can't provide detailed recovery procedures for every SaaS application; there are too many, they change too frequently, and each organization's implementation is unique. Instead, here's what you need to do:

Before an attack happens:

- Document your organization's specific SaaS recovery procedures as part of your IRP.
- Test these procedures regularly.
- Understand the API limits and estimate realistic recovery timeframes.
- Know what your third-party backup solution can and cannot restore.
- Identify who at the vendor you can contact for support during an emergency.

During recovery:

- Work closely with your third-party backup vendor's support team.
- Be prepared for recovery to take much longer than traditional infrastructure.
- Monitor for signs of compromise in the restored data (unusual sharing, modified permissions, suspicious workflows).
- Consider engaging the SaaS vendor's incident response team (IRT) if they offer one.

Choose a Restore Method for Filesystems

Filesystem restores (e.g., home directories, fileservers) are quite different than databases. Restoring them after a ransomware attack requires special consideration.

If you have a normal encryption attack, where all files were instantly encrypted at roughly the same time, you simply need to restore the filesystem to the most recent backup prior to that moment. However, some ransomware is actually quite tricky and will not encrypt all your files at the same time. Let's look at that challenge.

One of the biggest challenges with filesystem restores after ransomware is figuring out when the encryption started. Some attackers don't just encrypt everything at once; they often gradually encrypt files over time to avoid detection. This means you might have backups where some files are encrypted and others aren't. You need to restore from a point in time when all the files were still unencrypted, which might be much earlier than you think.

I (Curtis) have worked with organizations that discovered files were being encrypted weeks before the main ransomware attack. Perhaps the attackers were testing their tools and methods, encrypting a few files here and there to see if anyone noticed. Or perhaps they were simply being methodical and hoping that if they only restore a few files here and there, they could encrypt quite a lot before anyone noticed. If your attack has a long dwell time, which is the time between initial infection and discovery of the ransomware, a restore from a backup taken during the dwell time will restore some encrypted files along with some good ones.

Restore Before Infection, Followed by Many Individual Restores

One approach is to restore the entire filesystem from a backup taken before any encryption occurred, then use individual file restores to bring specific files up to a more recent state.

For example, you might restore everything from a month-old backup, then use individual restores to update important files that changed since then. This gives you a clean baseline while minimizing data loss for the most important files.

The challenge with this approach is identifying which files need to be updated and which backups contain clean versions of those files. You need detailed knowledge of what was happening in your environment leading up to the attack.

What is also likely to happen is that you miss some files that were encrypted, and users will contact support during the coming months as they discover an encrypted file. While this may sound bad, remember an encrypted file isn't the same as an infection of malware. It's the result of the malware, not the malware itself. So missing some encrypted files is more likely to just annoy people, rather than risk reinfection.

Curated Restore

A more sophisticated approach is curated restore, which restores the latest version of each file before it was encrypted.

One way to do this is utilizing the services of someone good at scripting. You could write a script that scans the filesystem for encrypted files, identifies the date they were encrypted, then issues a restore request for that file just prior to that date and time. It's usually very easy to find the encrypted files, because they are typically all stored with the same extension, as you saw in the case studies in Chapters 9 and 10.

Example 15-1 contains a quick example script for Linux or MacOS that finds all files with a *.given* extension, gets their epoch date (number of seconds since January 1, 1970), subtracts one hour and one year from it, converts that into regular date formats, deletes the encrypted file, then passes the dates to NetBackup's `bprestore` command, telling it to restore the file to the latest backup from as far back as a year ago, and up to one hour before the encryption happened. I used the `-K` option because I'm guessing at what the old file used to be.

> Example 15-1 is a very basic effort that I (Curtis) put together just to show you the kind of thing you could do. It is not intended to be used as actual code; it's intended to show that this could be coded. This script also uses macOS syntax because I wrote it on a Mac. Linux systems would use `stat -c '%Y %n'` instead of `stat -f '%m %N'`.

Anyone good with scripting should be able to easily adapt that for their backup tool. Once again, please don't let your worst day before the first time you're trying to build such a script.

Example 15-1. A basic curated restore script

```
echo "What is the extension of the encrypted files (e.g. .lock)?"
read extension

find . -type f -name "*${extension}" |while read line
do

#get this epoch date and filename of the file
data=`stat -f "%m %N" "$line"`

#grab just the epoch date
oldepoch=`echo $data|awk '{print $1}'`

#subtract one hour and one year from that date
newepoch=`expr $oldepoch - 60`
```

```
yearagoepoch=`expr $oldepoch - 31556952`

#convert the new times to a date/time format
hourago=`date -r $newepoch`
lastyear=`date -r $yearagoepoch`

#Get the filename
file=`echo $data|awk '{print $2}'|sed "s/\$extension//"`
pwd=`pwd`

#remove the encrypted file
rm -f $pwd/$file

#guess at the other files.
#The -K option will not overwrite a file if it is there
bprestore -K -s $lastyear -e $hourago $pwd/$file.docx
bprestore -K -s $lastyear -e $hourago $pwd/$file.pptx
bprestore -K -s $lastyear -e $hourago $pwd/$file.xlsx

done
```

Some backup systems can do this for you automatically. It's basically the same as the scripted approach, but automated via your backup system. It has all the metadata and the information over time. It knows when a file got encrypted, and it can easily figure out the most recent version of each file before it was encrypted. If your backup system supports this feature, it should work perfectly. It may take a while, but it should be completely automated. Unfortunately, as of this writing, very few products support this kind of restore. Perhaps that will change over time.

Use a Sandbox Area for All Restores

We also recommend using a *sandbox environment*, also known as a *clean room*, for all recovery activities after a ransomware attack. It's a place where you can restore your data and work on it without contaminating your production environment.

The concept is simple: restore everything to an isolated network first, scan it for malware, test it, and only then move it to production. This gives you multiple layers of protection against reinfection.

We already covered setting up a sandbox in "Playing in a Sandbox" on page 225, but that was for a different purpose. That was a training environment with simulated threats. This is an isolation environment for handling potentially real malware during actual recovery. So it's even more important to keep this sandbox completely isolated.

Like with the other sandbox, there should be no shared storage and no network connections between this network and your production network or the Internet. It is highly possible that some of your systems were infected before they were backed up.

Restoring will restore the infected version, and you don't want it reaching back out to its C2 servers for instructions.

The easiest way to set up a sandbox is in the cloud, and like many other activities in this book, you should practice doing this before you need to do so. You can spin up a completely separate virtual network in AWS, Azure, or Google Cloud, restore your systems there, and test them to your heart's content. When you're satisfied they're clean, you can either migrate them back to production or use them as the foundation for rebuilding your environment. This may seem like we're going against my previous statements about not having network connections, but this can be done in such a way that there is only one way in and out of the virtual data center you create in the cloud, and you will manage that connection. There will still be no network route between that virtual data center and any other network. If necessary, consult a cyber professional or network security person for help. The best thing about using the cloud is that you can create a pristine environment that has never been touched. Infrastructure as code is a beautiful thing.

If you're doing this on premises, you'll need dedicated hardware that was not connected to your production network at the time of the incident. I've seen organizations use old lab equipment for this purpose. It doesn't need to be super fast; it just needs to be functional and isolated. This can be difficult to achieve, but it is possible.

Scan for Malware

You really need to be scanning for malware as much as you can when doing a restore, because if you're restoring from backups that were taken after the initial compromise, there's a good chance those backups contain the malware that got you into this mess in the first place.

Scanning During the Restore

Modern backup systems are starting to include malware scanning capabilities. Some products will scan backups as they're being taken and flag any that contain known malware signatures. Others will scan during the restore process, which would be our preference. We say this because you will likely be able to tell the scanner what to look for, by using the signatures of the particular malware products you found during the containment and eradication phase. These backup features are still relatively new, but they're becoming more common.

You can also scan for known malware signatures during the restore process using some type of EDR or XDR system, such as those discussed in Chapter 8. The best way to do this is to create a list of file hashes for malware that you discovered during the containment and eradication phase in Chapter 11 and telling your scanning products to specifically check for those signatures.

As previously mentioned, this is becoming easier as backup vendors build these capabilities into their products. But remember that hash-based scanning only catches known malware. If the attackers used custom tools or modified existing malware, hash-based scanning won't detect it. This is why scanning is just one part of a comprehensive recovery strategy.

Scanning After Restore

You can also scan again for known malware hashes. The reason for scanning twice is that some malware doesn't fully activate until the system is running. Files that looked innocent during the restore might reveal their true nature once the system boots up and the malware starts executing.

This is also when you can run more sophisticated analysis tools like those discussed in Chapter 12. Static analysis looks at files on disk; dynamic analysis looks at what those files do when they're executed. Both have their place in a comprehensive security strategy.

Restore Your OS and Data

We once again want to reiterate that the safest way to do this is to build your OS disks from a golden image, and then restore your data disks. We do not recommend restoring your operating system from backups (including backups of your VM boot disk), because it is too easy to reintroduce malware from your backups. Then you can restore your databases and filesystem data.

The actual restore process in your sandbox depends on what kind of backup system you're using, but the principles are the same regardless. You want to restore to a known good point in time, which means going back to before the attack started.

Pick Your Restore Point

Another very important decision is picking the point in time to which you are going to restore your data. Restore too late and you risk reinfection. Restore too early and you lose valuable data.

This is where having good monitoring and logging pays off. If you know the attack started on Tuesday at 3 p.m., it would be best if you restored from Monday night's backup. But if the attackers were in your environment for weeks or months before launching their ransomware (which is common), you might need to go back much further. The more you learn in the analysis, containment, and eradication phases, the easier this decision is going to be.

Some organizations discover they need to go back six months or more to find a clean restore point. This is painful, but it's better than restoring infected systems and having to start the whole process over again.

You may find yourself in a position where you are forced to choose between a known good backup—where you will definitely lose weeks or months of data—or a backup that is suspected to be infected, which you will have to clean in every way you can imagine to ensure it's safe. Only you can make the decision of what's right to do at that moment. Again, we recommend working with a cyber professional when making this decision.

The safest way to do such a restore is to restore to media that you do not have to boot. This means you performed the procedure mentioned above in "Booting from alternate media" on page 426, mounted a drive to that clean OS, then restored your data to that drive. This method reduces the risk that anything on the drive might execute and reinfect anything. Once you're sure the data drive is clean, you can boot the entire system with its attached data drive.

Test Functionality

Once fully restored and scanned, it's time to actually start testing its functionality. This is where you'll discover whether your restores actually worked. Can you log in? Are authentication mechanisms functioning as you expect? Do the applications start? Can you access the data you need?

Don't assume that just because the restore completed without errors, everything is working correctly. I've seen restores that looked successful but resulted in corrupted databases or missing files. The only way to know for sure is to test.

We will once again mention the importance of recovery groups. In addition to testing the functionality of individual systems, you need to test how systems that depend on each other work together.

Monitor for Any Network Activity

You should be monitoring network activity from restored systems inside your sandbox. Even though you have designed the sandbox to block such traffic, it's important to see if any systems are trying to reach the outside world. What is the system trying to communicate with?

Set up network monitoring tools that can capture and analyze all traffic from your restored systems. Look for anything unusual: unexpected outbound connections, DNS queries for domains that weren't in use before the attack, attempts to communicate with IP addresses outside your normal business operations, or even attempts to talk to known C2 servers.

Restored systems can look clean and still try to phone home to attacker-controlled servers. Network activity is the smoke that indicates the proverbial fire. If you see any such activity, use standard forensics techniques to figure out what's causing it and snuff it out!

Recover to the Cloud

One of the most significant changes in disaster recovery over the past decade has been the rise of cloud-based recovery options. The cloud (e.g., AWS, Azure, Google Cloud) offers unique advantages for ransomware recovery, including unlimited capacity, geographic isolation from your primary environment, and the ability to quickly spin up temporary infrastructure.

Why Recover to the Cloud?

There are several compelling reasons to consider cloud-based recovery after a ransomware attack. The first and most obvious reason is speed. You can provision new infrastructure in the cloud much faster than you can acquire and configure physical hardware. When you're dealing with tight recovery time objectives, this speed advantage can be critical.

The second reason is isolation. If your on-premises environment has been compromised, recovering to the cloud gives you complete separation from the infected environment. The attackers have no way to reach your cloud-based recovery environment, assuming you set it up correctly. (Again, it should be a sandbox. Consult your cloud vendor on how best to do this.)

The third reason is cost. You only pay for cloud resources while you're using them. This makes cloud-based disaster recovery much more affordable than maintaining a full duplicate data center that sits idle most of the time.

But cloud recovery isn't without its challenges. Network bandwidth becomes a critical constraint when you're restoring large amounts of data over the internet. This is why having a copy of your backups already in the cloud can be crucial for success. Be sure to be careful about your security configuration, or you might create new vulnerabilities in your recovery environment. Ensure it has at least the same protections as production.

Planning Your Cloud Recovery

Before you need it, you should have a plan for how cloud recovery will work in your environment, and you should test it on a regular basis as part of your IRP testing. This means understanding which cloud services you'll use, how you'll get your data to the cloud, and how you'll configure networking and security in your recovery environment.

Start by choosing your cloud provider and region. Pick a region that's geographically separated from your primary data center but still accessible to your users. You don't want to recover to a region on the other side of the world if it means your users can't effectively access their applications.

Next, plan your network architecture. How will users connect to applications running in the cloud? Will you use VPN connections, direct network connections, or internet-based access? Each approach has different security and performance implications.

Finally, plan your data transfer strategy. How will you get backup data to the cloud? Can your backup system restore directly to cloud storage, or will you need to transfer backup files first and then restore from there?

Any advice in this book on the best way to set up a given cloud provider for this process would be out of date before it is published, and we would not have the space to go into the level of detail you need, either. Tell your preferred cloud vendor what your plans are and ask them to help guide you through this process. Take full advantage of every resource they offer.

Another best practice would be that running your production environment in the cloud should not be the first time you are using the cloud for production. Once you have selected what cloud environment you plan on using for recovery, consider moving at least a few apps into that world. That way, you'll be more familiar with how it works and you won't be blindsided during the recovery.

Setting Up Temporary Cloud Infrastructure

We think the best way to do disaster recovery for any reason these days is to use the cloud, and recovering into the cloud after a ransomware attack is no exception. If you work in an environment that is anti-cloud, it's time to find that out now and plan accordingly, which means having a full recovery site with contracted SLAs ready to go when you need it. But we are going to continue on with this chapter as if you've resolved that.

One of the biggest advantages of cloud recovery is how quickly you can set up temporary infrastructure. You can accomplish in an hour what might take weeks to procure and install in a physical data center.

But speed comes with a cost: it's easy to make security mistakes when you're moving fast. Take time to properly configure security groups, access controls, and network isolation. The last thing you want is to recover from a ransomware attack only to create new security vulnerabilities in your temporary environment. I know I'm beating this drum pretty heavily, but this is why this should all be planned, documented, automated, and tested well in advance of ever needing to use it.

Start with the minimum infrastructure you need to restore critical systems. You can always add more capacity later. It's better to start small and grow than to overprovision and waste money on resources you don't need.

Document everything you're doing. In the chaos of ransomware recovery, it's easy to lose track of what you've configured and how. Good documentation will help you manage your temporary environment and plan the eventual migration back to production.

It's also important to automate this as much as possible. Create recovery groups and automate the creation of those recovery groups one at a time. Again, consult your cloud vendor on how best to do this.

Networking Considerations

Network connectivity is often the biggest challenge in cloud-based recovery. Your users need to be able to access applications running in the cloud, which means setting up appropriate network connections. However, you also want to prevent any malware from getting in or out.

For temporary recovery situations, internet-based access is often the fastest to implement. Users can connect to cloud-based applications over VPN connections or through secure web interfaces. This approach works well for short-term recovery but may not provide the performance users expect for long-term operations.

If you need better performance or have compliance requirements that mandate private network connections, you'll need to set up dedicated network links to your cloud environment. This takes longer to implement—and is obviously more expensive—but provides better security and performance.

Before continuing, let's talk about regions and availability zones. In cloud parlance, a *region* is a geographic area that contains multiple physically separated data centers, with regions typically being hundreds or thousands of miles apart to protect against large-scale disasters. Within each region are multiple *availability zones*, which are independent data centers separated by miles with their own power and networking. They protect against individual data center failures while staying close enough for fast data transfer between them.

Applications that worked well on your internal network might behave differently when they're spread across multiple cloud availability zones or regions. Latency between availability zones should be negligible, but it's still not nothing. Latency between regions can be significant. Ensure that the performance of your intended cloud design is sufficient.

Data Transfer Challenges

Getting your backup data to the cloud can be a significant challenge, especially if you have large amounts of data and limited network bandwidth. A terabyte of data that restores quickly from local storage might take days to transfer over a typical internet connection.

Some backup vendors have partnerships with cloud providers that allow direct restoration to cloud storage without having to transfer data over the internet first. If your backup system supports this, it can dramatically speed up the recovery process.

Another option is physical data transfer services offered by cloud providers. You can ship hard drives or storage appliances to the cloud provider, who will upload your data to their storage systems. This is slower to initiate but can handle much larger data volumes than network-based transfers.

The best option, however, is to plan for this in advance and have your backup data located in the same cloud vendor and region as your recovery. Restoring this way can actually be faster than even the fastest on-prem restore.

Plan for these challenges before you need to use them. Test your data transfer methods and measure how long they take. This will help you set realistic expectations for recovery times and plan accordingly.

Failover and Failback Concepts

The final piece of the recovery puzzle is understanding how to fail over to your recovery environment and then fail back to your primary environment once it's been rebuilt. This process is more complex than it might seem at first glance.

Understanding Failover

Failover is the process of switching operations from your primary environment to your recovery environment. In the context of ransomware recovery, this happens after you've restored your systems in the recovery environment and verified they're working correctly.

But failover isn't just about technology; it's also about people and processes. Users need to know how to access applications in the new environment. Network connections need to be redirected. DNS entries will need to be updated. Security policies need to be reviewed and updated for the new environment.

The key to successful failover is preparation. You should have documented procedures for how failover will work in your environment. This includes technical procedures for redirecting network traffic and updating configurations, as well as communication plans for notifying users about changes.

Test your failover procedures regularly. Many organizations have great disaster recovery plans on paper but discover during an actual emergency that their procedures don't work as expected. Regular testing helps identify and fix these problems before you need to use them for real.

Managing the Transition Period

There's usually a transition period between when you start operating in your recovery environment and when you can return to normal operations. During this period, you're running your business from temporary infrastructure that might not have all the capabilities of your primary environment.

This transition period requires careful management. You need to monitor the performance and capacity of your temporary infrastructure. You need to manage costs, especially if you're using cloud resources that charge by usage. And you need to maintain security in an environment that was set up quickly under pressure.

Document any changes you make during the transition period. When you eventually migrate back to your primary environment, you'll need to replicate any configuration changes or data updates that happened while you were running in the recovery environment.

Consider this transition period an opportunity to test new configurations or approaches. Since you're already running in a temporary environment, it might be a good time to try new security configurations or application architectures that you've been considering.

Planning Your Return

Returning to normal operations, or "failback," requires just as much planning as the initial recovery. You need to decide when you're ready to return, how you'll migrate data and applications back to the primary environment, and how you'll handle any changes that occurred during the recovery period.

The timing of failback depends on several factors. Is your primary environment fully rebuilt and secured? Have you addressed the vulnerabilities that allowed the original attack? Do you have confidence that the attackers are completely out of your environment?

Don't rush the return to normal operations. It's better to spend extra time in your recovery environment while you properly rebuild and secure your primary environment than to return too early and risk another attack.

One more really important consideration: make sure you have a plan to regularly back up your infrastructure while it's running in the recovery environment! You could be there from days to months. If users have been working in the recovery environment, you need to make sure their work doesn't get lost when you switch back to the primary environment. This will require a separate backup plan, as well as careful coordination of the timing of the switch.

Testing Failback Procedures

Just like failover procedures, failback procedures should also be regularly tested. Many organizations focus their disaster recovery testing on the initial recovery but neglect to test the return to normal operations.

Failback testing can be more complex than failover testing because it requires coordinating between two environments. You need to test data synchronization, application migration, and user redirection—and you need to do all this without disrupting ongoing operations.

Consider using your regular disaster recovery tests as opportunities to practice failback procedures. Instead of just testing that you can recover to your backup site, test the complete cycle of failing over and then failing back.

Document lessons learned from both real events and tests. Each time you exercise your failover and failback procedures, you'll discover things that could be improved. Make sure these improvements get incorporated into your procedures for next time.

Long-Term Considerations

Some organizations discover during ransomware recovery that their temporary cloud-based infrastructure actually works better than their original on-premises environment. The cloud environment might be more scalable, more secure, or more cost-effective than what they had before.

If this happens, you might want to consider making your "temporary" recovery environment permanent. This effectively turns your disaster recovery event into a cloud migration.

But don't make this decision while you're still in crisis mode. Take time to properly evaluate the long-term implications of staying in the cloud. Consider factors like ongoing costs, compliance requirements, and user experience.

If you do decide to stay in the cloud, treat it like any other major infrastructure change. Develop a proper migration plan, address any remaining gaps in functionality, and make sure your security and operational procedures are updated for the new environment.

Summary

Recovery from ransomware is not a sprint; it's a marathon. You need to be methodical, careful, and patient. Rushing the recovery process increases the risk of reinfection and can undo all the work you've done to clean up your environment.

Start with your most critical systems and work your way down your priority list. Recover in groups to be able to test applications that use multiple systems. Test everything thoroughly before putting it back into production. And remember that recovery isn't just about restoring data; it's about rebuilding trust in your systems and processes.

The sandbox approach should be your default for all recovery activities. Yes, it takes longer than restoring directly to production, but the extra time is worth it for the additional security it provides.

Document everything you're doing during the recovery process. This documentation will be valuable for post-incident analysis and will help you improve your recovery procedures for next time. Because unfortunately, there might be a next time.

Most importantly, don't consider the recovery complete until you've addressed the vulnerabilities that allowed the attack in the first place. Restoring from backup without fixing the underlying security problems is just inviting the attackers back for round two.

Recovery from ransomware is one of the most challenging things you'll ever do in IT. But with proper preparation, the right tools, and a methodical approach, you can get your organization back on its feet and running better than before. The key is to not panic, stick to your procedures, and take the time to do things right.

Remember: the goal isn't just to get back to where you were before the attack. The goal is to get back to where you were, but more secure, more resilient, and better prepared for whatever comes next.

CHAPTER 16

Post-Mortem Analysis

The ransomware attack is over; the floodwaters have receded, and your body has started replenishing its supply of cortisol. The systems are rebuilt, and all the critical data has been restored, operations are back online, and we've come down from DEFCON 1[1] to an improved state of normal operational readiness and awareness. But the work isn't done. The post-mortem analysis phase is a critical step in ensuring your organization rises up from the ashes stronger, more resilient, and better prepared for future threats—like a phoenix, you have been transformed. This chapter focuses on the process of conducting a thorough post-mortem analysis of a ransomware attack, with an emphasis on documenting what happened, identifying lessons learned, updating your incident response plan (IRP), and enhancing your monitoring and response capabilities. By systematically analyzing the attack, your organization can transform a painful experience into an opportunity for growth and improvement. We'll explore practical steps, real-world examples, and actionable recommendations to help your organization not only recover but also benefit from the aftermath of a ransomware incident. Many organizations miss the post-mortem analysis step—to their detriment.

One final note about our companion site, *StopRansomware.com*. It's a great place to get template documents, like the example given later in this chapter.

---

1 Defense Condition 1, or DEFCON 1, is the highest readiness level in the US military's Defense Readiness Condition system, indicating that nuclear war is either imminent or already underway.

The Importance of Post-Mortem Analysis

A ransomware attack sucks and is one of the worst types of incidents you can endure. It >tests an organization's cybersecurity preparedness, response capabilities, and resilience. While the immediate focus is on containment, eradication, and recovery, the post-mortem analysis is where you extract value from the experience. Failing to conduct a thorough post-mortem analysis puts you at risk of repeating the same mistakes, leaving vulnerabilities unaddressed, and undermining stakeholder confidence. Post-mortem analysis will help to identify any gaps in your process and fix them.

The post-mortem process should be led by your chief information security officer (CISO) or senior cybersecurity manager. This leader coordinates the analysis, facilitates meetings, ensures documentation is completed, and tracks action items to completion. In smaller organizations without a CISO, the IT director or incident response team (IRT) leader should assume this role. The key is having one person accountable for ensuring the post-mortem happens and delivers results.

The post-mortem analysis serves several critical and valuable purposes:

Understanding the attack
Documenting how the attack unfolded, including the initial compromise (root cause, patient zero), lateral movement, and impact, provides clarity on what went wrong and why.

Identifying weaknesses
Analyzing gaps in your defenses, whether technical, procedural, or human, will help pinpoint areas for improvement.

Improving response
Evaluating the effectiveness of your IRP reveals what worked, what didn't, and how to optimize future responses.

Building resilience
Implementing lessons learned strengthens your cybersecurity posture, reducing the likelihood and impact of future attacks.

Restoring trust
A transparent and thorough post-mortem demonstrates to stakeholders (management, employees, customers, partners, and regulators) that you've taken the incident seriously and are committed to preventing it from happening again.

Regulatory compliance
Ensuring compliance with data breach notification laws and industry regulations, such as GDPR, HIPAA, or PCI-DSS, mitigates legal and financial risks.

The post-mortem is not about assigning blame but about fostering a culture of continuous improvement. By approaching the analysis with an open mind and a commitment to learning, you can turn a negative experience into a catalyst for positive change. You can then use anything you learn in the post-mortem to update your processes and procedures. For example, after the 2017 WannaCry attack, many organizations discovered critical gaps in their security program during post-mortems. They found that patches were often applied manually on irregular schedules, sometimes weeks or months after release, and that their networks lacked proper segmentation, allowing the ransomware to spread laterally across entire systems. In response, these organizations implemented automated patch management systems that deployed critical security updates within 24–48 hours of release, established regular patch testing protocols, and created network segments that isolated critical infrastructure from general user systems. These changes significantly reduced their exposure to similar threats.

Psychological and Organizational Impact

Ransomware attacks don't just disrupt systems; they take a toll on employees and organizational culture. The stress of managing an attack can lead to burnout, reduced morale, and turnover among IT and cybersecurity teams.

Human Factors

A post-mortem should address these human factors to ensure long-term recovery:

Assessing team well-being
Evaluate the emotional and psychological impact on staff. For instance, the engineering company reported high stress among IT staff due to their continuous 24/7 recovery efforts. Consider offering counseling or wellness programs to the IR teams that endure this level of involvement.

Rebuilding team confidence
Use the post-mortem to acknowledge team efforts and successes, no matter how small, to restore morale. Highlighting effective actions, like quick containment, can boost confidence.

Training for resilience
Incorporate stress management and crisis leadership training into the IRP to prepare teams for future incidents.

Action item: Schedule a debrief with HR within one month of post-recovery to assess team well-being and plan support measures, such as mental health resources or team-building activities.

Communicating Post-Mortem Results to Employees

Balance transparency with security when sharing post-mortem findings with staff. Employees need to understand what happened and how the organization is responding, but detailed technical information about vulnerabilities should be limited to those with a need to know.

What to share broadly:

- High-level timeline of what happened (without technical exploit details)
- Changes being implemented to prevent recurrence (improved training, new security tools)
- Acknowledgment of the team's efforts during the incident
- Updated security policies or procedures employees need to follow
- Success metrics showing the organization is more resilient

What to restrict:

- Specific vulnerabilities exploited or systems compromised
- Details about security tool configurations
- Names of individuals involved (maintain blame-free culture)
- Ransom payment amounts or negotiation details
- Specific indicators of compromise (IOCs) or attacker tools (restrict to security team)

Hold an all-hands meeting within 30 days of completing the post-mortem to reinforce cybersecurity awareness and build confidence in the organization's response.

Documenting What Happened

There is no point in having a post-mortem meeting if it's not going to be documented. In addition, documentation prepared in advance can help structure the post-mortem and make it easier to record lessons learned. Good documentation provides a clear record of the attack, response, and recovery efforts, serving as both a historical reference and a guide for future improvements. Documentation should be detailed, accurate, and organized to facilitate analysis and accountability. The next few pages contain an example post-mortem meeting template.

Example Post-Mortem Template

This is an example document that can be used to create a template for your post-mortem. Many of the items should obviously be followed up by blanks, but we have included explanatory text here where appropriate.

INCIDENT SUMMARY

Incident ID: [Unique identifier]

Date of Attack: [Date attack was discovered]

Date of Post-Mortem: [Date of post-mortem meeting]

Prepared By: [Name, Title]

Reviewed By: [Names of all participants]

Classification: [Confidential/Internal Use Only]

EXECUTIVE SUMMARY

[2–3 paragraph overview of the incident, impact, and key findings]

Total Cost: $[Amount]

Systems Affected: [Number/percentage]

Downtime: [Duration]

Data Loss: [Description]

INCIDENT TIMELINE

Priority	Action item	Owner	Due date	Status	Resources
CRITICAL	[Description]	[Name]	[Date]	[Status]	$[Amount]
HIGH	[Description]	[Name]	[Date]	[Status]	$[Amount]
MEDIUM	[Description]	[Name]	[Date]	[Status]	$[Amount]
LOW	[Description]	[Name]	[Date]	[Status]	$[Amount]

ATTACK DETAILS

Attack Vector: [Phishing email, exploited vulnerability, compromised credentials, other]

Initial Access Point: [Specific system, user account, or vulnerability]

Ransomware Variant: [Name and version, if identified]

Attacker Tools Identified: [List tools like Cobalt Strike, ExMatter, etc.]

Dwell Time: [Time between initial compromise and detection]

Indicators of Compromise (IOCs): [File hashes, IP addresses, domains, etc.]

IMPACT ASSESSMENT

Systems affected:

- Servers: [Number]—[List critical systems]
- Workstations: [Number]
- Cloud environments: [Description]
- Backup systems: [Status]
- Network infrastructure: [Impact]

Data impact:

- Data encrypted: [Volume/description]
- Data exfiltrated: [Volume/description if known]
- Data permanently lost: [Description]
- PII/PHI compromised: [Yes/No—Details]

Financial impact

- Ransom demanded: $[Amount]
- Ransom paid: $[Amount] (if applicable)
- Recovery costs: $[Amount breakdown]
  - Labor (internal): $[Amount]
  - Third-party services: $[Amount]
  - Hardware replacement: $[Amount]
  - Software licensing: $[Amount]
- Lost revenue: $[Amount]
- Regulatory fines (actual/potential): $[Amount]
- Total estimated cost: $[Amount]

Operational impact

- Total downtime: [Duration]
- Services disrupted: [List]
- Customer impact: [Description and number affected]
- Recovery time by system: [List]

Reputational impact

- Media coverage: [Yes/No—Description]
- Customer complaints: [Number/description]
- Public disclosure required: [Yes/No]
- Stock price impact (if applicable): [Percentage]

RESPONSE EFFECTIVENESS

What worked

    ✓ [Specific action]—[Why it was effective]
    ✓ [Specific action]—[Why it was effective]
    ✓ [Specific action]—[Why it was effective]

What failed

    ✗ [Specific gap]—[Impact of this failure]
    ✗ [Specific gap]—[Impact of this failure]
    ✗ [Specific gap]—[Impact of this failure]

Detection performance

- Time to detect: [Duration from compromise to detection]
- Detection method: [SIEM alert/User report/Backup notification/Other]
- Alert accuracy: [Were there false negatives? False positives?]
- Tool performance: [Assessment of EDR, XDR, SIEM, etc.]

Containment performance

- Time to contain: [Duration from detection to containment]
- Containment methods used: [List]
- Containment effectiveness: [Did infection spread after detection?]
- Challenges encountered: [Description]

Recovery performance

- Time to restore critical systems: [Duration]
- Backup restore success rate: [Percentage]
- Reinfection incidents: [Yes/No—Details]
- Recovery method: [Backup restore/System rebuild/Decryption/Other]

External support

- Cyber insurance: [Role and effectiveness]
- Law enforcement (FBI/Local): [Role and effectiveness]
- Incident response firm: [Name and assessment]
- Forensic investigators: [Name and assessment]
- Legal counsel: [Role and effectiveness]
- Other vendors: [List and assessment]

ROOT CAUSE ANALYSIS

Primary root cause: [Description]

Contributing factors

1. [Factor]—[Explanation using Five Whys if applicable]
2. [Factor]—[Explanation]
3. [Factor]—[Explanation]

Technical failures

- [Specific vulnerability or gap]
- [Specific vulnerability or gap]

Procedural failures

- [Process gap or breakdown]
- [Process gap or breakdown]

Human factors

- [Training gap or error]
- [Training gap or error]

LESSONS LEARNED

Key insights

1. [Lesson]—[Supporting evidence from incident]
2. [Lesson]—[Supporting evidence from incident]
3. [Lesson]—[Supporting evidence from incident]

Best Practices Confirmed

- [Practice that proved valuable]
- [Practice that proved valuable]

Areas for Improvement

- [Specific area needing enhancement]
- [Specific area needing enhancement]

Unexpected Challenges

- [Challenge not anticipated in IR plan]
- [Challenge not anticipated in IR plan]

ACTION ITEMS

Priority	Action item	Owner	Due date	Status	Resources
CRITICAL	[Description]	[Name]	[Date]	[Status]	$[Amount]
HIGH	[Description]	[Name]	[Date]	[Status]	$[Amount]
MEDIUM	[Description]	[Name]	[Date]	[Status]	$[Amount]
LOW	[Description]	[Name]	[Date]	[Status]	$[Amount]

INCIDENT RESPONSE PLAN UPDATES

Updates required

- Roles and responsibilities section
- Detection and monitoring procedures
- Containment strategies
- Eradication processes
- Recovery procedures
- Communication plans
- Contact lists (internal and external)
- Escalation paths
- Tool configurations

Specific changes

1. [Section]—[Change description]—[Rationale]
2. [Section]—[Change description]—[Rationale]

REGULATORY AND LEGAL CONSIDERATIONS

Regulatory requirements

- GDPR notification: [Yes/No—Date completed]
- HIPAA notification: [Yes/No—Date completed]
- CCPA notification: [Yes/No—Date completed]
- Other: [Specify]

Legal actions

- Law enforcement report filed: [Yes/No—Case number]
- Insurance claim filed: [Yes/No—Claim number]
- Potential litigation: [Description]
- Regulatory investigation: [Status]

Compliance gaps identified

- [Gap and remediation plan]
- [Gap and remediation plan]

STAKEHOLDER COMMUNICATIONS SUMMARY

Internal communications

- Employees notified: [Date and method]
- Board briefed: [Date]
- Department updates: [Description]

External communications

- Customers notified: [Date, method, number affected]
- Regulators notified: [Date and agencies]
- Media response: [Description]
- Public statement issued: [Yes/No—Date]

Communication effectiveness

- What worked: [Description]
- What needs improvement: [Description]

MONITORING ENHANCEMENTS

New monitoring capabilities implemented

- [Tool/capability]—[Purpose and configuration]
- [Tool/capability]—[Purpose and configuration]

Alert tuning

- [Alert modified]—[Reason for change]
- [Alert modified]—[Reason for change]

Testing schedule

- Backup recovery tests: [Frequency]
- Penetration testing: [Next scheduled date]
- Tabletop exercises: [Next scheduled date]

KNOWLEDGE SHARING

Information shared externally

- IOCs shared with: [FBI IC3/ISAC/Other]
- Best practices contributed to: [Industry forum/Initiative]
- Case study published: [Yes/No]

Internal training updates

- Training modules updated: [List]
- New training required: [Description]
- Next training date: [Date]

METRICS AND KPIs

Pre-incident baseline

- MTTD: [Time]
- MTTR: [Time]
- Backup success rate: [Percentage]
- Phishing simulation success: [Percentage]

Post-incident targets

- MTTD target: [Time]
- MTTR target: [Time]
- Backup success rate target: [Percentage]
- Phishing simulation target: [Percentage]

FOLLOW-UP SCHEDULE

30-day review: [Date]

- Verify critical action items are in progress or completed
- Confirm technical fixes (patches, MFA, backup improvements) are deployed
- Check that high-priority security gaps are addressed
- Review early metrics (MTTD, MTTR improvements)

90-Day Review: [Date]

- Assess completion of medium-priority action items
- Evaluate effectiveness of new monitoring and detection tools
- Review results from first post-incident phishing training
- Conduct first tabletop exercise with updated IR plan

Annual Review: [Date]

- Confirm all action items completed or explicitly accepted as residual risk
- Review metrics showing year-over-year improvement
- Assess whether post-mortem changes prevented or mitigated subsequent incidents
- Update IR plan based on new threats and organizational changes

APPENDICES

- Appendix A: Forensic Report Summary
- Appendix B: Ransom Note and Communications
- Appendix C: Network Diagrams (Pre and Post-Incident)
- Appendix D: Cost Breakdown Details
- Appendix E: Stakeholder Feedback Summary
- Appendix F: Third-Party Assessment Reports

Key Elements to Document

Your documentation should capture the following information, and relay it back to the appropriate parties mentioned in "Who's Calling the Shots?" on page 201:

Attack timeline

Initial compromise
>   When and how did the attacker gain access? For example, was it a phishing email or an exploited vulnerability like EternalBlue?

Lateral movement
>   How did the attacker move through the network? Reference tools like Cobalt Strike or PowerShell Empire, if identified.

Detection
>   When was the attack detected, and by what means (e.g., SIEM alerts, user reports, backup system notifications)?

Response actions
>   When was the IRP activated? What containment measures were taken? When were systems wiped or replaced?

Recovery timeline
>   When were systems restored? Were there delays or issues during recovery?

Impact assessment

> *Systems affected*
>> List all compromised systems, including servers, workstations, firewalls, cloud environments, and backups. For example, the engineering company case study noted that 80% of their systems (2,300 workstations and servers) were infected.

> *Data loss*
>> Document any data that was permanently lost, such as the proprietary engineering data in the case study, or an encrypted executive's laptop that had to be rebuilt without a backup.

> *Financial costs*
>> Include ransom payments (e.g., $4.5 million in the Lorenz case), recovery costs (labor, software, hardware, etc.), lost revenue, and third-party expenses.

> *Operational impact*
>> Quantify downtime, disrupted services, and customer impact. For instance, the Colonial Pipeline attack caused a six-day fuel shortage.

> *Reputational damage*
>> Note any public backlash or loss of customer trust, as seen in high-profile attacks like NotPetya, or the 2023 retail attack that led to a 20% stock price drop after public disclosure.

Response effectiveness

> *What worked*
>> Highlight successful actions, such as effective isolation of infected systems or clean restores from immutable backups, or coordination with the FBI.

> *What failed*
>> Identify gaps, such as the engineering company's lack of offline backups for critical systems, or gaps in network visibility and defense.

> *External support*
>> Document the role of cyber insurance, law enforcement (e.g., FBI involvement in the Lorenz case), and third-party vendors like IT managed service providers (MSPs), incident response, or remediation support services.

Forensic findings

- Reference forensic reports from tools like system imagers or log analyzers. For example, did analysis using Hybrid Analysis or VirusTotal identify the ransomware variant?

- Note any attacker tools (e.g., TrickBot, ExMatter) found during eradication.

- Document evidence of exfiltration, such as unusual network traffic to C2 servers, dwell time, or techniques and tactics using SIEM and XDR behavioral analytics.

Stakeholder communications
- Record notifications to employees, customers, and regulators.

  Real-world example: Colonial Pipeline's 2021 ransomware attack, caused by a compromised VPN credential, led to a six-day fuel shortage across the southeastern US. Their post-mortem revealed weak MFA implementation and a lack of network segmentation. By sharing IOCs with the FBI and CISA, they contributed to industry-wide defenses, and their updated IRP included mandatory MFA and zero-trust architecture.

- Note any warnings issued about fake emails from your domain.

Tools for Documentation

Here are some tools you can use for documentation purposes:

Incident management platforms
Use tools like ServiceNow, Jira, or PagerDuty to centralize documentation and track action items.

Forensic tools
Leverage log analyzers (e.g., Splunk, ELK Stack) to correlate events and build a timeline.

Collaboration tools
Use Microsoft Teams, SharePoint, Slack, or Confluence to share and review documentation in real-time.

Templates
Create reusable templates for incident reports, ensuring consistency across incidents—there will be more.

Best Practices for Documentation

Store post-mortem documents for at least seven years to support regulatory compliance and potential litigation. If litigation is pending or threatened, implement a legal hold and consult your legal counsel before disposing of any incident-related materials. Post-mortem documents should be classified as "Confidential—Limited Distribution" and stored in an access-controlled repository separate from general IT documentation. Maintain both digital and printed copies in different locations to ensure availability if future incidents compromise your primary storage.

Here are some other best practices for your documentation:

Be specific
> Include dates/times (normalized across time zones), system names, and user accounts involved. For example, note that the Lorenz attack began at 8 a.m. CST on a Thursday.

Be objective
> Avoid subjective language or blame. Focus on facts and evidence.

Be comprehensive
> Document both technical and nontechnical aspects, such as communication breakdowns or leadership decisions.

Secure the documentation
> Store records in a secure, access-controlled location to protect sensitive information and ensure they are backed up.

Version control
> Track changes to the document to maintain an audit trail.

Conducting the Post-Mortem Meeting

The post-mortem meeting is the cornerstone of the analysis process. It brings together key stakeholders to review the incident, share perspectives, and identify actionable insights. This meeting should be structured, inclusive, and focused on collaboration to ensure that all relevant information is captured and analyzed. Ideally, the meeting should include an objective moderator (not you) and a scribe to take notes.

Step 1: Planning the Post-Mortem Meeting

Preparation is key to a productive post-mortem meeting. Here's how to set it up for success:

Identify participants
> Post-mortem analysis typically occurs in phases, starting with an internal review before expanding to include external stakeholders. Begin with your core internal teams: IT, cybersecurity, incident response, legal, communications, and senior leadership, to establish a baseline understanding of the incident and identify initial lessons learned. This internal session allows for candid discussion without external pressures.
>
> Once you've completed the internal analysis, consider holding a broader post-mortem meeting that includes external partners such as cyber insurance providers, forensic investigators, or law enforcement who were involved in the response. (Be sure to consult legal before involving outsiders in any post-mortem

discussions.) These external stakeholders can provide valuable perspectives on attacker tactics, industry trends, and regulatory considerations.

Additionally, you may want to conduct separate, more technical deep-dive sessions with smaller groups (e.g., just the security and IT teams) to examine specific technical details, vulnerabilities, and remediation steps without overwhelming nontechnical stakeholders. For example, in the case study of the engineering company compromised by the Lorenz group, the organization could start with an internal post-mortem, then hold a follow-up session with the FBI and cyber insurance negotiator to gain insights on the attacker's tactics and negotiation outcomes, while running parallel technical sessions to address specific security control failures.

Set a clear agenda

Define the meeting's objectives, such as documenting the attack timeline; evaluating response readiness and effectiveness, resources, and communications; and identifying lessons learned. Include a preamble to your agenda that defines the ground rules for participation and sets a clear focus on collaboration. Share the agenda in advance to ensure participants come prepared.

Choose a facilitator

Appoint a neutral and objective facilitator, ideally someone with experience in incident response or project management, to keep the discussion on track and prevent it from devolving into blame-shifting. The facilitator should encourage open dialogue and ensure all voices are heard.

Gather data

Collect all relevant documentation, including logs, forensic reports, ransom notes, communication records, the IRT's activity logs, and recovery timelines. For instance, logs from your SIEM or XDR systems can provide critical insights into the attack's progression.

Schedule promptly but thoughtfully

Hold the meeting as soon as possible after recovery, ideally within one to two weeks, to ensure details are fresh. However, avoid rushing into it while the team is still exhausted from the recovery effort. Allow enough time for participants to gather their thoughts and data, shower, and get some rest.

Step 2: Structuring the Post-Mortem Meeting

A well-structured meeting ensures comprehensive coverage of the incident and actionable outcomes. As mentioned in the previous section on documentation, one of the best ways to provide this structure is through an organizational document that lists the types of information you wish to gather, which allows the person taking notes to easily fill in the information. Use the following framework to guide the discussion:

1. Incident overview:

   - Present a detailed timeline of the attack, from initial compromise to recovery. Reference specific evidence, such as the ransom note or logs showing the attacker's entry point, phishing emails, EDR alerts, escalation communications (email, phone, etc.), and the expansion of the people involved.

   - Discuss the scope and impact, including affected systems, data loss, downtime, and financial costs. For example, the engineering company case study estimated a total cost of $7 million, including ransom, expenses, and lost revenue. Was $7M an accurate accounting of the impact? What about the value of reputation or client confidence? This is where some of the heavy analysis begins to show the gaps in your business impact analysis, inventories of your systems and data, and how data is classified and valued.

   - Highlight key events, such as when the attack was detected, when the IRP was activated, and when systems were restored. Include key decision points, such as engaging law enforcement, consulting third-party experts, disconnecting the internet, and resetting everyone's passwords.

2. Response evaluation:

   - Review the effectiveness of the IRP. Did the team follow the plan? Were there gaps or deviations? For instance, the engineering company's lack of an IRP beyond "Call Mike" highlights the need for a formalized process.

   - Assess the performance of detection tools, such as EDR, XDR, or SIEM, in identifying the attack. Did they provide timely alerts, or were there false negatives?

   - Evaluate containment and eradication efforts. Were infected systems properly isolated? Did wiping or replacing systems prevent reinfection? Were you able to make timely decisions on endpoint isolation, power down, and replacement?

   - Discuss recovery efforts. Were the system and data restored successful? Did the sandbox approach prevent reinfection? Were there issues with data integrity or malware persistence? How much time was lost doing paperwork or searching for help?

3. Root cause analysis:

   - In a typical post-mortem, you are simply recording the root cause that you have already determined. If you do not yet know your root cause, please identify that before beginning your post-mortem.

   - Identify the initial access point. Was it a phishing email, an unpatched vulnerability (e.g., the EternalBlue exploit used in WannaCry, or a zero day in your

Fortinet firewall), or compromised credentials sold by an initial access broker (IAB)?

- Analyze how the attacker moved laterally. For example, did they exploit weak network segmentation or use tools like Cobalt Strike?

- Determine why the attack succeeded. Were backups unprotected? Did phishing-resistant MFA fail? Were junior administrators unprepared? Were there gaps or deficiencies in the alerting and escalation processes?

4. Lessons learned:

- Identify what went well. For example, did your cyber insurance provider facilitate a swift response? Did automated recovery processes reduce downtime? Were there benefits to your network architecture that limited the damage?

- Highlight what went wrong. For instance, the engineering company's failure to act on tabletop exercise recommendations exacerbated the attack's impact. Missing or outdated procedures and system information. Poor visibility across the environment. Untested response and recovery plans. No agreements or relationships with third-party experts.

- Discuss unexpected challenges, such as the proprietary engineering system that couldn't be decrypted. Restoring from bare metal. Working with outsourced managed service vendors that are not available 24/7. The need for third-party or out-of-band support for communications when the entire network is compromised. No personal contact information for employees (e.g., Gmail or cell phone) to communicate incident updates.

5. Action items:

- Assign specific tasks to address identified weaknesses, such as patching vulnerabilities, enhancing MFA, or improving backup immutability.

- Set timelines and owners for each action item. Each action item needs a specific owner who is responsible for completion, not just coordination. Set realistic deadlines based on complexity and available resources. For items delayed beyond their due date, the owner must provide a status update explaining the delay and a revised timeline. Executive leadership should review action item status in monthly security briefings to maintain accountability.

- Prioritize immediate fixes (e.g., patching critical vulnerabilities) and long-term improvements (e.g., redesigning network architecture).

- Items that cannot be completed due to budget or resource constraints should be formally documented as accepted residual risk with executive approval.

6. Stakeholder feedback loop:

- Again, a standard document (e.g., survey form) can be used to gather feedback from stakeholders.

- Collect anonymous feedback from participants to identify unspoken concerns, such as fear of blame or resource constraints. Use tools like Microsoft Forms or SurveyMonkey to ensure honesty.

- Review feedback to refine the IRP and address cultural barriers, such as reluctance to report phishing due to fear of reprimand.

Step 3: Facilitating Open Discussion

Establish a blame-free environment where participants feel safe sharing honest feedback. The following activities can help foster open dialogue:

Techniques for engagement
Use structured discussion methods like the "Five Whys" or SWOT analysis (Strengths, Weaknesses, Opportunities, Threats) to uncover root causes. For example, if backups were compromised, ask:

- Why were backups compromised? (They were stored on a network share.)

- Why were they on a network share? (Lack of immutable storage.)

- Why was immutable storage not implemented? (Budget constraints.)

- Why were budget constraints an issue? (Cybersecurity was not prioritized.)

- Why was cybersecurity not prioritized? (Lack of executive buy-in.)

Conflict resolution
If tensions arise, the facilitator should redirect focus to solutions. For instance, if IT blames users for phishing, pivot to discussing training improvements.

External perspectives
Encourage external partners (e.g., FBI, MSSPs) to share insights on attacker tactics, such as double extortion trends seen in 2024 ALPHV attacks.

These activities can uncover systemic issues that can be addressed through policy changes, budget reallocation, or cultural shifts.

Step 4: Documenting the Meeting

Assign a scribe to capture detailed notes, including key findings, decisions, and action items. Use a standardized template to ensure consistency, such as:

Incident summary
Date, scope, and impact of the attack

Timeline
Key events and response actions

Root causes
> Technical, procedural, and human factors

Lessons learned
> What worked, what didn't, and why

Action items
> Specific tasks, owners, and deadlines

Recommendations
> Strategic improvements for long-term resilience

Share the draft with participants for feedback within 48 hours to ensure accuracy and completeness. Finalize the document and distribute it to all stakeholders, including senior leadership and external partners, if appropriate.

Regulatory and Legal Considerations

Ransomware attacks often trigger regulatory obligations. The post-mortem exercise should consider the following activities, if applicable:

Compliance requirements
> Review obligations under GDPR, HIPAA, or CCPA. For example, GDPR requires 72-hour breach notifications. Document compliance actions taken and gaps, such as delayed customer notifications in the Lorenz case.

Legal implications
> Assess potential lawsuits or fines. For instance, a 2024 healthcare breach led to a $10 million class-action settlement due to delayed notifications.

Action items
> Assign the legal team to update breach notification procedures and review cyber insurance policies for compliance coverage.

Action item: Conduct a compliance audit within 30 days of your post-recovery to ensure regulatory adherence and updated legal protocols.

Learning from Your Mistakes

The post-mortem analysis is an opportunity to learn from mistakes and turn weaknesses into strengths. By identifying what went wrong and why, you can implement targeted improvements to prevent recurrence. These mistakes must be converted to corrective actions with clear, time-bound tasks assigned to convert the mistakes to opportunities. (We discuss this in more detail at the end of this section.)

Common Mistakes

This section examines common mistakes encountered in ransomware attacks and provides guidance on how to address them.

1. Failure to act on prior recommendations:

   - Example: The engineering company ignored tabletop exercise recommendations, leading to unprotected backups and a prolonged recovery.

   - Lesson: Prioritize and implement recommendations from tabletop exercises, penetration tests, and red team assessments. Assign clear ownership and timelines to ensure accountability.

   - Action: Review past security assessments and create a prioritized remediation plan. For instance, implement immutable backups if previously recommended. Escalate overdue remediation activities to ensure continued or renewed focus.

2. Inadequate backup protection:

   - Example: The engineering company's critical engineering data had no offline backups, resulting in permanent loss.

   - Lesson: Backup systems are prime targets for attackers. Ensure backups are immutable, stored offline or on separate storage, and regularly tested.

   - Action: Deploy truly immutable backups with MFA and multi-party authorization (MPA) for restores. Conduct regular recovery tests to verify data integrity and restore effectiveness.

3. Weak initial access controls:

   - Example: Many attacks, including WannaCry, exploited unpatched vulnerabilities or weak credentials.

   - Lesson: Robust patch management, phishing-resistant MFA, and password management are critical to preventing initial access.

   - Action: Implement automated patch management, enforce strong passwords via a separate privileged password manager, and deploy phishing-resistant MFA across all systems. Ideally, also enforce MFA policy that prohibits browsers from allowing "Trust this Device," "Remember Me," or "Stay Logged In," or to generally save credentials.

4. Poor network segmentation:

   - Example: The Lorenz attack spread rapidly due to insufficient network segmentation, infecting 80% of their systems.

   - Lesson: Network segmentation limits lateral movement. Laptops and desktops should be on separate VLANs, and unnecessary communication should be blocked. Backup or archive network segments should require additional credentials.

- Action: Redesign network architecture to enforce least privilege and whitelisting of ports. Conduct penetration tests to validate segmentation.

5. Delayed detection:

- Example: The Lorenz group had access for three months before detection, allowing extensive reconnaissance and exfiltration.
- Lesson: Effective detection tools (e.g., EDR, XDR, SIEM) and backup system notifications are essential for early detection.
- Action: Enhance monitoring with XDR and SIEM solutions, configuring thresholds for downloads from O365, firewall data volumes, and backup systems to trigger alerts on anomalies, such as excessive restores or deletions.

6. Lack of a formal IRP:

- Example: The engineering company's IRP was limited to "Call Mike," leading to an informal and chaotic response.
- Lesson: A well-defined IRP with clear roles, responsibilities, and procedures is critical for an effective response.
- Action: Develop and test a comprehensive IRP, including tabletop exercises and playbooks, and the establishment of your incident response ecosystem of resources and service providers.

7. Insufficient staff training:

- Example: Phishing remains a common entry point for ransomware, often due to untrained users clicking malicious links.
- Lesson: Ongoing user training and testing reduce the risk of phishing attacks, as well as a company culture that prioritizes protection over criticism—if you make a mistake, report it as soon as possible without fear of retribution.
- Action: Implement regular phishing simulations and cybersecurity awareness training for all employees, along with management messaging that supports a collaborative culture of protection.

Prioritizing Improvements with Limited Resources

Post-mortems typically identify more problems than you can immediately fix. If budget constraints force you to prioritize, focus on:

What the attackers actually exploited
Fix the initial access point and lateral movement paths first. If they got in through phishing, that's priority one. If they moved laterally due to poor segmentation, that's priority two.

Quick wins that reduce risk significantly
Implementing MFA on admin accounts costs little but prevents many attacks. Immutable backups are relatively inexpensive compared to ransom payments.

Gaps that regulators care about
If compliance violations contributed to the attack, fix those first to avoid fines on top of recovery costs.

What your cyber insurance requires
Many policies now mandate specific controls (MFA, EDR, offline backups). Implement these to maintain coverage.

Create a simple matrix scoring each improvement on two factors: implementation cost (Low/Medium/High) and risk reduction (Low/Medium/High). Focus first on High risk reduction items that are Low or Medium cost. Document what you couldn't fix as accepted residual risk and present this to leadership.

Turning Mistakes into Opportunities

Each mistake is an opportunity to improve. Use the post-mortem to create a prioritized list of improvements, such as:

Technical upgrades
Deploy advanced detection tools, immutable backups, or application whitelisting.

Process improvements
Formalize IRPs, automate patch management, and test recovery processes.

Cultural changes
Foster a security-first culture by engaging leadership and prioritizing cybersecurity investments.

Training enhancements
Expand training to cover not only phishing but also incident response roles and responsibilities.

Case Study: What Maersk Learned from the 2017 NotPetya Attack

After suffering the devastating NotPetya attack in 2017 that cost between $250 and $300 million, the shipping giant Maersk conducted an extensive post-mortem that revealed critical gaps: all 150 domain controllers were wiped out simultaneously due to a lack of network segmentation, backup strategies weren't designed for a global simultaneous attack, and security baselines were inconsistently applied across the organization. Rather than accepting these failures, Maersk transformed their approach to cybersecurity, implementing a two-part strategy balancing proactive and reactive capabilities, assuming future incidents would occur, and focusing on rapid

---

recovery rather than attempting to stop every attack. The company's CISO stated that their new goal will be: "If the business was hit again, we can recover quicker," reducing their target Active Directory recovery time from 9 days to 24 hours.

Maersk also embraced transparency as a core principle, openly communicating with customers throughout the crisis, which resulted in their stock price actually increasing after the attack and strengthened customer relationships. The company enshrined these lessons in five organizational principles relating to resilience, board-room accountability, and secure-by-design practices, and now conducts computer forensics even for seemingly minor incidents. While we cannot document whether Maersk has prevented subsequent attacks, their transformation from relying on luck (a power outage in Ghana that saved their last domain controller) to implementing systematic resilience demonstrates how a thorough post-mortem can fundamentally reshape an organization's security posture.

Adapting Your Incident Response Plan

The post-mortem analysis should directly translate into updates to your IRP. An effective IRP is a living document that evolves with each incident, incorporating lessons learned to improve future responses. This section outlines how to adapt your IRP based on the post-mortem findings.

Key Components to Update

The post-mortem analysis should directly inform specific updates to your IRP. Don't let your findings gather dust in a report; translate them into concrete changes that will improve your response to the next incident. Focus on the areas where gaps were identified, but also reinforce what worked well to ensure those practices are formalized and repeatable:

Roles and responsibilities
- Clarify roles for all team members, including IT, cybersecurity, legal, and communications. For example, the engineering company's lack of clear roles led to reliance on external support.
- Define escalation paths and decision-making authority, particularly for critical actions such as isolating networks, shutting down critical systems, disconnecting the company from the internet, or paying ransoms.

Detection and monitoring
- Incorporate new detection tools or configurations identified during the post-mortem. For instance, if SIEM alerts failed to detect the attack, adjust rules or integrate an XDR solution with behavioral analytics.

- Add backup system notifications for anomalies, such as excessive restores or deletions. Implement alerting for any file stores, like SharePoint or OneDrive, to identify downloads or deletions that exceed a threshold.

Containment strategies
- Update containment procedures based on what worked or failed. For example, if isolating affected networks was effective, formalize the process with specific tools and triggers.
- Address gaps, such as the need to pause VMs immediately to stop the spread, or power down systems to get them offline and halt any potential infection. Physically disconnecting network segments, turning off VPN or other remote services, and updating firewall rules are additional considerations.

Eradication processes
- Refine eradication methods based on the tools found (e.g., Cobalt Strike, ExMatter) and hiding places (e.g., boot sectors, firmware). These attributes should also be used to update EDR and firewall detection capabilities.
- Document specific wiping and replacement protocols for different system types. Ensure that related operating procedures are referenced to guide these specific recovery activities (i.e., SQL server rebuild guide).

Recovery procedures
- Update recovery plans to include sandbox restores, malware scanning, and cloud-based recovery options.
- Specify golden image creation and maintenance for faster, safer restores. Ensure that your golden image is labeled to ensure you are using the correct version.

Communication plans
- Revise stakeholder notification procedures based on feedback from the attack. For example, implement an expectation for updates to executive management, and improve initial and ongoing notifications to customers and regulators.
- Include warnings about fake emails from your domain to prevent secondary attacks. Prohibit employees from disclosing incident details to third parties and from posting on social media.

Testing and training
- Schedule tabletop exercises to test the updated IRP as soon as it is approved.
- Expand training to cover new threats, such as AI-driven ransomware or supply chain attacks. Provide employees with an update on the results of the recent incident and the changes being implemented to enhance the company's resilience.

Automation and tooling
Incorporate automation to streamline future responses. For example:

- Use scripts to automate network isolation or system imaging.
- Deploy backup systems with built-in malware scanning and curated recovery.
- Leverage infrastructure-as-code for cloud-based recovery to reduce manual errors.

Testing the updated plan

Test the revised IRP through tabletop exercises and simulations to ensure it addresses the identified weaknesses. For example, simulate a Lorenz-style attack with double extortion to verify improved detection and response capabilities. Document the results and repeat as needed.

Implementing strict monitoring

Post-ransomware monitoring is critical to detect residual threats, prevent reinfection, and ensure long-term security. The post-mortem analysis should translate into a robust monitoring strategy that addresses the attack's root causes and vulnerabilities.

Key Monitoring Areas

Effective monitoring demands a strategic approach that focuses on the specific weaknesses exposed during your attack. Use your post-mortem findings to prioritize monitoring in the areas where attackers gained access, moved laterally, or achieved their objectives. The goal is to detect the next attack earlier in the kill chain, before it can cause significant damage. Configure your monitoring to address the following key areas:

Network traffic
- Monitor for unusual outbound connections, DNS queries, or C2 communications. For example, look for traffic to known malicious domains identified during the attack, or any suspicious IP addresses, ports, or protocols (e.g., if your company only does business in Kansas, then internet traffic to Europe could be suspect).
- Deploy network monitoring tools like Zeek or Wireshark to capture and analyze traffic. Consider implementing a true network detection and response (NDR) solution or an XDR platform that is capable of real-time analysis, alerting, and automated response.

Endpoint activity
- Use XDR to detect suspicious behavior, such as unauthorized privilege escalation or file encryption.
- Monitor endpoints for signs of reinfection, especially if cleaning was attempted instead of wiping.

Backup systems

- Configure backup systems to alert on anomalies, such as excessive restores, deletions, or exfiltration attempts.

- Regularly scan backups for malware to ensure clean restore points.

User behavior

- Monitor for phishing attempts or compromised credentials, which are common entry points.

- Use user behavior analytics (UBA) to detect anomalies, such as unusual login times or locations.

System logs

- Centralize logs in a SIEM system for real-time analysis and correlation.

- Retain logs for at least six months to support forensic analysis of future incidents. If you have regulatory compliance requirements, the SIEM could be configured to retain logs for at least a year.

Implementing Monitoring Tools

Proper configuration and integration are what make monitoring tools effective. Many organizations make the mistake of implementing powerful security tools but leaving them with default settings or failing to connect them to their broader security ecosystem. Your post-mortem findings should guide how you tune these tools to detect the specific tactics, techniques, and procedures (TTPs) used in your attack. The following tools and configurations will help you build a comprehensive monitoring strategy:

SIEM
Use Splunk, QRadar, or Elastic SIEM to aggregate and analyze logs from all systems.

XDR
Deploy platforms like Stellar Cyber to connect with all your data sources, including SIEM, EDR, NDR, firewalls, and cloud environments.

Backup monitoring
Configure backup systems (e.g., Veeam) to alert on suspicious activity.

DLP
Enhance DLP controls to detect exfiltration attempts, especially within backup traffic. Office 365's Purview is essential for Microsoft Cloud event auditing.

Regular Audits and Testing

Monitoring tools and configurations degrade over time: systems change, new applications are deployed, employees come and go, and attack techniques evolve. All of these issues can create blind spots in your monitoring coverage. Without regular audits and testing, you cannot be confident that your monitoring will actually detect the next attack. Establish a cadence of reviews and tests that validates your monitoring effectiveness and ensures configurations remain aligned with your current environment and threat landscape. Implement the following audit and testing practices:

- Conduct monthly reviews and quarterly audits of monitoring configurations to ensure they align with the latest threat intelligence.

- Conduct penetration tests and red team exercises as often as possible to validate the effectiveness of monitoring. Organizations that have recently suffered a ransomware attack should increase testing frequency and rigor for at least the next two years (e.g., quarterly versus annual), as threat actors often retarget previously compromised organizations or share intelligence about vulnerable victims within criminal networks.

- Test backup system alerts and recovery processes monthly to quarterly, depending on the criticality of your data and your recovery objectives.

Sharing Threat Intelligence

Share post-mortem findings with industry peers, cybersecurity firms, and law enforcement to contribute to collective defenses. For example:

- Report the attack to the FBI's IC3 (IC3.gov).
- Share IOCs with ISACs or ISOs, after consulting with legal.
- Participate in initiatives like No More Ransom to help develop decryption tools.

Recommendations for Long-Term Resilience

The post-mortem analysis is not a one-time event but the start of a continuous improvement process. To build long-term resilience, consider the following recommendations:

Invest in cybersecurity culture.
- Engage leadership to secure budget for cybersecurity. For example, post-Lorenz, the engineering company allocated $2 million for XDR and training.

- Foster a blame-free culture with anonymous reporting channels for phishing or errors.

- Conduct quarterly all-hands meetings to reinforce cybersecurity awareness.

Enhance technical defenses.
- Deploy offsite, truly immutable backups with MFA and MPA (as discussed in Chapter 6), tested at least quarterly.

- Implement application whitelisting and network segmentation.

- Use advanced detection tools like XDR and SIEM that have automated response capabilities.

- Adopt a zero-trust architecture with micro-segmentation, validated by annual penetration testing.

Regular testing and training.
- Conduct tabletop exercises and red team assessments at least annually. Include a broad audience, where possible, to allow employees to observe how the incident is handled.

- Expand phishing training to include AI-generated deepfake emails, a growing threat.

- Train nontechnical staff (e.g., legal, HR) on IR roles to improve coordination.

Collaborate with external partners.
- Work with cyber insurance providers to align coverage with post-mortem findings.

- Share IOCs with ISACs and law enforcement. For example, the healthcare case study shared ALPHV IOCs with the US Department of Health and Human Services (HHS).

- Join initiatives like NoMoreRansom or CISA's Joint Cyber Defense Collaborative.

Monitor emerging threats.
- Subscribe to threat intelligence feeds (e.g., Recorded Future, ThreatConnect) to track ransomware variants like Cl0p or LockBit 4.0.

- Monitor dark web forums for IAB activity targeting your industry, using services like Flashpoint, Search Light, or a managed service from Blackswan Cybersecurity.

- Prepare for AI-driven ransomware, such as automated phishing or evasion of EDR.

Document and review.
- Maintain a living IRP that evolves with each incident. Ensure this plan is available offline.

- Create a centralized repository for post-mortem reports, accessible to key stakeholders.

- Conduct annual reviews of post-mortem findings to ensure action items are completed.

Metrics for measuring improvement.
To ensure post-mortem action items translate into resilience, define KPIs:

Mean time to detect (MTTD)
Target a reduction from 90 days (Lorenz case) to under 24 hours with XDR and SIEM enhancements.

Mean time to respond (MTTR)
Aim to reduce containment time from 48 hours to 4 hours through automated isolation.

Backup recovery success rate
Target 100% successful restores in quarterly tests.

Employee phishing resistance
Achieve a 90% success rate in phishing simulations within six months.

Chart: Post-mortem action item progress.
To track action item completion, use a chart similar to the one in Figure 16-1 to visualize the progress of key activities. This will help stakeholders track improvements and establish accountability.

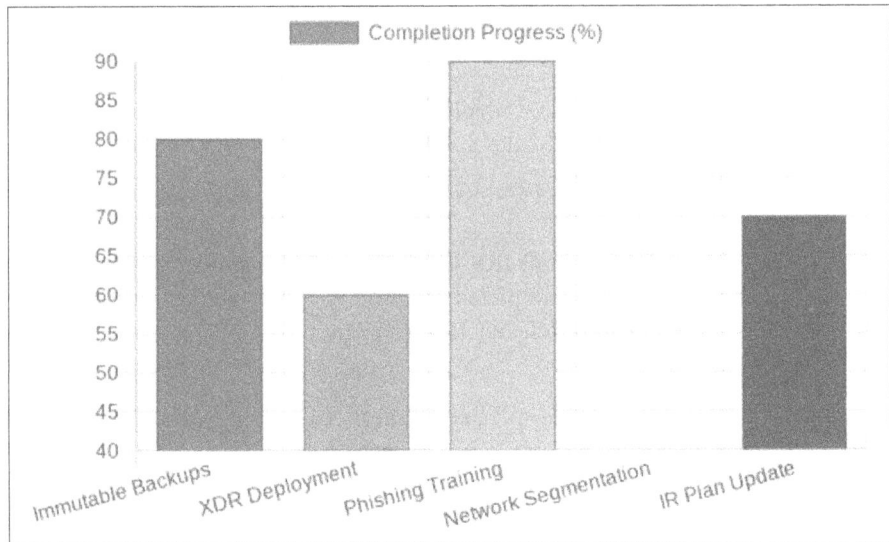

Figure 16-1. Tracking action items

Post-Mortem Analysis Case Studies

To illustrate the post-mortem process, let's look at a couple of case studies based on some of the examples we've discussed throughout.

The Lorenz Attack

To illustrate the post-mortem process, let's revisit the engineering company case study from Chapter 1. The company suffered a devastating Lorenz ransomware attack that infected 80% of its systems, cost $7 million, and from which it took seven weeks to recover. The post-mortem analysis revealed critical lessons that shaped their future cybersecurity strategy:

Post-mortem meeting

Participants

IT team, cybersecurity manager, CIO, legal counsel, FBI, cyber insurance negotiator, and external forensic analysts.

Agenda

Review the attack timeline, evaluate response effectiveness, identify root causes, and assign action items.

Findings

Timeline

The Lorenz group compromised the network three months prior to the infection incident, exploiting a phishing email to gain initial access. They used Cobalt Strike for lateral movement and ExMatter for exfiltration.

Response

The lack of a formal IRP led to a chaotic response. Recommendations from a recently completed tabletop exercise (e.g., offline backups and communications deficiencies) were ignored.

Impact

2,300 systems were infected, critical engineering data was lost, and the company paid $4.5 million in ransom.

Root causes

Weak phishing defenses, no immutable backups, inadequate network segmentation, poor communications strategy, and delayed detection.

Documentation

Incident report

Detailed the attack timeline, from phishing email to ransom payment. Included forensic evidence (e.g., *.sz40* file extension) and ransom note.

Impact assessment

Quantified $7 million in costs, including ransom, recovery, and lost revenue. Noted reputational damage due to customer notifications.

Response evaluation

Highlighted successful FBI coordination but criticized the lack of an IRP and backup testing.

Lessons learned

Phishing vulnerability

Employees needed better training to recognize phishing emails.

Backup gaps

Critical systems lacked offline, immutable backups.

Delayed detection

Three months of undetected access underscored the need for expanded network and system visibility capabilities of XDR and SIEM platforms.

Response chaos

The absence of a formal IRP delayed containment and recovery.

IRP updates

Roles

Assigned clear roles for IT, cybersecurity, and legal teams. Designated a primary incident coordinator.

Detection

Deployed Stellar Cyber XDR platform and configured appropriate data sources, including SentinelOne, firewalls, O365, server syslogs, and Extrahop NDR for real-time alerts. Added backup system notifications for anomalies.

Containment

Formalized network isolation procedures, including automated system isolation, shunning IPs at the firewall, and pausing VMs immediately upon detection.

Recovery

Implemented immutable backups with MFA and MPA. Established a sandbox environment for system restore testing.

Testing

Scheduled annual tabletop exercises and annual penetration tests.

Monitoring enhancements

- Deployed Stellar Cyber XDR for monitoring and Splunk for log analysis.

- Configured Veeam to alert on excessive restores or deletions.
- Implemented UBA capabilities of Stellar Cyber to establish network, device, and user behavioral baselines from which suspicious activity can be detected.
- Conducted monthly reviews and quarterly audits of monitoring tools and quarterly recovery tests.

Outcomes
> The post-mortem transformed the company's cybersecurity posture. By addressing the identified weaknesses, they reduced the risk of future attacks, improved response times, and restored stakeholder confidence. The company also shared IOCs with the FBI and industry peers, contributing to collective defenses.

Healthcare Breach (2023)

Another mid-sized hospital (not Change Healthcare mentioned in Chapter 9) suffered a ransomware attack by the ALPHV/BlackCat group, encrypting 60% of its systems, including patient records. The post-mortem revealed:

Timeline
> Initial access via a spear-phishing email targeting a junior administrator. Attackers used Rclone for data exfiltration over a period of two weeks.

Impact
> $3 million ransom was paid, $5 million in recovery costs, and a two-week disruption to patient care. In addition, the indirect impact to the hospital was reputational damage, which led to a 10% drop in patient visits.

Root causes
> Lack of phishing-resistant MFA, a flat and unsegmented network, and untested backups.

Lessons learned
> The hospital implemented mandatory phishing training, deployed immutable backups with MFA, and adopted a zero-trust model.

Outcomes
> Reduced recovery time in a subsequent 2024 incident to three days and restored patient trust through transparent communication.

Summary

The post-mortem analysis is your opportunity to turn a ransomware attack into a learning experience that strengthens your organization. By conducting a thorough meeting, documenting what happened, learning from mistakes, adapting your IRP, and implementing enhanced and comprehensive monitoring, you can mitigate the risk of future attacks and build a more resilient cybersecurity posture. The engineering company case study demonstrates the transformative power of a well-executed post-mortem, turning a $7 million disaster into a catalyst for change.

As ransomware continues to evolve, with new variants like ALPHV and Cl0p and tactics like double extortion, organizations must remain vigilant. The post-mortem is not just about recovering from the past but preparing for the future. By embracing continuous improvement, collaborating with industry peers, and investing in robust defenses, you can ensure your organization is ready for whatever comes next.

Index

managed security service providers (MSSPs), 242, 255

managed service providers (MSPs), 255-258

master boot record (MBR), 411

mean time to detect (MTTD), 196

mean time to respond (MTTR), 197

mean time to restore (MTTR), 197

metamorphic code, 13

Metasploit tool, 409

metrics
    backup and recovery metrics, 66
    capacity metrics, 64
    included in IRPs, 196
    recovery metrics, 62-67
    RTO and RPO, 40

MFA (see multifactor authentication)

MFA fatigue, 166

Mimikatz (attacker tool), 29

mission-critical systems, 89

mistakes (see also common mistakes)
    learning from, 465
    turning into opportunities, 468

ML-based detection, 258

mobile devices, 118

Modern Data Protection (Preston), 53, 74

monitoring
    backup environments, 177
    cloud monitoring, 339
    continuous, 103-105
    critical nature of, 103
    data leaving your network, 140
    database auditing, 141
    defense in depth, 105
    endpoint activity, 126
    file access, 142
    firewall logs, 129, 339
    following containment actions, 398
    for data staging, 140
    incident response readiness, 230
    for network activity following restores, 437
    post-attack, 471
    tools for, 472

morale, maintaining, 299, 447

MOVEit (exfiltration tool), 277

MS-ISAC (Multi-State Information Sharing and Analysis Center), 331

MSPs (managed service providers), 255

MSSPs (see managed security service providers)

MTTD (mean time to detect), 196

MTTR (mean time to respond), 197

MTTR (mean time to restore), 197

multi-client intelligence, 256

Multi-State Information Sharing and Analysis Center (MS-ISAC), 331

multifactor authentication (MFA), 80-82, 94, 134, 165

multiplexing, 71

N

naming ransomware variants, 321-332, 352-356

National Checklist Program (NCP), 96

national cybersecurity agencies, 190

National Institute of Standards and Technology (NIST), 96, 122

National Vulnerability Database (NVD), 26

near-continuous data protection (near-CDP), 73

negotiations, 36, 358-362

network connectivity, 440

network device logs, 252

network interface cards, 413

network reconfiguration, 183

network security
    analyzing network traffic, 326-330
    case study, 127, 130
    disconnecting infected hardware, 390
    DNS filtering, 131
    firewalls and traffic control, 129, 339
    limiting lateral movement of ransomware, 126
    monitoring following restores, 437
    network mapping, 31
    network monitoring, 130, 394
    network propagation, 7, 31
    network scanning, 25, 30, 117
    network segmentation, 127
    network-based DLP, 140
    spikes in outbound traffic, 205
    vulnerability assessments, 132

network shares, 118, 391

Network Time Protocol (NTP), 255

next-generation firewalls (NGFWs), 129

NIST (see National Institute of Standards and Technology)

NIST Cybersecurity Framework 2.0, xviii, 1, 51, 197, 233, 263, 419

NoMoreRansom.org, 270, 341

updates, 80, 168
USB storage devices, 123
user accounts, disabling, 389
user and entity behavior analytics (UEBA), 131, 258
user permissions, 124
user-agent detection, 15
UVM Health Network, 381

V

variant identification, 321-332, 352-356
Veeam's Direct SAN Access, 171
vendor-dependent recovery capabilities, 429
vendors, 189, 301
verification, second level with MFA, 81
VirLock ransomware, 9-11
virtualization, 75, 144, 376, 382-385
virtualization layers, 413
Volatility Framework, 362-365
Volume Shadow Copy Service (VSS), 141
volume snapshots, 142
VPN-like mechanisms, 32
vulnerabilities (see also software vulnerabilities)
    assessing, 132
    of backup systems, 42, 44-47
    known vulnerabilities, 80

scanning for, 97, 117

W

Walker, Shawn, 235
WannaCry attack (2017), 8, 18, 31, 80, 334
war games, 223-230
wellness programs, 447
whitelists/allowlists, 118
Wireshark, 335, 339
workload usage, 64
write-ahead logs, 427

X

XDR (see extended detection and response)

Y

YARA (Yet Another Recursive Acronym) rules, 350
Yuba County attack (2021), 175

Z

Zellis attack (2025), 277
zero-day threats, 104, 277
zero-trust architecture, 274

About the Authors

W. Curtis Preston, widely known as Mr. Backup, has dedicated his career to educating organizations on how to protect their data from threats, from user error to natural disasters, terrorist attacks, and now the growing wave of cyber threats. Widely recognized as the industry's leading independent expert in backup and disaster recovery technology and strategies, Preston has spent over 30 years helping hundreds of companies safeguard their critical data, including Amazon, Intuit, Standard & Poor's, ExxonMobil, and Turner Broadcasting.

Preston is the author of five O'Reilly books on data protection and recovery, and the founder of *backupcentral.com*, a site dedicated to backup and recovery education for over 20 years. As the founder and CEO of Truth in IT, he produced hundreds of educational seminars worldwide. He is the host of *The Backup Wrap-Up* podcast, where he discusses data protection strategies and interviews industry experts.

Preston has served in technical evangelism and advisory roles at leading data protection companies, including seven years as chief technical evangelist at Druva, Inc., a data protection-as-a-service company. He has also served as an expert witness in data protection litigation, helping several litigants win their cases.

Now, Preston is bringing that educational mission to the fight against ransomware. He is currently developing the Stop Ransomware Academy, an educational platform that will help organizations prepare for and recover from ransomware attacks.

Dr. Mike Saylor is a seasoned cybersecurity expert with over 30 years of experience in IT and cybersecurity and over 25 years as a college cybersecurity and digital forensics professor. Dr. Saylor currently serves as the CEO and incident response lead at Blackswan Cybersecurity, which he cofounded, and the program director and chair of Business and Computer Science at Weatherford College. His career spans leadership roles in various organizations, including as a past CIO at Cornerstone Credit Union League, CEO and cofounder of Cyber Defense Labs, global IT audit leader for CitiGroup, director of threat and vulnerability management for Pricewaterhouse, and information security officer for a global telecom.

A respected figure in the cybersecurity community, Dr. Saylor is a 25-year member of the FBI's InfraGard program, where he has held leadership positions, including president, IT sector chief, and the current healthcare sector chief of the North Texas InfraGard Chapter. He also volunteers with the North Texas Fusion Center and the North Texas Crime Commission's Cybercrime Subcommittee.

Dr. Saylor has contributed to the field through his coauthorship of the 3rd, 4th, and 5th editions of the book *Cyber Crime and Cyber Terrorism*. In addition to his professional achievements, he holds a doctorate of business administration, computer and information systems security/information assurance.

Colophon

The animal on the cover of *Learning Ransomware Response & Recovery* is a tuatara (*Sphenodon punctatus*), a species of reptile native to New Zealand. Although it looks like a lizard, it is in fact in a separate branch of the reptile family tree and is the only surviving member of its order. Its name comes from Maori and means "peaks on the back," referring to its spiny crest. Males can erect their spines to attract mates or when fighting with other males.

The tuatara is New Zealand's largest reptile, with fully grown males reaching up to two feet in length and weighing over two pounds. Tuataras primarily eat intvertebrates such as insects and worms, though they are also known to eat lizards, seabird eggs, and chicks.

Although tuataras are considered a species of least concern, they are still at risk from habitat loss and introduced predators such as rats. Many of the animals on O'Reilly covers are endangered; all of them are important to the world.

The cover illustration is by José Marzan Jr., based on an antique line engraving from Lydekker's *Royal Natural History*. The series design is by Edie Freedman, Ellie Volckhausen, and Karen Montgomery. The cover fonts are Gilroy Semibold and Guardian Sans. The text font is Adobe Minion Pro; the heading font is Adobe Myriad Condensed; and the code font is Dalton Maag's Ubuntu Mono.

O'REILLY®

Learn from experts.
Become one yourself.

60,000+ titles | Live events with experts | Role-based courses
Interactive learning | Certification preparation | Verifiable skills

Try the O'Reilly learning platform free for 10 days.